Public Health Issues: Theory and Practices

Shalie Malik • Varun Chhachhar
Manoj Kumar Mishra
Editors

Public Health Issues: Theory and Practices

Springer

Editors
Shalie Malik
Department of Zoology
University of Lucknow
Lucknow, Uttar Pradesh, India

Varun Chhachhar
Faculty of Law
University of Lucknow
Lucknow, Uttar Pradesh, India

Manoj Kumar Mishra
Cancer Research Center,
Department of Biological Sciences
Alabama State University
Montgomery, AL, USA

ISBN 978-981-96-6649-2 ISBN 978-981-96-6650-8 (eBook)
https://doi.org/10.1007/978-981-96-6650-8

This Springer imprint is published by the registered company Springer Nature Singapore Pte Ltd.
The registered company address is: 152 Beach Road, #21-01/04 Gateway East, Singapore 189721, Singapore

Foreword

In an era marked by rapid globalization, environmental changes, and unprecedented public health challenges, the need for a nuanced understanding of public health has never been more pressing. *Public Health Issues: Theory and Practices*, edited by Shalie Malik, Varun Chhachhar, and Manoj Kumar Mishra, emerges as a comprehensive resource that not only chronicles the historical evolution of public health but also addresses the multifaceted issues that confront societies today.

The book is thoughtfully divided into four parts, each meticulously crafted to explore the vast landscape of public health. The first section guides readers through the history and foundational public health concepts. The editors have skillfully highlighted key milestones, showing how significant events, from pandemics to innovations, have shaped health practices. This historical context is essential for anyone seeking to understand the present state of public health and the dynamics that influence it.

The second part delves into the socioeconomic implications of public health, illuminating how factors like income, education, and environmental conditions affect health outcomes. This section is particularly relevant as it underscores the interconnectedness of social determinants and public health policies. By providing insights into economic impacts and patient burdens, the authors advocate for a more equitable healthcare system, an urgent call to action in today's world.

The third part shifts focus to environment and gender concerns, recognizing that health is not solely a matter of individual behavior but is profoundly influenced by broader societal structures. The chapters address critical issues such as gender-specific health challenges and the role of international environmental treaties, reinforcing the need for inclusive solutions in public health strategies.

The fourth part discusses the intersection of public health, policy, and law to create frameworks that protect and improve the health of populations. Overall, public health relies on well-crafted policies backed by strong legal frameworks to ensure that health initiatives are successfully implemented and sustained.

Finally, the book tackles the complex legal and policy frameworks that govern public health. In the wake of the COVID-19 pandemic, discussions surrounding infectious disease response and public health laws have gained newfound urgency.

The editors have provided a comprehensive analysis of these topics, ensuring that readers are equipped with knowledge about both the challenges and the opportunities for the improvement in public health policy.

As you engage with *Public Health Issues: Theory and Practices*, I encourage you to reflect on the themes' interconnectedness. The editors and contributors have successfully created a work that serves as an academic resource and a guide for practitioners and policymakers striving to create healthier communities.

In conclusion, *Public Health Issues: Theory and Practices* is an invaluable contribution to the field of public health, bridging the gap between historical insights and contemporary challenges. It offers a holistic perspective that will inform and inspire a new generation of public health leaders and advocates. As we navigate the complexities of health in our globalized world, let this volume serve as a beacon of knowledge and a call for collaborative action.

Interim Dean, Graduate College of Social Work
University of Houston
Houston, TX, USA

President Emerita
Stillman College
Tuscaloosa, AL, USA
November 5, 2024

Cynthia Warrick

Preface

The authors in this edited book, *Public Health Issues: Theory and Practice*, set the stage for exploring the dynamic landscape of public health. They emphasize the crucial interplay between theoretical framework and practical applications, illustrating how robust theories inform effective public health strategies. Recognizing the urgent challenges of emerging infectious diseases, health disparities, and environmental changes, the authors have highlighted the importance of a multidisciplinary approach. This book aims to equip readers—whether students, practitioners, or policymakers—with the knowledge and tools needed to address contemporary public health issues. By bridging theory and practice, the authors inspire innovative solutions and foster a deeper understanding of the factors that influence community health, ultimately promoting a healthier, more equitable society.

Part I lays the groundwork for understanding public health by tracing its historical milestones and conceptual evolution. Chapter 1 highlights significant achievements, emphasizing how historical events like pandemics and innovations have influenced health practices. Chapter 2 examines the origin of public health, detailing the shift from individual health concerns to community-oriented approaches. Chapter 3 discusses health literacy, a critical factor in empowering communities to make informed health choices. Finally, Chap. 4, titled "Clocks and Human Health," explores how time perception affects health behaviors and outcomes, illustrating the influence of societal rhythms on public health.

Part II addresses the socioeconomic dimensions of public health. Chapter 5 analyzes the economic impacts of environmental regulations during pandemics, highlighting the need for a balance between health policy and economic sustainability. Chapter 6 focuses on social determinants of health, emphasizing how income, education, and environment shape health outcomes. Chapter 7 provides insights into the financial implications of public health initiatives, which are crucial for policymakers' effective resource allocation. Chapter 8 examines patients' burdens, mainly due to socioeconomic disparities, advocating for a more equitable approach to healthcare.

Part III recognizes the intertwined roles of gender and environment in health. Chap. 9 addresses gender-specific health issues, advocating for inclusive solutions.

Chapter 10 discusses international environmental treaties and their relevance to public health, reinforcing the connection between health and environmental policies.

Part IV, the final section, delves into the legal and policy frameworks governing public health. Chapter 11 reviews wellness programs, assessing their effectiveness in promoting community health. Chapter 12 discusses infectious disease response planning, particularly relevant to the COVID-19 pandemic. Chapter 13 critiques public health laws in India, focusing on the challenges faced during the pandemic. Chapter 14 compares public health insurance policies in developing countries, while Chap. 15 reflects on lessons learned from the pandemic in developed nations, emphasizing the need for adaptable health systems.

We extend our heartfelt gratitude to all contributing authors whose expertise and dedication have shaped the discussion within these pages. Each chapter reflects a unique perspective, and the collaborative spirit of this work underscores the importance of interdisciplinary approaches in addressing public health issues. We appreciate the time and effort each author invested in their research, insights, and reflections, enriching the dialogue on theory and practice in public health. Additionally, we thank our reviewers for their invaluable feedback, which has enhanced the quality of this book. We hope this collective effort will inspire readers to engage with the pressing challenges of public health and contribute to meaningful change in their communities.

Lucknow, India Shalie Malik
Lucknow, India Varun Chhachhar
Montgomery, AL, USA Manoj Kumar Mishra

About the Book

Public Health Issues: Theory and Practice delves into the critical challenges public health is facing today, offering a comprehensive examination of both theoretical framework and practical applications. The book addresses pressing topics such as infectious diseases, chronic health conditions, and health disparities, emphasizing the importance of evidence-based approaches to intervention and policy formulation. It explores the role of social determinants of health, the impact of environmental factors, and the need for adequate health communication strategies. The book illustrates successful public health initiatives through case studies and real-world examples while highlighting areas requiring improvement. Overall, it is a vital resource for practitioners, policymakers, and students, providing the tools necessary to navigate the complexities of public health practice in a rapidly changing world.

Contents

Part I Public Health: History, Concepts, Scope

1 **Public Health Milestones Through the Years** 3
Jamal Masood and Reshma Masood

2 **The Origin and Practice of Public Health** 17
Ayush Lohiya

3 **Health Literacy** 27
Parul Dubey and Manoj Kumar Mishra

4 **Clocks and Human Health** 39
Sayantan Sur, Jyoti Tiwari, and Shalie Malik

Part II Public Health: Social and Economic Implication

5 **Pandemics and Policy: The Economic Impacts of Environmental Regulations** 65
Girjesh Shukla and Shubham Singh Bagla

6 **Social Determinants of Health (SDoH) and Their Impact on Human Well-Being** 79
Sreelakshmi Krishnakumar, Ritis K. Shyanti, Shalie Malik, and Manoj Kumar Mishra

7 **The Economics of Health: Understanding the Financial Implications of Public Health Initiatives** 91
Anamika Kumar Kulbhaskar

8 **Socio-economic Status Driven Social, Behavioral, and Financial Burden on Patients: A Critical Assessment of Health Equity** 111
Ritis K. Shyanti, Ram Alagan, Seela Aladuwaka, Shalie Malik, and Manoj Kumar Mishra

Part III Public Health: Environment and Gender Concerns

9 Policy and Governance in Public Health: Gender Concerns and Remedies 129
Anu Mehra

10 International Environmental Treaties and Public Health in the Context of Global Climate Change Crisis: Challenges and Mitigation 143
Ram Alagan, Seela Aladuwaka, Sandhu Aladuwaka, Parul Dubey, Shalie Malik, and Manoj Kumar Mishra

Part IV Public Health: Policy and Law

11 Wellness Programs 165
Chahal Anjali and Sandeep Kumar

12 Infectious Disease and Emergency Response Planning 187
Vipul Shah, Chahal Anjali, and Shalie Malik

13 Public Health Laws in India: Issues and Challenges in Covid-19 203
Jyoti Rattan and Anshula Rattan

14 A Comparative Analysis of Public Health Insurance Laws and Policies in Developing Countries 221
Manoj Kumar

15 Public Health in Developed Countries: A Lesson to Be Learnt from the COVID-19 Pandemic 237
Varun Chhachhar and Niharika Kumar

Index 255

Editors and Contributors

About the Editors

Shalie Malik is a Professor in the Department of Zoology at the University of Lucknow and is the Director of Dr. Giri Lal Gupta Institute of Public Health & Public Affairs. She is a Visiting Scientist at Alabama State University, having visited in 2023 and 2018, and was awarded the prestigious UGC Raman Fellowship (2016–2017) to conduct research at Alabama State University. Additionally, she received the DST-DAAD exchange scholarship (2001–2002) for work at the Max-Planck Institute for Ornithology in Germany and the Indian Society of Chronomedicine Fellowship Award in 2022. She is currently the Vice President of the Indian Society for Chronobiology and has previously served as Treasurer (2019–2022). She has received multiple university awards for her contributions to Avian Chronobiology (2016–2023) and has authored more than 80 widely cited peer-reviewed research articles in prestigious scientific journals, including Philosophical Transactions of the Royal Society B, Proceedings of the Royal Society B, Biology of Reproduction. Neuroendocrinology, Comparative Biochemistry and Physiology A, Photochemistry and Photobiology, Cancer Letters, Chronobiology International, among others. She has presented her research at numerous national and international conferences. Her research is funded by several organizations, including Science and Engineering Research Board (SERB), University Grants Commission (UGC), Department of Science & Technology (DST), Council of Science and Technology (CST), Center of Excellence (COE), and Research and Development Grant (R&D) (Govt. of U.P.). Her interests focus on how daily light, altered night environments, food availability, temperature, and social factors influence daily and seasonal behaviors regulated by endogenous clocks. Currently, her lab investigates the ecological impacts of artificial night lighting and anthropogenic noise on bird behavior and physiology as well as the intricate interplay between human lifestyle patterns and circadian rhythm regulated functions.

Varun Chhachhar is a Professor in the Faculty of Law, University of Lucknow, and Director of Dr. Shankar Dayal Sharma Institute of Democracy, University of Lucknow. He is a member of the Higher Education Council, Govt. of Uttar Pradesh, India. He is also the Director of RTI Cell at the University of Lucknow. He had also worked with Law Centre- I, Faculty of Law, University of Delhi, for 5 years as an Assistant Professor. He has published six books, including two on the Right to Information and another on the Right to Food, Competition Law, and Law and Governance. He had also published 20 research papers on various aspects of law, Public Policy specifically the Right to Information, Constitutional Law, and Environment Law, in various reputed journals and contributed chapters in books edited by legal luminaries across the country. He regularly delivers lectures at various government universities and national law universities across India. Apart from that, he is a speaker on RTI for many public institutions across India, training people in public institutions. He has more than 12 years of teaching experience. He received his LLB from Delhi University in 2006 and LLM from Jamia Millia Islamia in 2009. He also received the Post Graduate Scholarship for Professional Studies (LLM) for the years 2007–2009 by the University Grant Commission. He was a Junior Research Fellow at the University Grant Commission (2009). He was awarded a PhD on "Right to Information, Accountability and Administration of Justice" in 2016 by the Faculty of Law, Jamia Millia Islamia, New Delhi.

Manoj Kumar Mishra is a Professor at the Department of Biological Sciences, Alabama State University, Montgomery, AL, USA. He is also the founding director of the Cancer Research Center at Alabama State University. He received his MSc and PhD from Banaras Hindu University, Varanasi, India. After obtaining his doctorate, he moved to the United States and did his postdoctoral training in the Division of Biology, Kansas State University, Manhattan, KS; Division of Allergy and Immunology, Department of Pediatrics, Washington University School of Medicine, St. Louis, MO; and Division of Rheumatology, Department of Pediatrics at Medical College of Wisconsin, Milwaukee, WI. Before moving to Alabama State University in early 2009, he continued at the Medical College of Wisconsin as a Research Scientist in the Division of Allergy and Clinical Immunology within the Department of Pediatrics. He also holds a secondary appointment at the Division of Molecular and Cellular Pathology within the Department of Pathology, School of Medicine at the University of Alabama Birmingham, Birmingham, AL. He serves on several NIH study sections and the editorial board of scientific peer-reviewed journals. Research and educational grants from the National Institutes of Health and the National Science Foundation support Dr. Mishra's lab. He has several awards and recognition for his teaching and research. In 2015, he received the Faculty of the Year award at Alabama State University. In 2013, he was selected as one of the top 25 professors among mid-sized universities in the United States. He was a faculty scholar in cancer research at the American Association of Cancer Research in 2013, 2014, and 2016. In 2022, he received outstanding achievement awards from the Society of American Asian Scientists in Cancer Research (SAASCR). His education interests revolve around training, mentoring, and providing opportunities to undergraduate and graduate students, mainly from underrepresented populations. His research interest focuses on broader areas of immunology, tumor biology, and health disparity, using prostate cancer as a model system. His lab currently investigates the roles of dietary compounds, microbial metabolites, and immune cells, especially regulatory T and NK cells, in prostate cancer development and progression.

Contributors

Ram Alagan Department of Advancement Studies and W.E.B. Du Bois Honors Program, Alabama State University, Montgomery, AL, USA

Sandhu Aladuwaka Department of Political Science (MPA), University of Alabama, Tuscaloosa, AL, USA

Seela Aladuwaka Department of Advancement Studies and W.E.B. Du Bois Honors Program, Alabama State University, Montgomery, AL, USA

Chahal Anjali Dr. Giri Lal Gupta Institute of Public Health and Public Affairs, University of Lucknow, Lucknow, Uttar Pradesh, India

Shubham Singh Bagla SRM University, Delhi-NCR, Sonepat, Haryana, India

Varun Chhachhar Faculty of Law, University of Lucknow, Lucknow, Uttar Pradesh, India

Parul Dubey Cancer Research Center, Department of Biological Sciences, Alabama State University, Montgomery, AL, USA

Sreelakshmi Krishnakumar Cancer Research Center, Department of Biological Sciences, Alabama State University, Montgomery, AL, USA

Manoj Kumar Dr. Ram Manohar Lohiya National Law University, Lucknow, Uttar Pradesh, India

Sandeep Kumar Surgery and Epidemiology, King George's Medical University, Lucknow, India

AIIMS Bhopal, Bhopal, India

Anamika Kumar Kulbhaskar Department of Management Studies, Indian Institute of Technology Roorkee, Uttarakhand, India

Ayush Lohiya Kalyan Singh Super Specialty Cancer Institute, Lucknow, India

Shalie Malik Department of Zoology, University of Lucknow, Lucknow, Uttar Pradesh, India

Jamal Masood Era's Lucknow Medical College & Hospital, Department of Community Medicine and Public Health, King George's Medical University, Lucknow, Uttar Pradesh, India

Reshma Masood National Health Mission, Government of Uttar Pradesh, Uttar Pradesh, India

Anu Mehra Law Centre 1, Faculty of Law, University of Delhi, New Delhi, India

Manoj Kumar Mishra Cancer Research Center, Department of Biological Sciences, Alabama State University, Montgomery, AL, USA

Niharika Kumar Faculty of Law, University of Lucknow, Lucknow, Uttar Pradesh, India

Anshula Rattan University of Auckland, Auckland, New Zealand

Jyoti Rattan Department of Laws, Panjab University, Chandigarh, India

Vipul Shah R.P. Shah Memorial Trust for Global Health and Paediatric Disabilities, Lucknow, Uttar Pradesh, India

Girjesh Shukla Himachal Pradesh National Law University, Shimla, India

Ritis K. Shyanti Cancer Research Center, Department of Biological Sciences, Alabama State University, Montgomery, AL, USA

Sayantan Sur School of Biodiversity, One Health, and Veterinary Medicine, University of Glasgow, Glasgow, UK

Jyoti Tiwari Department of Zoology, University of Lucknow, Lucknow, Uttar Pradesh, India

Abbreviations

AANAT	Arylalkylamine N-Acetyltransferase
AB-NHPM	Ayushman Bharat-National Health Protection Mission
ABP	Ayushman Bharat Program
ACE	Adverse Childhood Experiences
ADE	Anno Domini Era
AIDS	Acquired Immune Deficiency Syndrome
ALLS	Adult Literacy and Life Skills
APHA	The American Public Health Association
AQI	Air Quality Index
ARI	Acute Respiratory Infection
ASPD	Advanced Sleep Phase Disorder
AVP	Arginine Vasopressin
BC	Before Christ
BCE	Before Common Era
BCG	Bacillus Calmette Guerin
BISP	Benazir Income Support Program
BNS	Bharatiya Nyaya Sanhita
BNSS	Bharatiya Nagarik Suraksha Sanhita
bOPV	Bivalent Oral Polio Vaccine
BPHU	Block Public Health Units
BPL	Below Poverty Line
BRICS	Brazil, Russia, India, China, and South Africa
BSA	Bharatiya Sakshya Adhiniyam
CBHI	Community-Based Health Insurance
CDC	Centers for Disease Control
CE	Common Era
CEA	Clinical Establishment Act
CGHS	Central Government Health Scheme
CH	Community Health
CHC	Community Health Centre
CHE	Current Health Expenditure

Clk	*Clock*
CM	Community Medicine
CO	Carbon Monoxide
CO_2	Carbon Dioxide
COVAX	COVID-19 Vaccines Global Access
COVID-19	Corona Virus Disease 2019
CrPC	Code of Criminal Procedure
CRSDs	Circadian Rhythm Sleep Disorders
Cry	*Cryptochrome*
CSSM	Child Survival and Safe Motherhood Programme
CVD	Cardiovascular Diseases
DALYs	Disability Adjusted Life Years
DBP	D-box Binding Protein
DDMA	District Disaster Management
DH	District Hospital
dLGN	Dorsal Lateral Geniculate Nucleus
DMA	Disaster Management Act
DOTS	Directly Observed Therapy Short-Course
DSPD	Delayed Sleep Phase Disorder
EAG	Empowered Action Groups
EDA	Epidemic Diseases Act
ENT	Ear Nose Throat
EPA	Environmental Protection Agency
EPI	Expanded Program on Immunization
EPIC	Environmental Policy Integrated Climate
ESI	Employee State Insurance
ESIS	Employees' State Insurance Scheme
FAO	Food and Agriculture Organization
FIL3	Nuclear Factor Interleukin 3
FPH	Faculty of Public Health
FRD	Free-Running Disorder
FRUs	First Referral Units
FY	Financial Year
GABA	γ-Aminobutyric Acid
GBV	Gender-Based Violence
GCF	Green Climate Fund
GDHS	Global Digital Health Summit
GDP	Gross Domestic Product
GFHIS	Government-Funded Health Insurance Schemes
GHT	Geniculo Hypothalamic Tract
GIS	Geographic Information System
GNI	Gross National Income
GOBI – FFF	Growth Monitoring, Oral Rehydration, Breastfeeding, Immunisation, Fertility Promotion, Feeding Programme, and Female Development

GOBI	Growth Monitoring, Oral Rehydration, Breastfeeding and Immunisation
GOI	Government of India
GP	General Practitioners
GPA	Global Programme on AIDS
GRP	Gastrin-Releasing Peptide
GWI	Global Wellness Institute
H1N1	Influenza A Virus
H5N1	Avian Influenza A
HEIDI	Health and Environmental Interplay Database
HFD	High-Fat Diet
HHS	Health and Human Services
HIA	Health Impact Assessment
HiAP	Health in All Policies
HIV	Human Immunodeficiency Virus
HLEG	High-Level Expert Group
HLF	Hepatic Leukemia Factor
HSR	Health Silk Road
HWCs	Health and Wellness Centers
ICCPR	International Covenant on Civil and Political Rights
ICMR	Indian Council of Medical Research
ICU	Intensive Care Units
IDF	International Diabetes Federation
IEA	Indian Evidence Act
IFA	Iron Folic Acid
IGL	Intergeniculate Leaflet
IHR	International Health Regulations
IMCI	Integrated Management of Childhood Diseases
IML	Intermediolateral Nucleus
INR	Indian National Rupee
IPC	Indian Penal Code
ipRGCs	Intrinsically Photosensitive Retinal Ganglion Cells
IPV	Inactivated Poliovirus Vaccine
IPV	Intimate Partner Violence
IRC	International Red Cross/Red Crescent
IRDAI	Insurance Regulatory and Development Authority of India
ISI	Indian Standards Institution
IUDs	Intra-Uterine Devices
IYCF	Infant and Young Child Feeding
JLD	Jet Lag Disorder
JSSK	Janani Shishu Suraksha Karyakram
JSY	Janani Suraksha Yojana
LGBTQ+	Lesbian, Gay, Bisexual, Transgender, Queer, Plus Other Diverse Identities
MBS	Medicare Benefit Schedule

MCH	Maternal and Child Health
MHM	Menstrual Hygiene Management
MMR	Maternal Mortality Ratio
MoHFW	Ministry of Health and Family Welfare
MoSPI	Ministry of Statistics and Programme Implementation
MTPA	Medical Termination of Pregnancy Act
NACI	National Advisory Committee on Immunizations
NACP	National AIDS Control Program
NCD	Non-communicable Diseases
NDCs	Nationally Determined Contributions
NDMA	National Disaster Management Authority
NDRF	National Disaster Response Force
NES	Night Eating Syndrome
NFHS	National Family Health Survey
NGO	Non-governmental Organizations
NHA	National Health Accounts
NHP	National Health Policy
NHPS	National Health Protection Scheme
NHRA	National Health Reform Agreement
NHS	National Health Service
NHSRC	National Health Systems Resource Centre
NITI	National Institute for Transforming India
NMEP	National Malaria Eradication Program
NMHP	National Mental Health Program
NO_2	Nitrogen Dioxide
NPCDCS	National Programme for Prevention and Control of Cancer, Diabetes, Cardiovascular Diseases, and Stroke
NPHCE	National Program for Health Care of the Elderly
NPMs	Nurse Practitioner Midwives
NPY	Neuropeptide Y
NTEP	National Tuberculosis Elimination Programme
NVPO	National Vaccine Program Office
O_3	Ozone
ODS	Ozone Depleting Substances
OOP	Out-of-Pocket
OOPE	Out-of-Pocket Expenditure
OPD	Out Patient Department
OPN	Olivary Pretectal Nucleus
OVLT	Organum Vasculosum Lamina Terminalis
PACS	Post Acute COVID-19 Syndrome
Per	*Period*
PERMA	Positive Emotions, Engagement, Relationships, Meaning, Accomplishment
PFHIS	Publicly Funded Health Insurance Schemes
PHAC	Public Health Agency of Canada

PHC	Primary Health Centre
PHSM	Public Health and Social Measures
PM	Particulate Matter
PMABHIM	PM-Ayushman Bharat Health Infrastructure Mission
PMJAY	Pradhan Mantri Jan Arogya Yojana
PMSMA	Pradhan Mantri Surakshit Matritva Abhiyan
PPE	Personal Protective Equipment
PPP	Public-Private Partnerships
PRC	Phase Response Curve
PRET	Preparedness and Resilience for Emerging Threats Initiative
PSM	Preventive and Social Medicine
PVN	Paraventricular Nucleus
RBSK	Rashtriya Bal Swasthya Karyakaram
REACH	Racial and Ethnic Approaches to Community Health
REALM	Rapid Estimate of Adult Literacy in Medicine
REM	Rapid Eye Movement
RGC	Regional Geriatric Center
RHT	Retino-Hypothalamic Tract
RMNCH+A-	Reproductive Maternal Neonatal Child and Adolescent Health
RSBY	Rashtriya Swasthya Bima Yojana
RSTV	Rajya Sabha Television
SARS	Severe Acute Respiratory Syndrome
SARS-CoV-2	Severe Acute Respiratory Syndrome-Coronavirus-Second Strain
SAS	Specialist and Academic Staff
SC	Statutes of Canada
SCG	Superior Cervical Ganglion
SCHIS	Senior Citizen Health Insurance Scheme
SCN	Suprachiasmatic Nuclei
SDC	Swiss Agency for Development and Cooperation
SDGs	Sustainable Development Goals
SDH	Social Determinants of Health
SDMA	State Disaster Management Authority
SDoH	Social Determinants of Health
SES	Socioeconomic Status
SHI	Social Health Insurance
SO_2	Sulfur Dioxide
SRHR	Sexual and Reproductive Health Rights
SUMAN	Surakshit Matritva Aashwasan
SVI	Social Vulnerability Index
Tele MANAS	Tele Mental Health Assistance and Networking Across States
THE	Total Health Expenditure
TOFHLA	Test of Functional Health Literacy in Adults
tOPV	Trivalent Oral Poliovirus Vaccine
TRIPS	Trade-Related Aspects of Intellectual Property Rights
TTFL	Transcriptional Translational Feedback Loop

UCL-IHE	University College London's Institute of Health Equity
UDHR	Universal Declaration of Human Rights
UHC	Universal Health Coverage
UHIS	Universal Health Insurance Scheme
UK	United Kingdom
UN	United Nation
UNFPA	United Nations Fund for Population Activities
UNICEF	United Nations International Children's Emergency Fund
UPI	Universal Programme of Immunization
US	United States
USA	United States of America
USGCRP	US Global Change Research Program
USSR	Union of Soviet Socialist Republics
UT	Union Territory
VIP	Vasoactive Intestinal Peptide
WASH	Water, Sanitation and Hygiene
WFSO	World Food Security Outlook
WHO	The World Health Organization

Part I
Public Health: History, Concepts, Scope

Chapter 1
Public Health Milestones Through the Years

Jamal Masood and Reshma Masood

1.1 Definition of Health

World Health Organization (WHO) provided a definition of health in the preamble to its constitution in 1948. It is "Health is a state of complete physical, mental and social well-being and not merely the absence of disease or infirmity".

1.2 Public Health

The term "Public Health" was coined around 1840. The aim was to protect the public from the spread of communicable diseases. Public Health Act was enacted in England in the year 1848.

Charles Edward Amory Winslow was the first chairman of the Department of Public Health at the Yale University School of Medicine in United States. In 1920, he defined Public Health as "The Science and art of preventing disease, prolonging life and promoting physical health and efficiency through organized community efforts".

The WHO Expert Committee on Public Health Administration (1952) has defined Public Health as "the science and art of preventing disease, prolonging life and promoting health and efficiency through organized community efforts for the sanitation of the environment, the control of communicable infections, the

J. Masood (✉)
Era's Lucknow Medical College & Hospital, Department of Community Medicine and Public Health, King George's Medical University, Lucknow, Uttar Pradesh, India

R. Masood
National Health Mission, Government of Uttar Pradesh, Lucknow, India

S. Malik et al. (eds.), *Public Health Issues: Theory and Practices*,
https://doi.org/10.1007/978-981-96-6650-8_1

education of the individual in personal hygiene, the organization of medical and nursing services for early diagnosis and preventive treatment of disease, and the development of social machinery to ensure for every individual a standard of living adequate for the maintenance of health, so organizing these benefits as to enable every citizen to realize his birthright of health and longevity".

1.3 History of Public Health

The history of Public health is a story of the search for effective means of securing health and preventing disease in the population. Public Health evolved with trial and error. Every culture had developed a system of public health [1]. The evolution of public health continues, pathogens change, as do the environment and the host. In order to face challenges ahead, it is important to have an understanding of the past [2].

Ancient Indian System of Public Health
Ancient Indian cities were planned and built with street paving and sewer drains. Ayurvedic medicine, medical schools and public hospitals were developed between 800 and 200 BCE. Personal hygiene was emphasized, and sanitation and water supply engineering were also developed during this period. Indian Medicine and Public Health played an important role in Asia. In ancient India, the celebrated authorities in Ayurvedic medicine were Atreya, Charaka, Sushruta, and Vaghbhatt. Atreya (800 BCE) is the first great Indian physician and teacher. Charaka (200 ADE) compiled "Charaka Samhita" which mentions 500 drugs. Sushruta is known as father of Indian surgery. He compiled the surgical knowledge in his classic "Sushruta Samhita". Samhitas of Charaka and Sushruta were translated into Persian and Arabic in about 800 ADE [3, 4].

Ancient Chinese System of Public Health
Chinese medicine and public health developed in 2700 BCE. Hygiene dietetics, hydrotherapy, massage, acupuncture, herbal drugs, and immunization against small pox were all used by Chinese physicians. Digging of wells for safe drinking water, destruction of rats, and rabid animals were the public health measures used by Chinese.

Ancient Egyptian System of Public Health
Egyptian medicine and public health have reached its peak around 2800 BCE. They built planned cities, public baths, and underground drains. They had knowledge of inoculation against smallpox, use of mosquito nets, and association of plague with rats. Personal hygiene was also emphasized [5].

Ancient Mesopotamian System of Public Health
Mesopotamia is a region in Iraq. Mesopotamian Public health was developed around 2100 BCE. Hygiene was of utmost importance to the Mesopotamians. They believed that an unclean and smelly body was impure. Regular bathing was

a common practice. Mesopotamians used soaps made from clay or ash mixed with scented oils. Mesopotamians understood that sickness is associated with uncleanliness [6].

Ancient Greek System of Public Health
The greatest physician in Greek medicine was Hippocrates (460–370 BCE). He is called Father of Medicine. Hippocrates was also an epidemiologist; he distinguished between diseases which were epidemic and those which were endemic. His book *Airs, Water and Places* is considered a treatise on social medicine and hygiene. Ancient Greece placed high emphasis on healthful living habits in terms of personal hygiene, nutrition, physical fitness, and community sanitation. City officials were appointed to look after public drains and water supply providing organized sanitary and public health services [7].

Ancient Roman System of Public Health
Roman Public Health developed by first century BCE. The Romans were extremely skilled in engineering of water supply, sewage, and drainage system. They built public baths and latrines. They also developed town planning, sanitation of military establishments, and medical care. Rome itself had access to clean water supplying ample water for the citizens. Marshlands were drained to reduce the malarial threat. Streets were paved there was organized garbage disposal system.

Ancient Arabic System of Public Health
The Golden age of Arabic Medicine and Public Health was between 800 and 1300 ADE. They developed their own system of medicine known as the Unani system of medicine. They founded schools of public health and hospitals in Baghdad, Damascus, and Cairo. Two great physicians Rhazes and Avicenna. Piped water supplies were documented in Cairo in the ninth century. The greatest contribution of Arabs was in the field of pharmacology. They developed pharmaceutical chemistry and introduced a large number of drugs, herbal and chemical. They introduced a wide range of syrups, oils, poultices, plasters, pills, powders, alcoholates, and aromatic water [4, 7].

1.4 Important International Public Health Events [8–12]

- **1348—1350 Black Death**

  Pandemic of Bubonic plague was called Black Death. Originated in Asia, spread by armies of Genghis Khan. This pandemic killed 60 million in fourteenth century.

- **1518**—Royal College of Physicians founded in London.
- **1639**—Massachusetts Law requires recording of births and deaths.
- **1661**—John Graunt founded Medical Statistics and Demography in London. He constructed the first mortality table.
- **1665**—Great Plague of London. The Great Plague killed an estimated 1,00,000 people almost a quarter of London's population in 18 months.

- **1667—**Pandemic of Malaria in Europe, Epidemic of Smallpox in London.
- **1747—**James Lind conducted case control study of scurvy in sailors.
- **1796—**Edward Jenner vaccinated 24 children against Smallpox.
- **1801—**First National Census in United Kingdom.
- **1854—**John Snow of England in his classic investigation of cholera epidemic Golden Square district of London was able to focus attention on the common water pump in broad street as the source of infection.
- **1854—**Florence Nightingale founded Modern nursing in Crimean War.
- **1858—**Public Health and Local Government Act in United Kingdom.
- **1864—**First International Geneva Convention and founding of International Committee of the Red Cross.
- **1872—**American Public Health Association founded.
- **1876—**Robert Koch discovered Anthrax bacillus.
- **1876—**Neisser discovered Gonococcus organism.
- **1880—**Laveran discovered Typhoid bacillus.
- **1880—**Hansen discovered Leprosy organism.
- **1882—**Robert Koch discovers the Tuberculosis organism.
- **1883—**Robert Koch discovers bacillus of cholera.
- **1883—**Louis Pasteur vaccinated against anthrax.
- **1885—**Louis Pasteur developed Rabies vaccine.
- **1897—**London School of Hygiene and Tropical Medicine founded.
- **1915—**John Hopkins and Harvard Schools of Public Health founded.
- **1918–1919—**Pandemic of Spanish flu (Influenza) killed 20 million people.
- **1926—**Pertussis vaccine developed.
- **1928—**Alexander Fleming discovered penicillin.
- **1946—**World Health Organization (WHO) founded.
- **1948**—United Kingdom establishes National Health Service.
- **1954—**Framingham study of heart disease risk factors.
- **1954—**Salk's inactivated poliomyelitis vaccine licensed.
- **1960—**Sabin's live poliomyelitis vaccine licensed.
- **1963—**Measles vaccine licensed.
- **1967—**Mumps vaccine licensed.
- **1970—**Rubella vaccine licensed.
- **1977—**WHO adopts Health for All by the Year 2000.
- **1977—**Last known outbreak of smallpox reported in Somalia.
- **1978—**Alma Ata Conference on Primary Health Care.
- **1978—**Hepatitis B vaccine licensed.
- **1979—**WHO declares Eradication of Smallpox.
- **1981—**First recognized case of AIDS in USA.
- **1987—**A worldwide "Safe Motherhood" campaign was launched by World Bank.
- **2002–2004—**Outbreak of SARS infected over 8000 people from 30 countries and resulted in 774 deaths.
- **2009—**Pandemic of Swine flu H1N1/Influenza virus.
- **2020—**COVID-19 Pandemic played havoc in the world.

1.5 Public Health in British India

- **1757**—The British had established their rule in India.
- **1825**—The Quarantine Act was promulgated.
- **1864**—Sanitary Commissioners were appointed in the three major provinces-Bombay, Madras and Bengal.
- **1869**—A Public Health Commissioner and a Statistical Officer were appointed with the Government of India.
- **1873**—Birth and Death Registration Act was promulgated.
- **1880**—The Vaccination Act was passed.
- **1881**—Indian Factories Act was passed.
- **1881**—The First All India Census was taken.
- **1896**—A severe epidemic of plague occurred in India which awakened the Government to the urgent need of improving public health.
- **1897**—The Epidemic Diseases Act was promulgated.
- **1909**—The Central Malaria Bureau was founded at Kasauli.
- **1911**—The Indian Research Fund Association (now I.C.M.R.) was established for the promotion of research.
- **1920**—Municipality and Local Board Acts, containing legal provisions for the advancement of public health were passed in several provinces.
- **1930**—The All India Institute of Hygiene and Public Health, Calcutta was established with aid from the Rockefeller Foundation.
- **1930**—The Child Marriage Restraint Act (Sarda Act) came into effect fixing the minimum age of marriage at 14 for girls and 18 for boys.
- **1937**—The Central Advisory Board of Health was set up with the Public Health Commissioner as Secretary and representative from the provinces and Indian States as members, to coordinate the public health activities in the country.
- **1939**—The Madras Public Health Act was passed.
- **1939**—The first Rural Health Training Centre was established at Singur, near Calcutta with aid from the Rockefeller Foundation.
- **1940**—The Drugs Act was passed.
- **1943**—The Health Survey and Development Committee (Bhore Committee) was appointed by the Government of India to survey the existing position in regard to health conditions and health organization in the country, and to make recommendations for the future development.
- **1946**—The Bhore Committee submitted its report. The health of the nation was reviewed under (1) Public Health (2) Medical Relief (3) Professional Education (4) Medical Research and (5) International Health. The Committee recommended a short-term and a long-term programme for the attainment of reasonable health services.

1.6 Evolution of Public Health in India Since Independence

India became independent in 1947. The Bhore Committee's report and recommendations became the basis for most of the planning and measures adopted by the national government. The significant events in the history of public health since India became free are as follows:

- **1947**—Ministries of Health were established at the Centre and States. The posts of Director General, Indian Medical Service, and of Public Health Commissioner with the Government of India were integrated in the post of Director General of Health Services, who is the principal adviser to the Union Government on both medical and public health matters. This example was followed by many States.
- **1948**—India joined the World Health Organization as a member state.
- **1948**—The Employees State Insurance Act. 1948 was passed.
- **1949**—The Constituent Assembly adopted the Constitution of India on 26 November, 1949. Article 246 of the Constitution of India covers all the health subjects; these have been enumerated in the seventh schedule under three lists—Union List, Concurrent List and State List.
- **1949**—Article 47 of the Constitution under the Directive Principles of State Policy states: "That the State shall regard the raising of the level of nutrition and standard of living of the people and the improvement of public health as among its primary duties".
- **1949**—The post of Registrar General of India was created in the Ministry of Home Affairs.
- **1949**—The South East Asia Regional Office of the WHO was established in New Delhi.
- **1949**—The Indian Research Fund Association was reconstituted into Indian Council of Medical Research.
- **1950**—The Constitution of India came into force and India became a Republic.
- **1950**—The Planning Commission was set up by the Government of India, which set to work immediately for drafting the first Five Year Plan.
- **1951**—The beginning of the first Five Year Plan, with a total outlay of Rs. 2356 crores. A sum of Rs.140 crores (5.9%) was allotted for health programmes.
- **1951**—The B.C.G. vaccination programme was launched in the country.
- **1952**—The Community Development Programme was launched on 2 October, 1952 for the all-round development of the rural areas. Provision of medical relief and preventive health services were part of the programme.
- **1952**—The Central Council of Health was constituted with the Union Health Minister as Chairman and the Health Ministers of the States as members to coordinate health policies between the Central and State Governments.
- **1952**—Primary Health Centres were set up.
- **1953**—The National Malaria Control Programme was commenced as part of the first Five-Year Plan.
- **1953**—National Family Planning Programme was started.
- **1954**—The Contributory Health Service Scheme was started at Delhi.

- **1954**—The Central Social Welfare Board was set up.
- **1954**—The National Water Supply and Sanitation Programme was inaugurated.
- **1954**—The National Leprosy Control Programme was started.
- **1954**—The Prevention of Food Adulteration Act was passed by Parliament.
- **1955**—The National Filaria Control Programme was started.
- **1955**—The Central Leprosy Teaching and Research Institute was established at Chingelput, Madras.
- **1955**—Filaria Training Centre was established at Ernakulam, Kerala.
- **1955**—The Hindu Marriage Act prescribed the minimum age for marriage 18 for boys and 15 for girls.
- **1955**—National TB sample survey commenced.
- **1956**—The Second Five Year Plan (1956–1961) was launched with an outlay of Rs.4800 crores, out of which Rs.225 crores (5.0%) were earmarked for health programmes.
- **1956**—The Model Public Health Act was published.
- **1956**—The Central Health Education Bureau was established in the Union Health Ministry.
- **1956**—Director, Family Planning was appointed in the Union Health Ministry.
- **1956**—The Demographic Training and Research Centre was established in Mumbai.
- **1956**—The Tuberculosis Chemotherapy Centre was established in Chennai.
- **1956**—The R.C.A projects were established by the Union Health Ministry with aid from the Ford Foundation.
- **1957**—Influenza pandemic swept the country.
- **1957**—The Demographic Research Centres were established in Calcutta, Delhi, and Trivandrum.
- **1958**—The National Malaria Control Programme was converted into National Malaria Eradication programme
- **1959**—The Mudaliar Committee was appointed by the Government of India to survey the progress made in the field of health since submission of the Bhore Committee's Report, and to make recommendations for future development and expansion of health services
- **1959**—The National Tuberculosis Institute was established at Bangalore.
- **1960**—The School Health Committee was constituted by the Union Health Ministry to assess the present standards of health and nutrition of school children and suggest ways and means to improve them.
- **1960**—National Nutrition Advisory Committee was constituted to tender advice regarding the nutritional policies to be adopted by the Government.
- **1960**—Vital statistics were transferred to the Registrar General of India, Ministry of Home Affairs, from the Directorate General Health Services.
- **1961**—The Third Five Year Plan (1961–66) was launched with an outlay of Rs.7500 crores out of which Rs.342 crores (4.3%) were provided for health programmes.
- **1961**—The Central Bureau of Health Intelligence was established.
- **1962**—The Central Family Planning Institute was established in Delhi.

- **1962**—The National Smallpox Eradication Programme was launched.
- **1962**—The School Health Programme was initiated.
- **1962**—The National Goitre control programme launched 1962.
- **1962**—The District Tuberculosis Programme was formulated.
- **1963**—The Applied Nutrition Programme was launched by the Government of India with aid from UNICEF, FAO, and WHO.
- **1963**—The National Institute of Communicable Diseases (formerly Malaria Institute of India) was inaugurated.
- **1963**—The National Trachoma Control Programme was launched.
- **1963**—The name "Contributory Health Service Scheme" was changed to "Central Government Health Scheme".
- **1963**—Extended Family Planning Programme was launched; emphasis in family planning was shifted from the clinic approach to "Extension approach".
- **1963**—The Chadha Committee established a norm of one Basic Health Worker for every 10,000 population.
- **1963**—Drinking Water Board was set up.
- **1964**—The National Institute of Health Administration and Education was opened in collaboration with the Ford Foundation.
- **1965**—Director ICMR, recommended Lippes Loop as safe and effective for a mass programme.
- **1965**—'Direct" BCG vaccination without prior tuberculin test, on a house to house basis, was introduced
- **1966**—Mukherjee Committee—Committee of Health Secretaries under the Chairmanship of Secretary, Ministry of Health, Government of India was constituted to look into the minimum additional staff required for the primary health centres to take over the maintenance work of malaria and smallpox.
- **1966**—A separate department of Family Planning was constituted in the Union Ministry of Health to coordinate family planning programme at the Centre and States.
- **1968**—A Bill of Registration of Births and Deaths was passed by the Parliament
- **1968**—The Govt. of India appointed the Medical Education Committee to study all aspects of medical education in the light of national needs and resources.
- **1969**—The Fourth Five Year Plan (1969–1974) was launched with an outlay of Rupees 16,774 crores, out of which Rs.840 crores were allocated to health and Rupees 315 crores to family planning.
- **1969**—Medical Education Committee said that the total period for MBBS course should be 4 ½ years and 1 year for internship, which should include posting in a rural centre for a period of at least 3 months.
- **1970**—The Drugs (Price Control) Order, 1970 was promulgated.
- **1970**—All India Hospital (Post-partum) Family Planning Programme was started.
- **1970**—The Registration of Births and Deaths Act, 1969 came into force from 1 April 1970.
- **1970**—The name of the Demographic Training and Research Centre, Mumbai was changed into International Institute for Population Studies.

- **1971**—The Medical Termination of Pregnancy Bill, 1969 was passed by Parliament.
- **1972**—The Medical Termination of Pregnancy Act came into force on 1 April 1972.
- **1972**—The National Nutrition Monitoring Bureau was set up under the Indian Council of Medical Research, with headquarters at the National Institute of Nutrition, Hyderabad. Regional units have also been established in the States.
- **1973**—The National Programme of Minimum Needs was incorporated in the Fifth Five Year Plan. A provision of Rs. 2803 crores was made for this programme, which covered elementary education, rural health, nutrition, rural roads and water supply, housing, slum improvement, and rural electrification.
- **1973**—The Government envisaged a scheme for setting up 30 bedded rural hospitals; one such hospital for every 4 primary health centres.
- **1973**—The Kartar Singh Committee submitted its report recommending the formation of a new cadre of health workers designated "Multi-purpose Health Workers" for the delivery of health, family planning, and nutrition services to the rural communities, who will replace in course of time the basic health workers, family planning health assistants, auxiliary nurse-mid-wives, etc.
- **1974**—The Fifth Five Year Plan was launched on 1 April 1974 with a total outlay of Rs.53,411 crores, of which Rs.37,250 crores were in the public sector and Rs.16,161 crores in the private sector. A sum of Rs.796 crores were allotted to health, and Rs.516 crores to family planning.
- **1974**—The United Nations designated 1974 as World Population Year.
- **1974**—Parliament enacted the Water (prevention and control pollution) Act, 1974.
- **1975**—India became smallpox-free on 5 July 1975.
- **1975**—The Government of India accepted the revised strategy for NMEP.
- **1975**—Integrated Child Development Services Scheme launched on October 2, 1975.
- **1975**—The ESI Act was amended.
- **1976**—Indian Factories Act of 1948 amended.
- **1976**—The Prevention of Food Adulteration (Amendment) Act 1975 came into force on 1 April 1976.
- **1976**—The Equal Remuneration Act, 1975 was promulgated providing for equal wages for men and women for the same work of a similar nature.
- **1976**—The Union Health Ministry announced a "new population policy".
- **1976**—The Central Council of Health proposed a three-tier plan for medical care in villages.
- **1976**—National Programme for Prevention of Blindness was formulated.
- **1977**—ROME scheme was launched.
- **1977**—Rural Health Scheme was launched; training of community health workers was taken up.
- **1977**—Revised Modified Plan of malaria eradication was put into operation.
- **1977**—National Institute of Health and Family Welfare, New Delhi established.
- **1977**—WHO adopted the goal of Health for All by 2000 A.D.

- **1978**—Bill on Air Pollution introduced in the Lok Sabha.
- **1978**—Parliament approved the Child Marriage Restraint (Amendment) Bill, 1978 fixing the minimum age at marriage 21 years for boys and 18 years for girls.
- **1978**—EPI was launched.
- **1978**—Declaration of Alma Ata underlined the primary health care approach.
- **1979**—World Health Assembly endorsed the Declaration of Alma Ata on primary health care.
- **1979**—The Regional offices of family welfare and NMEP of Govt. of India were merged and named as Regional Office for Health and Family Welfare.
- **1980**—On 8 May 1980, smallpox was officially declared eradicated from the entire world by World Health Assembly.
- **1980**—Sixth Five Year Plan (1980–1985) was launched.
- **1981**—The 1981 census was taken.
- **1981**—WHO and Member Countries adopted the Global strategy for Health for All.
- **1981**—India is committed to the goal of providing safe drinking water and adequate sanitation for all by 1990, under the International Drinking water Supply and Sanitation Decade 1981–1990.
- **1981**—The Air (Prevention and Control of Pollution) Act of 1981 was enacted.
- **1982**—The New 20 Point Programme was announced.
- **1982**—The Govt. of India announced its National Health Policy.
- **1983**—India launched a National Plan of Action against avoidable disablement, known as "IMPACT India".
- **1983**—National Leprosy Control Programme to be called National Leprosy Eradication Programme.
- **1983**—National Health Policy was approved by the Parliament.
- **1983**—Guinea-worm eradication Programme was launched.
- **1984**—Bhopal gas tragedy, the worst ever industrial accident in history occurred on the night of Dec. 2/3 taking a toll of at least 3000 people and 50,000 were affected.
- **1984**—The ESI (Amendment) Bill, 1984 was approved by Parliament.
- **1984**—The Workmen's Compensation (Amendment) Act, 1984 came into force from 1 July 1984.
- **1985**—Seventh Five Year Plan (1985–1990) was launched.
- **1985**—Universal Immunization Programme was launched.
- **1985**—The Lepers Act, 1898 was repealed by Parliament.
- **1985**—A separate Department of Women and Child Development was set up under the newly created Ministry of Human Resource Development.
- **1986**—The Environment (Protection) Act 1986 promulgated.
- **1986**—20-point plan restructured.
- **1986**—Parliament voted Mental Health Bill.
- **1986**—Juvenile Justice Act 1986 came into force.
- **1987**—New 20 point programme was launched.
- **1987**—Indian Standards institution (ISI) renamed: Bureau of Indian Standards.

- **1987**—National Diabetes Control Programme initiated.
- **1987**—National AIDS Control Programme launched.
- **1987**—The Factories (Amendment) Act 1987 operated—with provisions to protect employees exposed to hazardous processes.
- **1989**—Blood Safety Programme was launched.
- **1990**—Control of Acute Respiratory Infection (ARI) Programme initiated as a pilot project in 14 districts.
- **1992**—Eighth Five Year Plan (1992–1997) was launched.
- **1992**—Child Survival and Safe Motherhood Programme (CSSM) was launched on 20 August 1992.
- **1992**—The Infant Milk substitute, Feeding Bottles and Infant Foods (Regulation of Production, Supply and Distribution) Act 1992 came into force.
- **1993**—Revised National Tuberculosis Programme with DOTS introduced as Pilot Project in the country.
- **1993**—National Nutrition Policy 1993 was formulated.
- **1994**—The Panchayati Raj Act came into force with all States completing the process of legislation.
- **1995**—The legislation on Transplantation of Human Organs was enacted to regulate the removal, storage and transplantation of human organs for therapeutic purposes and for prevention of commercial dealings in human organs.
- **1996**—Pulse Polio Immunization, the largest single day public health event took place on 9 December 1995 and 20 January 1996. The second phase of PPI was conducted on 7 December 1996 and 18 January 1997.
- **1996**—Prenatal Diagnostic Technique (Regulation and Prevention of Misuse) Act 1994 came into force from January 1996.
- **1996**—Yaws eradication programme launched.
- **1997**—Reproductive and Child Health Programme launched.
- **1997**—Ninth five year plan launched, 1998–1999.
- **1997**—National Family Health Survey-2 undertaken covering 90,000 women aged 15–49 years.
- **1997**—National Malaria Eradication Programme renamed as National Anti-Malaria Programme.
- **1997**—Phase II of National AIDS Control Programme became effective.
- **2000**—Government of India announced National Population Policy-2000.
- **2000**—Certification of India as a Guinea Worm disease free country by WHO in February 2000.
- **2000**—Signatory to UN Millennium Declaration.
- **2000**—National Commission on Population constituted.
- **2001**—India stages first census of the century.
- **2001**—National Policy for empowerment of women launched on 20 March 2001.
- **2002**—National Health Policy 2002 announced.
- **2002**—Government announces National AIDS Prevention and Control Policy 2002.
- **2002**—Tenth Five Year Plan launched.

- **2002**—Emergence of SARS.
- **2003**—Parliament approves the Cigarettes and other Tobacco Products (Prohibition, Regulation of Trade and Commerce, Production, Supply and Distribution) Act.
- **2003**—National Vector Borne Disease Control Programme approved as umbrella programme for prevention of vector borne diseases, viz., malaria, filaria, Kala-azar, dengue/DHF, and Japanese encephalitis.
- **2004**—Vandemataram Scheme launched.
- **2004**—Revised Programme of Nutritional Support to Primary Education (Mid-day meal scheme) launched.
- **2004**—Low osmolarity oral rehydration salt replaces the existing formula.
- **2004**—Integrated Disease Surveillance Project launched.
- **2004**—National Guidelines on Infant and Young Child Feeding formulated in Aug. 2004
- **2005**—RCH II launched.
- **2005**—Janani Suraksha Yojana launched.
- **2005**—National Rural Health Mission launched.
- **2005**—Indian Public Health Standards for Community Health Centres formulated.
- **2005**—National Plan of Action for Children 2005 formulated.
- **2006**—WHO releases new paediatric growth chart based on breast-fed children.
- **2006**—Ban on child labour as domestic servant.
- **2006**—National Family Health Survey-3 conducted.
- **2006**—IMNCI was launched in 16 states.
- **2007**—11th Five-Year Plan launched.
- **2007**—NACP III launched.
- **2007**—Indian Public Health Standards for PHC and sub-centres formulated.
- **2008**—Non-communicable Disease Programme as pilot project launched.
- **2009**—Pandemic Influenza H1N1 outbreak
- **2010**—ICMR announces nutrients requirements and recommended dietary allowances for Indians
- **2011**—India stages second census of the century
- **2013**—National Health Mission launched, RMNCH+A strategy launched.
- **2014**—India Newborn Action Plan launched on 27th March.
- **2014**—India declared polio free country.
- **2014**—Mission Indradhanush launched on 25th December.
- **2015**—NITI Aayog replaces Yojana Aayog on 1 January 2015.
- **2015**—Use of IPV in immunization schedule from November 2015.
- **2015**—Juvenile Justice Act 2015.
- **2015**—Swachh Bharat Abhiyan launched.
- **2016**—Sustainable Development Goals officially came in to force on 1 January 2016.
- **2016**—Malaria eradication plan (2016–2030) launched.
- **2016**—Switch from tOPV to bOPV in April 2016.

- **2017**—Aadhaar number must for death certificate from October 2017.
- **2017**—National Health Policy 2017.
- **2018**—National Health Protection Scheme.
- **2018**—Ayushman Bharat launched.
- **2019**—RNTCP renamed National Tuberculosis Elimination Programme (NTEP).
- **2020**—"National Medical Commission" replaced MCI on 25.9.2020.
- **2020**—COVID-19 Pandemic played havoc in the world.
- **2021**—Digital Health ID project.
- **2021—PM-Ayushman Bharat Health Infrastructure Mission (PM-ABHIM)** was announced in the Budget 21–22 on 1 February 2021. The PM-ABHIM is a Centrally Sponsored Scheme. The components of the PM-ABHIM scheme are: **(1)** Rural Health and Wellness Centres: Under PM-ABHIM, provision is available for necessary infrastructure support for construction of Sub Health Centres level AB-HWCs in rural areas in seven High Focus States (Bihar, Jharkhand, Odisha, Punjab, Rajasthan, Uttar Pradesh and West Bengal) and three North-eastern States (Assam, Manipur and Meghalaya) cumulatively over a 5-year duration from FY 21–22 to FY 25–26. **(2)** Urban Health and Wellness Centres: Under PM-ABHIM, 11,024 Urban HWCs cumulatively over a 5-year duration from FY 21–22 to FY 25–26 are envisaged to be established across all the States and UTs to ensure provision of comprehensive primary health care to the urban population. **(3)** Block Public Health Units: Under the scheme, it is envisaged to establish 3382 BPHUs in all the Blocks of the 11 EAG States/UTs (Assam, Bihar, Chhattisgarh, Himachal Pradesh, UT–Jammu and Kashmir, Jharkhand, Madhya Pradesh, Odisha, Rajasthan, Uttar Pradesh and Uttarakhand) by 2025–2026 with the objective to equip the Block level health units to handle public health emergencies and to respond and monitor the healthcare services. **(4)** Integrated Public Health Labs: An Integrated Public Health Laboratories in all 730 districts will be set up under the scheme to optimize access to laboratory services, quality assurance efforts, cost-effectiveness, and efficient use of human resources.
- **2022—Tele MANAS program—**Tele Mental Health Assistance and Networking Across States (Tele Manas) initiative has been launched by Ministry of Health & Family Welfare, Government of India, during October 2022. It aims to provide free tele mental health services all over the country round the clock. A toll-free number (14416) is available in each state and union territory for easy access to mental health support [13].
- **2023—Aapke Dwar Ayushman—**Launched in September 2023 as part of the Ayushman Bhava campaign, this program includes the Ayushman app, which allows beneficiaries to self-verify their information [14].
- **2024**—National Tobacco Control Programme-Establishment of Tobacco Cessation Centres in all Medical Colleges of the country on 24 September 2024.
- **2024—Health-tech event in India—**The Global Digital Health Summit is the convening summit for global leaders and implementers across the industry, academia, and the government. GDHS-24, or the Global Digital Health Summit

2024, is a conference that will take place on 4–5 October 2024 at the Jio World Convention Centre in Mumbai, India. The summit will focus on the digital healthcare revolution and will include discussions, presentations, and an expo.

1.7 Conclusion

The history of Public Health is important because it can help us understand how public health concepts have evolved and how to improve public health today. It shows how public health workers can play a political role to lobby for changes that improve community health. It also shows how scientific discovery and social values have come together to shape public health approaches and how public health measures have evolved over time. It emphasizes how improving general social conditions like housing, food, water, and sanitation can improve population health.

References

1. Henry S. A history of medicine, vol. I. London: Oxford University Press; 1951.
2. Dubos RJ. Man, medicine and environment. New York: New American Library; 1969.
3. Jaggi OP. Indian system of medicine. Atma Ram and Sons; 1973.
4. Parke-Davis. Great moments in medicine. A history of medicine in pictures. Parke-Davis & Co; 1961.
5. WHO. World health, May 1970; 1970.
6. Anderson CL, et al. Community health. C.V. Mosby; 1978.
7. Douglas G. A history of medicine. London: Thomas Nelson & Sons; 1947.
8. WHO-UNICEF. Health for all, sr. no.1; 1978.
9. WHO. Health for all sr no 1; 1978.
10. UNDP. Human development report 2015. Oxford University Press.
11. UNDP. Human development report 2011. Oxford University Press; 2011.
12. UNDP. Human development report 2020; 2020.
13. Government of India. 2023. https://telemanas.mohfw.gov.in.
14. Government of India. 2024. https://mohfw.gov.in.

Chapter 2
The Origin and Practice of Public Health

Ayush Lohiya

2.1 Introduction

Historical practices along with trial and error in the medical science have influenced the history of public health. The origin and history of public health is the search of methods of preventing diseases. Public health has evolved historically with the changes in agent, host, and environment. This knowledge will facilitate the understanding of current and future landscape of public health.

2.2 Public Health in the Ancient and Medieval Period

2.2.1 Ancient World

The early civilizations combined practical knowledge of herbal medicine, midwifery, and treating wounds, to drive out "evil spirits" with mystical beliefs, divination, and shamanism. In Mesopotamia, the Code of Hammurabi (c. 1700 BCE) included practices of medical conduct. In China, digging wells for drinking water was a frequent practice in this era. India had ancient towns with street paving, construction rules, and covered sewer drains. Ayurvedic medicine also evolved during this period. Hippocrates developed a code of ethics for medical practice in addition to the clinical techniques of observation and reporting. He also explained the link between illness patterns and the physical environment—that is, the air, water, and places [1].

A. Lohiya (✉)
Kalyan Singh Super Specialty Cancer Institute, Lucknow, India

S. Malik et al. (eds.), *Public Health Issues: Theory and Practices*,
https://doi.org/10.1007/978-981-96-6650-8_2

2.2.2 Early Medieval Period

The early medieval era was dominated by the Church's practices in the field of health and medicine. Majority of the doctors were monks who followed the practices advocated by the Church. Most of the people had inadequate access to sanitary, hygienic homes, education, and nutrition. Muslim medicine developed during Islamic control in this period primarily in Persia, Central Asia, Baghdad and Cairo [1].

2.2.3 Late Medieval Period

Monastery hospitals were established during this period to medical care to the patients. In the tenth century, medical schools started emerging in Europe between the eleventh and sixteenth centuries. In Europe, leprosy was spreading, especially among the poor. Isolation was common in leprosaria throughout Europe. The public health act of quarantine was established as a government measure when seaport cities started to separate the leprosy patients. The ships having lepers were kept waiting in isolated parts of the harbor for 30 days (*treutina*), then for 40 days (*quarantina*).

Between 1200 and 1400 CE, plague (The Black Death), spread to China with Mongol invasions, and halved the population of China. Likewise, the disease affected majority of Europe between 1346 and 1350, killing between 24 and 50 million people, which was approximately one-third of the population at that time. Plague affected whole communities despite the known methods of disease prevention at that time. Similar outbreaks of syphilis, typhus, smallpox, measles, and the plague happened across Europe, in part due to the trade and the increasing movement of commodities and people. Malaria was also rampant across communities. Scurvy, scarlet fever, and rickets were also widespread, especially among seafarers [1].

2.2.4 The Germ and Miasma Theories

Miasmists held that noxious vapors or infectious mists emerging from the filth were the source of disease. Hence, the sanitary measures to remove waste and garbage was the best way to prevent infectious diseases. At that time, the miasma teachings of Galen were in direct opposition to the contagion theory of sickness, which was described by Fracastorus in 1546 and later by Paracelsus. This theory introduced the terms *infection* and *disinfection*. The work of Antony van Leeuwenhoek (1632–1723), who created the microscope in 1676, contributed to the strengthening of the germ theory. The germ theorists held that microorganisms were the source of diseases that could spread from person to person or through contact with contaminated water or sewage [1].

2.3 Public Health in the Modern Period (1600 CE Onwards)

It became evident during this time that innovative concepts and novel methods of thinking might be translated into useful practices and objects. The fields of clinical medicine, surgery, and therapeutics, as well as the sciences of chemistry, physics, physiology, and anatomy, rapidly expanded in this era.

2.3.1 *Applied Epidemiology*

On lengthy voyages, scurvy (Black Death of the Sea) posed a serious threat to sailors' health. In 1740–1744, a British naval fleet with seven ships and around two thousand soldiers set out to circumnavigate the earth. The squadron lost majority of its sailors to scurvy, and when it returned to England, it had only one ship and less than 200 men. James Lind conducted his groundbreaking epidemiological study on scurvy among sailors in 1747. Lind used a remarkable scientific methodology that included the formation of hypotheses, research design, meticulous observation and testing, recording, and publication. It is considered as the first clinical trial and epidemiological investigation of diet in public health. In 1795, the findings were translated into practice when the Royal Navy adopted routine issuance of lime juice to sailors to prevent scurvy [2].

2.3.2 *Vaccination*

The existence of smallpox was documented in history since the third century BCE. In ancient China, traditions of preventing a more virulent form of the disease by inoculation or transmission of the disease to healthy people were reported. This practice was known as variolation and brought to England from Constantinople. Edward Jenner (1749–1823) was the first to use vaccination with cowpox to prevent smallpox in 1796, initiating one of the most dramatically successful endeavors of public health. Vaccination later became compulsory in many countries, leading to the ultimate public health achievement: global eradication of smallpox in the late twentieth century [3].

2.3.3 *Foundations of Health Statistics and Epidemiology*

Demography, the study of birth and death rates, is the cornerstone of epidemiology. For military reasons, Peter the Great started registering male child births in Russia in 1722. Born into a family of mathematicians in Europe, Daniel Bernoulli

(1700–1782) created life tables based on information that indicated immunization against smallpox at infancy extended life expectancy and variolation against the disease offered lifetime immunity. Edwin Chadwick's work recognized the exceptional importance of precise statistical data in health planning and illness prevention. Due to his efforts, the Registrar-General's Office of Britain was established by legislation in 1836. Lemuel Shattuck started statewide vital statistics register in Boston, Massachusetts, in 1842. This initiative later served as a model for other states in the United States [1].

2.4 Sanitation and Public Health

The British government commissioned Edwin Chadwick to undertake a study on sanitation conditions in England. The study eventually led to the Chadwick report in the year 1842. Likewise, in 1850, the Massachusetts Sanitary Commission, chaired by Lemuel Shattuck, was established to investigate sanitary conditions. The Chadwick Report in Great Britain (1842) and the Shattuck Report in Massachusetts (1850) promoted the concept of municipal boards of health based on public health law with a public mandate to supervise and regulate community sanitation [4, 5].

2.4.1 John Snow and Cholera

The big cholera pandemics began in India between 1825 and 1854 and traveled to Europe and North America at an ever-increasing rate. During August and September of 1854, John Snow, who was Queen Victoria's anesthetist and a founding member of the London Epidemiological Society, looked into a cholera outbreak that had occurred near Broad Street. He tracked down around five hundred cholera deaths during a 10-day span. Snow looked into a second outbreak that occurred in September and October of 1854, this time with suspicions of water transmission. He classified cholera deaths according to the victims' residence and the water provider for the house. While nearby residences served by the Lambeth Company had rates lower than the rest of London, Southwark and Vauxhall Water Company-provided households experienced high rates of cholera deaths. This findings of the study provided strong epidemiological insights to Snow's theory that contaminated Thames water, which was supplied to households across a substantial portion of south London, was the source of the cholera epidemic. It also resulted in legislation in 1857 requiring water firms to filter their supply. This study was conducted 30 years before the discovery of causative organism was discovered. Even then, the Snow's study on cholera has become one of the classic epidemiological investigations, recognized to this day for its scientific rigor [6].

2.4.2 *Hospital Reform*

Semmelweiss (1818–1865), a Hungarian obstetrician at the Vienna Hospital, hypothesized in 1846 that the deaths caused by puerperal fever were caused by medical professionals who contaminated themselves and then passed on autopsy material to living patients. He brought the mortality rates of women receiving medical attention down to that of the group receiving midwifery care by mandating that physicians and medical students soak their hands in chlorinated lime following autopsies [6].

2.5 Infectious Diseases and Public Health

The French chemist Louis Pasteur is regarded as one of the important individuals in scientific history. He administered attenuated animal tissue, which produced antibodies that prevented the disease but not the infection. A boy received rabies vaccination from Pasteur. German medical officer Robert Koch created fundamental bacteriological procedures, such as how to culture and stain microorganisms. He proved the transmission of a particular disease by a specific germ by demonstrating the bacterium that causes anthrax, recovering it from sick animals, and passing it through multiple generations of animals. He also cultivated and exhibited the tubercle bacillus in 1882. After that, he separated and recognized Vibrio cholerae. He also developed “Koch’s postulates” which defined the criteria for causation of a disease by a specific organism. It substantiated the germ theory which was a long-lasting contribution to the science of medicine [3].

2.5.1 *Vector Borne Diseases*

The significance of carriers, those who can spread a disease without exhibiting clinical symptoms, has been shown by studies on disease transmission in the many infectious diseases. The plague bacillus was identified in 1894. P. L. Simmond in 1898 proved that the plague was a rat sickness that was transmitted to people by fleas. In 1880, Alphonse Laveran discovered malarial parasites. Malaria transmission by the Anopheles mosquito was demonstrated in 1897 by Benvenuto Grassi in Rome, Patrick Manson in England, and Ronald Ross, a British army doctor in India. After applying his understanding of transmission to vector control measures and shielding unwell individuals from mosquito bites, William Gorgas eradicated yellow fever in Havana in about 8 months. This study demonstrated the possibility of controlling diseases carried by vectors [4].

2.5.2 Microbiology and Immunology

Emile Roux and Alexandre Yersin, identified, cultured the diphtheria-causing bacteria, and proposed that it secreted a toxin or poison that was responsible for the disease's fatal consequences. Emile Behring created an antitoxin for passive immunization of an infected individual as well as a protective immunization against diphtheria in people with active immunization. Various pathogenic organisms were identified between 1876 and 1898, which laid a solid basis for advancements in the production of vaccines.

It became clear in the latter part of the nineteenth century that attenuated microbes might be injected into a host to create antibodies against the organism, so actively immunizing the host. A diseases individual may receive passive vaccination by receiving an injection of animals' serum containing attenuated germs. The vaccinations developed by Indian bacteriologist Waldemar Haffkine preceded Pasteur's. He developed the first vaccines against bubonic plague and cholera after testing them on himself. Together, bacteriologist Albert Calmette (1863–1933) and veterinarian Camille Guérin (1872–1961) investigated the intestinal route of tuberculosis. The TB vaccine, known as BCG (bacille Calmette–Guérin), was developed by the two, via the ongoing replanting of bacterial cultures, and was named after the two. Jonas Salk created an inactivated vaccine in 1955 and Albert Sabin developed a live attenuated vaccine in 1961, both of which were based on the techniques pioneered by John Enders and colleagues for isolating and cultivating the virus. Sabin's vaccine is still the cornerstone of the global effort to eradicate polio since it was more affordable and simpler to administer on a large scale [3].

2.6 Maternal and Child Health and Nutrition in Public Health

2.6.1 Maternal and Child Health

Preventive care as a service separate from curative medical services for women and children was initiated in the urban slums of industrial cities in nineteenth-century France, in the form of "milk stations" (*gouttes de lait*). The concept of the "milk station," combined with home visits, was pioneered by Lillian Wald (1867–1940) in Unites States, who coined the term *district nurse* or *public health nurse*. In the Soviet Union, maternal and child health was emphasized by institution of the state health plan in 1918 by Nikolai Semashko. The services were provided free as a state responsibility through an expanding network of antenatal and childcare centers. The scopes of the services include preventive checkups, home visits, and vaccinations and other services. The emphasis placed on maternal and child health continues to be a keystone and a major pillar of public health [6].

2.6.2 *Nutrition in Public Health*

The prevalence of beriberi in sailors' diets was decreased by incorporating meat and vegetables into their rice-based meals in 1882. Dutch medical officer, Christiaan Eijkman discovered that those prisoners who had polished rice in their camps had beriberi while the disease did not affect those who consumed unprocessed rice. Kasimir Funk (1884–1967) first used the name "vitamin" (or "vital amine") to refer to the substance in 1911. In 1916, US researchers first identified fat-soluble vitamin A and water-soluble vitamin B. The latter was subsequently shown to have many factors. In 1906, the Pure Food and Drug Act was passed in the United States. Federal power over food and labelling regulations was established by the legislation, initially for interstate trade and eventually extended to the entire nation [6].

2.7 Globalization of Health

Cooperation in health has been a part of international diplomacy from the first international conference on cholera in 1851 in Cairo to the health organization of the League of Nations after World War I, and further, into modern times. Established in 1948, the World Health Organization's (WHO's) constitution was signed in 1946, with the charter defining health as "the complete state of physical, social and mental well-being, and not merely the absence of disease." The tradition of international cooperation continues by organizations such as the WHO, the International Red Cross/Red Crescent (IRC), the United Nations Children's Fund (UNICEF), and a myriad of others. Global health issues and social disparities are by their very nature beyond the capacity of individual or even groups of countries to solve. Successes in the eradication of smallpox and the control of many other diseases by public health measures show the potential for concerted international cooperation and action targeted at specific objectives that reduce disease and suffering [7].

2.8 Creating and Managing Health Systems

One of the biggest problems facing public health is providing healthcare to the entire population. Governments have extensive duties for the health of the populace as insurers, providers, or regulators of health care. A country's health comprised not only illness preventive strategies but also prepayment and funding for medical and hospital services. Several European nations expanded their national health insurance programs in the 1920s. A more gradual evolution occurred in Canada between 1946 and 1971, during which time national health insurance and pensions were established.

All the nations in the first 10 years of the twenty-first century have made it their mission to ensure the social and health well-being of their citizens, yet there are still significant disparities and gaps in their accomplishments. Concerns about rising expenses are becoming more widespread across industrialized nations, as health care expenditures influence overall economic expansion. Ensuring universal access to healthcare for the populace is an elusive goal for developing nations. Despite this, significant strides have been made in the delivery of essential services like vaccination and prenatal care [7].

2.9 Summary

The latter part of the nineteenth and the early part of the twentieth centuries saw the establishment of the foundations for public health organizations. The development of food regulation, waste management, and water sanitation at the municipal and higher levels of government, along with the organization of local public health offices through state and federal subsidies and the advancement of vaccination technology, all helped to reduce the spread of infectious illnesses. While there were few effective medical therapies available at the start of the twentieth century, improved public health standards led to a decrease in mortality and an increase in longevity. With the development of antibiotics, antihypertensives, and psychotherapy medications after World War II, medical technology advanced and the gap between public health and medicine grew as the emphasis switched to curative medical care [8].

The 1960s and current age of public health have brought about a renewed emphasis on the epidemiology and prevention of non-infectious diseases. Modern public health has significantly reduced mortality and morbidity for a wide range of diseases through consumer advocacy and health promotion because of these and related investigations of environmentally associated disease and damage. Health for All is a goal shared by national and international health authorities, but it confronts significant challenges from disparities in access to resources, overdevelopment of some services at the expense of others, and conflicting agendas. The public, however, has high expectations for unrestricted access to healthcare, including highly technical and specialized treatments that may exceed the financial and human resources that are available.

References

1. Theodore H, Tulchinsky Elena A. Varavikova The New Public Health A History of Public Health Elsevier. 1–42.
2. Cook GC. Scurvy in the British mercantile marine in the 19th century, and the contribution of the Seamen's Hospital Society. Postgrad Med J. 2004;80:224–9. Available at: http://pmj.bmj.com/content/80/942/224.long.
3. Plotkin SA, Orenstein WA, Offit PA. Vaccines. 5th ed. Philadelphia: Saunders/Elsevier; 2008.

4. Centers for Disease Control and Prevention. Achievements in public health, 1900–1999: control of infectious diseases. MMWR Morb Mortal Wkly Rep. 1999;48:621–9. Available at: http://www.cdc.gov/mmwr/preview/mmwrhtml/mm4829a1.htm.
5. Krishnan A. Community medicine in India – Which way forward? Indian J Community Med. 2016;41:5–10.
6. Rosen G. A history of public health. Expanded ed. Baltimore: Johns Hopkins University Press; 1993.
7. Labisch A. History of public health-history in public health: looking back and looking forward. Soc Hist Med. 1998;11(1):1–13. https://doi.org/10.1093/shm/11.1.1.
8. Centers for Disease Control and Prevention. Ten great public health achievements – worldwide, 2001–2010. MMWR Morb Mortal Wkly Rep. 2011;60:814–8. Available at: http://www.cdc.gov/mmwr/preview/mmwrhtml/mm6024a4.htm.

Chapter 3
Health Literacy

Parul Dubey and Manoj Kumar Mishra

Health literacy is similar to general literacy but distinct. Literacy is the ability to identify, understand, interpret, create, communicate, and compute using written text, verbal instructions, and numeracy skills in various contexts [1]. It encompasses essential competencies needed to function effectively and successfully in life. However, health literacy extends beyond crucial reading, comprehension, language, and math skills. It is critical in empowering, engaging, and activating individuals within a person-centered care model [2, 3]. Therefore, it is vital to understand and fully define the concept of health literacy.

3.1 Evolution of the Idea of Health Literacy

In the 1970s, health literacy first evolved when health education was seen as a social policy [4], and again, in the 1990s, the managed care payment systems in the USA evolved. Today, health literacy is recognized as a global public health [5] aimed at augmenting health promotion through better education and communication strategies and facilitating patient outcomes with rudimentary health literacy [4, 6]. With a growing focus on population health, prevention of diseases, health promotion, and managing acute and chronic illness, it is crucial to incorporate health literacy interventions into all strategies. Although health literacy significantly impacts patient's health care experiences, it is not solely dependent on individual skills. Providers may not entirely recognize the importance of health literacy in advancing patient

P. Dubey · M. K. Mishra (✉)
Cancer Research Center, Department of Biological Sciences, Alabama State University, Montgomery, AL, USA
e-mail: mmishra@alasu.edu

S. Malik et al. (eds.), *Public Health Issues: Theory and Practices*,
https://doi.org/10.1007/978-981-96-6650-8_3

outcomes, which secures patient safety and adheres to medications and treatments, enabling patients to act in their best interest [1]. Health literacy is also contemplated as a social determinant of health [7], fundamental for accomplishing value-driven health care and managing risk in bundled care programs dictated by Medicare [1]. In a population-based healthcare strategy, evaluating the population's health literacy aids healthcare systems in determining the needed educational and promotional activities. This approach helps regulate population health, alleviate the risks associated with costly in-hospital diagnostic and treatment services, and reduce 30-day readmissions [8].

3.2 How Can Improved Health Literacy Help in Enhancing Health?

Health Literacy has been defined by the US Department of Health and Human Services (HHS) as "the extent to which individuals can procure, process, and understand the fundamental health information and assistance needed to make appropriate health decisions" [9]. People with inadequate health literacy may struggle to read and comprehend food labels, complete health assessment forms, communicate with a clinician about the symptoms, measure medications, navigate the healthcare system, or abide by self-care instructions. Several studies have established the correlation between low health literacy and poor health status. Insufficient health literacy leads to underusing preventive resources like vaccinations and routine screenings. This insufficiency affects the patient's comprehension of all the instructions given by a clinician on medication, leading to the mismanagement of chronic conditions, for example, diabetes, asthma, or high blood pressure [10]. Sanders et al. (2009) demonstrated an undeviating correlation between low health literacy and a poor understanding of prophylactic care information and the use of preventive care services, particularly among adults [11]. A strong link between health literacy and health disparities has also been observed. According to HHS, cultural and linguistic differences among patients significantly influence their health literacy levels, leading to ameliorated health disparities [9], particularly among elderly adults, racial and ethnic minorities, recent refugees and immigrants, low-income individuals, and non-native English speakers. Therefore, promoting health literacy not only helps reduce disparities but also enhances the provision of patient-centered care [12]. Health literacy is not only crucial for patients but for clinicians as well. Health professionals who can speak and understand not only the language but also the culture of their patients are more likely to overcome the gap between the medical information provided to the patients and its practical implementation. Since it is often difficult for clinicians to identify who among their patients have insufficient health literacy, adopting transparent communication practices and removing literacy-related barriers will enhance care for all patients [9].

3.3 Various Dimensions of Health Literacy

Health literacy extends beyond fundamental reading, writing, and numeracy skills within the health context. It is an umbrella term encompassing various aspects of patient interaction from their perspective with the healthcare system, including the capability to communicate, engage in clinical care, and access healthcare [13]. Health literacy is divided into three main aspects: functional health literacy, interactive health literacy, and critical health literacy, each increasing in complexity. "Functional health literacy" is comprehending the provided health information. "Interactive health literacy" involves combining social and functional health literacy skills to engage in effective health-seeking behavior. "Critical health literacy" is the most advanced aspect of health literacy, referring to the capability to critically analyze health information and make informed decisions about personal healthcare based on functional and interactive skills [14].

3.4 Assessment of Health Literacy

Recognizing the importance of health literacy in clinical practice, researchers have increasingly focused on measuring it. For this purpose, several tools have been developed, including proxy assessments, direct testing of individual health literacy abilities, and self-report measures [15]. While some studies use proxies like education level to assess health literacy [16, 17], numerous tools have been created to directly measure personal health literacy abilities [18–20]. Self-report measures are less commonly preferred because patients with poor health literacy often feel embarrassed to admit their difficulties [21–24].

Using socioeconomic factors as proxy measurements of health literacy is convenient but often inadequate. For instance, studies have shown a significant mismatch between education attainment and reading ability [25]. Buchbinder et al. reported that relying solely on education level alone as a proxy for health literacy would have misclassified more than 10% of their survey respondents [22]. An international study on adult literacy and life skills (ALLS) coordinated by Statistics Canada and the Organization for Economic Co-operation and Development included a domain measuring health literacy [14]. Other direct health literacy testing tools include the Rapid Estimate of Adult Literacy in Medicine (REALM), which assesses the ability to pronounce standard medical terms, and the Test of Functional Health Literacy in Adults (TOFHLA), which evaluates reading comprehension and numeracy skills using hospital materials [18].

Direct testing instruments, such as the Newest Vital Sign [26], and simpler tools used for screening questions have also been developed to distinguish patients with poor health literacy [13, 27]. These instruments are generally easy to administer and can be used quickly, making them suitable for routine clinical practice. However, the sensitivity and specificity of these testing instruments are subpar compared to TOFHLA, which is often considered the standard for health literacy assessment [28]. Despite the universal use of TOFHLA, there is no concurrence on the best instrument for precisely measuring health literacy levels [15]. Therefore, a combination of different instruments may be beneficial.

3.5 Significance of Health Literacy in Oncology

Over the past few decades, healthcare delivery has undergone significant changes, notably shifting towards a more patient-centered approach that emphasizes effective partnerships between healthcare providers and patients [29–32]. This approach necessitates that information and resources be tailored to each patient's understanding of health information and their ability to navigate the health system, a concept known as "health literacy." Based on the information provided by health professionals, patients often make crucial decisions about disease prevention, screening, and treatment. The advent of new technologies, a shift to outpatient care, pressures on the healthcare system, and a rise in treatment options have unavoidably made the health system more intricate and disintegrated [29, 30]. These changes pose significant challenges for patients in making informed healthcare decisions. This is important, particularly in oncology, where the high disease burden, the accessibility of cancer screening programs, the complexity of multimodal therapies, and the emphasis on cancer clinical trials add to the intricacies of patient care.

3.6 Frequency of Inadequate Health Literacy

Several studies have investigated the prevalence of health literacy in various clinical settings, particularly at the population level [16, 20, 29]. The differences in the prevalence of limited health literacy have been reported, and variability in measurement methods supposedly contributed to these differences. Consistent high rates of limited health literacy at a population level and in specific clinical settings have been observed using the TOFHLA [24, 33–35]. However, some reports demonstrated limited health literacy among the moderate segment of the population (5–10%) [21, 22, 36, 37].

Despite these discrepancies, TOFHLA assessments have consistently shown that many individuals struggle to perform simple health tasks, including reading and construing a prescription label or an appointment card. For example, a cross-sectional survey was conducted with 2659 patients in two different urban hospitals in the USA. The survey's outcome exhibited that up to 41.6% of patients struggle with comprehending the recommended instructions for taking medicines on an empty stomach, and 26% of patients failed to understand the information about their next appointment [33]. Numerous cross-sectional surveys have been conducted in rheumatology, general practice, pediatrics, and geriatrics at the population level [22, 29, 34, 38–40]. Differences in socioeconomic characteristics and different kinds of illness are the factors that may result in varying extent of health literacy. Therefore, these studies were conducted to enhance understanding of inadequate health literacy in specific clinical settings [41]. However, research exploring health literacy has been very limited in cancer patients [42–44]. There have been a handful of studies centered only on cancer patients and cancer survivors that mainly investigate the insights of cancer recurrence risk or contentment with the medical decision-making process [42–44]. Previously, studies on health literacy and cancer have primarily explored the association between levels of health literacy and contribution to cancer screening programs among non-cancer patients [45–49]. There was a recent study that measured health literacy in patients with head and neck cancer who survived while undergoing total laryngectomy. However, the study was conducted retrospectively with only eight participants [50]. Additionally, studies on health literacy and cancer conducted previously have often used convenience sampling or targeted certain groups, particularly elderly individuals or specific ethnic groups, like African Americans, who are more likely to have lower educational levels [37, 45–49, 51].

3.7 Connections and Outcomes Linked to Restricted Health Literacy

Inadequate individual abilities and/or high health literacy stipulations could lead to poor health literacy. Jordan et al. exhibited that health literacy influences the interplay between personal capacities, the healthcare system, and society [13]. Consequently, beyond an individual's intrinsic abilities, the intricate healthcare system and societal services can place high demands on patients' health literacy. Several investigations revealed that people with poor health literacy often struggle to obtain, understand, and retain health information [43, 52]. Suboptimal health literacy is considered an independent risk factor for poorer health outcomes and increases the risk of hospitalization [38, 53].

Several reports demonstrated a strong correlation between insufficient health literacy, patient's socioeconomic characteristics, particularly older adults, and low education levels [18, 21, 36, 37]. One study reported that individuals without a methodical education are seven times more likely to have inadequate health literacy than people with proper education [36]. On the contrary, Helitzer et al. noted that even people with high education levels can struggle with health-related detailed facts, direction, and decisions [54]. Furthermore, particularly in cancer care, this link between old age and poor health literacy is found to be significant, as 60% of new cancer cases and 70% of deaths due to cancer occur in patients over 65 years old [55]. However, studies on the correlation between health literacy levels and gender have produced inconsistent results [36, 56].

Cancer patients being unable to understand their health information thoroughly is likely to exacerbate their distress levels, leading to dissatisfaction with care and could also minimize their overall well-being [32]. A study with early-stage breast cancer female patients demonstrated that patients who perceived themselves as inadequately informed were twofold more prone to experience depression or anxiety in contrast to patients who perceived themselves as well informed [57]. Gamble stated that patients without sufficient information about treatment side effects or who expected only minor side effects experienced greater anxiety [58]. Moreover, a study of prostate cancer patients revealed that patients with substandard health literacy often associated prostate cancer with death, fear, and suffering, regardless of the disease's stage and nature [59]. Consequently, cancer patients who are well-informed about their condition are more likely to manage their disease effectively compared to those who lack sufficient information [57].

3.8 Barriers in Communication that Impede Comprehension and Informed Decision-Making

Ineffective communication by physicians can impose substantial health literacy challenges on patients [60]. Doctors frequently employ medical terminology and intricate sentence structures when interacting with patients [61]. Terms that healthcare professionals perceive as straightforward can pose difficulties for individuals with restricted health literacy [52]. Physicians might not be aware of how widespread low health literacy is in the community, leading them to overlook the challenges patients face in understanding due to their limited capacity to learn [62], thereby imposing significant health literacy demands on them.

Research on cancer patients' comprehension of informed consent revealed that just 60% could recall the purpose and details of a recommended treatment procedure the day after it was explained [63]. When patients are confronted with an initial cancer diagnosis or negative news, their emotional reactions can hinder their ability to process additional information effectively [64]. Patients often seek information elsewhere because they lack proper communication with their healthcare providers. Those with limited health literacy frequently rely on the experiences of family and friends, who may themselves have advanced-stage cancer and find it challenging to discuss their worries with healthcare professionals [52, 60].

According to a population-based survey conducted in the United States by Gansler et al., there are several misunderstandings regarding cancer treatment [65]. These misunderstandings can influence how patients accept and adhere to their treatment plans. For instance, nearly half of the survey respondents believed that cancer treatment involving surgery could lead to metastasis throughout the body [65]. At the same time, 27% were under the impression that the medical industry deliberately withheld a cure for cancer to maximize profits. While this survey did not directly evaluate health literacy levels, its findings indicate that a considerable segment of the population had a limited grasp of established medical knowledge about cancer, suggesting low health literacy. Indeed, individuals with low health literacy are 1.5 to three times more prone to experiencing adverse health outcomes than those with adequate health literacy [66].

3.9 Impact of Inadequate Health Literacy on Cancer Treatment

Health literacy is pivotal in the realm of cancer, where decisions regarding prevention, screening, and treatment have become increasingly intricate [67]. Sufficient health literacy is crucial for effective disease prevention and managing chronic conditions [68]. Cancer patients frequently encounter complex and personalized treatment options [69], which can pose challenges for those with limited health literacy. During discussions with healthcare providers, patients with substandard health literacy may struggle to grasp information about their disease.

Recent research indicates that over 60% of patients have overestimated their chances of cancer cure by more than 20% compared to their doctors' assessments [60, 69]. Mackillop et al. discovered that more than half of patients had inflated expectations regarding their likelihood of cure [70], with many patients with metastatic cancer inadvertently believing their cancer was localized. Furthermore, a significant number of patients receiving palliative treatments mistakenly thought they were undergoing curative care [70]. In this research, 46% of patients did not have a high school education, and they were markedly more prone to misapprehending the sole purpose of their treatments than those who had completed high school (50% vs. 25%) [70].

Likewise, 72% of patients lacking a high school diploma inflated their likelihood of cure, compared to 38% of those with a high school education [70]. Nonetheless, misapprehensions remained even among patients with higher levels of education. These misconceptions may cause patients to form inaccurate opinions regarding the efficacy of their cancer treatments [52], possibly leading to irrelevant interventions or insufficient treatment [44].

3.10 Approaches to Assist Individuals with Low Health Literacy

Several initiatives have targeted specific groups of patients with limited health literacy. Han et al. investigated the effectiveness of employing lay health workers to educate, counsel, and guide first-generation Korean-Americans through breast cancer screening. Following the intervention, mammography participation rates showed a notable 30% increase [71]. Several strategies have been proposed for healthcare providers to improve patient comprehension during consultations. These methods involve utilizing decision aids written in simple language to present information about cancer treatment or screening programs in a clear, text-based, and numerical format [72, 73]. Other approaches include employing the "teach-back technique," where patients are asked to summarize the information they received during a medical visit in their own words to confirm their understanding [60, 74]. The U.S. Department of Health and Human Services recently announced a national action plan to enhance the general public's health literacy, outlining multiple goals and strategies for achieving this objective [14].

3.11 Forthcoming Studies

Recent research has seen a surge in health literacy studies, encompassing investigations into its prevalence, socioeconomic factors influencing it, the impact of limited health literacy, and interventions to aid individuals with low health literacy. However, much of this research has primarily focused on the general population or other medical disciplines besides oncology. Studies examining health literacy among cancer patients have often been less rigorous, employing less reliable measurement instruments or poorly selected cohorts of patients. It is critical to thoroughly explore the prevalence of limited health literacy across different cancer types using rigorous methodologies and to identify predictors of poor health literacy in oncology to identify disadvantaged patients within the healthcare system better.

Challenges persist in comprehensively measuring health literacy due to its multifaceted nature. There is a need for further research to develop and validate tools that comprehensively assess health literacy across all dimensions. These tools should also be quick to administer to enable routine use in clinical practice. Current interventions to support patients with inadequate health literacy have predominantly focused on functional health literacy in various clinical contexts. More specific interventions are necessary to enhance patient's interactive and critical health literacy, empowering them to voice concerns or questions to their healthcare providers comfortably and actively discuss their health status, treatment plans, and outcomes.

Moreover, considering the broader scope of health literacy, including access to healthcare and government screening programs, developing interventions tailored to support patients with low health literacy would be beneficial. Ultimately, integrating health literacy into every facet of cancer care by healthcare professionals is essential to guaranteeing sufficient support and optimal information delivery to all cancer patients, regardless of their health literacy levels. This approach aims to enhance patient satisfaction, improve *quality of life, and promote adherence to treatment* plans.

References

1. Parnell TA, Stichler JF, Barton AJ, et al. A concept analysis of health literacy. Nurs Forum. 2019;54(3):315–27.
2. Pelletier LR, Stichler JF. Action brief: patient engagement and activation: a health reform imperative and improvement opportunity for nursing. Nurs Outlook. 2013;61(1):51–4.
3. Pelletier LR, Stichler JF. Patient-centered care and engagement: nurse leaders' imperative for health reform. J Nurs Adm. 2014;44(9):473–80.
4. Sørensen K, Van den Broucke S, Fullam J, et al. Health literacy and public health: a systematic review and integration of definitions and models. BMC Public Health. 2012;12:80.
5. Ratzan SC. Health literacy: communication for the public good. Health Promot Int. 2001;16(2):207–14.
6. Kim SH, Lee A. Health-literacy-sensitive diabetes self-management interventions: a systematic review and meta-analysis. Worldviews Evid-Based Nurs. 2016;13(4):324–33.
7. Rowlands G, Shaw A, Jaswal S, et al. Health literacy and the social determinants of health: a qualitative model from adult learners. Health Promot Int. 2017;32(1):130–8.
8. Weiss ME, Bobay KL, Bahr SJ, et al. A model for hospital discharge preparation: from case management to care transition. J Nurs Adm. 2015;45(12):606–14.
9. Benjamin RM. Improving health by improving health literacy. Public Health Rep. 2010;125(6):784–5.
10. Berkman ND, Dewalt DA, Pignone MP, et al. Literacy and health outcomes. Evid Rep Technol Assess (Summ). 2004;87:1–8.
11. Sanders LM, Shaw JS, Guez G, et al. Health literacy and child health promotion: implications for research, clinical care, and public policy. Pediatrics. 2009;124(Suppl 3):S306–14.
12. Hasnain-Wynia R, Wolf MS. Promoting health care equity: is health literacy a missing link? Health Serv Res. 2010;45(4):897–903.
13. Jordan JE, Buchbinder R, Osborne RH. Conceptualizing health literacy from the patient perspective. Patient Educ Couns. 2010;79(1):36–42.
14. Koay K, Schofield P, Jefford M. Importance of health literacy in oncology. Asia Pac J Clin Oncol. 2012;8(1):14–23.
15. Jordan JE, Osborne RH, Buchbinder R. Critical appraisal of health literacy indices revealed variable underlying constructs, narrow content, and psychometric weaknesses. J Clin Epidemiol. 2011;64(4):366–79.
16. Hanchate AD, Ash AS, Gazmararian JA, et al. The Demographic Assessment for Health Literacy (DAHL): a new tool for estimating associations between health literacy and outcomes in national surveys. J Gen Intern Med. 2008;23(10):1561–6.
17. Hoffman-Goetz L, Meissner HI, Thomson MD. Literacy and cancer anxiety as predictors of health status: an exploratory study. J Cancer Educ. 2009;24(3):218–24.
18. Parker RM, Baker DW, Williams MV, et al. The test of functional health literacy in adults: a new instrument for measuring patients' literacy skills. J Gen Intern Med. 1995;10(10):537–41.
19. Baker DW, Williams MV, Parker RM, et al. Development of a brief test to measure functional health literacy. Patient Educ Couns. 1999;38(1):33–42.
20. Davis TC, Crouch MA, Long SW, et al. Rapid assessment of literacy levels of adult primary care patients. Fam Med. 1991;23(6):433–5.
21. Barber MN, Staples M, Osborne RH, et al. Up to a quarter of the Australian population may have suboptimal health literacy depending upon the measurement tool: results from a population-based survey. Health Promot Int. 2009;24(3):252–61.
22. Buchbinder R, Hall S, Youd JM. Functional health literacy of patients with rheumatoid arthritis attending a community-based rheumatology practice. J Rheumatol. 2006;33(5):879–86.
23. Baker DW, Parker RM, Williams MV, et al. The health care experience of patients with low literacy. Arch Fam Med. 1996;5(6):329–34.

24. Parikh NS, Parker RM, Nurss JR, et al. Shame and health literacy: the unspoken connection. Patient Educ Couns. 1996;27(1):33–9.
25. Larson I, Schumacher HR. Comparison of literacy level of patients in a VA arthritis center with the reading level required by educational materials. Arthritis Care Res. 1992;5(1):13–6.
26. Weiss BD, Mays MZ, Martz W, et al. Quick assessment of literacy in primary care: the newest vital sign. Ann Fam Med. 2005;3(6):514–22.
27. Schwartz LM, Woloshin S, Black WC, et al. The role of numeracy in understanding the benefit of screening mammography. Ann Intern Med. 1997;127(11):966–72.
28. Mancuso JM. Assessment and measurement of health literacy: an integrative review of the literature. Nurs Health Sci. 2009;11(1):77–89.
29. Eysenbach G, Kohler C. How do consumers search for and appraise health information on the world wide web? Qualitative study using focus groups, usability tests, and in-depth interviews. BMJ. 2002;324(7337):573–7.
30. Rees CE, Ford JE, Sheard CE. Evaluating the reliability of DISCERN: a tool for assessing the quality of written patient information on treatment choices. Patient Educ Couns. 2002;47(3):273–5.
31. Laine C, Davidoff F. Patient-centered medicine. A professional evolution. JAMA. 1996;275(2):152–6.
32. Jefford M, Tattersall MH. Informing and involving cancer patients in their own care. Lancet Oncol. 2002;3(10):629–37.
33. Williams MV, Parker RM, Baker DW, et al. Inadequate functional health literacy among patients at two public hospitals. JAMA. 1995;274(21):1677–82.
34. Downey LV, Zun LS. Assessing adult health literacy in urban healthcare settings. J Natl Med Assoc. 2008;100(11):1304–8.
35. Juzych MS, Randhawa S, Shukairy A, et al. Functional health literacy in patients with glaucoma in urban settings. Arch Ophthalmol. 2008;126(5):718–24.
36. von Wagner C, Knight C, Steptoe A, et al. Functional health literacy and health-promoting behaviour in a national sample of British adults. J Epidemiol Community Health. 2007;61(12):1086–90.
37. Donelle L, Arocha JF, Hoffman-Goetz L. Health literacy and numeracy: key factors in cancer risk comprehension. Chronic Dis Can. 2008;29(1):1–8.
38. Baker DW, Gazmararian JA, Willaims MV, et al. Functional health literacy and the risk of hospital admission among Medicare managed care enrollees. Am J Public Health. 2002;92(8):1278–83.
39. Baker DW, Wolf MS, Feinglass J, et al. Health literacy and mortality among elderly persons. Arch Intern Med. 2007;167(14):1503–9.
40. Federman AD, Sano M, Wolf MS, et al. Health literacy and cognitive performance in older adults. J Am Geriatr Soc. 2009;57(8):1475–80.
41. Gazmararian JA, Baker DW, Williams MV, et al. Health literacy among Medicare enrollees in a managed care organization. JAMA. 1999;281(6):545–51.
42. Mohan R, Beydoun H, Barnes-Ely ML, et al. Patients' survival expectations before localized prostate cancer treatment by treatment status. J Am Board Fam Med. 2009;22(3):247–56.
43. Lillie SE, Brewer NT, O'Neill SC, et al. Retention and use of breast cancer recurrence risk information from genomic tests: the role of health literacy. Cancer Epidemiol Biomarkers Prev. 2007;16(2):249–55.
44. Brewer NT, Tzeng JP, Lillie SE, et al. Health literacy and cancer risk perception: implications for genomic risk communication. Med Decis Mak. 2009;29(2):157–66.
45. Holmes-Rovner M, Price C, Rovner DR, et al. Men's theories about benign prostatic hyperplasia and prostate cancer following a benign prostatic hyperplasia decision aid. J Gen Intern Med. 2006;21(1):56–60.
46. Miller DP Jr, Brownlee CD, McCoy TP, et al. The effect of health literacy on knowledge and receipt of colorectal cancer screening: a survey study. BMC Fam Pract. 2007;8:16.

47. von Wagner C, Semmler C, Good A, et al. Health literacy and self-efficacy for participating in colorectal cancer screening: the role of information processing. Patient Educ Couns. 2009;75(3):352–7.
48. Guerra CE, Dominguez F, Shea JA. Literacy and knowledge, attitudes, and behavior about colorectal cancer screening. J Health Commun. 2005;10(7):651–63.
49. Peterson NB, Dwyer KA, Mulvaney SA, et al. The influence of health literacy on colorectal cancer screening knowledge, beliefs, and behavior. J Natl Med Assoc. 2007;99(10):1105–12.
50. Beitler JJ, Chen AY, Jacobson K, et al. Health literacy and health care in an inner-city, total laryngectomy population. Am J Otolaryngol. 2010;31(1):29–31.
51. Friedman DB, Corwin SJ, Dominick GM, et al. African American men's understanding and perceptions about prostate cancer: why multiple dimensions of health literacy are important in cancer communication. J Community Health. 2009;34(5):449–60.
52. Doak CC, Doak LG, Friedell GH, et al. Improving comprehension for cancer patients with low literacy skills: strategies for clinicians. CA Cancer J Clin. 1998;48(3):151–62.
53. Baker DW, Parker RM, Williams MV, et al. Health literacy and the risk of hospital admission. J Gen Intern Med. 1998;13(12):791–8.
54. Helitzer D, Hollis C, Cotner J, et al. Health literacy demands of written health information materials: an assessment of cervical cancer prevention materials. Cancer Control. 2009;16(1):70–8.
55. Cohen HJ. The cancer aging interface: a research agenda. J Clin Oncol. 2007;25(14):1945–8.
56. Paasche-Orlow MK, Parker RM, Gazmararian MJ, et al. The prevalence of limited health literacy. J Gen Intern Med. 2005;20(2):175–84.
57. Fallowfield LJ, Hall A, Maguire GP, et al. Psychological outcomes of different treatment policies in women with early breast cancer outside a clinical trial. BMJ. 1990;301(6752):575–80.
58. Gamble K. Communication and information: the experience of radiotherapy patients. Eur J Cancer Care. 1998;7(3):153–61.
59. Dale W. Evaluating focus group data: barriers to screening for prostate cancer patients. Cancer Treat Res. 1998;97:115–28.
60. Davis TC, Williams MV, Marine E, et al. Health literacy and cancer communication. CA Cancer J Clin. 2002;52(3):134–49.
61. Kilbridge KL, Fraser G, Krahn M, et al. Lack of comprehension of common prostate cancer terms in an underserved population. J Clin Oncol. 2009;27(12):2015–21.
62. Rogers ES, Wallace LS, Weiss BD. Misperceptions of medical understanding in low-literacy patients: implications for cancer prevention. Cancer Control. 2006;13(3):225–9.
63. Cassileth BR, Zupkis RV, Sutton-Smith K, et al. Informed consent – why are its goals imperfectly realized? N Engl J Med. 1980;302(16):896–900.
64. Maguire P, Faulkner A. Communicating with cancer patients. BMJ. 1988;297(6663):1610.
65. Gansler T, Henley SJ, Stein K, et al. Sociodemographic determinants of cancer treatment health literacy. Cancer. 2005;104(3):653–60.
66. Dewalt DA, Berkman ND, Sheridan S, et al. Literacy and health outcomes: a systematic review of the literature. J Gen Intern Med. 2004;19(12):1228–39.
67. Goodwin PJ, Sridhar SS. Health-related quality of life in cancer patients–more answers but many questions remain. J Natl Cancer Inst. 2009;101(12):838–9.
68. Adams RJ, Stocks NP, Wilson DH, et al. Health literacy–a new concept for general practice? Aust Fam Physician. 2009;38(3):144–7.
69. Amalraj S, Starkweather C, Nguyen C, et al. Health literacy, communication, and treatment decision-making in older cancer patients. Oncology (Williston Park). 2009;23(4):369–75.
70. Mackillop WJ, Stewart WE, Ginsburg AD, et al. Cancer patients' perceptions of their disease and its treatment. Br J Cancer. 1988;58(3):355–8.
71. Han H-R, Lee H, Kim MT, et al. Tailored lay health worker intervention improves breast cancer screening outcomes in non-adherent Korean-American women. Health Educ Res. 2009;24(2):318–29.

72. Juraskova I, Butow P, Lopez AL, et al. Improving informed consent in clinical trials: successful piloting of a decision aid. J Clin Oncol. 2007;25(11):1443–4. author reply 1444
73. Holmes-Rovner M, Stableford S, Fagerlin A, et al. Evidence-based patient choice: a prostate cancer decision aid in plain language. BMC Med Inform Decis Mak. 2005;5:16.
74. Jefford M, Moore R. Improvement of informed consent and the quality of consent documents. Lancet Oncol. 2008;9(5):485–93.

Chapter 4
Clocks and Human Health

Sayantan Sur, Jyoti Tiwari, and Shalie Malik

4.1 Introduction

Circadian Rhythms and Evolution of Circadian Research

Life on Earth has evolved under a 24-h solar day, comprising daily cycles of light and dark periods. All organisms exhibit diurnal changes in physiology and behavior following the variability of this geophysical environment [1]. To optimally time their physiological events, organisms utilize an endogenous time-keeping mechanism that can approximately measure the diel time scale [2]. These endogenous rhythms are known as circadian (circa = about; *dies* = day) rhythm, which (i) has an inherent periodicity of ~24 h, (ii) can be reset to oscillate (known as *entrainment*) with the environmental cycle and (iii) are protected from changes in temperature, pH, and nutrition within physiological limits [2]. Circadian rhythms are critical to the survival and welfare of organisms including humans as they aid in timing biological and behavioral processes and synchronizing the internal environment [3]. Disruption of the circadian rhythmicity can lead to various mental and physical disorders in humans. The importance of circadian health is being further recognized after the 2017 Nobel Prize in Physiology or Medicine was awarded to Jeffrey Hall, Michael Rosbash, and Michael W. Young for discovering the molecular machinery regulating the circadian rhythm.

S. Sur
School of Biodiversity, One Health, and Veterinary Medicine, University of Glasgow, Glasgow, UK
e-mail: sayantan.sur@glasgow.ac.uk

J. Tiwari · S. Malik (✉)
Department of Zoology, University of Lucknow, Lucknow, Uttar Pradesh, India
e-mail: malik_shalie@lkouniv.ac.in

S. Malik et al. (eds.), *Public Health Issues: Theory and Practices*,
https://doi.org/10.1007/978-981-96-6650-8_4

The first observations of circadian rhythm were made by an astronomer Jean-Jacques d'Ortous de Mairan in 1729, who discovered that in constant darkness the leaves of the mimosa plant continued to unfold and close [4]. The persistence of the leaf movements in darkness indicated that the rhythm was "endogenous" in nature and could persist without the presence of external stimuli. Two hundred years later Erwin Bünning determined the characteristics and genetic basis of circadian rhythms [5]. Thereafter in the early to mid-twentieth century, endogenous rhythms started to be discovered in primates [6], rodents [7], insects [8], birds [9], and humans [10]. The term "circadian" was coined in 1959 by Franz Halberg to define these endogenous rhythms [4]. The pursuit to discover the molecular basis of circadian rhythms started when Seymour Benzer identified different mutant phenotypes of two circadian behaviors: pupal eclosion and locomotor activity in *Drosophila melanogaster* [11]. They observed three *Drosophila* mutants, one was arrhythmic, the other had a period of 19 h (<24 h), and the third had a period of 28 h (>24 h). Following this discovery, in 1984, Jeffery Hall, Michael Rosbash, and Michael Young independently cloned and restored the first clock gene, period (*per*) [12–14]. Subsequently, the second clock gene, timeless (*tim*) was identified by Young, which explained how PER protein enters the nucleus [15]. The positive elements of the clock machinery, *clock* and *bmal1*, were identified in the mouse by Joseph Takahashi and colleagues [3, 16, 17]. The *Drosophila* clock (*Clk*) and cycle (*Cyc*) were finally discovered by Hall and Rosbash as positive elements for *per* and *tim* transcription [18, 19]. Later discoveries unveiled the molecular components of the parallel feedback loop of the circadian clock. The core transcription-translation feedback loop (TTFL) established in *Drosophila*, where PER/TIM binds and inhibits their own transcription through CLOCK/CYCLE is a conserved model for circadian clocks, although the core proteins differ between species [5]. The presence of circadian clocks in almost all forms of unicellular and multicellular organisms advocates the evolutionary advantage of anticipation and adaptation to the daily variability of the environment. In this chapter, we will discuss the mechanisms of entrainment, the role of encephalic centers, and molecular regulation of circadian oscillations and then explore how disruptions of daily circadian rhythms can manifest as physiological and mental ailments in humans.

4.2 An Overview of the Circadian System

4.2.1 Retinal Light Detection

The functional interaction between the body and the external environment requires input pathways that relay external and internal information to the brain. The external cue that synchronizes or entrains the endogenous circadian rhythm with the daily 24-h day/night cycle is known as *zeitgeber* (from German, "time giver"). The most important zeitgeber in the natural environment is the ambient light. The retina at the back of our eyes relays the photic information to the central pacemaker in mammals, including humans, i.e., suprachiasmatic nuclei (SCN). The retina which is a thin layer of nerve tissue contains specialized photoreceptors, that include rods and cones [20]. During the daytime rods are suppressed, but during twilight and darker periods they are activated, whereas during the daytime cones allow us to detect colors, movement, and spatial details [20]. Besides, the rods and cones, secondary retinal neurons, known as intrinsically photosensitive retinal ganglion cells (ipRGCs, containing melanopsin photopigment) integrate and relay photic information to the SCN (Fig. 4.1) [22, 23]. Photostimulation activates melanopsin and triggers G-protein cascade leading to membrane depolarization, which differs from rods and cones that show hyperpolarization [24]. However, ipRGCs also receive photic information from the rods and cones, integrating photic information relating to spectrum and illuminance. They also innervate other encephalic regions such as the olivary pretectal nucleus (OPN) and dorsal lateral geniculate nucleus (dLGN) involved in pupillary constriction and visual perception, respectively [24].

4.2.2 Suprachiasmatic Nucleus: The Central Pacemaker

The suprachiasmatic nucleus (SCN) is the central pacemaker that regulates the circadian timing. It consists of two nuclei on each side of the third ventricle in the anterior hypothalamus, right above the optic chiasm [25]. The retinohypothalamic tract (RHT) originating from the ipRGCs in the retina projects directly into the SCN. Lesion studies established that damage to the SCN severely compromises behavioral, physiological, and seasonal rhythms [26]. The SCN is divided into ventrolateral “core” and dorsomedial “shell” subregions, where the retino-recipient core contains vasoactive intestinal peptide (VIP) and gastrin-releasing peptide (GRP) and the shell contains arginine vasopressin (AVP)-expressing cells (Fig. 4.1b) [27]. Direct inputs originating from the ipRGCs modulate the activation of core neurons, where GRP increases during the photophase (light period) and VIP increases during the scotophase (dark period) (Fig. 4.1b) [27]. VIP signaling mediates the spatiotemporal expression of circadian genes which is a critical feature of the circuit-level function of SCN [28]. AVP neurons of the shell project into the paraventricular nucleus (PVN) and regulate the daily feeding rhythms [29]. AVP neurons also innervate the organum vasculosum lamina terminalis (OVLT) regulating anticipatory thirst before sleep [30]. All SCN neurons produce γ-aminobutyric acid (GABA) which modulates the day-to-day phase relationship of the neurons across seasons [31]. GABA is proposed to oppose synchrony within the SCN, opposing the actions of VIP. The coordination between VIP and GABA keeps the membrane potential of SCN neurons within an operating range that allows neuronal communication [26]. Studies on rodents further suggest dual actions of GABA on SCN neurons, where it is inhibitory at night and excitatory during daytime [32]. Besides RHT, the SCN receives photic cues from the intergeniculate leaflet (IGL)

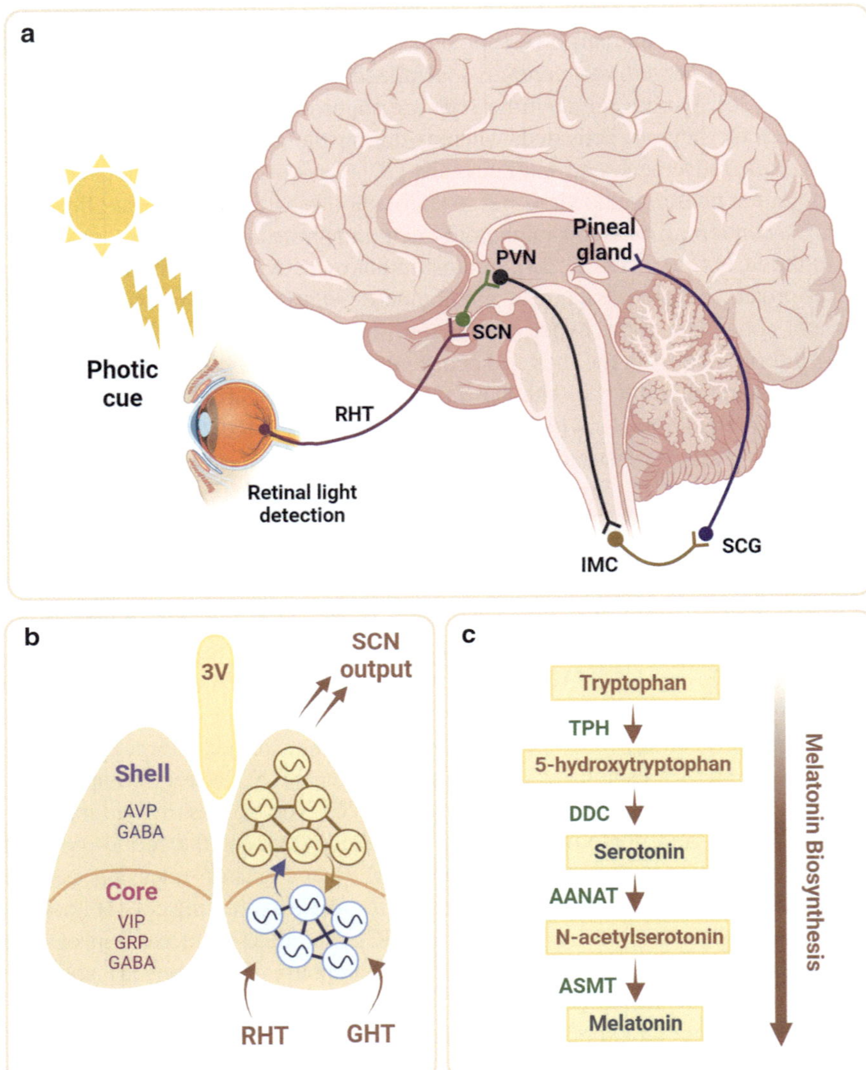

Fig. 4.1 (**a**) Schematic illustration of the neuroanatomical pathway of photic regulation of the pineal gland. External photic information is perceived by intrinsically photosensitive retinal ganglion cells (ipRGC) in the retina and subsequently relayed to the suprachiasmatic nucleus (SCN) through the retinohypothalamic tract (RHT). Efferent projections from the SCN innervate the paraventricular nucleus (PVN). Neuronal signaling from PVN activates neurons of the intermediolateral column (IMC) in the spinal cord which via superior cervical ganglion (SCG) promotes melatonin secretion from the pineal gland. (**b**) Anatomical structure of the SCN. The SCN is divided into a ventrolateral core and a dorsomedial shell. The core harbors vasoactive intestinal peptide (VIP), gastrin-releasing peptide (GRP), and γ-aminobutyric acid (GABA) expressing neurons, whereas the shell expresses arginine vasopressin (AVP) and GABA. The core receives inputs from the RHT and geniculohypothalamic tract (GHT). The activity of core and shell neurons is synchronized through intracellular communication, which generates outputs to entrain the peripheral clock. (Adapted from Cheng and Cheng [21]). 3V: Third Ventricle. (**c**) Biosynthesis of melatonin in the pineal gland. TPH Tryptophan hydroxylase, DDC DOPA decarboxylase, AANAT Arylalkylamine N-acetyltransferase, ASMT Acetylserotonin O-Methyltransferase

via the geniculohypothalamic tract (GHT) (Fig. 4.1b) [25]. Neuropeptide Y (NPY) is the primary GHT neurotransmitter that acts directly on SCN neurons. GHT and RHT show partial overlap in their innervations within the SCN [25]. The majority of the monosynaptic efferent projections of the SCN terminate within the thalamic and hypothalamic nuclei. The polysynaptic projections terminate in the pineal gland where they release norepinephrine during the nighttime and stimulate postsynaptic adrenergic receptors, leading to the production of melatonin.

4.2.3 *Pineal Gland and Melatonin Rhythm*

The pineal gland or epiphysis cerebri is a neuroendocrine gland located in the midline of the brain, between the cerebral hemispheres. It is unpaired and pine cone-shaped with the major function of synthesis and secretion of melatonin. Melatonin is synthesized from tryptophan through four sequential enzymatic steps (Fig. 4.1c) [33]. It transduces the external photic information to the whole body system. Arylalkylamine N-acetyltransferase (AANAT) is the rate-limiting enzyme in the four-step melatonin synthesis pathway and catalyzes the acetylation of serotonin. Serotonin within the pineal is present in high levels during the daytime and is reduced during nighttime due to melatonin synthesis. The increase in serotonin synthesis is mediated by β-adrenergic signaling, while the increase in serotonin release is controlled by α-adrenergic receptors [34]. Circadian signals originating from the SCN are transmitted to the pineal gland, sequentially through the paraventricular nuclei (PVN), spinal intermediolateral nucleus (IML), and superior cervical ganglion (SCG) (Fig. 4.1) [33]. During the daytime, synaptic GABAergic input from the SCN blocks glutamatergic inputs from the PVN which ultimately suppresses melatonin synthesis. However, at nighttime glutamatergic SCN outputs to the PVN stimulate melatonin production [35]. Circadian melatonin production and secretion in the pineal is abolished following bilateral lesions of the SCN [36]. Melatonin production persists under constant dark conditions and is entrained by the ambient light/dark cycle [37]. It binds to melatonin receptors present in many central and peripheral tissues and regulates daily and seasonal physiological functions including glucose homeostasis, reproduction, and the sleep-wake cycle.

4.2.4 *Molecular Clockwork in Mammals*

The molecular clockwork in mammalian cells is cell-autonomous and is driven by components of the positive and negative transcriptional-translational feedback loops (TTFLs) [38]. The primary feedback loop is composed of ten core clock genes, i.e., *Period* (*Per1*, *Per2*, *Per3*), *Cryptochrome* (*Cry1*, *Cry2*), *Bmal1*, and *Clock*. In the early photophase, genes of the positive limb of the feedback loop *Bmal1* and *Clock* are transcribed [3, 16, 39]. The translated products then dimerize to form the BMAL1:CLOCK protein complex which binds to CACGTG E/E'-box DNA response elements located in the promoter regions of the target genes leading to their transcription [5, 40]. The nuclear accumulation of the BMAL1:CLOCK complex peaks during the scotophase in the mouse [41]. One set of target genes that the BMAL1:CLOCK complex acts on includes genes from the negative limb of the feedback loop, *Period,* and *Cryptochrome*. The translated PER and CRY proteins form dimers and show peak cytoplasmic accumulation in the evening hours [41]. At night, the PER:CRY protein complex enters the nucleus and binds directly to CRY proteins to inhibit the activity of BMAL1:CLOCK complex [42, 43]. Additionally, Casein Kinase I delta (CK1δ) is shuttled within the nucleus which leads to further repression [44]. PER proteins, however, promote the dissociation of the BMAL1:CLOCK complex from the DNA binding elements [43, 45]. A secondary loop of the TTFL runs parallel to the primary TTFL. This loop starts with the BMAL1:CLOCK complex that drives the transcription of RORα/β and REV-ERBα/β orphan nuclear receptor genes [46, 47]. The translated protein ROR and REV-ERB compete for the RORE (retinoic acid-related orphan receptor response elements) binding sites located within the promoter region of Bmal1 [46, 47]. ROR and REV-ERB proteins bind to the RORE site and promote or inhibit the transcription of *Bmal1* respectively [48]. The BMAL1:CLOCK complex also initiates the transcription of the PAR bZIP genes with D-box elements, including nuclear factor interleukin 3 (NFIL3), hepatic leukemia factor (HLF), and D-box binding protein (DBP) [49]. The *computationally highlighted repressor of the network oscillator* (CHRONO) was additionally identified as a core clock gene. The expression of CHRONO is antiphasic to that of *Bmal1* and is similar to the CRY proteins, and it transcriptionally represses the BMAL1:CLOCK activity [38].

4.3 Circadian Clock, Lifestyle and Disease

4.3.1 Circadian Misalignment in Daily Life

4.3.1.1 General Mechanisms and Shift-Work

Circadian misalignment refers to a variety of disruptions in daily behavior and physiology that include sleep-wake cycle disturbances, altered feeding time, and misaligned central and peripheral rhythms in humans (Fig. 4.2) [50]. Our modern lifestyle consists of living in indoor environments during the daytime and under artificial light during nighttime, which reduces the diurnal contrast of our natural lightscape [51]. Light is the most critical zeitgeber that entrains our circadian clocks, and the alteration of ambient light conditions affects our internal biological timing. This leads to various health conditions including metabolic diseases, insulin resistance, cardiovascular diseases, and even cancer [51]. Circadian misalignment is more prevalent in shift workers leading to the desynchrony of the sleep-wake cycle and circadian physiology including diurnal cortisol, melatonin, and body temperature rhythms. In non-shift workers, with a normal sleep-wake cycle, the biological clock drives the diurnal wakefulness where circadian rhythmicity is observed with

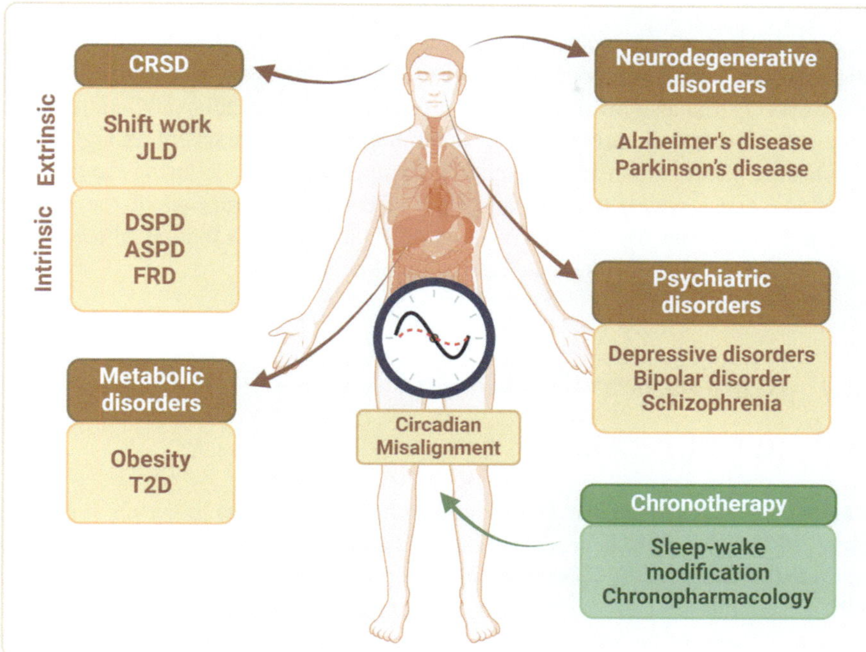

Fig. 4.2 Circadian misalignment/disruptions lead to the development of various circadian rhythm sleep disorders (CRSD), metabolic disorders, neurodegenerative disorders, and psychiatric disorders. The implementation of chronotherapy through bright light therapy, melatonin treatment, and chronopharmacology can boost therapeutic outcomes while minimizing harmful side effects. JLD Jet Lag Disorder, DSPD Delayed Sleep Phase Disorder, ASPD Advanced Sleep Phase Disorder, FRD Free-Running Disorder, T2D Type 2 Diabetes

increased and decreased daytime alertness in the day- and nighttime respectively [52]. This circadian drive is counteracted by the homeostatic drive for sleep, which starts accumulating during the daytime [53]. In daytime workers, these two contrasting processes work in synchrony with the external photic cycle to ensure that alertness is high during work and sleep is induced during the nighttime [52]. However, shift workers working during the nighttime remain awake opposing their natural biological rhythm. This leads to fragmentation and disruption of the sleep cycle and drowsiness during the morning hours [54].

4.3.1.2 Jetlag Disorder

Circadian misalignment is also observed in passengers who undergo transmeridian jet travel. Travelers develop a circadian sleep disorder known as Jet Lag Disorder (JLD), characterized by daytime drowsiness and insomnia [55]. JLD develops due to rapid travel across the time zones which is too fast for the circadian clock to reset. Thus, there is a mismatch between the endogenous circadian rhythm and the local schedule for arousal and sleep. The circadian misalignment is accompanied by a reduced amount of sleep during long-time travel in a sitting position and travel fatigue which further compounds its effect [55]. Similar to circadian disruptions in shift workers, JLD also involves the misalignment of the circadian and homeostatic processes. Homeostatic drive to sleep accumulates due to persistent jet lag insomnia. Further, the circadian arousal signal is dampened or absent during the daytime or waking hours which triggers mistimed sleepiness. Disruption of the natural sleep-wake cycle due to circadian misalignment can increases the risk of accidents, work-related errors, injuries, and degradation of health [52].

4.3.2 Neurodegenerative Disorders

4.3.2.1 Alzheimer's Disease

In aging adults, circadian disruptions are common occurrences; however, it is more severe in people with neurodegenerative disorders including Alzheimer's and Parkinson's diseases [56]. The circadian disruption in older adults in part results due to the degeneration of the central pacemaker or SCN. These disruptions can manifest as alterations of the sleep-wake cycle with heightened activity during the night time coupled with lower activity during the day. For example, patients with Alzheimer's show fragmented sleep, decreased amplitude of the circadian rhythms, and delayed onset of sleep and awake [57]. The physical activity of the patients is scattered throughout the 24-h day suggesting circadian rhythm fragmentation [58, 59], whereas, in a study in Italy, patients with moderate to severe Alzheimer's showed an advance in bedtime compared to controls without dementia [60]. The magnitude of circadian disruption seems to depend on the severity of Alzheimer's, with severe Alzheimer's causing critical rhythm disruption, while preclinical or mild Alzheimer's leads to moderate circadian changes [56]. A few studies on post-mortem tissues have shown that the methylation and expression of the *BMAL1* gene in fibroblast cultures [61] and clock gene expression in brain regions [62] are altered in Alzheimer's. Epigenetic alterations in preclinical Alzheimer's are a regulatory mechanism that can lead to neurodegeneration and cognitive impairment through disruptions of circadian rhythmicity [61]. SCN neuronal population expressing AVP and VIP show significant loss in Alzheimer's disease [63, 64]. The amyloid β peptide has been suggested to mediate circadian disruption through the degradation of the core clock protein BMAL1 [65, 66].

4.3.2.2 Parkinson's Disease

Unlike Alzheimer's disease, patients with Parkinson's disease show reduced amplitude of circadian rhythm, but no significant circadian phase-shifts [56]. The most common non-motor symptom that affects Parkinson's patients is an altered sleep-wake cycle, which predominantly includes daytime sleepiness [67, 68]. A study reported that the mesor and amplitude of core body temperature are reduced in patients compared to healthy individuals [69]. The circulatory melatonin levels are also significantly reduced in patients with Parkinson's compared to age-matched controls [67]. The nighttime circadian dip in blood pressure is also lost in patients, which might lead to nocturnal hypertension [70]. However, dopaminergic treatment in Parkinson's disease can itself lead to circadian changes, as studies have shown the treatment can cause phase advancement of the melatonin rhythm [71, 72]. Dopaminergic treatment can also cause excessive daytime sleepiness [68]. However, it is debatable whether neurodegeneration is caused by or leads to circadian disruptions. Growing evidence suggests that circadian disruptions precede the development of symptoms of neurodegenerative diseases, suggesting that the disruptions contribute to neuropathology [56].

4.3.3 Psychiatric Disorders

4.3.3.1 Depressive Disorders

Several psychiatric disorders including depression, bipolar, and schizophrenia show severe sleep-wake disruptions [73]. However, similar to neurodegenerative disorders, it is not well understood whether the disruptions are merely symptomatic or contribute to the manifestation of psychiatric disorders. Earlier research on major depression observed shortened Rapid eye movement (REM) latency and advancement of morning awakenings [53, 74]. The intensity of the major depressive disorder has also been correlated with circadian disruption as severe depression causes more phase delay of circadian rhythm [75]. The use of antidepressants can also affect circadian rhythmicity. For example, agomelatine, a melatonin agonist, is known to act as a "resynchronizer" of the circadian rhythm in models of depressive disorder [76, 77]. Agomelatine in human studies has been observed to increase the amplitude of the circadian activity-rest cycle with parallel improvement of depressive symptoms [78]. The changes in the light-dark cycle have also been linked to the development of seasonal affective disorder [79]. Likely, the relationship between circadian disruption and depression is bidirectional with complex interaction and synergization of various physiological pathways [73].

4.3.3.2 Bipolar Disorder

One of the key features of bipolar disorder is the disruption of activity and rest cycle [50]. Specifically, during manic episodes in bipolar disorder, the sleep patterns show drastic alterations [73]. Studies utilizing wrist actigraphy have demonstrated that individuals with bipolar disorder have fragmented nighttime sleep, lower amplitude of circadian rhythm, and reduced daytime activity [80, 81]. The core body temperature minimum and the timing of the onset of melatonin under dim light conditions (dim light melatonin onset or DLMO) are frequently used as circadian timing markers [50]. Compared to unipolar disorder, individuals with bipolar disorder have later DLMO [82]. However, there was no phase angle difference between uni- and bipolar individuals [82]. In laboratory hamster studies, treatment with lithium chloride (a pharmacological agent used to treat bipolar disorders) significantly lengthened the period of the circadian clock [83–85]. Lithium treatment has also been shown to alter glycogen synthase kinase-3beta, which is a key link to the molecular clockwork [86, 87]. Alteration of core clock genes has been associated with manic symptoms. For example, mutations in the Clock gene [88] and site-specific knockdown of Clock in the ventral tegmental area [89] can lead to mania-like behaviors.

4.3.3.3 Schizophrenia

Individuals with schizophrenia show significant circadian disruptions [90]. However, compared to depressive and bipolar disorders, the circadian alterations at mechanistic and epidemiological levels are less understood in schizophrenia. For example, the circadian rhythm in individuals with schizophrenia is misaligned [91, 92], phase advanced [93], and delayed or free running [94]. A reason for the variability and lack of mechanistic understanding is that the causes of schizophrenia remain elusive and are likely a combination of genetic and external factors [73]. A correlation between the phase of melatonin rhythm and the sleep-wake cycle is observed in schizophrenic patients [93, 95]. To understand the mechanistic details of the interaction of the circadian clock and schizophrenia, many animal models are being utilized. One such model is the "blind-drunk" (Bdr) mouse line possessing schizophrenic-like symptoms [96]. Bdr mouse showed phase-advancement of the activity-rest cycle and fragmentation of the circadian rhythmicity [97]. In humans, variation in the receptor for VIP (Vipr2) can cause an increased risk of development of schizophrenia [98].

4.3.4 Circadian Rhythm Sleep Disorders

International Classification of Sleep Disorders Second Edition (International Classification of Sleep Disorders, Second Edition: Diagnostic and Coding Manual, 2005) has categorized circadian rhythm sleep disorders into extrinsic and intrinsic disorders [50]. Extrinsic CRSDs include sleep disorders caused by changes in external factors, such as shift work and Jet lag. Intrinsic CRSDs are caused by disruptions of daily functions due to changes in internal circadian rhythm and include delayed sleep phase disorder (DSPD), advanced sleep phase disorder (ASPD), and free-running disorder (FRD) which will be covered in this section.

4.3.4.1 Delayed Sleep Phase Disorder

DSPD is an intrinsic CRSD that is characterized by a 3- to 6-h phase delay in the sleep-wake cycle resulting in the onset of insomnia and daytime sleepiness. DSPD individuals are reported as having evening chronotype; however, they show significant distress and sleep abnormalities [50]. Depending on the population survey, DSPD is prevalent in 0.2–10% population, making it one of the most common CRSD [99–101]. Individuals with DSPD show delayed sleep-wake timing and circadian markers compared to the control population [102–104]. The etiology of DSPD is not well understood. Some studies suggest that the disorder includes an intrinsic circadian period longer than that found in healthy populations [105]. Other explanations include abnormality in the phase response curve (PRC) [105]. The circadian phase delay is possibly maintained by hypersensitivity to the evening-time light [106]. Studies have shown that misalignment of sleep and circadian timing marker core body temperature minimum occurs in DSPD [104]. However, another study did not observe changes in DLMO and core body temperature minimum between healthy and DSPD individuals [102]. DSPD is also associated with the presence of psychiatric disorders. A study observed that 64% of individuals diagnosed with DSPD show clinical depressive symptoms [107]. DSPD is also common in individuals with bipolar disorder compared to healthy and unipolar controls [82].

4.3.4.2 Advanced Sleep Phase Disorder

ASPD is characterized by a sleep-wake schedule that is several hours advanced compared to the average or desired time [105]. Individuals with ASPD can experience early evening sleepiness and early morning awakenings. The markers for biological timing such as melatonin are also advanced in ASPD [108]. ASPD is much less prevalent compared to DSPD and its effect on physiology and mental health is poorly understood. ASPD has been estimated to be present in ~1% of the general population [109]. One of the reasons that ASPD is documented less than DSPD is that it leads to fewer social conflicts as going early to work is not punished as compared to going late [105]. The mechanisms leading to ASPD are not known; however, the shortening of the circadian period can be one reason [110].

4.3.4.3 Free-Running Disorder

FRD is an intrinsic CRSD, where the sleep-wake cycle does not entrain to a stable time but rather shows progressive delay every day [50]. FRD can lead to fragmented sleep, periods of insomnia, and daytime sleepiness depending on the individual. Earlier studies conducted in constant environments determined that the intrinsic circadian period of humans is longer than 24 h, which is now estimated to be around 24.15 h [111]. Individuals with FRD show similarities with subjects under constant environmental conditions, which highlights their failure to entrainment [105]. FRD is common in blind people and is more observed in complete blindness as retinal inputs are critical for circadian rhythm entrainment [112]. FRD is also present in sighted individuals, for example in a large case study, 34% of sighted individuals with FRD were reported to develop major depression [113]. In sighted people, FRD usually occurs during their teenage and is very rare after 30 years of age [105]. Is unclear if the free-running period in humans changes from childhood to adulthood, which might lead to modifications of the periodicity in FRD individuals.

4.3.5 Metabolic Disorders

Metabolic disorders are conditions where the body's ability to process and distribute macronutrients is negatively altered [114]. It can be inherited where the disorders are triggered by genetic variations and/or it might be acquired due to changes in external factors. Obesity and Type 2 Diabetes (T2D) are the most prevalent metabolic disorder globally. To understand how metabolic disorders develop, it is necessary to understand how external factors influence the timing of clock gene expressions and thereby the physiology. Similar to the hypothalamus, peripheral metabolic organs such as the liver show rhythmic oscillations of genes [115]. External cues such as feeding time or jetlag can influence these peripheral oscillators leading to acquired changes and inherited genetic variation of the clock genes can further lead to metabolic diseases [116]. In humans, polymorphism in the *CLOCK* gene has been associated with a predisposition to obesity [117, 118]. Single nucleotide polymorphisms in the *BMAL1* gene have been implicated in the development of hypertension and T2D [119]. Similarly, polymorphisms in the *CRY2* gene are associated with increased fasting glucose [120, 121]. Besides the primary TTFL, genes of the secondary loop of TTFL are also linked with the development of metabolic disorders. For example, in men, polymorphism of REV-ERBα is associated with obesity [122]. Melatonin also seems to be a key regulator of metabolism as polymorphisms of melatonin receptor 1B (*MTNR1B*) affect fasting glucose, insulin secretion-related traits, and the risk of T2D [123–125].

Various studies on models of metabolic disorders show that circadian clocks respond to metabolic cues. In nocturnal mice, an obesogenic diet negatively affected the circadian system, shifting the timing of food intake to the light period [126]. High-fat diet (HFD) consumption during the "incorrect" time (i.e., light period for nocturnal animals) aggravates the development of obesity compared to feeding during the "appropriate" circadian time (i.e., dark period) [127]. In humans, one of the most common misalignments of feeding time is night eating syndrome (NES) [50]. NES is characterized as an eating disorder characterized by delayed eating timing during the evening and night relative to sleep timing [128]. Compared to other age groups, adolescents show a higher prevalence of NES. Individuals with NES consume higher calories during nighttime and show delayed onset of sleep, melatonin, and insulin rhythms [129, 130]. NES is associated with gradual weight gain [131] and the development of depressive symptoms [132]. Additionally, individuals with NES show poorer weight loss outcomes in weight loss programs [133]. In animal models, feeding at the wrong time has been shown to alter the circadian rhythmicity. Mice with day- and nighttime-restricted feeding show dramatic phase shifts of clock genes (ranging from 6–11 h) between the restricted feeding groups in the liver tissue [134]. The effects of feeding time on clock gene expressions were most prominent in the liver compared to muscle, heart, and epididymal fat [134]. Similarly, rats fed during the light phase showed drastic alterations in physiology and desynchrony of metabolic and clock gene expressions in liver and muscle tissue [135]. Time-restricted feeding appears to cause a desynchrony of the central pacemaker SCN and the peripheral organs leading to metabolic changes [136].

4.4 Circadian Clock and Chronotherapy

Chronotherapy involves optimizations of the timing of medical treatments following the body's circadian rhythms (Fig. 4.2). It aims to maximize the effectiveness and minimize the potential side effects of the medical treatment. Chronotherapy is practiced in two major ways, (a) to alter the sleep-wake timing of the patients and (b) to time therapeutic taking the patient's body rhythm into account [137], which we are going to cover in the following sections.

4.4.1 Modifications of the Sleep-Wake Cycle

In humans, the sleep-wake cycle reflects the functionality of the circadian clock [137]. As discussed in the previous sections, it is evident that circadian misalignments can lead to various neurological, psychiatric, and metabolic disorders that are generally associated with some form of disruption of the natural sleep-wake cycle. Manipulation of the sleep-wake rhythmicity has been shown to have robust effects on depression in individuals with affective disorders [138]. Sleep deprivation in general builds up the homeostatic drive to sleep. Acute sleep deprivation of a single night increased the cerebrospinal fluid β-Amyloid 42 levels, increasing the risk of Alzheimer's disease [139]. Various chronotechniques have been advocated to modify the disrupted sleep-wake cycle and concomitant pathology, which includes the use of light therapy and melatonin treatment.

4.4.1.1 Light Therapy and Sleep Disorders

In CRSDs, the sleep-wake rhythm shows misalignment with the circadian system and environmental cycles. The symptoms of these sleep disorders can be treated by optimally timed artificial light exposure, which can realign the circadian rhythms of sleep and alertness to the desired schedule of the patient [140]. Light treatment is mediated by the retinal photoreceptors that convey the photic signal directly to the SCN. The spectral composition and illuminance of the artificial light also play a significant role in the circadian phase shifts. For example, exposure to blue light (~460 nm) shows better results in suppressing nighttime melatonin secretions and phase-resetting circadian rhythms than green light (~555 nm) [141, 142]. Bright light therapies also seem to improve mood and sleep quality compared to dim light [140]. The timing of the light therapy is also critical for the treatment of CRSDs. In humans, light exposure in the early biological night causes phase delay, while exposure in the late biological night phase advances the circadian system [111]. Applying these principles, light therapy can be used to mediate phase shifts in the circadian processes of individuals with DSPD or ASPD. For example, early morning light therapy with reduced evening-time light led to the phase advancement of body temperature rhythm, early sleep onset, and augmentation of daytime alertness [143]. Similarly, patients with ASPD show improved sleep quality, total sleep duration, and delay of body temperature and melatonin rhythms when exposed to evening-time light therapy [144]. Light therapy can also minimize the symptoms of jet lag disorder. For eastward travel, a phase advancement is required mediated by bright-light exposure in the morning, whereas for westward travel a phase delay is ideal which is achieved by evening-time light therapy [140].

4.4.1.2 Melatonin Treatment and Circadian Entrainment

Pharmacological agents that can alter the circadian phase and thereby the output of the circadian clock are called chronobiotics [137]. Melatonin is a prototype chronobiotic that regulates the synchronization of the circadian system [145]. It is well tolerated and unlike other sleep-inducing drugs has a low potential dependence [146]. Even large doses of melatonin supplementation (20–100 mg/day) resulted in no clinically significant alterations to physiology and biochemical parameters [147]. Similar to light therapy, the direction and magnitude of circadian phase shifts depend on the timing of the melatonin administration. Melatonin treatment during the morning leads to circadian phase delay, while treatment during the evening hours advances the circadian rhythms [137]. In DSPD patients, melatonin secretion was less prominent between DLMO and rhythm peak compared to healthy individuals [148]. This indicates that a diminished surge of melatonin secretion after DLMO might contribute to the etiology of DSPD [149]. In sighted individuals likely to develop FRD, daily doses of melatonin (2–5 mg) timed to phase-advance the circadian clock through interactions with melatonin receptors in the SCN maintain the entrainment of the circadian rhythms with the 24-h environmental cycle [150]. In blind individuals with FRD, melatonin administration stabilized the sleep-wake cycle with improvements in sleep quality and mood [151]. The phase-shifting effects of melatonin can be further utilized to treat symptoms of DSPD and JLD and other sleep disorders [137]. Clinical trials of melatonin treatment have been shown to effectively treat insomnia in children with Autism spectrum disorder (ASD) [152] and adolescents with depression [153].

4.4.2 Chronopharmacology

Chronopharmacology is a branch of medical chronobiology that investigates the effectiveness of a drug administration as a function of biological time [137]. The efficacy of the drug treatment majorly depends on a) the chronopharmacokinetics, i.e., circadian changes in the bioavailability of the drug, and b) the chronesthesia, i.e., circadian changes in the drug susceptibility. Applying these principle concepts, clinical chronophramacology aims to purposefully alter the drug level to match the circadian rhythm of the body and maximize the therapeutic outcome with minimal side effects [137]. The liver is the primary metabolic organ that governs daily physiological processes and is critical to the detoxification of drugs. It is achieved through two phases, where in phase I, reactive or polar groups are introduced into xenobiotics, and in phase II, modified compounds are conjugated with polar compounds. The enzyme driving the phase I and II categories of drug metabolism was observed to show circadian variations [154]. The timing of drug administration thus has a crucial impact on how it is metabolized and detoxified. The circadian variability of arterial blood pressure is one of the most well-documented circadian rhythms. The blood pressure (BP) is known to peak during the late morning to early afternoon hours, and decline from the late evening to midnight [155]. Thus, patients with hypertension should be treated with higher doses of antihypertensive drugs during the morning period when the BP is the highest and should be administered in lesser doses during the night when the BP is lowest [156]. The specific guidelines for the chronotherapy of hypertension rely on the nature of the hypertension in the patient. Furthermore, the distribution of drugs depends on the circulation of blood and the binding capacities of drugs with erythrocytes, plasma proteins, and tissues. Circadian changes in the cardiac output and blood flow influence how the xenobiotics and drugs are distributed to the tissues. The increased blood flow during the circadian active period can be utilized in cancer treatment to deliver drugs to tumor tissues [157]. The binding capacities of plasma proteins also show circadian rhythm, for example, transcortin which binds to corticosteroids has the lowest binding capacity between night and early morning and the highest during the circadian evening [158, 159]. Thus, the circadian changes in the drug effectiveness or chronergy are determined by an interplay of changes in chronopharmacokinetics and chronesthesia of the particular drug; the study and implementation of chronotherapy will magnify therapeutic outcomes of known drugs and aid in personalized medical treatments.

Author Contribution Conceptualization, SM, SS; writing-original draft preparation, SM, SS, JT; Figures: SM, SS, JT.

Acknowledgments All figures were created using BioRender.com.

Conflicts of Interest The authors declare no conflict of interest.

Disclosure Statement The authors have nothing to disclose.

Funding The present work was supported by a research grant from the Council of Science & Technology, U.P. (Ref. No. CST/AAS/2021/D-2321) to SM.

References

1. Walker WH, Walton JC, DeVries AC, Nelson RJ. Circadian rhythm disruption and mental health. Transl Psychiatry. 2020;10(1):1–13. https://doi.org/10.1038/s41398-020-0694-0.
2. Paranjpe DA, Sharma VK. Evolution of temporal order in living organisms. J Circadian Rhythms. 2005;3:7. https://doi.org/10.1186/1740-3391-3-7.
3. Vitaterna MH, Takahashi JS, Turek FW. Overview of circadian rhythms. Alcohol Res Health. 2001;25(2):85–93.
4. Kuhlman SJ, Craig LM, Duffy JF. Introduction to chronobiology. Cold Spring Harb Perspect Biol. 2018;10(9):a033613. https://doi.org/10.1101/cshperspect.a033613.
5. Huang R-C. The discoveries of molecular mechanisms for the circadian rhythm: the 2017 Nobel Prize in physiology or medicine. Biom J. 2018;41(1):5–8. https://doi.org/10.1016/j.bj.2018.02.003.
6. Simpson S, Galbraith JJ. IV.—Observations on the normal temperature of the monkey and its diurnal variation, and on the effect of changes in the daily routine on this variation. Earth Environ Sci Trans R Soc Edinb. 1906;45(1):65–104. https://doi.org/10.1017/S0080456800011649.
7. Richter CP. A behavioristic study of the activity of the rat. Williams & Wilkins; 1922. (No. 2).
8. Beling I. Über das Zeitgedächtnis der Bienen. Z f vergl Physiologie. 1929;9(2):259–338. https://doi.org/10.1007/BF00340159.
9. Kramer G. Experiments on Bird orientation *. Ibis. 1952;94(2):265–85. https://doi.org/10.1111/j.1474-919X.1952.tb01817.x.
10. Von Aschoff J, Wever R. Spontanperiodik des Menschen bei Ausschluß aller Zeitgeber. Naturwissenschaften. 1962;49(15):337–42. https://doi.org/10.1007/BF01185109.
11. Konopka RJ, Benzer S. Clock mutants of Drosophila melanogaster. Proc Natl Acad Sci. 1971;68(9):2112–6. https://doi.org/10.1073/pnas.68.9.2112.
12. Bargiello TA, Young MW. Molecular genetics of a biological clock in drosophila. Proc Natl Acad Sci. 1984;81(7):2142–6. https://doi.org/10.1073/pnas.81.7.2142.
13. Reddy P, Zehring WA, Wheeler DA, Pirrotta V, Hadfield C, Hall JC, Rosbash M. Molecular analysis of the period locus in Drosophila melanogaster and identification of a transcript involved in biological rhythms. Cell. 1984;38(3):701–10. https://doi.org/10.1016/0092-8674(84)90265-4.
14. Zehring WA, Wheeler DA, Reddy P, Konopka RJ, Kyriacou CP, Rosbash M, Hall JC. P-element transformation with period locus DNA restores rhythmicity to mutant, arrhythmic drosophila melanogaster. Cell. 1984;39(2):369–76. https://doi.org/10.1016/0092-8674(84)90015-1.
15. Myers MP, Wager-Smith K, Wesley CS, Young MW, Sehgal A. Positional cloning and sequence analysis of the drosophila clock gene, timeless. Science. 1995;270(5237):805–8. https://doi.org/10.1126/science.270.5237.805.
16. Antoch MP, Song E-J, Chang A-M, Vitaterna MH, Zhao Y, Wilsbacher LD, Sangoram AM, King DP, Pinto LH, Takahashi JS. Functional identification of the mouse circadian clock gene by transgenic BAC rescue. Cell. 1997;89(4):655–67. https://doi.org/10.1016/S0092-8674(00)80246-9.
17. Gekakis N, Staknis D, Nguyen HB, Davis FC, Wilsbacher LD, King DP, Takahashi JS, Weitz CJ. Role of the CLOCK protein in the mammalian circadian mechanism. Science. 1998;280(5369):1564–9. https://doi.org/10.1126/science.280.5369.1564.
18. Allada R, White NE, So WV, Hall JC, Rosbash M. A mutant drosophila homolog of mammalian clock disrupts circadian rhythms and transcription of period and timeless. Cell. 1998;93(5):791–804. https://doi.org/10.1016/S0092-8674(00)81440-3.
19. Rutila JE, Suri V, Le M, So WV, Rosbash M, Hall JC. CYCLE is a second bHLH-PAS clock protein essential for circadian rhythmicity and transcription of drosophila period and timeless. Cell. 1998;93(5):805–14. https://doi.org/10.1016/S0092-8674(00)81441-5.

20. Blume C, Garbazza C, Spitschan M. Effects of light on human circadian rhythms, sleep and mood. Somnologie (Berl). 2019;23(3):147–56. https://doi.org/10.1007/s11818-019-00215-x.
21. Cheng A, Cheng H-Y. Genesis of the master circadian pacemaker in mice. Front Neurosci. 2021;15. https://doi.org/10.3389/fnins.2021.659974.
22. Provencio I, Jiang G, De Grip WJ, Hayes WP, Rollag MD. Melanopsin: an opsin in melanophores, brain, and eye. Proc Natl Acad Sci. 1998;95(1):340–5. https://doi.org/10.1073/pnas.95.1.340.
23. Provencio I, Rodriguez IR, Jiang G, Hayes WP, Moreira EF, Rollag MD. A novel human opsin in the inner retina. J Neurosci. 2000;20(2):600–5. https://doi.org/10.1523/JNEUROSCI.20-02-00600.2000.
24. Do MTH. MELANOPSIN and the intrinsically photosensitive retinal ganglion cells: biophysics to behavior. Neuron. 2019;104(2):205–26. https://doi.org/10.1016/j.neuron.2019.07.016.
25. Ma MA, Morrison EH. Neuroanatomy, nucleus suprachiasmatic. In: StatPearls. Treasure Island: StatPearls Publishing; 2024.
26. Herzog ED, Hermanstyne T, Smyllie NJ, Hastings MH. Regulating the Suprachiasmatic Nucleus (SCN) circadian clockwork: interplay between cell-autonomous and circuit-level mechanisms. Cold Spring Harb Perspect Biol. 2017;9(1):a027706. https://doi.org/10.1101/cshperspect.a027706.
27. Hastings MH, Maywood ES, Brancaccio M. Generation of circadian rhythms in the suprachiasmatic nucleus. Nat Rev Neurosci. 2018;19(8):453–69. https://doi.org/10.1038/s41583-018-0026-z.
28. Pauls S, Foley NC, Foley DK, LeSauter J, Hastings MH, Maywood ES, Silver R. Differential contributions of intra-cellular and inter-cellular mechanisms to the spatial and temporal architecture of the suprachiasmatic nucleus circadian circuitry in wild-type, cryptochrome-null and vasoactive intestinal peptide receptor 2-null mutant mice. Eur J Neurosci. 2014;40(3):2528–40. https://doi.org/10.1111/ejn.12631.
29. Santoso P, Nakata M, Ueta Y, Yada T. Suprachiasmatic vasopressin to paraventricular oxytocin neurocircuit in the hypothalamus relays light reception to inhibit feeding behavior. Am J Physiol Endocrinol Metab. 2018;315(4):E478–88. https://doi.org/10.1152/ajpendo.00338.2016.
30. Gizowski C, Zaelzer C, Bourque CW. Clock-driven vasopressin neurotransmission mediates anticipatory thirst prior to sleep. Nature. 2016;537(7622):685–8. https://doi.org/10.1038/nature19756.
31. Moldavan M, Cravetchi O, Williams M, Irwin RP, Aicher SA, Allen CN. Localization and expression of GABA transporters in the suprachiasmatic nucleus. Eur J Neurosci. 2015;42(12):3018–32. https://doi.org/10.1111/ejn.13083.
32. Wagner S, Sagiv N, Yarom Y. GABA-induced current and circadian regulation of chloride in neurones of the rat suprachiasmatic nucleus. J Physiol. 2001;537(Pt 3):853–69. https://doi.org/10.1111/j.1469-7793.2001.00853.x.
33. Borjigin J, Li X, Snyder SH. The pineal gland and melatonin: molecular and pharmacologic regulation. Annu Rev Pharmacol Toxicol. 1999;39:53–65. https://doi.org/10.1146/annurev.pharmtox.39.1.53.
34. Sun X, Deng J, Liu T, Borjigin J. Circadian 5-HT production regulated by adrenergic signaling. Proc Natl Acad Sci. 2002;99(7):4686–91. https://doi.org/10.1073/pnas.062585499.
35. Borjigin J, Zhang LS, Calinescu A-A. Circadian regulation of pineal gland rhythmicity. Mol Cell Endocrinol. 2012;349(1):13–9. https://doi.org/10.1016/j.mce.2011.07.009.
36. Kalsbeek A, Garidou M-L, Palm IF, Van Der Vliet J, Simonneaux V, Pévet P, Buijs RM. Melatonin sees the light: blocking GABA-ergic transmission in the paraventricular nucleus induces daytime secretion of melatonin. Eur J Neurosci. 2000;12(9):3146–54. https://doi.org/10.1046/j.1460-9568.2000.00202.x.
37. Liu T, Borjigin J. Free-running rhythms of pineal circadian output. J Biol Rhythm. 2005;20(5):430–40. https://doi.org/10.1177/0748730405277868.

38. Yi JS, Díaz NM, D'Souza S, Buhr ED. The molecular clockwork of mammalian cells. Semin Cell Dev Biol. 2022;126:87–96. https://doi.org/10.1016/j.semcdb.2021.03.012.
39. Bunger MK, Wilsbacher LD, Moran SM, Clendenin C, Radcliffe LA, Hogenesch JB, Simon MC, Takahashi JS, Bradfield CA. Mop3 is an essential component of the master circadian pacemaker in mammals. Cell. 2000;103(7):1009–17. https://doi.org/10.1016/S0092-8674(00)00205-1.
40. Hogenesch JB, Gu Y-Z, Jain S, Bradfield CA. The basic-helix–loop–helix-PAS orphan MOP3 forms transcriptionally active complexes with circadian and hypoxia factors. Proc Natl Acad Sci. 1998;95(10):5474–9. https://doi.org/10.1073/pnas.95.10.5474.
41. Lee C, Etchegaray J-P, Cagampang FRA, Loudon ASI, Reppert SM. Posttranslational mechanisms regulate the mammalian circadian clock. Cell. 2001;107(7):855–67. https://doi.org/10.1016/S0092-8674(01)00610-9.
42. Xu H, Gustafson CL, Sammons PJ, Khan SK, Parsley NC, Ramanathan C, Lee H-W, Liu AC, Partch CL. Cryptochrome 1 regulates the circadian clock through dynamic interactions with the BMAL1 C terminus. Nat Struct Mol Biol. 2015;22(6):476–84. https://doi.org/10.1038/nsmb.3018.
43. Ye R, Selby CP, Ozturk N, Annayev Y, Sancar A. Biochemical analysis of the canonical model for the mammalian circadian clock *. J Biol Chem. 2011;286(29):25891–902. https://doi.org/10.1074/jbc.M111.254680.
44. Etchegaray J-P, Machida KK, Noton E, Constance CM, Dallmann R, Di Napoli MN, DeBruyne JP, Lambert CM, Yu EA, Reppert SM, Weaver DR. Casein kinase 1 Delta regulates the pace of the mammalian circadian clock. Mol Cell Biol. 2009;29(14):3853–66. https://doi.org/10.1128/MCB.00338-09.
45. Chiou Y-Y, Yang Y, Rashid N, Ye R, Selby CP, Sancar A. Mammalian period represses and de-represses transcription by displacing CLOCK–BMAL1 from promoters in a Cryptochrome-dependent manner. Proc Natl Acad Sci. 2016;113(41):E6072–9. https://doi.org/10.1073/pnas.1612917113.
46. Guillaumond F, Dardente H, Giguère V, Cermakian N. Differential control of Bmal1 circadian transcription by REV-ERB and ROR nuclear receptors. J Biol Rhythm. 2005;20(5):391–403. https://doi.org/10.1177/0748730405277232.
47. Preitner N, Damiola F, Luis-Lopez-Molina ZJ, Duboule D, Albrecht U, Schibler U. The orphan nuclear receptor REV-ERBα controls circadian transcription within the positive limb of the mammalian circadian oscillator. Cell. 2002;110(2):251–60. https://doi.org/10.1016/S0092-8674(02)00825-5.
48. Cho H, Zhao X, Hatori M, Yu RT, Barish GD, Lam MT, Chong L-W, DiTacchio L, Atkins AR, Glass CK, Liddle C, Auwerx J, Downes M, Panda S, Evans RM. Regulation of circadian behaviour and metabolism by REV-ERB-α and REV-ERB-β. Nature. 2012;485(7396):123–7. https://doi.org/10.1038/nature11048.
49. Yoshitane H, Asano Y, Sagami A, Sakai S, Suzuki Y, Okamura H, Iwasaki W, Ozaki H, Fukada Y. Functional D-box sequences reset the circadian clock and drive mRNA rhythms. Commun Biol. 2019;2(1):1–10. https://doi.org/10.1038/s42003-019-0522-3.
50. Baron KG, Reid KJ. Circadian misalignment and health. Int Rev Psychiatry. 2014;26(2):139–54. https://doi.org/10.3109/09540261.2014.911149.
51. Fischer D, Vetter C, Roenneberg T. A novel method to visualise and quantify circadian misalignment. Sci Rep. 2016;6(1):38601. https://doi.org/10.1038/srep38601.
52. James SM, Honn KA, Gaddameedhi S, Van Dongen HPA. Shift work: disrupted circadian rhythms and sleep—implications for health and Well-being. Curr Sleep Med Rep. 2017;3(2):104–12. https://doi.org/10.1007/s40675-017-0071-6.
53. Borbely AA. A two process model of sleep regulation. Hum Neurobiol. 1982;1(3):195–204.
54. Åkerstedt T. Shift work and disturbed sleep/wakefulness. Occup Med. 2003;53(2):89–94. https://doi.org/10.1093/occmed/kqg046.
55. Sack RL. The pathophysiology of jet lag. Travel Med Infect Dis. 2009;7(2):102–10. https://doi.org/10.1016/j.tmaid.2009.01.006.

56. Leng Y, Musiek ES, Hu K, Cappuccio FP, Yaffe K. Association between circadian rhythms and neurodegenerative diseases. Lancet Neurol. 2019;18(3):307–18. https://doi.org/10.1016/S1474-4422(18)30461-7.
57. Videnovic A, Lazar AS, Barker RA, Overeem S. 'The clocks that time us'—circadian rhythms in neurodegenerative disorders. Nat Rev Neurol. 2014;10(12):683–93. https://doi.org/10.1038/nrneurol.2014.206.
58. Hooghiemstra AM, Eggermont LHP, Scheltens P, van der Flier WM, Scherder EJA. The rest-activity rhythm and physical activity in early-onset dementia. Alzheimer Dis Assoc Disord. 2015;29(1):45. https://doi.org/10.1097/WAD.0000000000000037.
59. Musiek ES, Bhimasani M, Zangrilli MA, Morris JC, Holtzman DM, Ju Y-ES. Circadian rest-activity pattern changes in aging and preclinical Alzheimer disease. JAMA Neurol. 2018;75(5):582–90. https://doi.org/10.1001/jamaneurol.2017.4719.
60. Liguori C, Romigi A, Nuccetelli M, Zannino S, Sancesario G, Martorana A, Albanese M, Mercuri NB, Izzi F, Bernardini S, Nitti A, Sancesario GM, Sica F, Marciani MG, Placidi F. Orexinergic system dysregulation, sleep impairment, and cognitive decline in Alzheimer disease. JAMA Neurol. 2014;71(12):1498–505. https://doi.org/10.1001/jamaneurol.2014.2510.
61. Cronin P, McCarthy MJ, Lim ASP, Salmon DP, Galasko D, Masliah E, De Jager PL, Bennett DA, Desplats P. Circadian alterations during early stages of Alzheimer's disease are associated with aberrant cycles of DNA methylation in BMAL1. Alzheimers Dement. 2017;13(6):689–700. https://doi.org/10.1016/j.jalz.2016.10.003.
62. Cermakian N, Waddington Lamont E, Boudreau P, Boivin DB. Circadian clock gene expression in brain regions of Alzheimer's disease patients and control subjects. J Biol Rhythm. 2011;26(2):160–70. https://doi.org/10.1177/0748730410395732.
63. Wang JL, Lim AS, Chiang W-Y, Hsieh W-H, Lo M-T, Schneider JA, Buchman AS, Bennett DA, Hu K, Saper CB. Suprachiasmatic neuron numbers and rest–activity circadian rhythms in older humans. Ann Neurol. 2015;78(2):317–22. https://doi.org/10.1002/ana.24432.
64. Zhou J-N, Hofman MA, Swaab DF. VIP neurons in the human SCN in relation to sex, age, and Alzheimer's disease. Neurobiol Aging. 1995;16(4):571–6. https://doi.org/10.1016/0197-4580(95)00043-E.
65. Schmitt K, Grimm A, Eckert A. Amyloid-β–induced changes in molecular clock properties and cellular bioenergetics. Front Neurosci. 2017;11. https://doi.org/10.3389/fnins.2017.00124.
66. Song H, Moon M, Choe HK, Han D-H, Jang C, Kim A, Cho S, Kim K, Mook-Jung I. Aβ-induced degradation of BMAL1 and CBP leads to circadian rhythm disruption in Alzheimer's disease. Mol Neurodegener. 2015;10(1):13. https://doi.org/10.1186/s13024-015-0007-x.
67. Breen DP, Vuono R, Nawarathna U, Fisher K, Shneerson JM, Reddy AB, Barker RA. Sleep and circadian rhythm regulation in early Parkinson disease. JAMA Neurol. 2014;71(5):589–95. https://doi.org/10.1001/jamaneurol.2014.65.
68. Tholfsen LK, Larsen JP, Schulz J, Tysnes O-B, Gjerstad MD. Development of excessive daytime sleepiness in early Parkinson disease. Neurology. 2015;85(2):162–8. https://doi.org/10.1212/WNL.0000000000001737.
69. Zhong G, Bolitho S, Grunstein R, Naismith SL, Lewis SJG. The relationship between thermoregulation and REM sleep behaviour disorder in Parkinson's disease. PLoS One. 2013;8(8):e72661. https://doi.org/10.1371/journal.pone.0072661.
70. Berganzo K, Díez-Arrola B, Tijero B, Somme J, Lezcano E, Llorens V, Ugarriza I, Ciordia R, Gómez-Esteban JC, Zarranz JJ. Nocturnal hypertension and dysautonomia in patients with Parkinson's disease: are they related? J Neurol. 2013;260(7):1752–6. https://doi.org/10.1007/s00415-013-6859-5.
71. Bordet R, Devos D, Brique S, Touitou Y, Guieu JD, Libersa C, Destée A. Study of circadian melatonin secretion pattern at different stages of Parkinson's disease. Clin Neuropharmacol. 2003;26(2):65.
72. Fertl E, Auff E, Doppelbauer A, Waldhauser F. Circadian secretion pattern of melatonin in de novo Parkinsonian patients: evidence for phase-shifting properties of l-dopa. J Neural Transm Gen Sect. 1993;5(3):227–34. https://doi.org/10.1007/BF02257677.

73. Karatsoreos IN. Links between circadian rhythms and psychiatric disease. Front Behav Neurosci. 2014;8. https://doi.org/10.3389/fnbeh.2014.00162.
74. Germain A, Kupfer DJ. Circadian rhythm disturbances in depression. Hum Psychopharmacol Clin Exp. 2008;23(7):571–85. https://doi.org/10.1002/hup.964.
75. Emens J, Lewy A, Kinzie JM, Arntz D, Rough J. Circadian misalignment in major depressive disorder. Psychiatry Res. 2009;168(3):259–61.
76. Koresh O, Kozlovsky N, Kaplan Z, Zohar J, Matar MA, Cohen H. The long-term abnormalities in circadian expression of period 1 and period 2 genes in response to stress is normalized by agomelatine administered immediately after exposure. Eur Neuropsychopharmacol. 2012;22(3):205–21.
77. Morley-Fletcher S, Mairesse J, Soumier A, Banasr M, Fagioli F, Gabriel C, Mocaer E, Daszuta A, McEwen B, Nicoletti F. Chronic agomelatine treatment corrects behavioral, cellular, and biochemical abnormalities induced by prenatal stress in rats. Psychopharmacology. 2011;217:301–13.
78. Kasper S, Hajak G, Wulff K, Hoogendijk WJ, Montejo AL, Smeraldi E, Rybakowski JK, Quera-Salva M-A, Wirz-Justice AM, Picarel-Blanchot F. Efficacy of the novel antidepressant agomelatine on the circadian rest-activity cycle and depressive and anxiety symptoms in patients with major depressive disorder: a randomized, double-blind comparison with sertraline. J Clin Psychiatry. 2010;71(2):6060.
79. Rosenthal NE, Sack DA, Gillin JC, Lewy AJ, Goodwin FK, Davenport Y, Mueller PS, Newsome DA, Wehr TA. Seasonal affective disorder: a description of the syndrome and preliminary findings with light therapy. Arch Gen Psychiatry. 1984;41(1):72–80. https://doi.org/10.1001/archpsyc.1984.01790120076010.
80. Jones SH, Hare DJ, Evershed K. Actigraphic assessment of circadian activity and sleep patterns in bipolar disorder. Bipolar Disord. 2005;7(2):176–86. https://doi.org/10.1111/j.1399-5618.2005.00187.x.
81. Rock P, Goodwin G, Harmer C, Wulff K. Daily rest-activity patterns in the bipolar phenotype: a controlled actigraphy study. Chronobiol Int. 2014;31(2):290–6. https://doi.org/10.3109/07420528.2013.843542.
82. Robillard R, Naismith SL, Rogers NL, Ip TK, Hermens DF, Scott EM, Hickie IB. Delayed sleep phase in young people with unipolar or bipolar affective disorders. J Affect Disord. 2013;145(2):260–3.
83. Iwahana E, Hamada T, Uchida A, Shibata S. Differential effect of lithium on the circadian oscillator in young and old hamsters. Biochem Biophys Res Commun. 2007;354(3):752–6.
84. LeSauter J, Silver R. Lithium lengthens the period of circadian rhythms in lesioned hamsters bearing SCN grafts. Biol Psychiatry. 1993;34(1–2):75–83.
85. Terao T. Calcium, lithium, and circadian rhythms. Biol Psychiatry. 1992;32(1):105–6.
86. Iwahana E, Akiyama M, Miyakawa K, Uchida A, Kasahara J, Fukunaga K, Hamada T, Shibata S. Effect of lithium on the circadian rhythms of locomotor activity and glycogen synthase kinase-3 protein expression in the mouse suprachiasmatic nuclei. Eur J Neurosci. 2004;19(8):2281–7. https://doi.org/10.1111/j.0953-816X.2004.03322.x.
87. Padiath QS, Paranjpe D, Jain S, Sharma VK. Glycogen synthase kinase 3β as a likely target for the action of lithium on circadian clocks. Chronobiol Int. 2004;21(1):43–55. https://doi.org/10.1081/CBI-120027981.
88. Roybal K, Theobold D, Graham A, DiNieri JA, Russo SJ, Krishnan V, Chakravarty S, Peevey J, Oehrlein N, Birnbaum S, Vitaterna MH, Orsulak P, Takahashi JS, Nestler EJ, Carlezon WA, McClung CA. Mania-like behavior induced by disruption of *CLOCK*. Proc Natl Acad Sci USA. 2007;104(15):6406–11. https://doi.org/10.1073/pnas.0609625104.
89. Mukherjee S, Coque L, Cao J-L, Kumar J, Chakravarty S, Asaithamby A, Graham A, Gordon E, Enwright JF III, DiLeone RJ. Knockdown of clock in the ventral tegmental area through RNA interference results in a mixed state of mania and depression-like behavior. Biol Psychiatry. 2010;68(6):503–11.

90. Monti JM, BaHammam AS, Pandi-Perumal SR, Bromundt V, Spence DW, Cardinali DP, Brown GM. Sleep and circadian rhythm dysregulation in schizophrenia. Prog Neuro-Psychopharmacol Biol Psychiatry. 2013;43:209–16.
91. Afonso P, Brissos S, Figueira ML, Paiva T. Schizophrenia patients with predominantly positive symptoms have more disturbed sleep–wake cycles measured by actigraphy. Psychiatry Res. 2011;189(1):62–6.
92. Bromundt V, Köster M, Georgiev-Kill A, Opwis K, Wirz-Justice A, Stoppe G, Cajochen C. Sleep–wake cycles and cognitive functioning in schizophrenia. Br J Psychiatry. 2011;198(4):269–76.
93. Rao ML, Gross G, Strebel B, Halaris A, Huber G, Bräunig P, Marler M. Circadian rhythm of tryptophan, serotonin, melatonin, and pituitary hormones in schizophrenia. Biol Psychiatry. 1994;35(3):151–63.
94. Wulff K, Dijk D-J, Middleton B, Foster RG, Joyce EM. Sleep and circadian rhythm disruption in schizophrenia. Br J Psychiatry. 2012;200(4):308–16.
95. Mills JN, Morgan R, Minors DS, Waterhouse JM. The free-running circadian rhythms of two schizophrenics. Chronobiologia. 1977;4(4):353–60.
96. Jeans AF, Oliver PL, Johnson R, Capogna M, Vikman J, Molnár Z, Babbs A, Partridge CJ, Salehi A, Bengtsson M, Eliasson L, Rorsman P, Davies KE. A dominant mutation in *Snap25* causes impaired vesicle trafficking, sensorimotor gating, and ataxia in the blind-drunk mouse. Proc Natl Acad Sci USA. 2007;104(7):2431–6. https://doi.org/10.1073/pnas.0610222104.
97. Oliver PL, Sobczyk MV, Maywood ES, Edwards B, Lee S, Livieratos A, Oster H, Butler R, Godinho SI, Wulff K. Disrupted circadian rhythms in a mouse model of schizophrenia. Curr Biol. 2012;22(4):314–9.
98. Vacic V, McCarthy S, Malhotra D, Murray F, Chou H-H, Peoples A, Makarov V, Yoon S, Bhandari A, Corominas R. Duplications of the neuropeptide receptor gene VIPR2 confer significant risk for schizophrenia. Nature. 2011;471(7339):499–503.
99. Regestein QR, Monk TH. Delayed sleep phase syndrome: a review of its clinical aspects. Am J Psychiatry. 1995;152(4):602–8.
100. Schrader H, Bovim G, Sand T. The prevalence of delayed and advanced sleep phase syndromes. J Sleep Res. 1993;2(1):51–5. https://doi.org/10.1111/j.1365-2869.1993.tb00061.x.
101. Weitzman ED, Czeisler CA, Coleman RM, Spielman AJ, Zimmerman JC, Dement W, Pollak CP. Delayed sleep phase syndrome: a chronobiological disorder with sleep-onset insomnia. Arch Gen Psychiatry. 1981;38(7):737–46.
102. Chang A-M, Reid KJ, Gourineni R, Zee PC. Sleep timing and circadian phase in delayed sleep phase syndrome. J Biol Rhythm. 2009;24(4):313–21. https://doi.org/10.1177/0748730409339611.
103. Ozaki S, Uchiyama M, Shirakawa S, Okawa M. Prolonged interval from body temperature nadir to sleep offset in patients with delayed sleep phase syndrome. Sleep. 1996;19(1):36–40.
104. Uchiyama M, Okawa M, Shibui K, Kim K, Tagaya H, Kudo Y, Kamei Y, Hayakawa T, Urata J, Takahashi K. Altered phase relation between sleep timing and core body temperature rhythm in delayed sleep phase syndrome and non-24-hour sleep–wake syndrome in humans. Neurosci Lett. 2000;294(2):101–4.
105. Sack RL, Auckley D, Auger RR, Carskadon MA, Wright KP Jr, Vitiello MV, Zhdanova IV. Circadian rhythm sleep disorders: part II, advanced sleep phase disorder, delayed sleep phase disorder, free-running disorder, and irregular sleep-wake rhythm. Sleep. 2007;30(11):1484–501.
106. Aoki H, Ozeki Y, Yamada N. Hypersensitivity of melatonin suppression in response to light in patients with delayed sleep phase syndrome*. Chronobiol Int. 2001;18(2):263–71. https://doi.org/10.1081/CBI-100103190.
107. Abe T, Inoue Y, Komada Y, Nakamura M, Asaoka S, Kanno M, Shibui K, Hayashida K, Usui A, Takahashi K. Relation between morningness–eveningness score and depressive symptoms among patients with delayed sleep phase syndrome. Sleep Med. 2011;12(7):680–4.

108. Reid KJ, Chang A-M, Dubocovich ML, Turek FW, Takahashi JS, Zee PC. Familial advanced sleep phase syndrome. Arch Neurol. 2001;58(7):1089–94.
109. Ando K, Kripke DF, Ancoli-Israel S. Delayed and advanced sleep phase symptoms. Isr J Psychiatry. 2002;39(1):11.
110. Jones CR, Campbell SS, Zone SE, Cooper F, DeSano A, Murphy PJ, Jones B, Czajkowski L, Ptček LJ. Familial advanced sleep-phase syndrome: a short-period circadian rhythm variant in humans. Nat Med. 1999;5(9):1062–5.
111. Czeisler CA, Duffy JF, Shanahan TL, Brown EN, Mitchell JF, Rimmer DW, Ronda JM, Silva EJ, Allan JS, Emens JS, Dijk D-J, Kronauer RE. Stability, precision, and Near-24-hour period of the human circadian pacemaker. Science. 1999;284(5423):2177–81. https://doi.org/10.1126/science.284.5423.2177.
112. Lockley SW, Skene DJ, Arendt J, Tabandeh H, Bird AC, Defrance R. Relationship between melatonin rhythms and visual loss in the blind. J Clin Endocrinol Metabol. 1997;82(11):3763–70.
113. Hayakawa T, Uchiyama M, Kamei Y, Shibui K, Tagaya H, Asada T, Okawa M, Urata J, Takahashi K. Clinical analyses of sighted patients with non-24-hour sleep-wake syndrome: a study of 57 consecutively diagnosed cases. Sleep. 2005;28(8):945–52.
114. Zakir F, Mohapatra S, Farooq U, MohdA M, Iqbal Z. Chapter 1 – Introduction to metabolic disorders. In: Dureja H, Murthy SN, Wich PR, Dua K, editors. Drug delivery systems for metabolic disorders. Academic Press; 2022. p. 1–20.
115. Zhang R, Lahens NF, Ballance HI, Hughes ME, Hogenesch JB. A circadian gene expression atlas in mammals: implications for biology and medicine. Proc Natl Acad Sci USA. 2014;111(45):16219–24. https://doi.org/10.1073/pnas.1408886111.
116. Maury E. Off the clock: from circadian disruption to metabolic disease. Int J Mol Sci. 2019;20(7):1597. https://doi.org/10.3390/ijms20071597.
117. Scott EM, Carter AM, Grant PJ. Association between polymorphisms in the clock gene, obesity and the metabolic syndrome in man. Int J Obes. 2008;32(4):658–62.
118. Sookoian S, Gemma C, Gianotti TF, Burgueno A, Castano G, Pirola CJ. Genetic variants of clock transcription factor are associated with individual susceptibility to obesity. Am J Clin Nutr. 2008;87(6):1606–15.
119. Woon PY, Kaisaki PJ, Bragança J, Bihoreau M-T, Levy JC, Farrall M, Gauguier D. Aryl hydrocarbon receptor nuclear translocator-like (BMAL1) is associated with susceptibility to hypertension and type 2 diabetes. Proc Natl Acad Sci USA. 2007;104(36):14412–7. https://doi.org/10.1073/pnas.0703247104.
120. Barker A, Sharp SJ, Timpson NJ, Bouatia-Naji N, Warrington NM, Kanoni S, Beilin LJ, Brage S, Deloukas P, Evans DM. Association of genetic Loci with glucose levels in childhood and adolescence: a meta-analysis of over 6,000 children. Diabetes. 2011;60(6):1805–12.
121. Dupuis J, Langenberg C, Prokopenko I, Saxena R, Soranzo N, Jackson AU, Wheeler E, Glazer NL, Bouatia-Naji N, Gloyn AL. New genetic loci implicated in fasting glucose homeostasis and their impact on type 2 diabetes risk. Nat Genet. 2010;42(2):105–16.
122. Ruano EG, Canivell S, Vieira E. REV-ERB ALPHA polymorphism is associated with obesity in the Spanish obese male population. PLoS One. 2014;9(8):e104065.
123. Bonnefond A, Clement N, Fawcett K, Yengo L, Vaillant E, Guillaume J-L, Dechaume A, Payne F, Roussel R, Czernichow S. Rare MTNR1B variants impairing melatonin receptor 1B function contribute to type 2 diabetes. Nat Genet. 2012;44(3):297–301.
124. Bouatia-Naji N, Bonnefond A, Cavalcanti-Proença C, Sparsø T, Holmkvist J, Marchand M, Delplanque J, Lobbens S, Rocheleau G, Durand E. A variant near MTNR1B is associated with increased fasting plasma glucose levels and type 2 diabetes risk. Nat Genet. 2009;41(1):89–94.
125. Lyssenko V, Nagorny CL, Erdos MR, Wierup N, Jonsson A, Spégel P, Bugliani M, Saxena R, Fex M, Pulizzi N. Common variant in MTNR1B associated with increased risk of type 2 diabetes and impaired early insulin secretion. Nat Genet. 2009;41(1):82–8.

126. Kohsaka A, Laposky AD, Ramsey KM, Estrada C, Joshu C, Kobayashi Y, Turek FW, Bass J. High-fat diet disrupts behavioral and molecular circadian rhythms in mice. Cell Metab. 2007;6(5):414–21.
127. Arble DM, Bass J, Laposky AD, Vitaterna MH, Turek FW. Circadian timing of food intake contributes to weight gain. Obesity. 2009;17(11):2100–2. https://doi.org/10.1038/oby.2009.264.
128. Hamdan M, Badrasawi M, Zidan S, Thawabteh R, Mohtaseb R, Arqoub KA. Night eating syndrome is associated with mental health issues among palestinian undergraduate students-cross sectional study. J Eat Disord. 2023;11(1):1. https://doi.org/10.1186/s40337-022-00727-2.
129. Goel N, Stunkard AJ, Rogers NL, Van Dongen HPA, Allison KC, O'Reardon JP, Ahima RS, Cummings DE, Heo M, Dinges DF. Circadian rhythm profiles in women with night eating syndrome. J Biol Rhythm. 2009;24(1):85–94. https://doi.org/10.1177/0748730408328914.
130. O'Reardon JP, Ringel BL, Dinges DF, Allison KC, Rogers NL, Martino NS, Stunkard AJ. Circadian eating and sleeping patterns in the night eating syndrome. Obes Res. 2004;12(11):1789–96. https://doi.org/10.1038/oby.2004.222.
131. Marshall HM, Allison KC, O'Reardon JP, Birketvedt G, Stunkard AJ. Night eating syndrome among nonobese persons. Int J Eat Disord. 2004;35(2):217–22. https://doi.org/10.1002/eat.10241.
132. Lundgren JD, Allison KC, O'Reardon JP, Stunkard AJ. A descriptive study of non-obese persons with night eating syndrome and a weight-matched comparison group. Eat Behav. 2008;9(3):343–51.
133. Gluck ME, Geliebter A, Satov T. Night eating syndrome is associated with depression, low self-esteem, reduced daytime hunger, and less weight loss in obese outpatients. Obes Res. 2001;9(4):264–7. https://doi.org/10.1038/oby.2001.31.
134. Bray MS, Ratcliffe WF, Grenett MH, Brewer RA, Gamble KL, Young ME. Quantitative analysis of light-phase restricted feeding reveals metabolic dyssynchrony in mice. Int J Obes. 2013;37(6):843–52.
135. Opperhuizen A, Wang D, Foppen E, Jansen R, Boudzovitch-Surovtseva O, De Vries J, Fliers E, Kalsbeek A. Feeding during the resting phase causes profound changes in physiology and desynchronization between liver and muscle rhythms of rats. Eur J Neurosci. 2016;44(10):2795–806. https://doi.org/10.1111/ejn.13377.
136. Woller A, Gonze D. Circadian misalignment and metabolic disorders: a story of twisted clocks. Biology. 2021;10(3):207.
137. Cardinali DP, Brown GM, Pandi-Perumal SR. Chapter 24 – Chronotherapy. In: Swaab DF, Kreier F, Lucassen PJ, Salehi A, Buijs RM, editors. Handbook of clinical neurology. Elsevier; 2021. p. 357–70.
138. Wirz-Justice A, Benedetti F. Perspectives in affective disorders: clocks and sleep. Eur J Neurosci. 2020;51(1):346–65. https://doi.org/10.1111/ejn.14362.
139. Ooms S, Overeem S, Besse K, Rikkert MO, Verbeek M, Claassen JAHR. Effect of 1 night of total sleep deprivation on cerebrospinal fluid β-amyloid 42 in healthy middle-aged men: a randomized clinical trial. JAMA Neurol. 2014;71(8):971–7. https://doi.org/10.1001/jamaneurol.2014.1173.
140. Gooley JJ. Treatment of circadian rhythm sleep disorders with light. Ann Acad Med Singap. 2008;37(8):669–76.
141. Cajochen C, Munch M, Kobialka S, Krauchi K, Steiner R, Oelhafen P, Orgul S, Wirz-Justice A. High sensitivity of human melatonin, alertness, thermoregulation, and heart rate to short wavelength light. J Clin Endocrinol Metabol. 2005;90(3):1311–6.
142. Lockley SW, Brainard GC, Czeisler CA. High sensitivity of the human circadian melatonin rhythm to resetting by short wavelength light. J Clin Endocrinol Metabol. 2003;88(9):4502–5.
143. Rosenthal NE, Joseph-Vanderpool JR, Levendosky AA, Johnston SH, Allen R, Kelly KA, Souetre E, Schultz PM, Starz KE. Phase-shifting effects of bright morning light as treatment for delayed sleep phase syndrome. Sleep. 1990;13(4):354–61.

144. Lack L, Wright H, Kemp K, Gibbon S. The treatment of early-morning awakening insomnia with 2 evenings of bright light. Sleep. 2005;28(5):616–23.
145. Pevet P, Klosen P, Felder-Schmittbuhl M-P. The hormone melatonin: animal studies. Best Pract Res Clin Endocrinol Metab. 2017;31(6):547–59.
146. Alexis Geoffroy P, Etain B, Micoulaud Franchi J-A, Bellivier F, Ritter P. Melatonin and melatonin agonists as adjunctive treatments in bipolar disorders. Curr Pharm Des. 2015;21(23):3352–8.
147. Galley HF, Lowes DA, Allen L, Cameron G, Aucott LS, Webster NR. Melatonin as a potential therapy for sepsis: a phase I dose escalation study and an ex vivo whole blood model under conditions of sepsis. J Pineal Res. 2014;56(4):427–38. https://doi.org/10.1111/jpi.12134.
148. Micic G, Lovato N, Gradisar M, Burgess HJ, Ferguson SA, Kennaway DJ, Lack L. Nocturnal melatonin profiles in patients with delayed sleep-wake phase disorder and control sleepers. J Biol Rhythm. 2015;30(5):437–48. https://doi.org/10.1177/0748730415591753.
149. Xie Z, Chen F, Li WA, Geng X, Li C, Meng X, Feng Y, Liu W, Yu F. A review of sleep disorders and melatonin. Neurol Res. 2017;39(6):559–65. https://doi.org/10.1080/01616412.2017.1315864.
150. Lewy A. Clinical implications of the melatonin phase response curve. J Clin Endocrinol Metabol. 2010;95:3158–60.
151. Skene DJ, Arendt J. Circadian rhythm sleep disorders in the blind and their treatment with melatonin. Sleep Med. 2007;8(6):651–5.
152. Goldman SE, Adkins KW, Calcutt MW, Carter MD, Goodpaster RL, Wang L, Shi Y, Burgess HJ, Hachey DL, Malow BA. Melatonin in children with autism spectrum disorders: endogenous and pharmacokinetic profiles in relation to sleep. J Autism Dev Disord. 2014;44(10):2525–35. https://doi.org/10.1007/s10803-014-2123-9.
153. Bartlett DJ, Biggs SN, Armstrong SM. Circadian rhythm disorders among adolescents: assessment and treatment options. Med J Aust. 2013;199:S16–20.
154. Zmrzljak UP, Rozman D. Circadian regulation of the hepatic endobiotic and xenobitoic detoxification pathways: the time matters. Chem Res Toxicol. 2012;25(4):811–24. https://doi.org/10.1021/tx200538r.
155. Smith DHG. Pharmacology of cardiovascular chronotherapeutic agents. Am J Hypertens. 2001;14(S6):296S–301S. https://doi.org/10.1016/S0895-7061(01)02176-8.
156. Dobrek L. Chronopharmacology in therapeutic drug monitoring—dependencies between the rhythmics of pharmacokinetic processes and drug concentration in blood. Pharmaceutics. 2021;13(11):1915.
157. Dallmann R, Okyar A, Lévi F. Dosing-time makes the poison: circadian regulation and pharmacotherapy. Trends Mol Med. 2016;22(5):430–45. https://doi.org/10.1016/j.molmed.2016.03.004.
158. Ayyar VS, Sukumaran S. Circadian rhythms: influence on physiology, pharmacology, and therapeutic interventions. J Pharmacokinet Pharmacodyn. 2021;48(3):321–38. https://doi.org/10.1007/s10928-021-09751-2.
159. Dallmann R, Brown SA, Gachon F. Chronopharmacology: new insights and therapeutic implications. Annu Rev Pharmacol Toxicol. 2014;54:339–61. https://doi.org/10.1146/annurev-pharmtox-011613-135923.

Part II
Public Health: Social and Economic Implication

Chapter 5
Pandemics and Policy: The Economic Impacts of Environmental Regulations

Girjesh Shukla and Shubham Singh Bagla

> … if the decision of competent matter is so unreasonable that no reasonable authority could ever come to it, then the courts can interfere.
> ~Wednesbury Principle of Reasonableness
> 'Associated Provincial Picture Houses Ltd. v. Wednesbury Corporation' [3]

5.1 Introduction

Environment protection is the act of preserving, conserving, and effectively managing natural entities. One of the objectives is to avoid the degradation of ecosystems, ensuring the survival of diverse nature and the maintenance of an ecological balance. It also regulates pollutants, conserves wildlife habitats, and ensures the sustainability of natural resources. Therefore, the primary aim should be to establish an equilibrium where the activities of humans do not degrade the environment so that it can still be used and enjoyed by the next generations to come. Human rights and environmental protection are essentially linked. Indeed, a healthy environment is a precondition or a requirement for the exercise of basic human rights, among them the rights to life, health, and well-being. Environmental degradation has been among the major causes of serious health problems and can cause displacement and a loss of means of subsistence, thereby infringing on fundamental human rights.

The chapter deals with some of the critical questions on environmental protection and administrative law. It discusses whether *ex-post-facto* approval may ever be

G. Shukla (✉)
Himachal Pradesh National Law University, Shimla, India
e-mail: girjesh@hpnlu.ac.in

S. S. Bagla
SRM University, Delhi-NCR, Sonepat, Haryana, India
e-mail: shubhamsingh@hpnlu.ac.in

S. Malik et al. (eds.), *Public Health Issues: Theory and Practices*,
https://doi.org/10.1007/978-981-96-6650-8_5

held sufficient for an activity that, per se, is dangerous and hazardous, thereby challenging the very legitimacy as well as safety of ex-post-facto authorisations. It also inquires if the application of logical reasoning arising under the rubric of administrative law applies correctly to environmental protection and whether the principles of administrative law efficiently protect the interests of the environment. Moreover, the work allows insight into the applicability of the Deep Pocket Theory in environmental situations, which holds that liability should occur where the money is. It concludes with the controversial issue of whether economic growth and development should come before environmental protection and whether this view could be justified concerning the world's long-term future. These questions are specifically designed to allow for a complex exploration of the complex relationships between legal frameworks, economic imperatives, and environmental sustainability.

5.2 The Environmental Regulations

Environmental legislation has undergone evolution based on raising awareness regarding the effects of industrialisation and urbanisation. Early legislation was more of a response to a specific incident of pollution or degradation. Only later did societies begin to develop an approach based on prevention, control, and mitigation. International conferences, remarkably the Stockholm Conference in 1972 and the Rio Earth Summit in 1992, have greatly moulded environmental legislation across borders. Internationally, Sustainable Development Goals consist of 17 interlinked global goals designed to act as a 'blueprint to achieve a better and more sustainable future for all'. Realising these goals will help in addressing world challenges such as related to poverty, inequality, climate, environmental degradation, peace, and justice. SDG 13 is directly linked to Climate Action, while SDG 14 and SDG 15 relate to Life Below Water and Life on Land, which is directly linked to environmental sustainability in combating climate change and preserving marine and terrestrial ecosystems [34].

In India, the protection of the environment is envisaged under the Constitution of India through various provisions. Article 48-A mandates the State to protect and improve the environment and safeguard the forests and wildlife. Article 51A(g) provides that it shall be the duty of every citizen to protect and improve the natural environment, including forests, lakes, rivers, and wildlife. It is on these constitutional provisions that several environmental laws and policies in India rest. The present framework of India's environmental laws consists of manifold legislation in the light of different environmental aspects. These include, amongst others, the Forest Conservation Act of 1980 [29], the Environment (Protection) Act of 1986, the Air (Prevention and Control of Pollution) Act of 1981 [26], the Water (Prevention and Control of Pollution) Act of 1974 [31], the Wildlife (Protection) Act of 1972 [32], and the National Green Tribunal Act of 2010 [31]. Every individual legislation has its own area of applicability, which requires separate clearances under respective legislation for any business or industry activity related to those areas. The judiciary in India has been very proactive with regard to environmental protection. On account of PILs, courts have expanded the interpretation of the right to life under Article 21 of the Constitution of India, 1950 [27], including the right to a healthy environment. The courts have also drawn upon the precautionary principle and the polluter pays principle to ensure effective enforcement of environmental regulations.

In the case of 'Rural Litigation and Entitlement Kendra Dehradun v. State of Uttar Pradesh' [22], also called the Doon Valley case, the Supreme Court finally ordered the closing of mining activities in the hilly areas after a lot of investigation quoted the following observation to the protection of the environment while doing sustainable development:

> …This would undoubtedly cause hardship to them, but it is a price that has to be paid for protecting and safeguarding the right of the people to live in a healthy environment with minimal disturbance of ecological balance and without avoidable hazard to them and to their cattle, homes and agricultural land and undue affection of air, water, and environment...

The case related to the issue that the tanneries in Tamil Nadu discharged their effluents into the Palar River, which was a main source of drinking water supply in the State. The Supreme Court, for the first time, applied the doctrine of Sustainable Development in 'Vellore Citizen Welfare Forum v. Union of India' [36] and held:

> ...Remediation of the damaged environment is part of the process of 'Sustainable Development' and as such polluter is liable to pay the cost to the individual sufferers as well as the cost of reversing the damaged ecology...

Furthermore, Kuldip Singh J. observed that:

> The onus of proof is on the actor or the industrialist/developer to show that his action is environmentally benign.

The Supreme Court reiterated the principle of absolute liability in the case of 'M. C. Mehta and Anr. v. Union of India & Ors.' [18] states that enterprises engaged in hazardous or inherently dangerous industries, under the absolute and non-delegable duties they owe to the community, take care that the activities do not affect workers or people residing near the concerned facility. Enterprises were absolutely liable for harm caused, and no amount of reasonable care taken or absence of negligence could be pleaded in its defence.

At its very core, sustainable development is ensuring that the needs of the present are met without endangering the generation of the future in meeting their own needs. It also establishes a harmonious integration of economic, social, and environmental considerations in development planning and decision-making [25]. Other major governing principles that can be derived from these include the precautionary principle, polluter pays principle, and intergenerational equity principle [25].

5.3 Regulatory Framework

The Environment (Protection) Act, 1986 (hereinafter referred to as 'the EP Act') was enacted in pursuance of the UN Conference on the Human Environment, 1972, prompted by concern over the environment. Per the powers conferred on the Central Government vide Sections 6 and 25 of the EP Act, the Central Government has made the Environment (Protection) Rules, 1986 (hereinafter referred to as 'the EP Rules'). In exercise of the powers conferred by Section 3(1) & (2) of the EP Act read with Rule 5 (3) (d) of the EP Rules, the Central Government issued an Environmental Impact Assessment Notification dated 27th January 1994, directing that on and from the date of publication of the said notification in the Official Gazette, '*expansion or modernisation of any activity or a new project listed in Schedule I to the said notification shall not be undertaken in any part of India, unless it has been accorded EC by the Central Government in accordance with the procedures specified in the said notification*'. This notification was revised dated 14th September 2006, being Notification S.O. 1533 (E) requiring prior environmental clearance (EC) from the Central Government or, as the case may be, by the State-Level Environment Assessment Authority, duly constituted by the Central Government under sub-section (3) of Section 3 of the EP Act. The Notification dated 14th September 2006 provides a four-stage process for environmental clearance, i.e. screening, scoping, public consultation, and appraisal.

Further, in exercise of power under Section 3(1) and Section 3(2) (v) of the EP Act read with Rule 5 (3) (d) of the EP Rules, the Central Government issued a notification being S.O. 804 (E) dated 14th March 2017 which provides for grant of ex post facto Environmental Clearance for project proponents who had commenced, continued or completed a project without obtaining EC under the EP Act/ EP Rules or the Environmental Impact Notification issued thereunder. Para (4) of the Notification reads as follows:

> (4) The cases of violation will be appraised by respective sector Expert Appraisal Committees constituted under sub-section (3) of Section 3 of the Environment (Protection) Act, 1986, with a view to assess that the project has been constructed at a site which under prevailing laws is permissible and expansion has been done which can be run sustainably under compliance of environmental norms with adequate environmental safeguards; and in case, where the finding of the Expert Appraisal Committee is negative, closure of the project will be recommended along with other actions under the law.

Thus, the ex post facto environmental clearance shall be subject to '*the finding of the Expert Appraisal Committee'*, and if the said findings are '*negative, closure of the project will be recommended along with other actions under the law'*.

The Ministry of Environment, Forest and Climate Change (MoEF&CC) issued a draft notification dated 23rd March 2020, which was duly published in the Gazette of India Extraordinary Part II. The Notification was proposed to be issued in the exercise of powers conferred by sub-section (1) and clause (v) of sub-section (2) of Section 3 of the EP Act for dealing with cases of violation of the notification concerning environmental clearance. Under this draft notification, cases of violations would be appraised by the Appraisal Committee to assess whether the project had been constructed or operated at a site that was permissible under prevailing laws and could be run sustainably in compliance with environmental norms with adequate environmental safeguards. However, Closure would be recommended if the findings of the Appraisal Committee were in the negative. If the Appraisal Committee found that such a unit had been running sustainably upon compliance with environmental norms with adequate environmental safeguards, the unit would be prescribed appropriate Terms of Reference, after which the procedure for grant of Environmental

Clearance would follow. The three notifications mentioned above provide ample scope for administrative discretion in providing the ex-post facto environmental clearance.

5.4 Environmental Regulations: Legislative Vs. Executive Control

Most of the environmental legislation gets passed by a legislature, but it requires proper implementation and execution at the hands of an executive. The legislature's control makes the regulation process democratic by incorporating the will of the people while making them. However, the executive tends to turn this into reality through policies, programmes, and enforcement mechanisms. The balancing of the executive-legislative intent equation must stride for the proper working of environmental governance. One fundamental concept given to us by the Roman etymologically, i.e. the doctrine of Public Trust, is a potential tool for citizens looking for a comprehensive legal framework for addressing how resources are managed. In order to be effective, Sax believes that doctrine has to (1) grant a legal right of the public, (2) be enforceable against the government, and (3) promote contemporary environmental quality concerns [4, 12, 13, 24].

'The public trust was a vehicle to ensure the democratisation of natural resources decision-making' These are the words of Joseph L. Sax in his first paper published by Michigan Law Review, asserting that a 'concerted minority' may influence the administrative decision-making at the cost of the 'diffuse majority' into enumerated cases concerning public resources. Hence, the courts do play a role in political democratisation by mandating the legislature and compelling it to follow fiduciary duties [4, 13, 21, 24].

In India, the Public Trust Doctrine is a part of the law of the land in the context of environmental conservation jurisprudence and declared in the case of M. C. Mehta v Kamal Nath [19] that:

> The State is the trustee of all natural resources which are by nature meant for public use and enjoyment. The public at large is the beneficiary of the sea shore, running waters, air, forests and ecologically fragile lands. The State as a trustee is under a legal duty to protect the natural resources. These resources meant for public use cannot be converted into private ownership.

5.5 Post-covid Environmental Regulation and Economic Challenges

Even as the global pandemic has been unravelling over the past years, the incumbent government has continued its push for the 'ease of doing business' agenda. In the period between 2011 and 2020, environmental laws in India were altered almost 300 times. While another version was proposed in 2020, with no decision on the proposal, the existing law was modified as many as 33 times between 2020 and 2021. The list of modifications just in the last decade showcases the depth of change India's environmental permission regulatory framework has gone through to make rules more conducive to businesses [16].

While India grapples with this complex challenge of balancing out these divergent needs, some Western countries are rightfully placing greater emphasis on the cause of conservation. In 2016, Canada set aside significant amounts in its budget for enhancing water, wastewater, and green infrastructure. More recently, last year itself, New Zealand introduced a law requiring carbon neutrality by 2050 through natural carbon sinks like forests that could absorb the emission. Almost wholly dependent on India to meet its requirements, Bhutan has reserved over 50% of its land as protected areas and, in effect, absorbs more carbon than it emits [23]. The cause of environmental conservation in India has been taken up in the last two decades only by the constitutional courts, while the executive is often seen to have either remained silent or passed executive orders in the form of circulars and office memorandums. This created an impression in the minds of the polluters that even if they do not comply with the judicial directions or statutory requirements, their non-compliance will be subsequently regularised and condoned [17].

Days prior to the strictest lockdown imposed in the world, the MoEF&CC released the draft EIA Notification 2020, a re-envisioned law detailing the procedures and requirements for industries and infrastructure projects to receive prior environmental clearance. Initially open for 2 months, this comment period was extended to 11 August 2020, after public uproar over its very bad timing. The draft parts company, with considerable relaxation of the environmental safeguards, makes provisions for not only ex-post-facto environmental clearance but also years of exemption to many project categories from public consultation. It increases central oversight of the expert appraisal committees. Be that as it may, despite the lockdown restrictions and the public's economic sufferings, more than two million comments were received on the draft, with the majority of them appealing for its withdrawal [16].

India has approved over 270 projects in its most protected environments since July 2014. The government has been weakening environmental protections simultaneously. The leading stakeholders are thus alert to threats not only to habitats and ecosystems but also to public health. Long before the outbreak of the COVID-19 pandemic, habitat destruction had already been warned by the WHO to change the infective transmission route. Events of emerging infectious diseases involving zoonotic pathogens, such as rabies, Nipah, Ebola, SARS, MERS, and recently COVID-19, have become frequent. Scientists hypothesised that the COVID-19-causing agent, the SARS-CoV-2 virus, most likely originated from bats and got into humans via an intermediate species before rapidly turning into a pandemic. This highly infectious disease has so far killed over 233,000 people worldwide and 1152 in India until 1 May 2020. The risk of getting exposed to these types of zoonotic diseases is extremely high in biodiversity hotspots where the variety, as well as the population, of animal species is very high, and so are the human contacts [23].

The Draft 2020 has a very stringent provision, '*ex post facto clearance*', applicable retrospectively to projects even before the March 2017 Notification that had condoned all environmental violations. It essentially allows units and projects now in operation illegally, without environmental clearance, to submit a remedial plan for their illegal status to be converted into a legal one. Moreover, this clearance would enable projects to get their EC ex post facto by simply paying penalties without adequate justification for practising in sheer violative ways. The move has rightly batted for validation of the very existence and continued operation of unlawful industries working without due environmental clearances. Again, the government has failed to come up with a credible justification for including such a clause, which ignores the potential environmental damage if projects of this nature were afforded a new legitimacy [17].

The draft EIA Notification 2020 seems to be a bold attempt to bypass the Supreme Court and offer concessions to different businesses that had been operating without relevant environmental clearances. A few such examples include IIT Madras, built on more than 52 acres of land by felling over 8100 trees; it has now planned more constructions necessitating the felling of 10,000 trees, and that too without any environmental clearance, and much later, it sought and got post-facto clearance [14]. The Kudankulam Nuclear Power Plant Units 1 and 2 were constructed without adherence to the Coastal Regulation Zone Notifications of 1991 and 2011 [10, 11]. In Assam's Dehing Patkai region, a coal mining project was allowed to go ahead even after 16 years of illegal mining were retrospectively regularised on the basis of a Rs 43 crore fine submitted by the Assam Forest Department [9, 14]. In another case, the Char Dham Pariyojana to expand the 900 kilometres to Badrinath and Kedarnath was broken up into 53 smaller projects to fall below 100 km in each one and thereby bypass the need for EIA requirements [5, 14].

In a recent analysis done by VIDHI, the findings have pointed out that immense amendments to the Environment Protection Act, 1986 were made from March 2020 to March 2022. These amendments numbered 39 and were brought about by 123 regulatory instruments like gazette notifications, OM, circulars, letters, orders, etc. Changes are essentially related to relaxations and exemptions from substantive statutory requirements that were marring their issuance through internal office memoranda, which are not public domain documents. It has been criticised for probable procedural flaws in making environmental law and administrative decisions in times of COVID-19 pandemic-induced challenges [15]. The report further illustrated how 16 gazette notifications waived the requirement of public notice for amendments to the EIA Notification, citing Rule 5(4) of the EP Rules, which provides for restrictions for environmental protection. According to the report, however, these amendments decreased environmental safeguards for polluting industries without proper environmental impact assessments to a considerable extent, hence totally going against the very mandate and legality enshrined under the EP Act [15].

It has been held by the Supreme Court in 'Alembic Pharmaceuticals Ltd. v. Rohit Prajapati & Ors.' [2] that any attempt to grant ex post facto clearance is legally unsustainable and invalid, and it has further gone on to hold that grants of such clearances are legally insupportable. Again, the judgment in 'Common Cause' (2017) fully established that an Ex Post Facto or Retrospective EC is completely alien to environmental jurisprudence. Further, the Apex Court in 'Pahwa Plastics (P) Ltd. v. Dastak NGO' [20] held that:

> 63. Ex post facto environmental clearance should not be granted routinely, but in exceptional circumstances taking into account all relevant environmental factors. Where the adverse consequences of denial of ex post facto approval outweigh the consequences of regularisation of operations by the grant of ex post facto approval, and the establishment concerned otherwise conforms to the requisite pollution norms, ex post facto approval should be given in accordance with the law, in strict conformity with the applicable rules, regulations and/or notifications…

Furthermore, the Supreme Court in 'Electrosteel Steels Limited v. Union of India and Ors.' [8] underline the precaution to provide EC and states that:

> 87.…Ex post facto environmental clearance should not however be granted routinely, but in exceptional circumstances taking into account all relevant environmental factors. Where the adverse consequences of ex post facto approval outweigh the consequences of regularization of operation of an industry by grant of ex post facto approval and the industry or establishment concerned otherwise conforms to the requisite pollution norms, ex post facto approval should be given in accordance with law, in strict conformity with the applicable Rules, Regulations and/or Notifications. Ex post facto approval should not be withheld only as a penal measure. The deviant industry may be penalised by an imposition of heavy penalty on the principle of 'polluter pays' and the cost of restoration of environment may be recovered from it.

From the above judgments, it is clear that Ex post facto environmental clearance should be granted in very few cases and only in exceptional circumstances after considering all the environmental factors. If the adverse effects of such approval are found to be less harmful than those of regularising the industry, and the industry adheres to the standards of pollution, the approval must be in accordance with the laws and rules applicable. It should not be denied solely as a punishment. Otherwise, the 'polluter pays' principle imposes a heavy penalty on industries that do not comply, including the cost of environmental restoration.

5.6 A Critique of the Relaxation of Environmental Regulations

Any critique of the present legal regime of *ex-post-facto* approval should begin by asking two fundamental questions. *First*, whether Rule 5 (4) of the EP Rules, 1986 violate the constitutional spirit by allowing the government to give supremacy to industrial policy over environmental protection? Even if it is assumed that such supremacy does not explicitly violate the constitutional provision or its spirit, the *second* question would be whether this *ex-post-facto* approval policy has necessary legitimacy from the parent Act, i.e. the Environmental (Protection) Act, 1986. If yes, then whether such protection could be completely rest on the discretion of the government or should have some rationality?

The Constitution of India, through Article 48A, explicitly makes the protection of the environment a directive principle of the state. Article 48A mandates the state to '*endeavour to protect and improve the environment and to safeguard the forests and wildlife of the country*'. This provision is supported by numerous judicial decisions of the apex court of India whereby a clean and green environment has been declared part 'right to life' guaranteed under Article 21 of the constitution. This directive principle is not without constitutional duties enshrined under Article 51A. One of the Fundamental Duties enumerated under Part IV-A of the Constitution directs the citizens to '*(g) to protect and improve the natural environment including forests, lakes, rivers, and wildlife, and to have compassion for living creatures*'. Thus, the protection of the environment is not only a state policy but also a duty of every citizen.

The Parliament, realising its constitutional duty along with the government being the signatory of the United Nations Conference on the Human Environment held in Stockholm in June 1972, enacted the Environment (Protection) Act, 1986 [28]. The Preamble of the Act sets the objective as:

> … to provide for the protection and improvement of environment and for matters connected therewith…. [and] to take appropriate steps for the protection and improvement of human environment…. [and whereas] it is considered necessary further to implement the decisions aforesaid in so far as they relate to the protection and improvement of environment and the prevention of hazards to human beings, other living creatures, plants and property.

The preamble of the Act unequivocally asserts that it is not merely a law to respond to domestic requirements but rather a legislation that vehemently affirms India's solemn commitment to environmental protection. This spirit is so categorically reiterated through Section 24(1) of the Act. The *non-obstante* clause enumerated through section 24(1) states that '*the provisions of [the Environment (Protection) Act, 1986] and the rules or orders made therein shall have effect notwithstanding anything inconsistent therewith contained in any enactment other than this Act*'. The bare reading of the above provisions indicates the expected supremacy of the law on environmental protection over any other (industrial) policies.

The second question is about the issue of *ex-post-facto* approval to EIA while giving supremacy to economic needs over environmental may be looking from the perspective of the Parent Act, i.e. the EP Act, 1986. In 'Pahwa Plastics Pvt. Ltd. v. Dastak NGO' [20], the Supreme Court, while dealing with the question of the mandatory nature of prior environmental clearance, ruled that the requirement to obtain environmental clearance is non-negotiable. However, the Bench, stated, took the view that '*an establishment contributing to the economy of the country and providing livelihood ought not to be closed down only on the ground of the technical irregularity of not obtaining prior Environmental Clearance irrespective of whether or not the unit actually causes pollution*'.

The court further says that the EP Act does not prohibit ex post facto *Environmental Clearance*. The Supreme Court of India seems to have completed a full circle from the 'M. C. Mehta v. Union of India' [18] (Oleum Gas Case) to the 'D. Swamy v. Karnataka State Pollution Control Board' [7] in respect of giving priority to human life over industrial development. It seems that through this policy, and while ignoring the objectives of the Environmental Protection Act, 1986, which eventually protects life and humans (present as well as future generations), the government has given environmental protection a secondary treatment over economic activity. Even though the court in 'M. C. Mehta v. Union of India' [18] allowed hazardous activities after fixing strict liability, the recent judgment of the Supreme Court permits presumably dangerous activity but without compliance with the law, with the assumption that these laws are mandating technical compliance and the same could be performed at the latter stage also. In the case of 'Vanashakti v. Union of India' [35], the Supreme Court of India, through its order dated 2nd January 2024, stayed the office memoranda issued by MoEF&CC that permitted ex-post-facto environmental clearances [33]. The court explained that the order would not come in the way of or block competent authorities from considering applications for amendments or change in Environmental Clearances, subject to the caveat that the concerned project had a valid environmental clearance prior to 7 July 2021. It clarified further that such applications would be considered by the competent authorities only in strict conformity with the law. Thus, this move on the part of the Apex Court does suggest that such prior environmental clearances may not be in consonance with constitutional ethos and legislative intent to prioritise economic development over ecological deterioration.

Several existing arguments against the relaxation of environmental regulations during the COVID-19 pandemic. Primarily, it was supposed to balance the position between the economy and long-term environmental sustainability. This sort of stand may undermine years of progress in saving the environment and might precipitate severe ecological and health repercussions. The second point is that, at times, these regulatory relaxations are non-transparent and have had very little consultation with relevant stakeholders. It was part of the process of tattering public trust and creating questions about the commitment of different governments with regard to environmental governance. This has differential effects on poor and marginalised communities, who are the most vulnerable to environmental degradation. Finally, it is wrong to assume that environmental regulations are naturally burdensome and drag economic growth. Actually, strong environmental policies can be a very good spur to innovation, green jobs, and strategies for resilient and sustainable economies. Indeed, the pandemic provided an opportunity to enhance, rather than lower, the enforcement of environmental laws and regulations, putting them at the heart of economic recovery plans, like green stimulus measures and sustainable development strategies.

5.7 Conclusion and Suggestions

From time and again reiterated by the apex court, sustainable development is an inalienable part of the right to life and a clean environment. Therefore, before the commencement of any activity, the possible environmental impacts have to be assessed and mitigated. If one looks into the approach of post-facto approvals followed by 'Vanashakti v. Union of India' [35], 'Electrosteel Steels Limited v. Union of India and Ors.' [8] and 'D. Swamy v. Karnataka State Pollution Control Board and Ors.' [7] judgments permit the activity to go on without the aforementioned evaluation, which undoubtedly goes against judgments like 'Common Cause v. Union of India and Ors.' [6] and 'Alembic Pharmaceuticals Ltd. v. Rohit Prajapati & Ors.' [2], which hold that there was something 'inherently illogical' and legal provisions violated in such approvals. These rulings give scarce regard to the objectives behind environmental impact assessments and clearances, culminating in the frontal assault against the integrity of environmental laws. Besides, they send an extremely damaging signal to the public at large that non-compliance with environmental conditions can be retrospectively condoned, often on grounds of economic benefits and thereby serving to nurture a 'pollute and pay' philosophy fundamentally hostile to principles of environmental stewardship.

India has actively participated in most of the major international environmental conferences, starting with the 1972 UN Conference on Human, Environment, and Development in Stockholm. The 1992 Rio Summit, UN Framework Convention on Climate Change, and Paris Climate Accord have substantially boosted its environmental governance through such engagements. However, the recent steps taken by India towards the potential weakening of its EIA regime are in complete disobedience to these international frameworks that put the country in a state of cognitive dissonance. There is a dilemma between international pledges and domestic actions that lower the country's leadership at the global level over matters concerning the environment and climate change.

Constitutional courts must intervene and also lay down a regulatory framework on those very rare occasions like the Madras High Court in the case of 'A Periyakaruppan v. The Principal Secretary & Anr' [1] invoked the 'parens patriae jurisdiction' (parent of the nation) and pronounced 'Mother Nature' as a juristic person/juridical person/legal person that was raised to the position of a living being with all related rights, duties, and liabilities. This landmark judgment has been important in giving a legal voice to nature in securing its preservation and conservation. Such judgments are very significant and creditable opportunities since the rights of nature are unable to advocate for themselves.

Some critical recommendations include restorations of relaxed environmental regulations to avoid long-term damage, introduction of green recovery plans to incorporate economic recovery with the promotion of green technologies and sustainable practices, and improvement on accessibility and stakeholder consultation in environmental decision-making processes to enhance public trust and consensus. The pandemic has stressed the tensions between economic development and environmental protection, which offers a unique opportunity to redesign how we scale up our development strategy. Such an approach, in simplest terms, aims to ensure that future economic growth will be sustainable and not at the detriment of our planet's health and well-being.

References

1. A Periyakaruppan v. The Principal Secretary & Anr, (Writ Petition (Mandamus) case no. 18636 of 2013).
2. Alembic Pharmaceuticals Ltd. v. Rohit Prajapati & Orsx. 2020. 17 SCC 157.
3. Associated Provincial Picture Houses Ltd. v. Wednesbury Corporation. 1948. 1 KB 223.
4. Blumm M, Guthrie R. Internationalizing the public trust doctrine: natural law and constitutional and statutory approaches to fulfilling the Saxion vision. UC Davis Law Review; 2012.
5. Citizens for Green Doon v. Union of India, 2021 SCC OnLine SC 1243.
6. Common Cause v. Union of India and Ors., Writ Petition (Civil) no. 114 of 2014.
7. D. Swamy v. Karnataka State Pollution Control Board and Ors., 2022 SCC OnLine SC 1278.
8. Electrosteel Steels Limited v. Union of India and Ors, 2023. 6 SCC 615.
9. ET Energyworld. Coal India slapped Rs 43.25 cr fine for illegal mining in Assam forest – ET EnergyWorld. In: ETEnergyworld.com. 2020. https://energy.economictimes.indiatimes.com/news/coal/coal-india-slapped-rs-43-25-cr-fine-for-illegal-mining-in-assam-forest/75590061. Accessed 2 July 2024.
10. G. Sundarrajan v. Union of India, 2013. 6 SCC 620.
11. Gajubha Jadeja Jesar v. Union of India and Others, 2022 SCC OnLine SC 993.
12. Ghosh S. Indian environmental law key concepts and principles. Hyderabad Orient Blackswan; 2019.
13. Jaffe LL, Sax JL. Defending the environment: a strategy for citizen action. Harv Law Rev. 1971;84:1562. https://doi.org/10.2307/1339618.
14. Jayaraman N. "Ex-post facto prior environmental clearances": how a nonsensical phrase was used to flout the law. In: Scroll.in. 2015. https://scroll.in/article/740252/ex-post-facto-prior-environmental-clearances-how-a-nonsensical-phrase-was-used-to-flout-the-law. Accessed 2 July 2024.
15. Jha S. Environment (Protection) Act: 39 changes made to rules in 2 years of pandemic, shows report. In: Down To Earth. 2022. https://www.downtoearth.org.in/governance/environment-protection-act-39-changes-made-to-rules-in-2-years-of-pandemic-shows-report-86591. Accessed 3 July 2024.
16. Kapoor M, Dinesh KA. Throughout the pandemic, environmental clearance law has been under the chopping block. In: The Wire. 2021. https://thewire.in/environment/throughout-the-pandemic-environmental-clearance-law-has-been-under-the-chopping-block#:~:text=2020%2D2021%20%E2%80%93%20No%20decision%20on. Accessed 1 July 2024.
17. Kumar N. Story of the forgotten mandamus: the opportunity to fulfil the need of a regulator. In: SCC Times. 2022. https://www.scconline.com/blog/post/2022/08/01/story-of-the-forgotten-mandamus-the-opportunity-to-fulfil-the-need-of-a-regulator/. Accessed 2 July 2024.
18. M. C. Mehta and Anr. v. Union of India & Ors., 1987. 1 SCC 395.
19. M. C. Mehta v. Kamal Nath and Others, 1997. 1 SCC 388.

20. Pahwa Plastics (P) Ltd. v. Dastak NGO, 2022 SCC OnLine SC 362.
21. Rose CM. Joseph Sax and the idea of the public trust. Issues in legal scholarship 3; 2003. https://doi.org/10.2202/1539-8323.1050.
22. Rural Litigation and Entitlement Kendra Dehradun v. State of Uttar Pradesh, 1985. 2 SCC 431.
23. Sanghera T. Environment vs economy: an approach that exposes India to COVID-19-like infections. In: IndiaSpend. 2020. https://www.indiaspend.com/environment-vs-economy-indias-flawed-logic-that-exposes-it-to-covid-19-like-infections/. Accessed 3 July 2024.
24. Sax JL. The public trust doctrine in natural resource law: effective judicial intervention. Mich Law Rev. 1970;68:471. https://doi.org/10.2307/1287556.
25. Singh S, Sharma R. An overview of environmental jurisprudence in India. J Gen Manag Res. 2014;1:1–13.
26. The Air (Prevention and Control of Pollution) Act, 1981.
27. The Constitution of India, 1950.
28. The Environment (Protection) Act, 1986.
29. The Forest Conservation Act, 1980.
30. The National Green Tribunal Act, 2010.
31. The Water (Prevention and Control of Pollution) Act, 1974.
32. The Wildlife (Protection) Act, 1972.
33. Thomas A. SC stays ex-post facto mining clearance without prior environmental clearance. In: Hindustan Times. 2024. https://www.hindustantimes.com/india-news/sc-stays-ex-post-facto-mining-clearance-without-prior-environmental-clearance-101704252518222.html. Accessed 3 July 2024.
34. United Nations. The 17 sustainable development goals. In: United Nations. 2015. https://sdgs.un.org/goals. Accessed 4 July 2024.
35. Vanashakti v. Union of India, 2024 SCC OnLine SC 139.
36. Vellore Citizen Welfare Forum v. Union of India, 1996. 5 SCC 647.

Chapter 6
Social Determinants of Health (SDoH) and Their Impact on Human Well-Being

Sreelakshmi Krishnakumar, Ritis K. Shyanti, Shalie Malik, and Manoj Kumar Mishra

6.1 SDoH and its Domains

SDoH encompasses all non-clinical factors that can affect an individual's physical and mental well-being and influence their overall quality of life. The World Health Organization (WHO) defines it as "the conditions in which people are born, grow, work, live, and age," which includes the socioeconomic and political norms governing the individual at regional, national, and international levels [1]. An initiative of the U.S. Department of Health and Human Services called The Healthy People 2030 has classified SDoH into five significant domains, i.e., economic stability, education access and quality, healthcare access and quality, neighborhood and built environment, and social and community context, which will be discussed in detail further [2].

6.1.1 Economic Stability

Poverty and unemployment are inevitably linked to high health risks and poor health outcomes. People without a stable income and those who have physical limitations to work struggle to cover expenses for necessities like housing,

S. Krishnakumar · R. K. Shyanti · M. K. Mishra (✉)
Cancer Research Center, Department of Biological Sciences, Alabama State University, Montgomery, AL, USA
e-mail: mmishra@alasu.edu

S. Malik
Department of Zoology, University of Lucknow, Lucknow, Uttar Pradesh, India

S. Malik et al. (eds.), *Public Health Issues: Theory and Practices*,
https://doi.org/10.1007/978-981-96-6650-8_6

clothing, food, utilities, and medicines, resulting in stress, anxiety, and depression [3, 4]. According to World Bank records, there was an increase of 23 million people living below the poverty line in 2022 compared to 2019 owing to the ill-fated pandemic hit [5]. Housing instabilities like overcrowding, poor maintenance, inadequate facilities/utilities, and homelessness expose low-income people to severe weather conditions as well as unhealthy or unhygienic environments. This can trigger the spread of infectious and contagious diseases and pose serious health concerns. Financial pressure also leads to food insecurity (poor intake or access to healthy food), which is one of the top global challenges and is estimated to be 11.6% of the world population as recorded by the World Food Security Outlook (WFSO) published in October 2023 [6]. Uncontrollable individual factors like race, ethnicity, and other demographic variables can push specific communities to unequal economic and employment opportunities, driving them to poverty. Children and adolescents are the worst hit due to such financial disparities in society, and several studies have reported adverse health impacts like malnutrition, developmental delays, behavioral disorders, mental illnesses associated with anxiety and depression, the onset of chronic illnesses like asthma, diabetes, and even cardiovascular diseases [7, 8]. Delayed or neglected medical attention not only worsens health conditions but also results in an increased number of premature deaths.

According to a study by The Health Foundation, unemployed people are 5 times more likely to be associated with poor health conditions than their employed counterparts [9]. Also, it is evidenced that employment positively impacts overall life expectancy [10]. However, the work-health relationship varies extensively in age, gender, education level, social status, household income, and geographical location [11, 12]. Policies to increase employment opportunities that ensure a steady income and other financial support like rental and healthcare allowances can invariably improve the quality of public life. At the same time, it is necessary to ensure proper worker safety measures are undertaken at all work sites to reduce workplace injuries and lethality.

6.1.2 Education Access and Quality

The inclusion of education as a health-determining factor is relatively new, and its importance comes into play through its direct influence on socioeconomic indicators like promising careers, steady income, and better living conditions. At the individual level, education develops social, academic, and technical skills and gives a better perspective of life and well-being. Beyond the ability to read, write, understand, and communicate, education helps people make affirmative decisions concerning their health and prompt healthy behaviors like regular exercise and a balanced diet. From reading medical labels to choosing healthy food ingredients, educated people reflect better insights on maintaining fitness and tend to show more acceptance of health-related communications [13, 14]. The relevance and scope of health literacy and its challenges are discussed elaborately in Chap. 1. Thus, access to good quality education invariably impacts health outcomes in society.

Disparities in attaining quality education between and within countries exist mainly due to cultural barriers, economic instability, inadequate resources, and lack of proper infrastructure. These factors are prominent in countries with low per capita income and also in several parts of developed countries [15, 16]. Grossman's theoretical model of health capital (1972) recognized a health production function wherein individuals can choose factors to predict health outcomes [17]. Higher income does not necessarily correspond to better health. The ability to spend more can have a negative impact on health if the wrong choices are made, like buying more cigarettes and alcoholic drinks than fresh vegetables and fruits. Though education defines a person's job profile, the job requirements and the working environment can have undesirable effects on personal health. For example, a person working long hours on the computer will inadvertently face risks of developing musculoskeletal problems, visual problems, sleep disorders, and also obesity [18, 19]. Therefore, education should not only be considered a means for attaining more financial margins but also be targeted to guide people into practicing healthy behavior and following healthy lifestyles.

6.1.3 Healthcare Access and Quality

Healthcare comprehensively encompasses preventive, curative, rehabilitative, and palliative medical services. Affordability, availability, and accessibility to timely healthcare services, from regular vaccinations and screenings to chronic disease management procedures, can reduce disease incidences, health complications, and mortality rates. The significant challenges encountered by healthcare facilities in providing quality services include language barriers, cultural competencies, and social discrimination [20, 21]. Also, inadequate infrastructural support and insufficient qualified professionals can delay care and timely medical interventions, thus increasing health risks.

The consequences of disregard for preventive or curative medical care are most reflected in children [22]. Recommendations and provisions for vaccination in children and adolescents are undertaken by responsible health advisory committees and regulatory bodies in every country. Similarly, comprehensive health checkup schedules are also outlined for older adults. Primary care visits and regular age-appropriate screening procedures can go a long way in facilitating early detection and disease management [23]. However, several barriers, including social and cultural stigma, can hamper proper medical conduct and administration to a great extent. Lack of affordable insurance coverage for healthcare expenses can cause a significant setback in accessing medical care among several classes of society [24]. People who have to spend out-of-pocket for medical costs avoid routine health checkups and neglect symptoms that can further worsen into chronic illnesses. Mobility issues due to lack of transportation facilities, geographical limitations, or residential segregation can also obstruct access to appropriate medical attention [25].

6.1.4 Neighborhood and Built Environment

Several factors can contribute to the influence of the living environment on personal health. One of them of primary importance is food security, which considers access to nutritious food in adequate quantities. According to the WHO guidelines, a healthy diet should include a daily intake of 400 g of fruits and vegetables, limiting total fats to less than 30% and free sugars to less than 10% of energy consumption per day [26]. It is also suggested that salt uptake be restricted to an upper limit of 5 g per day. The 2020–2025 dietary guidelines for Americans recommend customizing food preferences that include all core health elements based on cultural and traditional choices. It stresses the importance of staying within calorie limits and watching portion sizes. A healthy diet with the right proportion of nutrients can prevent non-communicable diseases (NCDs) and reduce risks of diabetes, hypertension, and obesity. People living in or near neighborhoods and societies with extensive farming, cultivation, and production activities have cheap and convenient access to fresh produce and healthy foods. However, several studies have shown that people in urban cities who rely on nontraditional food retailers and who have monetary and travel constraints to purchase farm fresh or organic foods are prone to nutritional deficits, metabolic syndrome, and risks of cancer [27, 28]. A large cohort study conducted in the UK with over 0.5 million participants concluded that a significant number of people in areas dense with ready-to-eat outlets developed type 2 diabetes and risks to chronic diseases [29]. Community-level interventions facilitating local food markets can help reduce regional health disparities and improve diet and nutrition regimes.

Elements of crime and violence in society are alarming factors that can have devastating long-term health adversities. People who live in areas with higher crime rates are under constant stress and fear of danger. Experiences of robbery, homicide, sexual abuse, kidnapping, or even stalking can be mentally and physically catastrophic [30, 31]. Both victims and witnesses, particularly children, suffer from post-traumatic stress disorders requiring social and medical support and extended remedial measures. Adverse childhood experiences (ACEs) can adversely affect brain development, neural responses, learning, cognitive skills, and social behavior [32, 33]. It can also increase the risks of chronic illnesses such as cardiovascular diseases and even premature deaths. The Burke Foundation, which focuses on transformative trauma care services, states that life expectancy in persons with ACEs can decrease by 20 years. Domestic violence, both physical and psychological, is also being recognized as a public health crisis around the world [34]. It also includes controlling behaviors that restrict the partner/victim physically, emotionally, financially, socially, and culturally, resulting in anxiety disorders and suicidal tendencies. Violence intervention programs in schools and hospitals have proven to be beneficial and cost-effective in reducing episodes of violence, retaliation, and injury recidivism [35, 36].

Housing quality and climatic/environmental conditions can also contribute to poor health management. Houses with poor structure and built quality can cause water leaks, mold build-up, exposure to paint and rust, poor insulation during harsh weather, etc., which can trigger health issues in the residents. Improper maintenance, repair, and replacement of damaged household accessories can hamper resilience and compromise health. Damaged electrical wiring and appliances can increase the risk of short circuits and fire hazards. Poor ecological conditions like water shortages and substandard air quality can also deteriorate health [37, 38]. Changing weather patterns, exposure to extreme temperatures, floods, landslides, etc., can harm health and well-being.

6.1.5 Social and Community Context

Discrimination based on race (racism), age (ageism), gender (sexism), sexual orientation (sexualism), and even disabilities (ableism) has shown adverse health impacts explicitly on marginalized communities [39]. The differences are apparent when weighed in terms of infant mortality rates, blood pressure and hypertension, obesity and diabetes, and even cases of depression and suicides. A history of incarceration and recidivism also has profound implications on the extent of disease burden. The risks of chronic disease conditions, including sexually transmitted diseases, are higher in women who experienced incarcerations than in men, suggesting women's protection schemes and empowering measures to be laid in places of concern [40, 41].

Involving in social works and community-level interactive and informative programs can, directly and indirectly, uphold physical and mental fitness. Community support networks and cultural norms can mitigate social isolation and discrimination [42]. Social institutions like family and friends generate social capital, an indicator of social cohesion that creates a sense of solidarity, trust, and support among individuals. A study conducted by Shah et al. has portrayed that social support is associated with lower risks of atherosclerotic plaques and cardiovascular complications [43]. Active civic participation has proven advantageous effects on subjective health, as determined by a multi-level analysis of 44 countries, with the democracy index being a significant contributing factor [44]. Volunteering in social and charitable activities has been shown to enhance emotional well-being, relieve stress and anxiety, and reduce cognitive impairment in older adults [45, 46]. Organizing regular health promotion and nutrition programs for different age groups can help spread awareness on maintaining health and hygiene responsibly and also keep a check on the overall health status in the community.

6.2 Health Equity—Challenges and Opportunities

As the name implies, health equity is a proposition that emphasizes fairness and justice in the distribution of healthcare. Beyond equal access to healthcare services, it also addresses underlying factors contributing to health disparities, such as socioeconomic status, education, housing, and environmental conditions, as discussed earlier. Ensuring everyone has equal access and opportunity to attain their full health potential is essential. Achieving health equity remains a critical global challenge that requires concerted efforts from government bodies, private organizations, both national and international, and other civil societies [47].

A combination of factors classified and recognized as the social determinants of health, as discussed above, can interchangeably regulate the local, regional, and demographic discrepancies that exist in the different realms of healthcare. The financial burden is a significant barrier that hinders the public's ability to avail themselves of timely healthcare services. Providing affordable medication, screening, and therapy remains challenging in successful prevention. People living in rural and underserved locations face limitations in accessing quality healthcare services, nutritious food, safe housing, and education, which can all perpetuate health inequities. Shortage of sufficient workforce to attend to the medical needs of the patients, inadequate infrastructure, and poor technological advancements have alarmingly resulted in health complications, medical malpractices, and deaths [48]. When communicating a person's medical condition or medical history, a language barrier is an unavoidable obstruction that can cause misinterpretations and improper medical management [49]. Also, using complex medical terms, phrases, and translations can be culturally incompetent and ineffective. Systemic racism, apart from interpersonal racism, plays a dominating role in the exacerbated levels of health disparities in ethnic minorities across the globe [50]. Ableism and transphobia also fall in line, increasing intricacies in the approach and attitude to healthcare from both the public and professionals.

Several strategies have been identified and implicated to promote health equity through a holistic approach [47]. As postulated, addressing the social determinants of health is the key to eliminating health-associated inequalities and reducing contemporary injustices. The government and policymakers should implement strategies to reduce poverty, increase educational and healthcare infrastructure investments, and facilitate unbiased healthcare coverage for all sections of society. Engaging communities in health promotion efforts and decision-making processes can empower individuals and foster partnerships to address local health inequities. Disaggregated data collection and stratification are essential to identify root causes and prioritize the targets for effective collaborative interventions. Health impact assessment (HIA) protocols should be advocated judiciously to guide stakeholders and decision-makers into implementing appropriate resolutions and evidence-based interventions to improve health outcomes productively [51]. Mapping medical health disparities using geographic information systems (GIS) can help strengthen investigations and identify areas that require immediate multisector collaborations to culminate health equity [52].

6.3 Global Initiatives and Policies Addressing SDoH

Basic healthcare needs are the primary rights of all human beings, and as discussed above, they are affected in multiple ways. Altogether, it is the combined responsibility of the government, the public, and other non-governmental organizations to ensure that everyone is endowed with equal rights and benefits concerning basic health requirements without bias. This requires collective efforts from experts in the field so that policies and reforms are made, warranting equality in all aspects relating to health. The RIO political declaration affirming global commitment to reduce health disparities was consented to by 125 member states in 2011. The WHO Commission on SDoH, in collaboration with the Swiss Agency for Development and Cooperation (SDC) and the University College London's Institute of Health Equity (UCL-IHE), had taken up transnational initiatives to demonstrate effective strategies for health reforms and disease recovery policies, especially for pandemics like COVID 19 by 2028 [53].

Many countries have adopted the Health in All Policies (HiAP) approach for collaborative inter-sectorial action plans emphasizing health implications in policy-making [54]. Pioneering efforts and progress have been made and appreciated in countries like Finland, Thailand, and South Australia. The Centers for Disease Control and Prevention (CDC) have implemented programs like the Racial and Ethnic Approaches to Community Health (REACH) to reduce disease rates in disadvantaged communities within urban, rural, and tribal settings [55]. Other CDC initiatives like the Environmental Health Tracking Network and PLACES have played instrumental roles in bringing justice to local health disparities. The grounds on which concrete actions are being undertaken will be discussed further.

6.3.1 Structural Discrimination and Racism

Addressing structural inequality and racism is a crucial step to reducing social and health burdens. From an economic point of view, direct or indirect discrimination and racism are reflected in several dimensions, which ultimately initiate disturbances in mental health and trigger other disorders. These factors can be emphasized when making any kind of reforms or policies for the affected populations globally. The Universal Declaration of Human Rights (UDHR), compiled and proclaimed by the United Nations, remains the standard reference for adopting fundamental treaties to uphold the freedom, equality, and dignity of people all around the globe [56]. The International Day for the Elimination of Racial Discrimination is observed annually on 21st March. UNESCO Network of Anti-Racism and Anti-Discrimination Officials was launched in December 2023, aiming to build an inclusive society. Based on the outcomes from different societal, scientific, and economic studies, it is proven that equitable employment opportunities for all will invariably produce a positive health impact in society and propagate sustainable development. This can be achieved by developing a skillful workforce and providing basic wages through various schemes [57].

6.3.2 Food Security

Health equity is essential to achieve momentum for healthy well-being. Considering the discrepancies among the populations of different communities, races, sexes, or lower socioeconomic status (SES), much effort is needed to facilitate access to healthy foods at affordable prices through investments and integrated collaborations among local and state-level committees and non-governmental organizations. The focus should be on strengthening economic, health, academic, and community networks to achieve equality on humanitarian grounds. American Public Health Association (APHA) aims to reach its health equity goal by 2030 by observing the responses from several inductive measures taken to attain food safety and security with a high priority [58]. The APHA team has created several policies to manage the inequity in earnings and wages, homelessness, children's environmental health, early childhood education, health workers' community, and racial and ethnic disparities. The Healthy People 2030 campaign aims to achieve similar goals to provide quality and nutritious food for all to engender a long and healthy life span.

6.3.3 Sustainable Mental Health

Psychological stress and mental health issues are growing worldwide, posing a considerable challenge in public health management. Limited public awareness and discussions addressing mental health problems remain obstacles in the path of sustainable emotional well-being. Many studies have pointed out preventive measures to tackle mental distress and maintain psychological resilience [59–61]. It is similar to adopting sequence-wise approaches for deadly diseases like cancer, such as going through symptoms, preventive screening, early identification, and confirmatory diagnosis. Per the WHO criteria, prevention is initiated in three different phases, i.e., primary, secondary, and tertiary. The naïve state of mental health is the phase that can culminate into the incidence of mental deterioration or suicidal temptation. Further, the US Institute of Medicine postulates ways to tackle this phase by intervening in universal, selective, and indicated modalities depending upon the diagnosis and risk of mental illness. The secondary and tertiary phases involve escalated mental disorders and associated disabilities that need multiple strategies, including social prescribing and interventions in vocational, family, trauma-informed care, etc., along with increased rehabilitation therapies. Addressing social determinants of health and uplifting mental health mediated through the eradication of poverty, gender biases, and social discrimination are the primary goals of the United Nations Sustainable Development Agenda, which aims to achieve its targets by 2030 [62].

6.4 Challenges and Future Prospective

Though remarkable progress has been made through regional and global interventions addressing the interlinked factors affecting public health, insufficient data collection, inappropriate cross-sector collaborations, poor political commitment, and inadequate resource allocation remain. Also, unforeseen situations and emergencies like climate changes, natural calamities, disease outbreaks, political warfare, and international conflicts can all disrupt advances made in efforts to establish health equity and integrity. Knowledge sharing through global conferences and academic partnerships can facilitate evidence-based research stratification and propose pertinent solutions. Strengthening multisector fraternities, developing data and technology-sharing platforms to improve data collection and tracking mechanisms, and engaging local communities and civil societies in decision-making can help accelerate progress. Thus, a global perspective, continued efforts, and active participation at all levels involving activities from data collection to policy making is essential to recognize the goal of health equity for all populations worldwide.

References

1. Marmot M, et al. WHO European review of social determinants of health and the health divide. Lancet. 2012;380(9846):1011–29.
2. Gómez CA, et al. Addressing health equity and social determinants of health through healthy people 2030. J Public Health Manag Pract. 2021;27(Supplement 6):S249–57.
3. Renahy E, et al. Connections between unemployment insurance, poverty and health: a systematic review. Europ J Public Health. 2018;28(2):269–75.
4. Vaalavuo M. Deterioration in health: what is the role of unemployment and poverty? Scand J Public Health. 2016;44(4):347–53.
5. Bank W. Poverty and shared prosperity 2022: correcting course. The World Bank; 2022.
6. Andree B. Food security trends in 2024 and beyond, in agriculture and food. World Bank Blogs; 2024.
7. De France K, Stack DM, Serbin LA. Associations between early poverty exposure and adolescent well-being: the role of childhood negative emotionality. Dev Psychopathol. 2023;35(4):1808–20.

8. Zhang L, et al. Early childhood income instability, food insecurity, and adolescents' behavioral health. Fam Relat. 2023;72(3):1186–200.
9. The Health Foundation. Employment and unemployment. Available from: https://www.health.org.uk/news-and-comment/charts-and-infographics/unemployment
10. Chetty R, et al. The association between income and life expectancy in the United States, 2001–2014. JAMA. 2016;315(16):1750–66.
11. Galos DR, Coppock A. Gender composition predicts gender bias: a meta-reanalysis of hiring discrimination audit experiments. Sci Adv. 2023;9(18):eade7979.
12. Fuentes K, et al. More than just double discrimination: a scoping review of the experiences and impact of ableism and racism in employment. Disabil Rehabil. 2024;46(4):650–71.
13. Barcellos SH, Carvalho LS, Turley P. Distributional effects of education on health. J Hum Resour. 2023;58(4):1273–306.
14. Hahn RA, Truman BI. Education improves public health and promotes health equity. Int J Health Serv. 2015;45(4):657–78.
15. Makhlouf Y. Trends in income inequality: evidence from developing and developed countries. Soc Indic Res. 2023;165(1):213–43.
16. Dessy S, Tiberti L, Zoundi D. The gender education gap in developing countries: roles of income shocks and culture. J Comp Econ. 2023;51(1):160–80.
17. Zweifel P. The Grossman model after 40 years. Eur J Health Econ. 2012;13(6):677–82.
18. Anbesu EW, Lema AK. Prevalence of computer vision syndrome: a systematic review and meta-analysis. Sci Rep. 2023;13(1):1801.
19. Christensen SWM, et al. Prolonged slumped sitting causes neck pain and increased axioscapular muscle activity during a computer task in healthy participants–a randomized crossover study. Appl Ergon. 2023;110:104020.
20. Lippert-Rasmussen K. Cost-effectiveness and the avoidance of discrimination in healthcare: can we have both? Camb Q Healthc Ethics. 2023;32(2):202–15.
21. Ramirez N, et al. Access to care among adults with limited English proficiency. J Gen Intern Med. 2023;38(3):592–9.
22. Zaidman EA, et al. Impact of parental health literacy on the health outcomes of children with chronic disease globally: a systematic review. J Paediatr Child Health. 2023;59(1):12–31.
23. Porter J, et al. Revisiting the time needed to provide adult primary care. J Gen Intern Med. 2023;38(1):147–55.
24. Suleman S, et al. Comparison of healthcare quality for uninsured and underinsured children through community health centres in Canada and the USA: a scoping review protocol. BMJ Open. 2024;14(1):e075340.
25. Kershaw KN, Albrecht SS. Racial/ethnic residential segregation and cardiovascular disease risk. Curr Cardiovasc Risk Rep. 2015;9:1–12.
26. World Health Organization. Carbohydrate intake for adults and children: WHO guideline. World Health Organization; 2023.
27. Clemente-Suárez VJ, et al. Global impacts of western diet and its effects on metabolism and health: a narrative review. Nutrients. 2023;15(12):2749.
28. Ahern M, Brown C, Dukas S. A National Study of the association between food environments and county-level health outcomes. J Rural Health. 2011;27(4):367–79.
29. Sarkar C, Webster C, Gallacher J. Are exposures to ready-to-eat food environments associated with type 2 diabetes? A cross-sectional study of 347 551 UK Biobank adult participants. Lancet Planetary Health. 2018;2(10):e438–50.
30. Borg BA, Rabinak CA, Marusak HA. Violence exposure and mental health consequences among urban youth. Curr Psychol. 2023;42(10):8176–85.
31. Hoppen TH, et al. Efficacy of psychological interventions for post-traumatic stress disorder in children and adolescents exposed to single versus multiple traumas: meta-analysis of randomised controlled trials. Br J Psychiatry. 2023;222(5):196–203.
32. Metzler M, et al. Adverse childhood experiences and life opportunities: shifting the narrative. Child Youth Serv Rev. 2017;72:141–9.

33. Moffitt TE. Childhood exposure to violence and lifelong health: clinical intervention science and stress-biology research join forces. Dev Psychopathol. 2013;25(4pt2):1619–34.
34. Sugg N. Intimate partner violence: prevalence, health consequences, and intervention. Med Clin North Am. 2015;99(3):629–49.
35. O'Toole MJ, Schnippel K, Larson B. Hospital-based violence intervention programs: an analysis of costs and key components. 2024.
36. Messman E, et al. Anonymous reporting systems for school-based violence prevention: a systematic review. Health Educ Behav. 2024;51(1):62–70.
37. Louis S, et al. Impacts of climate change and air pollution on neurologic health, disease, and practice: a scoping review. Neurology. 2023;100(10):474–83.
38. Holden KA, et al. The impact of poor housing and indoor air quality on respiratory health in children. Breathe. 2023;19(2):230058.
39. OASH. Discrimination. Available from: https://health.gov/healthypeople/priority-areas/social-determinants-health/literature-summaries/discrimination
40. Braithwaite RL, Treadwell HM, Arriola KR. Health disparities and incarcerated women: a population ignored. Am J Public Health. 2005;95(10):1679–81.
41. Erickson M, et al. Women, incarceration and HIV: a systematic review of HIV treatment access, continuity of care and health outcomes across incarceration trajectories. AIDS. 2019;33(1):101–11.
42. Chuang Y-C, Chuang K-Y, Yang T-H. Social cohesion matters in health. Int J Equity Health. 2013;12:1–12.
43. Shah AS, et al. Association of Psychosocial Factors with Short-Term Resting Heart Rate Variability: the atherosclerosis risk in communities study. J Am Heart Assoc. 2021;10(5):e017172.
44. Kim S, Kim C-y, You MS. Civic participation and self-rated health: a cross-national multi-level analysis using the world value survey. J Prev Med Public Health. 2015;48(1):18.
45. Cooney A, et al. Exploration of the meaning of connectedness for older people in long-term care in context of their quality of life: a review and commentary. Int J Older People Nursing. 2014;9(3):192–9.
46. Chen-Edinboro LP, et al. Neighborhood physical disorder, social cohesion, and insomnia: results from participants over age 50 in the health and retirement study. Int Psychogeriatr. 2015;27(2):289–96.
47. August E, et al. What is global health equity? A proposed definition. Ann Glob Health. 2022;88(1):50.
48. Kruk ME, et al. Mortality due to low-quality health systems in the universal health coverage era: a systematic analysis of amenable deaths in 137 countries. Lancet. 2018;392(10160):2203–12.
49. Al Shamsi H, et al. Implications of language barriers for healthcare: a systematic review. Oman Med J. 2020;35(2):e122.
50. Castle B, et al. Public health's approach to systemic racism: a systematic literature review. J Racial Ethn Health Disparities. 2019;6:27–36.
51. Harris-Roxas B, et al. Health impact assessment: the state of the art. Impact Assess Proj Apprais. 2012;30(1):43–52.
52. Wang F. Why public health needs GIS: a methodological overview. Ann GIS. 2020;26(1):1–12.
53. WHO. Action on social determinants of heath equity. 2024. Available from: https://www.who.int/initiatives/action-on-the-social-determinants-of-health-for-advancing-equity
54. Baum F, et al. Evaluation of health in all policies: concept, theory and application. Health Promot Int. 2014;29(suppl_1):i130–42.
55. O'Toole TP, et al. State and local chronic disease programs adapt and pivot to address community needs during the COVID-19 pandemic: examples from CDC funded SPAN, REACH, and HOP programs. Health Promot Pract. 2022;23(1_suppl):12S–20S.
56. Assembly UNG. Universal declaration of human rights, vol. 3381. Department of State; 1949.
57. Egede LE, Walker RJ, Williams JS. Addressing structural inequalities, structural racism, and social determinants of health: a vision for the future. J Gen Intern Med. 2024;39(3):487–91.

58. Investing in what works for America's communities. 2012: Federal Reserve Bank of San Francisco and Low Income Investment Fund.
59. Singh V, Kumar A, Gupta S. Mental health prevention and promotion—a narrative review. Front Psych. 2022;13:898009.
60. Fusar-Poli P, et al. Preventive psychiatry: a blueprint for improving the mental health of young people. World Psychiatry. 2021;20(2):200–21.
61. Kirkbride JB, et al. The social determinants of mental health and disorder: evidence, prevention and recommendations. World Psychiatry. 2024;23(1):58.
62. Weiland S, et al. The 2030 agenda for sustainable development: transformative change through the sustainable development goals? Politics Governance. 2021;9(1):90–5.

Chapter 7
The Economics of Health: Understanding the Financial Implications of Public Health Initiatives

Anamika Kumar Kulbhaskar

7.1 Introduction to Health Economics

Health economics applies economic theories, models, and empirical methods to examine how individuals, healthcare providers, and governments make decisions regarding health and healthcare [42]. The importance and interest in this field arise from three main factors: (1) the significant role the health sector plays in the overall economy, (2) the national policy challenges that emerge from the economic difficulties people encounter in managing and maintaining their health, and (3) the various health issues that are strongly influenced by economic factors [14].

7.1.1 Size of the Health Sector in the Overall Economy

The healthcare sector is a substantial part of the economy, consuming a significant portion of the GDP and requiring considerable investment [14].

According to a 2023 report from the Press Information Bureau,[1] India, the government's share of total health expenditure increased from 28.6% in Financial Year 2014 to 40.6% in Financial Year 2019. Moreover, the percentage of health spending within social services rose from 21% in Financial Year 2019 to 26% in Financial

[1] Press Information Bureau [46]; https://pib.gov.in/PressReleasePage.aspx?PRID=1894902; Posted On: 31 Jan 2023 by PIB Delhi.

A. K. Kulbhaskar (✉)
Department of Management Studies, Indian Institute of Technology Roorkee, Uttarakhand, India
e-mail: anamika.kulbhaskar@ms.iitr.ac.in

S. Malik et al. (eds.), *Public Health Issues: Theory and Practices*,
https://doi.org/10.1007/978-981-96-6650-8_7

Year 2023. Out-of-pocket expenses as a share of total health expenditure dropped from 64.2% in Financial Year 2014 to 48.2% in Financial Year 2019.

The National Health Policy (2017) called for government health expenditure to grow from 1.2% to 2.5% of GDP by 2025. Table 7.1 highlights the trends in government health spending in India.

Table 7.2 shows the current health expenditure expressed as a percentage of GDP of various countries worldwide. United States spends the highest with a current health expenditure of 18.8% of the GDP. Many other developed countries, such as the United Kingdom, Sweden, Norway, Japan, Canada, Netherlands, Switzerland, Australia, etc., also spend a substantial percentage of GDP on health expenditure. In contrast, the expenditure on current health by developing and underdeveloped countries is deficient (as a percentage of GDP).

The United States allocates the largest portion of its GDP to healthcare spending, with per capita spending exceeding $8000, significantly higher than any other nation. Many health economists attribute this high level of spending to the rapid adoption of new technologies in the U.S. Healthcare costs [14]. In contrast, India's public healthcare financing is minimal compared to other nations. All G20 nations, with the exception of Indonesia, invest at least ten times more per capita in public healthcare. Indonesia spends three times more than India. Among 55 low- and middle-income countries, India is ranked near the bottom, coming in tenth from last regarding public healthcare expenditure as a percentage of GDP [17, 28].

7.1.2 Economic Problems Related to Health Care

India's healthcare system is often defined by fragmented financing, with individuals primarily relying on out-of-pocket (OOP) payments to cover medical expenses. In this OOP-based model, families tend to dip into their savings, sell assets, or take on debt when a member falls ill to cover healthcare costs [28].

A primary goal of health systems is to protect households from financial burdens related to healthcare costs. India is working toward universal health coverage (UHC), with financial protection as a key component. According to Table 7.3, India ranks among the top three countries in the Southeast Asia region for out-of-pocket expenditure (OOPE) on health, accounting for about 62.6% of total health spending—one of the highest rates globally.[2] These costs significantly impact household budgets, often forcing reductions in essential expenditures and overall welfare [54].

Many studies have shown that OOPE significantly affects the economic status of a household, many times pushing them into poverty. Out-of-pocket (OOP) payments not only drive many individuals into poverty but also significantly worsen the living conditions of households that are already below the poverty line. In urban

[2] National health accounts estimates for India 2014–15, Ministry of Health and Family Welfare, Government of India.

Table 7.1 Trends in social services expenditure by general government (combined centre and states) in India

Items	2015–2016	2016–2017	2017–2018	2018–2019	2019–2020	2020–2021	2021–2022	2022–2023
Total Expenditure (Crores)	3,760,611	4,265,969	4,515,946	5,040,747	5,410,887	6,353,359	7,453,320	8,008,684
of which:								
Health (Crores)	175,272	213,119	243,388	265,813	272,648	317,687	516,427	548,855
As % of total expenditure								
Expenditure on Social Services	24.3	24.4	25.2	25.4	25.2	23.3	26.1	26.6
of which:								
Health	4.7	5	5.4	5.3	5	5	6.9	6.9
As % of GDP								
Expenditure on Social Services	6.6	6.8	6.7	6.8	6.8	7.5	8.2	8.3
of which:								
Health	1.3	1.4	1.4	1.4	1.4	1.6	2.2	2.1

Sources: Press Information Bureau [46], Budget Documents of Union and State Governments
Notes: The ratios to GDP at current market prices are calculated using the 2011–12 base up until 2021–22. The GDP for 2022–23 is based on figures from the Union Budget 2022–23

Table 7.2 Current health expenditure (% of GDP)

Country	2010	2011	2012	2013	2014	2015	2016	2017	2018	2019	2020	2021
Afghanistan	8.6	8.6	7.9	8.8	9.5	10.1	11.8	12.6	14.2	14.8	15.5	16.8
United Arab Emirates	3.9	3.7	3.4	3.6	3.6	3.6	3.5	4.1	4.1	4.3	5.7	
Argentina	9.4	9.4	9.8	9.8	9.7	10.2	9.0	10.4	9.5	9.5	10.0	
Australia	8.4	8.5	8.7	8.8	9.8	10.2	10.1	10.1	10.1	10.2	10.6	
Austria	10.2	10.0	10.2	10.3	10.4	10.4	10.4	10.4	10.3	10.5	11.5	12.2
Belgium	10.2	10.4	10.5	10.5	10.6	10.8	10.8	10.8	10.8	10.7	11.1	
Bangladesh	2.7	2.8	2.8	2.8	2.7	2.7	2.9	2.8	2.7	2.6	2.6	
Bahrain	4.1	3.9	4.1	4.3	4.4	5.0	4.9	4.5	4.1	4.0	4.7	
Brazil	7.9	7.8	7.7	8.0	8.4	8.9	9.2	9.5	9.5	9.6	10.3	
Bhutan	3.6	3.3	3.6	3.7	3.6	3.8	3.6	3.3	3.2	3.6	4.4	
Canada	10.7	10.4	10.5	10.4	10.3	10.7	11.0	10.9	10.8	11.0	12.9	11.7
Switzerland	9.9	10.0	10.2	10.5	10.6	11.0	11.3	11.5	11.4	11.3	11.8	
Chile	6.8	6.8	7.0	7.4	7.8	8.3	8.5	9.1	9.2	9.3	9.8	9.1
China	4.2	4.3	4.6	4.7	4.8	4.9	5.0	5.1	5.2	5.4	5.6	
Germany	11.1	10.8	10.9	11.0	11.0	11.2	11.2	11.3	11.5	11.7	12.8	12.8
Djibouti	3.1	3.4	3.3	2.9	3.0	3.1	2.7	2.5	2.3	2.0	2.0	
Denmark	10.6	10.4	10.5	10.3	10.3	10.3	10.3	10.1	10.1	10.1	10.5	10.8
Egypt, Arab Rep.	4.2	4.4	4.7	4.9	5.0	5.3	5.4	5.6	5.0	4.8	4.4	
Spain	9.1	9.2	9.2	9.1	9.1	9.1	9.0	8.9	9.0	9.1	10.7	
Ethiopia	5.5	4.5	4.5	4.1	4.0	3.8	3.6	3.5	3.3	3.2	3.5	
Finland	9.1	9.2	9.6	9.8	9.8	9.6	9.4	9.1	9.0	9.2	9.6	
France	11.2	11.2	11.3	11.4	11.5	11.4	11.5	11.4	11.2	11.1	12.2	
United Kingdom	10.0	9.9	9.9	9.8	9.8	9.8	9.7	9.6	9.7	9.9	12.0	11.9
Greece	9.6	9.2	8.9	8.4	7.9	8.2	8.4	8.1	8.1	8.2	9.5	
Croatia	8.0	7.7	7.7	6.4	6.6	6.7	6.7	6.7	6.8	6.8	7.8	
Hungary	7.4	7.5	7.4	7.2	7.0	6.9	7.0	6.7	6.6	6.3	7.3	
Indonesia	2.8	3.0	2.9	2.9	3.0	2.9	3.0	2.9	2.9	2.9	3.4	
India	3.3	3.2	3.3	3.7	3.6	3.6	3.5	2.9	2.9	2.9	3.0	
Ireland	10.5	10.6	10.6	10.3	9.5	7.3	7.4	7.1	6.9	6.7	7.1	6.7
Iran, Islamic Rep.	6.3	6.1	6.1	5.5	6.4	7.3	7.8	7.8	7.5	5.9	5.3	
Iraq	3.2	2.8	2.7	2.8	2.8	3.1	3.3	4.2	4.1	4.3	5.1	
Iceland	8.4	8.2	8.2	8.2	8.2	8.1	8.1	8.3	8.4	8.5	9.6	9.7
Israel	7.0	7.0	7.1	7.0	7.1	7.1	7.2	7.2	7.3	7.5	8.3	
Italy	8.9	8.8	8.8	8.8	8.9	8.9	8.7	8.7	8.7	8.7	9.6	9.5
Jamaica	5.3	5.2	4.9	5.0	5.2	5.6	5.7	6.1	6.0	6.1	6.6	
Japan	9.1	10.5	10.7	10.7	10.7	10.7	10.7	10.7	10.7	10.8	10.9	
Kenya	5.4	5.2	5.0	4.9	4.9	4.8	4.8	4.0	4.1	4.4	4.3	

(continued)

Table 7.2 (continued)

Country	2010	2011	2012	2013	2014	2015	2016	2017	2018	2019	2020	2021
Korea, Rep.	5.9	6.0	6.1	6.2	6.5	6.7	6.9	7.1	7.5	8.1	8.4	
Kuwait	2.7	2.3	2.3	2.5	2.9	4.2	4.7	4.7	5.2	5.4	6.3	
Sri Lanka	3.9	3.7	3.4	3.8	3.6	3.9	3.9	3.6	3.9	3.7	4.1	
Luxembourg	6.7	6.0	5.3	5.2	5.2	5.1	5.1	5.1	5.3	5.4	5.8	5.4
Maldives	8.5	7.9	8.7	8.2	7.9	8.7	10.3	9.3	7.4	7.7	11.3	
Mexico	5.7	5.5	5.7	5.8	5.6	5.7	5.6	5.5	5.4	5.4	6.2	
Myanmar	2.0	1.9	2.4	3.2	4.4	5.5	5.1	5.1	4.9	4.7	4.6	
Mauritius	4.6	4.3	4.3	4.7	5.5	5.7	5.7	5.8	5.9	6.2	6.7	
Malaysia	3.2	3.3	3.5	3.5	3.7	3.8	3.7	3.7	3.8	3.8	4.1	
Namibia	9.7	9.8	9.3	9.1	8.4	10.0	9.3	8.7	8.3	8.5	8.9	
Nigeria	3.3	3.3	3.4	3.4	3.3	3.6	3.6	3.7	3.1	3.0	3.4	
Netherlands	10.2	10.2	10.5	10.6	10.6	10.3	10.3	10.1	10.0	10.1	11.1	11.2
Norway	8.9	8.8	8.8	8.9	9.3	10.1	10.6	10.3	10.0	10.5	11.4	10.1
Nepal	4.4	4.4	4.5	4.6	5.1	5.5	5.4	4.7	4.5	4.4	5.2	
New Zealand	9.6	9.5	9.7	9.4	9.4	9.3	9.2	9.0	9.0	9.5	10.0	
Oman	2.8	2.5	2.6	2.9	3.6	4.7	4.8	4.5	3.7	4.4	5.3	
Pakistan	2.4	2.1	2.2	2.4	2.5	2.5	2.6	2.8	2.8	2.8	3.0	
Philippines	4.1	4.0	4.2	4.3	3.7	3.9	4.0	4.0	4.0	4.2	5.1	5.6
Portugal	10.0	9.7	9.7	9.4	9.3	9.3	9.4	9.3	9.4	9.5	10.5	11.2
Qatar	1.9	1.6	1.7	2.1	2.4	3.7	3.7	3.4	3.3	3.5	4.2	
South Asia	3.2	3.2	3.2	3.6	3.5	3.5	3.4	3.0	3.0	3.0	3.1	
Saudi Arabia	3.6	3.7	4.0	4.5	5.2	6.0	6.4	6.3	5.5			
Singapore	3.2	3.2	3.3	3.7	3.9	4.2	4.4	4.4	4.1	4.4	6.1	
Sweden	8.3	10.4	10.7	10.9	10.9	10.8	10.9	10.8	10.9	10.8	11.4	11.3
Thailand	3.4	3.6	3.5	3.5	3.7	3.9	3.9	3.9	3.9	3.9	4.4	
Ukraine	6.8	6.8	7.1	6.9	7.2	7.8	7.5	7.4	7.5	7.1	7.6	
United States	16.2	16.1	16.1	16.0	16.2	16.5	16.8	16.8	16.6	16.7	18.8	
Vietnam	4.7	4.6	5.0	5.1	4.6	4.6	4.5	4.7	5.0	5.0	4.7	
South Africa	7.8	7.9	8.0	8.1	7.9	8.1	8.1	8.0	8.1	8.2	8.6	

Source: World Health Organization Global Health Expenditure database (apps.who.int/nha/database)

Notes: This table presents the percentage of GDP represented by current health expenditure. The estimates account for healthcare goods and services utilized annually but exclude capital expenditures like infrastructure, equipment, information technology, and emergency vaccine reserves

areas, those experiencing poverty tend to have a greater average shortfall in consumption compared to their rural counterparts. The detrimental impact of health-related payments on poverty is particularly pronounced in poorer states, especially in rural regions [17]. According to Hooda [26], the substantial OOP expenses for healthcare contribute directly to an increase in India's overall poverty headcount ratio, with rural households disproportionately affected compared to those in urban areas.

Table 7.3 Out-of-pocket expenditure as percentage of current health expenditure (CHE) of South East Asia Region

	Bangladesh	Bhutan	India	Indonesia	Maldives	Myanmar	Nepal	Sri Lanka	Thailand	Timor-Leste
2000	61.82	11.54	71.70	45.20	62.99	85.66	55.78	40.04	34.19	
2001	65.81	7.93	74.11	40.49	57.46	85.90	51.27	41.09	33.99	
2002	62.94	10.30	73.37	46.38	51.88	82.23	51.96	40.45	27.90	
2003	63.01	19.01	73.42	46.02	53.81	83.17	53.81	37.61	27.17	41.25
2004	63.10	16.25	72.48	45.91	59.50	78.88	51.60	41.03	26.41	34.59
2005	65.38	16.79	73.15	55.33	55.66	82.50	49.22	40.50	27.58	33.20
2006	65.64	14.79	72.26	53.38	49.92	75.02	42.50	40.95	17.66	22.02
2007	66.41	14.34	70.82	49.55	47.23	82.16	60.96	44.85	14.81	18.26
2008	67.83	15.47	69.15	49.37	33.10	82.46	61.63	50.64	14.70	11.52
2009	67.94	16.58	66.76	49.22	34.32	82.27	57.62	53.29	15.90	8.84
2010	67.96	16.48	65.18	60.58	40.08	80.74	56.20	53.30	14.50	11.56
2011	68.18	16.34	62.22	56.22	39.69	77.28	58.38	51.22	13.01	9.92
2012	68.28	20.51	63.00	53.62	32.19	76.70	56.08	51.93	13.42	9.49
2013	69.62	20.31	69.07	50.90	32.29	72.23	63.53	48.93	12.54	6.97
2014	70.76	21.17	67.01	45.25	28.12	66.04	60.05	48.68	12.86	7.91
2015	72.68	19.79	64.66	43.05	19.45	70.45	59.44	48.93	11.91	7.36
2016	71.49	20.13	63.21	38.52	18.93	76.67	55.44	50.12	10.81	7.90
2017	70.09	13.31	55.11	36.60	20.59	75.69	57.38	49.25	11.84	8.34
2018	70.68	13.16	53.23	35.64	19.78	76.45	57.73	46.82	10.11	10.16
2019	72.05	17.79	52.00	35.07	17.46	79.52	57.91	45.51	8.67	10.48
2020	74.00	15.42	49.45	31.70	16.91	79.18	54.17	43.76	10.54	6.68
2021	72.99	18.80	49.82	27.49	14.33	70.25	51.26	43.64	9.04	5.89

Source: WHO, Global Health Expenditure Database (South East Asia Region)

Key factors impacting equity in health financing and financial protection include inadequate public funding, lack of comprehensive risk pooling, and high out-of-pocket expenses amid rising healthcare costs. National expenditure surveys reveal that disparities in health financing have worsened over the last two decades [1]. It is crucial for public policies to address these inequities, as effective health systems are essential for promoting both equity and efficiency in healthcare [1, 59]. Without a unified public healthcare framework or universal health insurance, high health expenditures can push even relatively affluent individuals into poverty [53].

7.1.3 *The Economic Element in Health*

Production, costs, and insurance are central economic issues in healthcare, but there are many other health-related factors with economic implications. Decisions regarding treatment options are influenced not only by medical considerations but also by cost comparisons of different therapies. Additionally, physicians are becoming more aware of the economic aspects of their patient interactions [13].

Out-of-pocket (OOP) payments made at a specific moment do not account for additional costs such as transportation to healthcare facilities, long-term indirect expenses related to managing care, or other health-related payments by households [48]. Another important economic factor that limits access to healthcare services and affects financing equity is the rising inflation in health expenditures. Over time, spending on medications has increased, with drug costs representing a larger share of out-of-pocket expenses for poorer individuals compared to those with higher incomes [1]. Ineffective regulation of drug prices, along with poor oversight of the pharmaceutical market and distribution systems, further worsens unequal access to affordable, high-quality medications [51].

Another factor that has economic implications is the financial uncertainty regarding health-care affordability.

Uncertainty can diminish individuals' peace of mind and overall well-being, often leading to behavioral changes that are typically negative. For instance, worries about the affordability of necessary healthcare may compel families to save substantial amounts of money that they might have otherwise used to increase the standard of living. While responses to uncertainty can vary from person to person, most people generally prefer less uncertainty rather than more [33, 48]. Insurance serves as a mechanism to manage financial uncertainty related to health. However, constraints within insurance—such as deductibles, copayments, and coverage limits—often shift a greater portion of the risk of illness and financial loss onto consumers [10].

7.2 Economic Inequalities and Health Disparities

The intergenerational transmission of earnings and income inequality remains robust today, possibly even more so than in previous generations [44]. Many health disparities stem from various social, economic, and political conditions that unevenly influence health distribution across populations. Additionally, some of these health inequities arise from the unjust allocation of essential social goods, power, and resources [1].

Herd et al. [25] suggest that financial resources can significantly impact health, particularly for those at the lower end of the income or wealth spectrum. Having adequate income and wealth facilitates access to medical care, which can enhance overall health maintenance. Additionally, wealthier individuals are more likely to opt for safer living and working conditions, as safety is considered a normal good [57].

It is crucial to acknowledge income disparities as a major contributor to poor health outcomes in vulnerable populations. Individuals with lower incomes face a higher overall disease burden, regardless of specific health conditions. The cumulative risk of poor health and disability increases throughout a person's life and is significantly worsened by rising income inequality. Health risks are deeply rooted in societal structures, and achieving health equity necessitates addressing economic inequality [5, 56].

Wealth, income, and education influence health behaviors by enhancing the perceived value of health. Essentially, greater wealth and income can ease financial constraints. At elevated levels of wealth and consumption, the additional benefit gained from consuming more diminishes, making further consumption less advantageous. In contrast, good health prolongs life, allowing for more time to enjoy consumption, leisure, and well-being. Consequently, individuals with higher socioeconomic status tend to assign greater importance to their health and are more likely to invest in it [2, 15, 24].

Since income plays a crucial role in health disparities, the recent decline in average income and other indicators of economic distress are concerning. The gap between the wealthy and the poor has been expanding since 1968, particularly in recent years. From 2005 to 2009, the proportion of wealth owned by the top 10% of the population rose from 49% to 56% [58].

Rapidly developing countries like India have experienced significant socioeconomic inequalities in the last two decades [7], leading to disparities in health system responsiveness [39]. The wealthiest 10% control 57% of the national income, while the bottom 50% hold just 13% (Economic Times, 2021). Estimates from the Reserve Bank of India in 2012 indicated that approximately 270 million people, or 21.92%, live below the poverty line [8].

India's healthcare system comprises both public and private facilities. About 80% of the population seeks outpatient care from private providers, primarily due to the perceived higher quality of care [11, 37, 49]. However, only about 10% have access to any form of social or voluntary health insurance, primarily through government schemes like the Employee State Insurance Scheme and the Central Government Health Scheme [1].

Public health facilities, which provide low-cost healthcare, are predominantly utilized by poorer individuals who cannot afford private care [37]. Research indicates that users of public health services typically have lower income and education levels compared to those who opt for private facilities. A significant factor contributing to the underutilization of primary healthcare in public facilities is their poor responsiveness. The socio-economic disparities in the responsiveness of public health services undermine the foundational principle of these facilities, which is to provide equitable access to healthcare for all, regardless of their financial means[3] [39].

Poverty not only prevents individuals from accessing healthcare systems but also limits their ability to influence decisions that impact their health. Achieving greater equity in health requires active participation from the community. It is essential for individuals to be empowered to advocate for their inclusion in healthcare systems and to demand the quality of care they deserve. This emphasizes the importance of placing people at the core of public health initiatives and practices [38].

7.3 Public Health Initiatives and Implications: Global Perspective

7.3.1 Evolution of Public Health-Care Overtime

Following World War II, the Soviet Union pioneered universal health coverage with its Semashko system, which had roots in the 1930s. Other countries adopted various strategies to achieve similar goals, ranging from state-funded models to market-based approaches. These initiatives led to marked improvements in living standards, education, healthcare, and public health policies, particularly in the United States, Western Europe, and Japan. Socialist countries followed suit, though with some delay. In contrast, low-income nations in Africa, Latin America, and Asia remained significantly behind in healthcare access and outcomes. The globalization of the 1990s and early 2000s spurred healthcare reforms focused on preventive care and outpatient services [32].

In the early twentieth century, awareness grew regarding the importance of addressing population-level factors affecting health. This led to widespread support for public health principles, culminating in the Declaration of Alma-Ata in 1978, which emphasized that health should be achievable for all people in an inclusive manner. Shortly after Alma-Ata, a number of selectively designed initiatives from northern countries were introduced (as enlisted in Table 7.4) [38].

---

[3] Financing and Delivery of Health Care Services in India. Background papers of the National Commission on Macroeconomics and Health, 2005; New Delhi, Ministry of Health and Family Welfare, Government of India.

Table 7.4 Chronology of some major international public-health initiatives initiated after the international conference on primary health care, Alma Ata, USSR, 1978

1978		International conference on primary health care, Alma Ata, USSR
1979	WHO	Health For All
	WHO	Selective primary health care
1980	World Bank	Structural adjustment/health-sector reform
1981	WHO	Guinea worm eradication
1983	UNICEF	Growth monitoring, oral rehydration, breastfeeding and immunisation (GOBI)
1985	UNICEF	Growth monitoring, oral rehydration, breastfeeding, immunisation, fertility promotion, feeding programme, and female development (GOBI-FFF)
	UNICEF	Universal programme of immunisation (UPI)
1986	WHO	Special programme on AIDS
1987	WHO, World Bank, UNFPA	Safe motherhood initiative
1988	WHO	Polio eradication initiative
	WHO	Global programme on AIDS (GPA; formerly special programme on AIDS)
1992	WHO, UNICEF	Integrated management of childhood diseases (IMCI)
1997	WHO	Lymphatic filariasis elimination
1998	WHO	Roll Back Malaria campaign
	WHO	Stop tuberculosis campaign

Source: Macfarlane et al. [38] "Public health in developing countries"

There is a general consensus that investing in healthcare capacities offers substantial long-term returns in terms of population health and societal productivity [31]. Health systems have been created to enable individuals to access necessary services while shielding them from the financial risks associated with medical expenses. This principle is commonly referred to as universal health coverage (UHC). It has inspired the development of social health insurance systems across Europe, the establishment of the National Health Service in the UK, and the healthcare reforms in the USA known as the Obama Care [9, 43, 47]. UHC also motivates many recent changes to health systems and financing in low- and middle-income nations [48].

The BRICS nations—Brazil, Russia, India, China, and South Africa—constitute 43% of the global population. At the World Health Assembly in May 2012, they emphasized the critical role of universal health coverage (UHC) in ensuring the right to health and endorsed global efforts towards UHC and sustainable development.[4] These countries face challenges such as inadequate public funding, the complexity of mixed healthcare systems, ensuring equity, workforce shortages,

[4]Instituto de Relaciones Internacionales; Joint Communique of the BRICS Members States on Health; May (2012).

Table 7.5 Overview of financial health protection programs in BRICS countries

	Brazil	Russia	India	China	South Africa
Out-of-pocket spending on health (% of total health expenditure, 2011)	57·8%	35%	59%	35%	7%
Gini index (year)	54·7 (2009)	40·1 (2009)	33·4 (2005)	47 (2007)	63·1 (2009)
GNI per head (US$, 2011)	$11,420	$20,560	$3590	$8390	$10,710
Annual GDP growth rate (5-year average; 2007–2011)	4·4%	2·8%	7·8%	10·4%	2·8%
Public expenditure on health (% of GDP, year)	3·3% (2005), 4·1% (2011)	3·2% (2005), 3·7% (2011)	0·9% (2005), 1·2% (2011)	1·8% (2005), 2·9% (2011)	3·4% (2005), 4·1% (2011)
Private expenditure on health (% of GDP, 2009)	4·9%	1·9%	2·8%	2·3%	5·1%
Health expenditure (% total of GDP, 2010)	9%	5·1%	4·1%	5·1%	8·9%

Source: Marten et al. [40] (The Lancet)
Notes: *BRICS* Brazil, Russia, India, China, and South Africa, *GNI* gross national income, *GDP* gross domestic product

demographic shifts, and addressing social determinants of health. The contentious nature of health reform is apparent across all BRICS nations [40].

Table 7.5 shows that all BRICS countries have raised public health funding recently, with China experiencing the largest increase from a low baseline, likely driven by its fast economic growth. Conversely, India, despite being the second fastest-growing economy in the group, has seen the least improvement in health funding. Each BRICS nation is dedicated to the right to health and is working toward universal health coverage (UHC), but all still have significant progress to make [40].

7.3.2 *Implications of Public Health Initiatives Globally*

Public health expenditure significantly impacts health system performance and patient satisfaction [39, 62]. Irving et al. [29] found that national healthcare spending is linked to consultation duration, patient health, and physician burnout, indicating that budget constraints leading to shorter consultations negatively affect both patient outcomes and healthcare workers' well-being. Corchero and Rubio (2022) [14] demonstrate that policy measures, like public health spending, affect healthcare quality, advising policymakers to avoid compromising health resource levels. To improve health system satisfaction, increased spending—particularly on clinical staff—may be necessary, especially given the pre-existing shortages of healthcare personnel in many countries before the COVID-19 pandemic.[5]

Private healthcare providers are essential in delivering services to many low-income countries, including marginalized communities [3]. South Asia has particularly witnessed substantial growth in the private sector over the last two decades, resulting in the highest rates of private healthcare usage globally [52, 55]. For example, in India, 93% of health facilities are privately owned [6]. Government public health agencies acknowledge that the private sector reaches populations that public institutions cannot, playing a vital role in advancing universal health coverage. Private facilities often have better geographic distribution and more convenient hours than public ones, driving interest in public-private partnerships (PPPs) [34].

The complex nature of international health inequalities demands a new public health approach that recognizes the interdependence of countries and their shared resources, as well as the collective responsibility for global health. Effective international cooperation involves exchanging ideas, expertise, and resources to combat health disparities worldwide [38]. An example of this collaboration is China's Health Silk Road (HSR) initiative, which utilizes Belt and Road Initiative transportation networks—such as railroads and ports—to provide medical assistance to partner countries and enhance China's influence in global health [27].

7.4 Public Health Initiatives and Implications: Indian Perspective

7.4.1 Brief Overview of Public Health Initiatives, Policies, and Schemes

India, a federal republic with 28 states and eight union territories, has a population of 1.428 billion,[6] with 64% residing in rural areas.[7] In 2010, healthcare costs pushed 60 million Indians below the poverty line [40]. The country's commitment to universal health coverage (UHC) began in 1946, prior to independence[8] [8]. The Employees' State Insurance Scheme (ESIS) was introduced in 1948 to provide health insurance for organized sector workers, with the intention of expanding as the economy developed [45]. In 1954, the Central Government Health Scheme was established to offer selective coverage for central government employees. The 1983 National Health

[5] International Labour Organization (2021). ilostat.ilo.org

[6] WHO [60]: Health data overview for the Republic of India. https://data.who.int/countries/356

[7] World Bank [61]: Rural population (% of total population); World Bank staff estimates based on the United Nations Population Division's World Urbanization Prospects: 2018 Revision. https://data.worldbank.org/indicator/SP.RUR.TOTL.ZS

[8] Bhore committee, National health portal of India. https://www.nhp.gov.in/bhore-committee-1946_pg; Date: 1946.

Policy [30] reaffirmed the aim of achieving "health for all by 2000″ and suggested the implementation of state-level Government-Funded Health Insurance schemes (GFHIS). In 1997, the Rashtriya Aarogya Nidhi Scheme insured individuals in the unorganized sector for life-threatening illnesses treated in government hospitals.

In 2003, India's Ministry of Finance launched the Universal Health Insurance Scheme (UHIS), the country's first national Government-Funded Health Insurance Scheme (GFHIS). Originally intended for universal coverage, it was revised the next year to serve only the below-poverty-line (BPL) population. In 2004, an initiative aimed at providing health security for unorganized sector workers was discontinued after its pilot phase. This progression led to the launch of the Rashtriya Swasthya Bima Yojana (RSBY) in 2008, aimed at providing secondary and tertiary care for the BPL population in public and contracted private hospitals. The 2012 High-level Expert Group (HLEG) report recommended expanding Government-Funded Health Insurance schemes (GFHIS) to cover all primary and select secondary and tertiary services for all citizens. However, the 2017 National Health Policy shifted focus to vulnerable populations, culminating in the launch of the Pradhan Mantri Jan Arogya Yojana (PMJAY) in 2018. These policies strive to encompass socially disadvantaged groups beyond just the BPL. While service providers now include both public and private sectors, the focus has largely remained on secondary and tertiary care, often overlooking primary care. PMJAY is funded entirely by both state and central governments, with the central budget allocating 1.8% of GDP to health for 2022–223 [8].

A major feature of the 2018–2019 union budget was the introduction of the Ayushman Bharat Program (ABP), which includes two main components: (a) the establishment of 150,000 health and wellness centers (HWCs) to deliver comprehensive primary healthcare by 2022 and (b) financial protection for secondary and tertiary hospitalizations under the National Health Protection Scheme (NHPS) [35, 36].

The second part of the Ayushman Bharat Program (ABP), known as the National Health Protection Scheme (NHPS) or Ayushman Bharat-National Health Protection Mission (AB-NHPM), is described as "the world's largest government-funded health insurance program."[9] NHPS provides up to ₹500,000 (around US$7700) per family annually for secondary and tertiary hospitalization costs. This scheme will replace the Rashtriya Swasthya Bima Yojana (RSBY) and the Senior Citizen Health Insurance Scheme (SCHIS).[10,11,12] While RSBY offered ₹30,000 (US$470) in cover-

---

[9] Government of India. India Budget 2018–19 and Budget Speech. Ministry of Finance, New Delhi. Available from: http://www.indiabudget.gov.in/

[10] Press Information Bureau. Cabinet approves Ayushman Bharat—National Health Protection Mission. 21 March 2018; New Delhi. Available from: http://pib.nic.in/newsite/PrintRelease.aspx?relid=177816. Accessed February 15, 2018.

[11] Government of India. Rashtiya Swasthya Bima Yojana. Ministry of Health and Family Welfare, Nirman Bhawan, New Delhi. 2014.

[12] Highlights of union budget 2016–17. The Hindu, New Delhi; 29 March 2016.

age for up to five family members, targeting 60 million families, AB-NHPM aims to cover 107.4 million families, reaching approximately 535 million people, or about 40% of the Indian population [35, 36].

In a press release on January 24, 2024, the General Insurance Council introduced the "Cashless Everywhere" initiative. This allows policyholders to receive treatment at any hospital, even those outside their insurance network, with cashless options available under specific conditions.[13] However, differing treatment rates across hospitals complicate the implementation of this system. Consequently, the Supreme Court has directed the Central Government to quickly set standardized hospital treatment charges for patients.[14]

7.4.2 Key Health-Care Indicators

India's healthcare system combines public and private providers and has significant disparities across states. Total health expenditure (THE) is about 3.16% of GDP, with the public sector contributing 40.61%, out-of-pocket expenses at 48.21%, private health insurance at 6.57%, and the remainder from social security and external donors.[15] Since the introduction of National Health Accounts, THE as a percentage of GDP has decreased from 4% in 2013–2014 to 3.3% in 2019–2020 (as shown in Table 7.6). During this period, government contributions rose from 28.6% to 41.4%, while household out-of-pocket spending fell from 64.2% to 47.1%, and private health insurance increased from 3.4% to 7%. Overall, central and state health expenditures combined represent only 1.3% of GDP, well below the 5% needed for Universal Health Coverage [23].

Public health providers effectively met India's healthcare needs in 1986–1987, but their importance has declined. By 2014, only 50% of rural and 35% of urban populations relied on public services. In 2014–2015, private health insurance expenditure was ₹17,755.31 crores, while government schemes, including RSBY, totaled ₹4589.84 crores[16] [23].

[13] Press Release Launch of "Cashless Everywhere." (Jan, 2024). https://www.gicouncil.in/news-media/events/press-release-launch-of-cashless-everywhere/

[14] SC asks Centre to fix hospital treatment charges for entire country. (2024, March 4). The Indian Express. https://indianexpress.com/article/business/sc-asks-centre-to-fix-hospital-treatment-charges-for-entire-country-9194054/

[15] Government of India [20]. National health accounts estimates for India 2018–19, Ministry of Health and Family Welfare.

[16] Government of India. National Health Policy [21]. Ministry of Health and Family Welfare, Nirman Bhawan, New Delhi, 2017. p. 1–32.

Table 7.6 Key indicators for India from NHA estimates 2019–2020 with the last Six NHA rounds

S.no.	Indicators	NHA 2013–14	NHA 2014–15	NHA 2015–16	NHA 2016–17	NHA 2017–18	NHA 2018–19	NHA 2019–20
1	Total Health Expenditure (THE) as % of GDP	4	3.9	3.8	3.8	3.3	3.2	3.3
2	Total Health Expenditure (THE) Per capita (Rs.) at current prices	3638	3826	4116	4381	4297	4470	4863
3	Total Health Expenditure (THE) Per capita (Rs.) at constant prices2	3174	3231	3405	3503	3333	3314	3516
4	Current Health Expenditures (CHE) as % of THE	93	93.4	93.7	92.8	88.5	90.6	90.5
5	Government Health Expenditure (GHE) as % THE	28.6	29	30.6	32.4	40.8	40.6	41.4
6	Out of Pocket Expenditures (OOPE) as % of THE	64.2	62.6	60.6	58.7	48.8	48.2	47.1
7	Social Security Expenditure on health as % of THE	6	5.7	6.3	7.3	9	9.6	9.3
8	Private Health Insurance Expenditures as % of THE	3.4	3.7	4.2	4.7	5.8	6.6	7
9	External/ Donor Funding for health as % of THE	0.3	0.7	0.7	0.6	0.5	0.4	0.5

Source: NHA estimates for various years, NHSRC, MoHFW, MoSPI & Registrar General of India GDP Deflators were used to the constant series (2011–12 prices). GDP deflators were calculated from GDP series available at mospi.gov.in

Post-COVID-19, the Union Budget for health has decreased in real terms. In 2023–2024, allocations to the Ministry of Health fell by 2%, following a 7% decline the previous year. This drop means the care level from 2019 to 2020 is now unachievable amid rising costs.[17]

7.4.3 Implications of Public Health Initiatives

Access to public health services is essential for the impoverished, as limited options can lead to high out-of-pocket costs or avoidance of care [50]. In India, where private health spending averages 60%, the role of public providers is critical. The government promotes private sector involvement through tax incentives and subsidies for hospital construction [23].

The impact of health insurance on financial risk differs significantly. The Aarogyasri scheme in Andhra Pradesh has effectively reduced out-of-pocket inpatient costs [12], while the RSBY program has had difficulty shielding households from healthcare expenses in various states, particularly affecting the poor in Karnataka and Maharashtra. In contrast, some community-based health insurance initiatives have successfully attracted funding to address healthcare needs.

The effectiveness of health insurance in reducing financial risk varies. The Aarogyasri scheme in Andhra Pradesh notably lowered out-of-pocket inpatient expenses, while RSBY has struggled to protect households from healthcare costs in many states, especially among the poor in Karnataka and Maharashtra. Some community-based health insurance schemes have successfully secured funding to meet healthcare needs [30].

India needs to significantly increase government health spending to tackle its disease burden. Health service financing is divided between the federal and state governments: states fully fund primary healthcare and hospitals, while the federal government covers family welfare and medical education. National disease control programs are shared 50:50, but states typically bear around 75% of the costs, including administrative expenses. Capital investments are equally shared, and the federal contribution to medical education is just over 40%. This arrangement means that state economic conditions and resources directly influence health outcomes. [23].

[17] Implications of the Union Budget 2022–23 for Health – JSA Press Release Link: Implications of the Union Budget 2022–23 for Health – JSA Press Release https://phmindia.org/2022/02/02/implicationsof-the-union-budget-2022-23-for-health-jsa-press-release/

7.5 Way Forward

Established in late 2020 by WHO Director-General Dr. Tedros Adhanom Ghebreyesus, the WHO Council on the Economics of Health for All aims to position health for all as a key public policy goal. It seeks to align national and global economies to support this vision, viewing investments in health systems as long-term benefits rather than short-term costs.[18] To eliminate health disparities, policies must address income inequality and wealth differentials. Improving health for low-income populations requires better coordination of public and private resources, backed by comprehensive public policies promoting income and health equity [4, 56].

To enhance health services in rural areas and impoverished states, it's essential to rationalize high drug expenditures. Key needs include improved survey designs for poverty assessments, rationalized drug policies (such as free supplies), and pro-poor health financing. Innovative financing mechanisms should focus on collection, pooling, and purchasing to alleviate poverty impacts from out-of-pocket (OOP) payments. Targeting specific areas and populations where OOP payments have the greatest effect is crucial [17]. Initiatives to strengthen universal health coverage (UHC) in India should prioritize budget allocations, develop new public health resources, leverage information technology, and promote efficient use of limited health resources [18].

The main challenge of the national health protection scheme lies in its effective implementation by state governments, which already have their own health insurance programs. A critical barrier is improving hospital infrastructure and staffing to enhance access, particularly in remote areas. Consistent enforcement of the Clinical Establishment Act 2010 (CEA) across states would ensure that hospital services are priced according to government guidelines and that quality standards are maintained in both public and private hospitals. This would facilitate uniform policy application and fair compensation for healthcare providers, helping to close the price gap between public and private services. To achieve Sustainable Development Goal 3—ensuring healthy lives and promoting well-being for all—it is vital to allocate resources not only for post-illness care but also for primary and preventive healthcare [23].

To enhance healthcare, it is crucial to strengthen ongoing initiatives such as free medicines and diagnostics, expand services in urban areas, address non-communicable diseases, and improve referral linkages [35, 36]. Creating synergy between the Ayushman Bharat-National Health Protection Mission (AB-NHPM) and Health and Wellness Centres will integrate secondary and tertiary care with comprehensive primary care, helping to mitigate demand-side moral hazards and control costs. Moving forward, it is essential to reinforce regulatory frameworks and institutions like the Insurance Regulatory and Development Authority and the Competition Commission of India, along with public health facilities, to promote competition and choice in the healthcare market [63].

---

[18] "Health for All: Transforming economies to deliver what matters." World Health Organisation, 2023.

References

1. Balarajan Y, Selvaraj S, Subramanian S. Health care and equity in India. Lancet. 2011;377(9764):505–15. https://doi.org/10.1016/S0140-6736(10)61894-6.
2. Becker G. Health as human capital: synthesis and extensions. Oxf Econ Pap. 2007;59(3):379–410.
3. Bennett S, Mcpake B, Mills A. Private Health Providers in Developing Countries: Serving the Public Interest? LondonZed Books; 1997.
4. Bor J, Cohen GH, Galea S. Population health in an era of rising income inequality: USA, 1980–2015. Lancet. 2017;389(10077):1475–90.
5. Case A, Deaton A. Rising morbidity and mortality in midlife among white non-Hispanic Americans in the 21st century. Proc Natl Acad Sci USA. 2015;112(49):15078–83.
6. Chakraborty D. The private sector's role in acheiving Universal Health Coverage in India, 2013; Institute for Democracy and Economic Affairs (Malaysia) Emerging Markets Health Network.
7. Deaton A, Dreze J. Poverty and inequality in India: a re-examination, Econ Polit Wkly, 2002, vol. 37 (pg. 3729–3748).
8. Dubey S, Deshpande S, Krishna L, Zadey S. Evolution of Government-funded health insurance for universal health coverage in India. Lancet Reg Health Southeast Asia. 2023;13 https://doi.org/10.1016/j.lansea.2023.100180.
9. Dunlop D, Martins J. An international assessment of health care financing: lessons for developing countries. 1996.
10. Ellis RP, McGuire TG. Supply-Side and Demand-Side Cost Sharing in Health Care. J Econ Perspect. 1993;7(4):135–51. https://doi.org/10.1257/jep.7.4.135.
11. Ergler CR, Sakdapolrak P, Bohle HG, Kearns RA. Entitlements to health care: why is there a preference for private facilities among poorer residents of Chennai, India? Soc Sci Med. 2010;72:pg. 327-37.
12. Fan VY, Karan A, Mahal A. State health insurance and out-of-pocket health expenditures in Andhra Pradesh, India. Int J Health Care Finance Econ. 2012;12(3):189–215. https://doi.org/10.1007/s10754-012-9110-5.
13. Folland S, Goodman AC, Stano M. The economics of health and health care. 7th ed. Pearson; 2013.
14. Folland, S., Goodman, A. C., & Stano, M. (2016). The economics of health and health care: pearson new international edition (7). Routledge https://doi.org/10.4324/9781315510736.
15. Galama TJ, van Kippersluis H. A theory of socio-economic disparities in health over the life cycle. Econ J. 2019;129(617):338–74. https://doi.org/10.1111/ecoj.12577.
16. García-Corchero JD, Jiménez-Rubio D. How do policy levers shape the quality of a national health system? J Policy Model. 2022;44(1):203–21. https://doi.org/10.1016/j.jpolmod.2021.09.003.
17. Garg CC, Karan AK. Reducing out-of-pocket expenditures to reduce poverty: a disaggregated analysis at rural-urban and state level in India. Health Policy Plan. 2009;24(2):116–28. https://doi.org/10.1093/heapol/czn046.
18. Garg S. Universal health coverage in India: newer innovations and the role of public health. Indian J Public Health. 2018;62(3):167. https://doi.org/10.4103/ijph.IJPH_221_18.
19. Global expenditure on health: public spending on the rise? Geneva: World Health Organization; 2021. Licence: CC BY-NC-SA 3.0 IGO. ISBN 978-92-4-004121-9 (electronic version); ISBN 978-92-4-004122-6 (print version).
20. Government of India. National health accounts estimates for India 2018–19. Ministry of Health and Family Welfare; 2022.
21. Government of India. National Health Policy. Ministry of Health and Family Welfare. New Delhi: Nirman Bhawan; 2017. p. 1–32.
22. Government of India. India Budget 2018–19 and Budget Speech. Ministry of Finance, New Delhi. Available from: http://www.indiabudget.gov.in/. Accessed Febuary 12, 2018b.

23. Gumber A, Lalitha N, Dhak B. Inter-state disparities in healthcare costs, health insurance coverage and financial protection in India: a comparative analysis of national sample surveys for 1986–87, 1995–96, 2004 and 2014. Int J Eng Technol Manag Res. 2023;10(5):Article 5. https://doi.org/10.29121/ijetmr.v10.i5.2023.1315.
24. Hall RE, Jones CI. The value of life and the rise in health spending. Q J Econ. 2007;122(1):39–72.
25. Herd P, Schoeni RF, House JS. Upstream solutions: does the supplemental security income program reduce disability in the elderly? Milbank Q. 2008;86(1):5–45.
26. Hooda SK. Out-of-pocket payments for healthcare in India: who have affected the most and why? J Health Manag. 2017;19(1):1–15. https://doi.org/10.1177/0972063416682535.
27. Huang Y. The Health Silk Road: How China Adapts the Belt and Road Initiative to the COVID-19 Pandemic. Am J Public Health. 2022;112(4):567–9. https://doi.org/10.2105/AJPH.2021.306647.
28. Indranil. State of Health Financing in India: the Myth of OOP reduction. State of Finance in India Report 2022–2023; Yoda Press; ISBN: 978-93-82579-21-2. 2023. https://www.cenfa.org/wp-content/uploads/2024/04/State-of-Finance-in-India-Report-2023.pdf
29. Irving G, Neves AL, Dambha-Miller H, Oishi A, Tagashira H, Verho A, et al. International variations in primary care physician consultation time: a systematic review of 67 countries. BMJ Open. 2017;7(10):Article e017902.
30. Jakab M, Krishnan C. Community involvement in health care financing: a survey of the literature on the impact, strengths, and weaknesses. HNP discussion paper series. Washington, DC: © World Bank; 2001. http://hdl.handle.net/10986/13706. License: CC BY 3.0 IGO
31. Jakovljevic MM, Ogura S. Health economics at the crossroads of centuries – from the past to the future. Front Public Health. 2016;4 https://doi.org/10.3389/fpubh.2016.00115.
32. Jakovljevic M, Groot W, Souliotis K. Health care financing and affordability in the emerging global markets. Front Public Health. 2016;4:2. https://doi.org/10.3389/fpubh.2016.00002.
33. Kahneman D, Tversky A. Prospect theory: an analysis of decision under risk. Econom J Econom Soc. 1979;47:263–91.
34. Khan MS, Salve S, Porter JD. Engaging for-profit providers in TB control: lessons learnt from initiatives in South Asia. Health Policy Plan. 2015;30(10):1289–95. https://doi.org/10.1093/heapol/czu137.
35. Lahariya C. 'Ayushman Bharat' Program and Universal Health Coverage in India. Indian Pediatr. 2018a;55(6):495–506. https://doi.org/10.1007/s13312-018-1341-1.
36. Lahariya C. Strengthening primary healthcare: From promises to reality. Ideas for India; 27 March 2018. 2018b. Available from: http://www.ideasforindia.in/topics/human-development/strengthening-primary-healthcarefrom-promises-to-reality.html
37. Levesque JF, Haddad S, Narayana D, Fournier P. Outpatient care utilization in urban Kerala, India. Health Policy Plan. 2006;21:289–301.
38. Macfarlane S, Racelis M, Muli-Muslime F. Public health in developing countries. Lancet. 2000;356(9232):841–6. https://doi.org/10.1016/S0140-6736(00)02664-7.
39. Malhotra C, Do YK. Socio-economic disparities in health system responsiveness in India. Health Policy Plan. 2013;28(2):197–205. https://doi.org/10.1093/heapol/czs051.
40. Marten R, McIntyre D, Travassos C, Shishkin S, Longde W, Reddy S, Vega J. An assessment of progress towards universal health coverage in Brazil, Russia, India, China, and South Africa (BRICS). Lancet. 2014;384(9960):2164–71. https://doi.org/10.1016/S0140-6736(14)60075-1.
41. Ministry of Health and Family Welfare, National health policy. Government of India, 1983. https://www.nhp.gov.in/sites/default/files/pdf/nhp_1983.pdf
42. Morris S, Devlin N, Parkin D, Spencer D. Economic analysis in healthcare. UK: Wiley; 2012.
43. Obama SB. Affordable health care for all Americans: the Obama-Biden plan. JAMA. 2008;300(16):1927–8. https://doi.org/10.1001/jama.2008.515.
44. Palloni A, Milesi C. Economic achievement, inequalities and health disparities: the intervening role of early health status. Res Soc Stratific Mobil. 2006;24(1):21–40. https://doi.org/10.1016/j.rssm.2005.02.001.

45. Patnaik I, Roy S, Shah A. The rise of government-funded health insurance in India. National Institute of Public Finance and Policy New Delhi; 2018. https://www.nipfp.org.in/media/medialibrary/2018/05/WP_231.pdf
46. Press Information Bureau. 2023. https://pib.gov.in/PressReleasePage.aspx?PRID=1894902; Posted on: 31 Jan 2023 by PIB Delhi.
47. Richard S, Ana R, Wienke B. Social health insurance systems in Western Europe. McGraw-Hill Education (UK); 2004.
48. Saksena P, Hsu J, Evans DB. Financial risk protection and universal health coverage: evidence and measurement challenges. PLoS Med. 2014;11(9):e1001701. https://doi.org/10.1371/journal.pmed.1001701.
49. Saksena P, Xu K, Elovainio R, Perrot J. Health services utilization and out-of-pocket expenditure at public and private facilities in low-income countries. World Health Report Background paper. Geneva World Health Organization; 2010.
50. Sen G, Iyer A, George A. Structural reforms and health equity: a comparison of NSS surveys, 1986-87 and 1995-96. Econ Polit Wkly. 2002;37(14):1342–52. http://www.jstor.org/stable/4411960
51. Selvaraj S, Nabar V. Access to medicines in India: issues, challenges and response. India health report. New Delhi: Business Standard Limited; 2010.
52. Shaikh B, Hatcher J. Health seeking behaviour and health services utilization trends in National Health Survey of Pakistan: what needs to be done? J Pak Med Assoc. 2007;57:411–4.
53. Selvaraj S, Karan AK. Deepening Health Insecurity in India: Evidence from National Sample Surveys since 1980s. Econ Polit Wkly. 2009;44(40):55–60.
54. Sriram S, Albadrani M. Impoverishing effects of out-of-pocket healthcare expenditures in India. J Family Med Prim Care. 2022;11(11):7120–8. https://doi.org/10.4103/jfmpc.jfmpc_590_22.
55. Sundar R. Household survey of health care utilisation and expenditure. Working Paper No. 53. New Delhi: National Council of Applied Economic Research (NCAER); 1995.
56. Vega WA, Sribney WM. Growing Economic Inequality Sustains Health Disparities. Am J Public Health. 2017;107(10):1606–7. https://doi.org/10.2105/AJPH.2017.304024.
57. Viscusi KW. Wealth effects and earnings premiums for job hazards. Rev Econ Stat. 1978;60(3):408–16.
58. Woolf SH, Braveman P. Where health disparities begin: the role of social and economic determinants—and why current policies may make matters worse. Health Aff. 2011;30(10):1852–9. https://doi.org/10.1377/hlthaff.2011.0685.
59. WHO. Health systems: improving performance. The world health report 2000. Geneva, Switzerland; 2000.
60. WHO. 2023: Health data overview for the Republic of India. https://data.who.int/countries/356
61. World Bank 2022: Rural population (% of total population); World Bank staff estimates based on the United Nations Population Division's World Urbanization Prospects: 2018 Revision. https://data.worldbank.org/indicator/SP.RUR.TOTL.ZS
62. Xesfingi S, Vozikis A. Patient satisfaction with the healthcare system: assessing the impact of socio-economic and healthcare provision factors. BMC Health Serv Res. 2016;16(1):1–7. https://doi.org/10.1186/s12913-016-1327-4.
63. Zodpey S, Farooqui HH. Universal health coverage in India: progress achieved & the way forward. Indian J Med Res. 2018;147(4):327. https://doi.org/10.4103/ijmr.IJMR_616_18.

Chapter 8
Socio-economic Status Driven Social, Behavioral, and Financial Burden on Patients: A Critical Assessment of Health Equity

Ritis K. Shyanti, Ram Alagan, Seela Aladuwaka, Shalie Malik, and Manoj Kumar Mishra

8.1 Background

Socioeconomic status (SES)-driven social, behavioral, and financial burdens on patients designate a crucial challenge in attaining healthcare and health equity. This research paper explores the various impacts of socioeconomic disparities on individuals' health outcomes, exploring how economic standing influences access to healthcare, health-related behaviors, and overall well-being.

At its essence, SES shapes the possibilities available to individuals, affecting their capability to afford healthcare services, medications, and preventive care. Lower SES often correlates with limited access to quality healthcare facilities and health insurance, exacerbating disparities in health outcomes across different socioeconomic groups [1]. Furthermore, financial constraints can lead to delays in seeking medical attention, resulting in exacerbated health conditions and higher healthcare costs in the long run.

Beyond financial barriers, SES also influences social determinants of health (SDH) such as education, employment opportunities, and neighborhood environments, all of which profoundly impact health behaviors and outcomes [2]. These factors collectively underline the need for targeted interventions to address socioeconomic disparities to promote health equity.

R. K. Shyanti · M. K. Mishra (✉)
Cancer Research Center, Department of Biological Sciences, Alabama State University, Montgomery, AL, USA
e-mail: mmishra@alasu.edu

R. Alagan · S. Aladuwaka
Department of Advancement Studies and W.E.B. Du Bois Honors Program, Alabama State University, Montgomery, AL, USA

S. Malik
Department of Zoology, University of Lucknow, Lucknow, Uttar Pradesh, India

S. Malik et al. (eds.), *Public Health Issues: Theory and Practices*,
https://doi.org/10.1007/978-981-96-6650-8_8

This research seeks to illustrate these complex dynamics, offering insights into effective strategies and policy recommendations that can mitigate socioeconomic-driven burdens on patients and advance the broader goal of achieving equitable health outcomes and health equity for all.

8.2 Method and Data

As a research method, this research used a qualitative method. Qualitative methods also provide rich insights into the complexities of human behavior, beliefs, and experiences, offering depth and context. This research employed secondary data sources and scholarly publications. Data is derived from diverse secondary published sources and international institutions such as the World Bank and the Centers for Disease Control and Prevention. Using such diverse secondary sources, this research examines SES-driven social, behavioral, and financial burdens on patients and how health disparities exacerbate patients' circumstances.

8.3 Hypothesis

SES significantly impacts the social, behavioral, and financial burdens experienced by patients, posing a critical barrier to achieving equitable healthcare access and health outcomes. Specifically, lower SES is hypothesized to correlate with increased difficulties in accessing healthcare services, higher levels of stress and unhealthy behaviors, and greater financial strain related to medical expenses, thereby worsening health disparities and hindering progress toward health equity.

8.3.1 Social Discrimination and Loneliness

Social isolation is defined as a situation of absence of healthy interaction and support among surrounding people, maybe close relatives or unknown [3, 4]. Missing emotional attachments and feeling lonely are important experiences mentioned in the literature that affect patients' well-being. Broadly, researchers defined social isolation as one-dimensional in the context of objective measures but multidimensional when including objective and perceived measures [5–7]. During treatments for different disorders and chronic diseases like cancer, utmost care is required because of the various physical and psychological abnormalities that can happen, which could lead to mild to severe depression and loneliness [8, 9]. Studies have found that during this period, social isolation from immediate family members and friends can deteriorate the patient's condition and pose a threat of going into a state of malnutrition, anxiety, aggressive behavior, suicidal tendencies, and even death observed in many patients [7, 10]. The emotional connections missing among cancer patients with the family or with the surrounding people can worsen the health conditions and raise several side effects in addition to cancer [7, 11]. This isolation process can be prolonged and, if not taken care, can lead to mental disability, malnutrition, unusually aggressive behavior, fear, depression, etc. Researchers and healthcare professionals are now devoting much of their attention to such events to integrate them into their strategies for better health outcomes (Fig. 8.1) [12–14]. Therefore, the rising cases of loneliness in chronic illnesses like cancer need group interventions [7, 15]. The group intervention strategy given by Stewart is based on psychological intervention specifically tailored for cancer patients experiencing social isolation. This approach will bring peers and professionals to one platform where they can handle and influence patients' emotions by sharing their previous

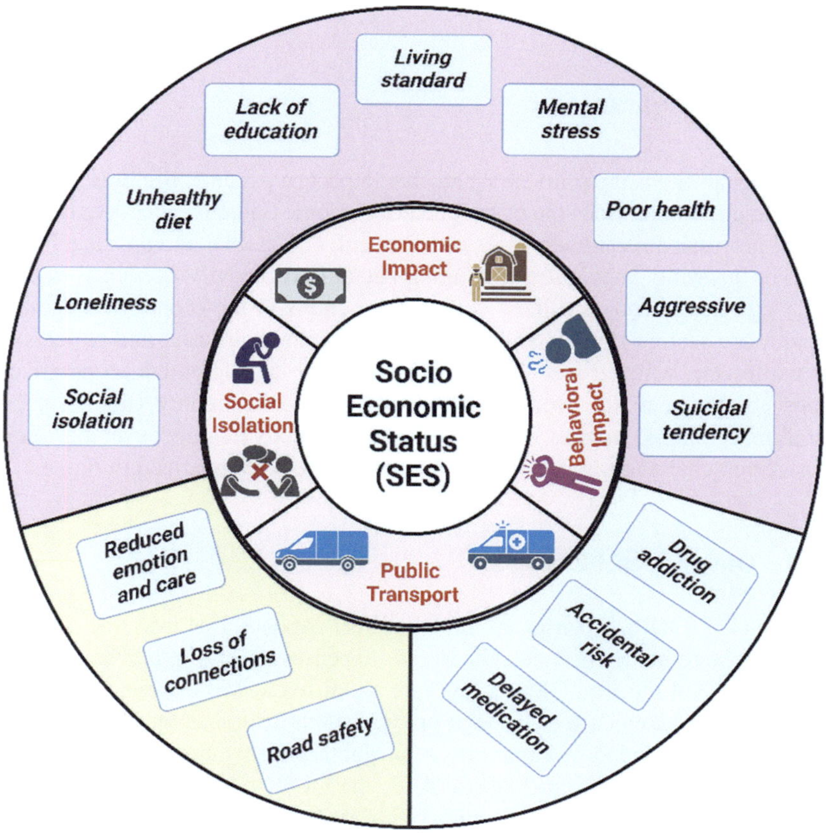

Fig. 8.1 SES in public health. Deciding socioeconomic status (SES) factors such as social isolation, economy, public transport and behavior influencing human health. The outcomes of the major SES factors on human life can be mild to severe with social discrimination, unhealthy diet, lack of education, mental stress, aggressiveness, suicidal tendency, drug addiction, loss of communication, risk of road accidents, and other health challenging events

experiences, valuable suggestions, resources, and practices. This multi-level intervention approach not only provides better support to patients to overcome depression and loneliness but in the long run, will improve social networking and receive valuable emotional support from their peers [16].

The novel Coronavirus (COVID-19) profoundly influenced global society through across-the-board isolation measures, deepening social, cultural, educational, and critical thinking challenges. Lockdowns and social distancing measures strived to curb the virus led to increased loneliness, depression, and anxiety [17]. Communities grappled with reduced social interactions, affecting mental health and exacerbating inequalities. The pandemic underscored the importance of social connections for well-being while highlighting disparities in access to resources and support systems. As societies navigate recovery, addressing the social impact of isolation remains crucial for rebuilding resilience and fostering inclusive environments that support mental and emotional health [18].

8.3.2 *Economic Impact*

Economic stability is the primary aspect that impacts a patient's life. It is the important parameter that decides the overall health outcome based on access to hospitals, medical professionals, nurses, types of treatment, and mental and physical burdens [19]. The growing population and aging factors are heavily burdened with the increasing rates of chronic illness, and a major chunk of the economy is dedicated to healthcare sectors [1, 20]. Still, the challenge with health care and patients persists worldwide, whether it is economically stable or in progressive economic conditions compared to the worst situations of a lower economy (Fig. 8.1) [21]. Therefore, economic stability both directly and indirectly influences socioeconomic status-driven challenges in addition to the other factors summarized in Fig. 8.1.

8.3.2.1 Out-of-Pocket Expenses

Out-of-pocket (OOP) expenses are mainly direct expenditures from the individual that cannot be reimbursed. In healthcare, the expenses are rising, and have globally reached 10.3% of the total GDP [22]. There are different ways of handling medical fees that can be taken care of through private health insurance, government plans, shared benefits provided by some private or public organizations, etc. [21]. As per the World Bank report from 2000 to 2017, the OOPs have been increasing, and people from low- and middle-income countries are spending double the amount. For poor people, it is incredibly hard to manage their expenses. In another report, there is a large shift in the OOPs from $24 billion dollars to $433 billion dollars during the period of 1970 to 2021 in the United States of America. Around 86% of the US population desires to reduce the burden of OOPs, which can help make them stable in handling their financial situation and dealing with routine medical expenses

[23]. This affects both household income and mental stress associated with treatments, further deteriorating economic conditions [21, 24, 25]. The indirect influence can bring mental illness and other diseases to the other family members, and the economic struggle continues to affect the patient's life [26, 27]. OOP is an issue for different patients at different levels depending upon the cost of medical facilities, income, and health insurance coverage, in addition to the racial disparities. Overall, OOP also burdens mental instability and can further impact health situations [23].

8.3.2.2 Household Finances

The household financial foundation is one of the characteristic features considered in the Social Vulnerability Index (SVI) as per the Centers for Disease Control and Prevention statement [28, 29]. Family income and expenditures are decisive factors in the family members' health outcomes and well-being. The impact of the household budget can be observed in children's development and behavior [30]. Economy and livelihood are directly proportionate to each other and are the biggest factors. Several indications of the economic burden ruined the physical and mental strength and shaped the home environment, either positively or negatively [31, 32]. The social taboo and stigma need to be reduced through interventions by providing financial support and engaging counselors will improve the conditions. It is always a broad scope for the responsible authorities to conduct timely surveys and provide necessary supplies to boost the family income of the economically deprived population. The message should be transferred in the community relevant to its economy and needs clarity so families can easily follow along with the surveys [33]. Financial management issues also need to be discussed and fixed, as well as the assessment of income and strategic expenditure so that low-income families can strategize how to save better [34].

8.3.2.3 Early Childhood Education

Children are the future that gets influenced by and leaves a broader impact on society, community, religion, and country [35, 36]. They are the most affected lives by SDH factors that depend on their status, such as place of birth, locality, gender, religion, financial condition, etc. The simplified concept of SDH is the nonmedical inputs that influence health output, as per the Centers for Disease Control and Prevention and the World Health Organization [29, 37]. Children coming from a poor economic background usually struggle to get proper food, hygiene, and sound health [38]. These limiting factors of the socioeconomic surroundings ultimately translate to personal behavior, social interactions, involvement in unwanted activities, poor health, lack of wealth, and poor well-being during adulthood [39]. Education should be a mandatory practice that ensures and provides a chance to uplift the future shape of life in a sustained manner [40, 41]. Education is where equal opportunities and treatment should be expected, which also helps in learning personal and professional behaviors in addition to the other subjects. There is sufficient evidence available that several children, especially from lower-income families, have difficulty attaining basic schooling or early childhood education. The absence rate is mostly due to poor health conditions in addition to other factors [39, 42]. The contribution of mothers to children's lives in learning, early education, and health hygiene is equally important compared to the role of the teacher. However, the work culture and financial situation nowadays make it very hard for women and single mothers to hold a dual role in managing their children and finances [43]. The characteristic features of well-nourished children are evident from the observations, creativity, and imagination that can be maintained when they have the opportunity to access all sorts of improved educational facilities. Therefore, focusing on mothers, teachers, and the surrounding environment to make roadmaps for better childhood education is essential [44, 45]. Actions to provide free or affordable education dedicated to every individual or at least to children should be a priority in many countries.

8.3.3 Public Transportation System

Public transportation is also a frequently associated factor in the SDH and health-related issues [46]. Transportation and connectivity services are the next set of things after wealth, education, and healthcare, which impact health outcomes [47]. Some important parameters of public transportation system includes the individual life style, work or business, the routes taken by individual to reach certain general facilities such as groceries, hospitals, and pharmacies affects SDH. The road infrastructure, location of the important services, and public transportation all count in the overall setup to obtain the regular needs. Unavailability or poor transportation facilities can lead to improper lifestyles and unwanted health-related issues [48]. This will further increase the mental stress and expenditures towards Medicare, resulting in unavoidable crunch economic situations. There are various reasons behind the shortage of healthcare associates in both rural and urban localities in the USA, and this shortage leads to heightened death rates in infants and critically ill patients. When a healthcare facility and its staff are inadequate to treat patients, they need an urgent and quick transportation system to send patients to a better facility. In rural areas, doctors usually refer patients and newborns with critical conditions to specialized pediatrics who need proper ambulances and nurses during transportation. In the absence of a less equipped transport system, the health risk of critically affected patients and newborns during travel is elevated (Fig. 8.1) [49]. The transport system may have several limitations, such as travel time, travel planning, communication, coordination, and proper care, which can lead to severe life-challenging health issues [50, 51]. Public transportation facilities must be better connected with the rural and urban healthcare facilities. While implementing any policy to support patients related to transport, coordinated efforts on public interest, affordable transportation services, internet access, and specific traffic routes should all be considered [52, 53]. Improving the transportation system and connectivity with the hospitals can positively impact patients' lives by mitigating stress, unwanted hospital visits, and postpartum depression and increasing hospital coordination and cohesiveness [53]. Betterment in transportation infrastructure will reduce the negative impacts on public health.

8.3.4 Behavioral Impact

SES status also determines the mental and physical behavior of individuals. It affects all age groups and genders. Closer observations of young children show they are more vulnerable to behavioral obstacles and, if ignored, can impact their future development [54, 55]. This commonly appears when the SES status is high or low [56, 57]. In the worldwide scenario, the existing psychological problems in children vary with respect to the SES spectrum. The low and middle-income countries, it is mainly due to the level of education, awareness, healthcare facility, and social culture, whereas in high-income countries, it is the peer's influence on the academic environment [58]. Behavioral changes are expected depending on the family income, education, neighborhood living style, food, and nutrition quality. It has been noticed in several poor SES cases that adolescents are found to be involved in criminal offenses that are most likely through drug, smoking, and alcohol habits (Fig. 8.1) [59]. The global percentage of affected children (2–6 years) and adolescents (6–18 years) is approximately 17.6% and 13.4%, respectively, with psychological stress-related problems describing the severity [60, 61]. The surrounding environment is where the individual starts experiencing different levels of external and internal stress from the guardian, school, and peers; additional factors should be emphasized to improve the situation [62]. To address and limit the SES-driven behavioral alterations, attention needs to focus and intervene in early childhood to identify behavioral disorders, followed by proper care and treatment [63, 64]. A recent study on early childhood development found that children significantly suffered from physiological disturbances in low and middle-income societies with a lack of standard education in mothers, low job opportunities, low financial stability, and high amounts of single-parenting [65].

8.3.5 SDH Interventions

Considering the significance of SDH as an integral part of life, various effective measures are being taken. The awareness among researchers, policymakers, political leaders, and health professionals is increasing day by day, and the priority is to get better outcomes. Continuous involvement of various stakeholders and policymakers to successfully implement policies targeting the issues of SDH is ongoing

[66]. Efforts have been focused on both medical and non-medical assistance, such as mobilizing people from high-poverty areas to low-poverty areas, providing support for food and regular requirements, free schooling, and medical supplies to those needy people. This, in turn, results in stabilizing mental and physical health conditions and thereby alleviates complex public health issues, disability percentage, and healthcare costs [67–69]. Healthy People is a foundation with an agenda to deliver health equity on various grounds by 2030. It started in 1990 when I worked with the associated organizations and experienced the possible changes needed promptly to provide a better environment that is more towards a healthy lifestyle [70]. Each decade of advancement, the foundation comes up with identified problems and a set of solutions to address disability, injury, premature mortality rate, enhancing independence, health disparities, health inequity, and literacy rate [2, 70, 71]. Public awareness about policies and benefits is equally important and needs to be circulated among communities through health literacy, advocacy, public gatherings, news bulletins, and social media platforms. Also, trust issues among society and healthcare personnel are a major hurdle and need attention among the authorities and beneficiaries to achieve successful health outcomes [72].

8.3.5.1 Managing Social Isolation Stress

Several organizations are working to achieve the decline or eliminate loneliness as one of the major SES factors. Different approaches are needed to recognize the types, factors behind them, and possible interventions for loneliness. Medication alone cannot always help social distress. It is more toward nonmedical interventions that, in some cases, require medication to resolve the loneliness problem [73]. Effective treatment begins with well-trained professionals and workers, clear guidelines to be followed, record keeping, and continuous support. The expert team's recommendation lies in the trust development during the survey, followed by personalized, detailed identification and treatment support [74]. Many times, direct engagement in building a social network is strong enough to reduce loneliness through existing relationships and new interactions [75]. Group intervention strategies also work better in some places where the identified problems are common in a particular group. Working on services like transportation, technology, and recreational places targeting different age groups with similar sensitive issues will provide fruitful outcomes in improving loneliness conditions. There is always a risk factor while dealing with inappropriate behavior from people who are mentally challenged and show aggression during the interaction. Also, in some cases, follow-up and continuous monitoring are required; otherwise, the chances of returning to the previously socially segregated position are very high [76]. Social prescribing is the strategy most frequently implemented by different organizations to reduce loneliness and increase emotional attachments.

8.3.5.2 Management of Economic Burden

Economic factors are central to life's overall health and well-being, and are the crucial SES determinants. There are various grounds on which the SES hierarchy is described. For example, the straightforward earnings of an individual or the whole family income decides economic strength [77]. However, in addition to that, other factors such as expense vs. saving plans decide the household budget on which more appropriate SES status can be measured [78, 79]. The real indicators of the economy in SES stand clear when occupational prestige is combined with family income and education [79–81]. To fix the economy, the public, private, and government sectors require the will and firm determination to recognize the exact areas where implementation can be done. Security of employment, food, and health in a coordinated manner can tackle the poverty issues in economically deprived families. Quality of food and the level of nutrition in several ways impact the immune system and health outcomes throughout life [82]. Sustaining the poor through aiding funding to get affordable shelter and food and providing medical insurance are important steps in resolving the economic burden. This, in turn, will also improve the future development of children by enhancing their health, skills, cognition, and productivity [83]. The health impact of the economy in low- and mid-income countries has always been a matter of concern. Several diseases can be avoidable through childhood immunization programs. Though economically sustainable countries can afford all such immunizations in many countries and localities, poor health immunization records prevail [84]. The World Health Organization (WHO) started a globalized Expanded Programme on Immunization (EPI) that has been working dedicatedly to improve immunization since 1974 [84, 85]. It is of utmost importance to invest in and prepare policies that can handle the vaccination of each individual so that the majority of the diseases and huge healthcare spending can be wiped out in the initial phases [86, 87]. Joblessness and crisis in employment sectors are the basis of increased economic burden which leads to an unstable mind, struggle in getting routine health care access, stigma, and social isolation. Economic assistance policies to support lower-income families can be achieved through different channels of creating opportunities, developing skills, direct cash distribution, social support, benefits in tax refunds, and better retirement plans [88–90]. Assistance in the field of education can build employment and financial strength in families with low income. Emphasis on strengthening primary and higher education with all the possible training and support can provide quality and productivity [91]. A fair and equitable resource of basic education and training for preschool, K-12 schooling, and advanced degrees will increase the probability of getting a job and substantially reduce the economic burden [92, 93]. In addition, housing assistance to homeless poor people and partial support to low and mid-income families will reduce mental and physical stress [94]. The affordable housing scheme to ensure a safe and secure shelter will be part of a healthy and economically stable society [95, 96].

8.3.5.3 Management of Transportation Services

Transportation service is very crucial in day-to-day life and is of maximum public dependency. Public transport not only interferes with the lifestyle, but its mismanagement can cause several health disturbances. Maximum use of public transport by the public is very useful from an environmental perspective as this will minimize traffic, fuel consumption, and noise and air pollution. It has a direct and major impact on climate change and associated adverse effects on nature and human health. Climate change raise global temperatures, greenhouse gases, and uneven precipitation throughout the years reducing the sustainable healthy lifestyle [97–99]. Severe health hazards related to respiration were observed in the poor air quality index (AQI) areas compared to those with good AQI. Eco-friendly and sustainable transportation is required to reduce the toxicity in the atmosphere. Focusing on the shared commute and micro-mobility mode of travel options, especially in urban areas with very high traffic can improve the situation [100–102]. Frequent government and public awareness programs in society can push the public mindset to adopt sharing or using public transport habits. The health-oriented advertisements and social media campaigns raising the benefits of public transport will further encourage public sentiments toward minimizing the use of personal vehicles [102]. Nowadays, electric vehicles are largely promoted by several countries looking towards sustainable green energy consumption, which can lower air pollution and improve health quality significantly [103]. However, the challenge here is to subsidize the cost through different schemes and increase charging stations at public places [104–106]. In alternative strategies, low carbon emitted fuel consumption for transportation is preferable. Biodiesel, hydrogen, and synthetic fuels are in focused research areas to minimize environmental pollution and health hazards [107, 108].

8.4 Conclusion

SES factors are the current demands in the context of public health and there is a landscape of opportunity for researchers, policymakers, stakeholders, and healthcare associates to advance on. In order to successfully address the issues to achieve a sustainable and healthy life, collaborative research on multiple areas is paramount. It is equally important to consider the obstacles arising from racism, gender, ethnicity, social relationships, and religious background to tackle the SDH. In addition to the upstream factors of SES, collective efforts and an integrated approach are required to maintain downstream factors like economic stability, quantity and quality of literacy, medical facilities, general services, and neighborhood environment. Involvement of Geographic Information System (GIS) technology and utilizing the benefits of the Artificial Intelligence approach can also enhance productivity in identifying the root cause of health problems and implementing intervention strategies. Enabling real-time tracking and information transmission of patient records and medical and nonmedical requirements in healthcare places will improve the quality of health. Diagnosis, prevention, therapeutics, recovery, and avoidance of relapse are the essential steps, and timely follow-up strategies will make families and communities healthier.

References

1. McMaughan DJ, Oloruntoba O, Smith ML. Socioeconomic status and access to healthcare: interrelated drivers for healthy aging. Front Public Health. 2020;8:231.
2. Chelak K, Chakole S. The role of social determinants of health in promoting health equality: a narrative review. Cureus. 2023;15
3. Berkman LF, Syme SL. Social networks, host resistance, and mortality: a nine-year follow-up study of Alameda County residents. Am J Epidemiol. 2017;185
4. Fine M, Spencer R. Social isolation: development of an assessment tool for HACC services. 2009.
5. Taylor HO, Cudjoe TK, Bu F, Lim MH. The state of loneliness and social isolation research: current knowledge and future directions. BMC Public Health. 2023;23:1049.
6. He C, Wu C, He Y, Yan J, Lin Y, Wan Y, Xue S, Gao F, Chang W, Liu R. Characteristics and influencing factors of social isolation in patients with breast cancer: a latent profile analysis. Support Care Cancer. 2023;31:363.
7. Wang C, Qiu X, Yang X, Mao J, Li Q. Factors influencing social isolation among cancer patients: a systematic review. Healthcare, MDPI. 2024;12:1042.
8. Beutel M, Brähler E, Wild P, Faber J, Merzenich H, Ernst M. Loneliness as a risk factor for suicidal ideation and anxiety in cancer survivor populations. J Psychosom Res. 2022;157:110827.
9. Papini C, Fayad AA, Wang M, Schulte FS, Huang IC, Chang YP, Howell RM, Srivastava D, Leisenring WM, Armstrong GT. Emotional, behavioral, and physical health consequences of loneliness in young adult survivors of childhood cancer: results from the Childhood Cancer Survivor Study. Cancer. 2023;129:1117–28.
10. Wang F, Gao Y, Han Z, Yu Y, Long Z, Jiang X, Wu Y, Pei B, Cao Y, Ye J. A systematic review and meta-analysis of 90 cohort studies of social isolation, loneliness and mortality. Nat Hum Behav. 2023;7:1307–19.
11. Fox RS, Armstrong GE, Gaumond JS, Vigoureux TF, Miller CH, Sanford SD, Salsman JM, Katsanis E, Badger TA, Reed DR. Social isolation and social connectedness among young adult cancer survivors: a systematic review. Cancer. 2023;129:2946–65.
12. Bonanno GA, Brewin CR, Kaniasty K, Greca AML. Weighing the costs of disaster: consequences, risks, and resilience in individuals, families, and communities. Psychol Sci Public Interest. 2010;11:1–49.
13. N.A.o.S. Engineering, Medicine, Risk and protective factors for social isolation and loneliness, Social Isolation and Loneliness in Older Adults: Opportunities for the Health Care System, 2020, 63–91.
14. Eating H, N. Blog-Inside, Social isolation, loneliness in older people pose health risks. 2020.
15. Murnaghan S, Scruton S, Urquhart R. Psychosocial interventions that target adult cancer survivors' reintegration into daily life after active cancer treatment: a scoping review. JBI Evidence Synthesis. 2024;22:607–56.
16. Stewart M, Craig D, MacPherson K, Alexander S. Promoting positive affect and diminishing loneliness of widowed seniors through a support intervention. Public Health Nurs. 2001;18:54–63.

17. Perez-Brumer A, Balasa R, Doshi A, Brogdon J, Doan T, Oldenburg CE. COVID-19 related shifts in social interaction, connection, and cohesion impact psychosocial health: longitudinal qualitative findings from COVID-19 treatment trial engaged participants. Int J Environ Res Public Health. 2022;19:10264.
18. Parenteau AM, Boyer CJ, Campos LJ, Carranza AF, Deer LK, Hartman DT, Bidwell JT, Hostinar CE. A review of mental health disparities during COVID-19: evidence, mechanisms, and policy recommendations for promoting societal resilience. Dev Psychopathol. 2022:1–22.
19. Desmedt M, Vertriest S, Hellings J, Bergs J, Dessers E, Vankrunkelsven P, Vrijhoef H, Annemans L, Verhaeghe N, Petrovic M. Economic impact of integrated care models for patients with chronic diseases: a systematic review. Value Health. 2016;19:892–902.
20. Pitchforth E, Nolte E. What is the evidence of economic impacts of integrated care. 2014.
21. Jalali FS, Bikineh P, Delavari S. Strategies for reducing out of pocket payments in the health system: a scoping review. Cost Effectiveness Resour Allocat. 2021;19:1–22.
22. W.H. Organization. Global spending on health: coping with the pandemic. World Health Organization; 2024.
23. Schmidt T, Juday C, Patel P, Karmarkar T, Smith-Howell ER, Fendrick AM. Expanding the catalog of patient and caregiver out-of-pocket costs: a systematic literature review. Popul Health Manag. 2024;27:70–83.
24. Baji P, Pavlova M, Gulácsi L, Groot W. Changes in equity in out-of-pocket payments during the period of health care reforms: evidence from Hungary. Int J Equity Health. 2012;11:1–11.
25. Saputra R, Ramadhani E, Laras PB, Suhardita K, Andrianie S. Economic burden on families: analyzing the financial impact of palliative care for cancer patients. Palliat Support Care. 2024:1–2.
26. Cameron EE, Joyce KM, Delaquis CP, Reynolds K, Protudjer JL, Roos LE. Maternal psychological distress & mental health service use during the COVID-19 pandemic. J Affect Disord. 2020;276:765–74.
27. Fegert JM, Vitiello B, Plener PL, Clemens V, Challenges and burden of the Coronavirus. (COVID-19) pandemic for child and adolescent mental health: a narrative review to highlight clinical and research needs in the acute phase and the long return to normality. Child Adolesc Psychiatry Ment Health. 2019;14(2020):1–11.
28. Gregory E, Hallisey E, Heitgerd J, Lewis B. A social vulnerability index for disaster management. J Homel Secur Emerg Manag. 2011;8
29. Brignone E, LeJeune K, Mihalko AE, Shannon AL, Sinoway LI. Self-reported social determinants of health and area-level social vulnerability. JAMA Netw Open. 2024;7:–e2412109.
30. Mood C, Jonsson JO. Trends in child poverty in Sweden: parental and child reports. Child Indic Res. 2016;9:825–54.
31. Cooper K, Stewart K. Does household income affect children's outcomes? A systematic review of the evidence. Child Indicators Res. 2021;14:981–1005.
32. Lai ET, Wickham S, Law C, Whitehead M, Barr B, Taylor-Robinson D. Poverty dynamics and health in late childhood in the UK: evidence from the Millennium Cohort Study. Arch Dis Child. 2019;104:1049–55.
33. Johansson N, Warner G, Avogadri N, Sarkadi A. Screening for economic hardship at Child Health Care Centres: a qualitative study of stakeholders' perceptions and experiences of the Healthier Wealthier Families model in Sweden. Scand J Public Health. 2024;14034948241252227:406.
34. Weida EB, Phojanakong P, Patel F, Chilton M. Financial health as a measurable social determinant of health. PLoS One. 2020;15:e0233359.
35. Larson K, Russ SA, Crall JJ, Halfon N. Influence of multiple social risks on children's health. Pediatrics. 2008;121:337–44.
36. Fuji KT, White ND, Packard KA, Kalkowski JC, Walters RW. Effect of a financial education and coaching program for low-income, Single Mother Households on Child Health Outcomes. Healthcare, MDPI. 2024;12:127.

37. Centers for Disease Control and Prevention. Social Determinants of Health at CDC. Available online: https://www.cdc.gov/about/sdoh/index.html. Accessed 22 Nov 2023.
38. French D, Vigne S. The causes and consequences of household financial strain: a systematic review. Int Rev Financ Anal. 2019;62:150–6.
39. Allison MA, Attisha E, Lerner M, De Pinto CD, Beers NS, Gibson EJ, Gorski P, Kjolhede C, O'Leary SC, Schumacher H. The link between school attendance and good health. Pediatrics. 2019;143
40. Smith A. Children and young people's participation rights in education. Int J Child Rights. 2007;15:147–64.
41. Burrows L, Wright J. Prescribing practices: shaping healthy children in schools. Int'l J Child Rts. 2007;15:83.
42. Schickedanz A, Dreyer BP, Halfon N. Childhood poverty: understanding and preventing the adverse impacts of a most-prevalent risk to pediatric health and well-being. Pediatr Clin. 2015;62:1111–35.
43. Packard KA, Kalkowski JC, White ND, Ryan-Haddad AM, Black LL, Flecky KA, Furze JA, Rusch LM, Qi Y. Effect of a financial education program on the health of single, low-income women and their children. Int Public Health J. 2015;7:37.
44. Yliverronen V. From story to product: pre-schoolers' designing and making processes in a holistic craft context, design and technology education: an. Int J. 2014;19:8–16.
45. Cooper KO, Lawler T, Raymond C, Stables K. Designerly play and the mud Pool: using Designerly play as a lens to view young children experiencing Forest School. Techne serien-Forskning i slöjdpedagogik och slöjdvetenskap. 2021;28:166–72.
46. Chi C, Hoque F. Impact of social determinants on health outcomes. J Bangladesh Med Associat North Am BMANA J. 2024:19–22.
47. Eder M, Henninger M, Durbin S, Iacocca MO, Martin A, Gottlieb LM, Lin JS. Screening and interventions for social risk factors: technical brief to support the US preventive services task force. JAMA. 2021;326:1416–28.
48. Riley T, Umoren R, Kotler A, Feltner J, Billimoria Z, James J, Mahankali A, White C, Brajkovic I, Gray MM. Disparities in access to healthcare services in a regional neonatal transport network. Int J Ind Ergon. 2024;99:103526.
49. Delacrétaz R, Fumeaux CJF, Stadelmann C, Trejo AR, Destaillats A, Giannoni E. Adverse events and associated factors during intrahospital transport of newborn infants. J Pediatr. 2022;240:44–50.
50. Greene ND, Riley T, Mastroianni R, Billimoria ZC, Enquobahrie DA, Baker C, Gray MM, Umoren RA. Neonatal vital sign trajectories and risk factors during transport within a regional care network. Air Med J. 2022;41:542–8.
51. Wooldridge AR, Carayon P, Hoonakker P, Hose B-Z, Eithun B, Brazelton T III, Ross J, Kohler JE, Kelly MM, Dean SM. Work system barriers and facilitators in inpatient care transitions of pediatric trauma patients. Appl Ergon. 2020;85:103059.
52. Smith VC, Love K, Goyer E. NICU discharge preparation and transition planning: guidelines and recommendations. J Perinatol. 2022;42:7–21.
53. Griffith T, Singh A, Naber M, Hummel P, Bartholomew C, Amin S, White-Traut R, Garfield L. Scoping review of interventions to support families with preterm infants post-NICU discharge. J Pediatr Nurs. 2022;67:e135–49.
54. Coley RL, Sims J, Dearing E, Spielvogel B. Locating economic risks for adolescent mental and behavioral health: poverty and affluence in families, neighborhoods, and schools. Child Dev. 2018;89:360–9.
55. Matar JL, Laletas S, Lubman DI. Mental health concerns and help-seeking behaviors among adolescents in high socioeconomic status groups: a scoping review. Adolesc Res Rev. 2024;9:93–134.
56. Lund TJ, Dearing E, Zachrisson HD. Is affluence a risk for adolescents in Norway? J Res Adolesc. 2017;27:628–43.

57. Zubrick SR, Hafekost J, Johnson SE, Sawyer MG, Patton G, Lawrence D. The continuity and duration of depression and its relationship to non-suicidal self-harm and suicidal ideation and behavior in adolescents 12–17. J Affect Disord. 2017;220:49–56.
58. Reiner RC, Olsen HE, Ikeda CT, Echko MM, Ballestreros KE, Manguerra H, Martopullo I, Millear A, Shields C, Smith A. Diseases, injuries, and risk factors in child and adolescent health, 1990 to 2017: findings from the global burden of diseases, injuries, and risk factors 2017 study. JAMA Pediatr. 2019;173:e190337.
59. Racz SJ, McMahon RJ, Luthar SS. Risky behavior in affluent youth: examining the co-occurrence and consequences of multiple problem behaviors. J Child Fam Stud. 2011;20:120–8.
60. Polanczyk GV, Salum GA, Sugaya LS, Caye A, Rohde LA. Annual research review: a meta-analysis of the worldwide prevalence of mental disorders in children and adolescents. J Child Psychol Psychiatry. 2015;56:345–65.
61. Reiss F, Meyrose A-K, Otto C, Lampert T, Klasen F, Ravens-Sieberer U. Socioeconomic status, stressful life situations and mental health problems in children and adolescents: results of the German BELLA cohort-study. PLoS One. 2019;14:e0213700.
62. Vélez-Agosto NM, Soto-Crespo JG, Vizcarrondo-Oppenheimer M, Vega-Molina S, García Coll C. Bronfenbrenner's bioecological theory revision: moving culture from the macro into the micro. Perspect Psychol Sci. 2017;12:900–10.
63. Divin N, Harper P, Curran E, Corry D, Leavey G. Help-seeking measures and their use in adolescents: a systematic review. Adolesc Res Rev. 2018;3:113–22.
64. Islam MI, Yunus FM, Isha SN, Kabir E, Khanam R, Martiniuk A. The gap between perceived mental health needs and actual service utilization in Australian adolescents. Sci Rep. 2022;12:5430.
65. Luo J, van Grieken A, Kruizinga I, Raat H. Longitudinal associations between socioeconomic status and psychosocial problems in preschool children. Eur Child Adolesc Psychiatry. 2024;33:1029–38.
66. Hatton CR, Kale R, Pollack Porter KM, Mui Y. Inclusive and intersectoral: community health improvement planning opportunities to advance the social determinants of health and health equity. BMC Public Health. 2024;24:170.
67. Thornton RL, Glover CM, Cené CW, Glik DC, Henderson JA, Williams DR. Evaluating strategies for reducing health disparities by addressing the social determinants of health. Health Aff. 2016;35:1416–23.
68. Butler SM. What is the outlook for addressing social determinants of health? JAMA Health Forum, American Medical Association. 2021;2:e213639.
69. Frank J, Abel T, Campostrini S, Cook S, Lin VK, McQueen DV. The social determinants of health: time to re-think? Int J Environ Res Public Health. 2020;17:5856.
70. Gómez CA, Kleinman DV, Pronk N, Gordon GLW, Ochiai E, Blakey C, Johnson A, Brewer KH. Addressing health equity and social determinants of health through healthy people 2030. J Public Health Manag Pract. 2021;27:S249–57.
71. Secretary's Advisory Committee on National Health Promotion and Disease Prevention Objectives for 2030. Recommendations for an approach to Healthy People 2020. https://www.healthypeople.gov/sites/default/files/Full%20Committee%20Report%20to%20Secretary%205-9-2017_1.pdf. Accessed 25 Nov 2020.
72. Ehlinger E. Health equity and social cohesion. MetroDoctors. 2017;September/October:12–3.
73. Moffatt S, Steer M, Lawson S, Penn L, O'Brien N. Link worker social prescribing to improve health and well-being for people with long-term conditions: qualitative study of service user perceptions. BMJ Open. 2017;7:e015203.
74. N.A.o. Sciences, D.o. Behavioral, S. Sciences, M. Division, B.o. Behavioral, S. Sciences, B.o.H.S. Policy, C.o.t. Health, M.D.o.S. Isolation, L.i.O. Adults. Social isolation and loneliness in older adults: opportunities for the health care system. National Academies Press; 2020.

75. Mann F, Bone JK, Lloyd-Evans B, Frerichs J, Pinfold V, Ma R, Wang J, Johnson S. A life less lonely: the state of the art in interventions to reduce loneliness in people with mental health problems. Soc Psychiatry Psychiatr Epidemiol. 2017;52:627–38.
76. Cacioppo JT, Cacioppo S, Capitanio JP, Cole SW. The neuroendocrinology of social isolation. Annu Rev Psychol. 2015;66:733–67.
77. Goudeau S, Croizet J-C. Hidden advantages and disadvantages of social class: how classroom settings reproduce social inequality by staging unfair comparison. Psychol Sci. 2017;28:162–70.
78. Davis-Kean PE, Tighe LA, Waters NE. The role of parent educational attainment in parenting and children's development. Curr Dir Psychol Sci. 2021;30:186–92.
79. Hughes BT, Srivastava S, Leszko M, Condon DM. Occupational prestige: the status component of socioeconomic status. Collabra Psychol. 2024;10
80. Warlaumont AS, Richards JA, Gilkerson J, Oller DK. A social feedback loop for speech development and its reduction in autism. Psychol Sci. 2014;25:1314–24.
81. Fujishiro K, Xu J, Gong F. What does "occupation" represent as an indicator of socioeconomic status?: exploring occupational prestige and health. Soc Sci Med. 2010;71:2100–7.
82. Shyanti RK, Greggs J, Malik S, Mishra M. Gut dysbiosis impacts the immune system and promotes prostate cancer. Immunol Lett. 2024;268:106883.
83. Hiam L, Klaber B, Sowemimo A, Marmot M. NHS and the whole of society must act on social determinants of health for a healthier future. BMJ. 2024;385:e079389.
84. Williams SV, Akande T, Abbas K. Systematic review of social determinants of childhood immunisation in low-and middle-income countries and equity impact analysis of childhood vaccination coverage in Nigeria. PLoS One. 2024;19:e0297326.
85. Keja K, Chan C, Hayden G, Henderson RH. Expanded programme on immunization, world health statistics quarterly. Rapp Trimest Stat Sanit Mond. 1988;41:59–63.
86. Piot P, Larson HJ, O'Brien KL, N'kengasong J, Ng E, Sow S, Kampmann B. Immunization: vital progress, unfinished agenda. Nature. 2019;575:119–29.
87. Rodrigues CM, Plotkin SA. Impact of vaccines; health, economic and social perspectives. Front Microbiol. 2020;11:1526.
88. Stringfellow EJ, Kim TW, Gordon AJ, Pollio DE, Grucza RA, Austin EL, Johnson NK, Kertesz SG. Substance use among persons with homeless experience in primary care. Subst Abus. 2016;37:534–41.
89. Hendriks A-M, Jansen MW, Gubbels JS, De Vries NK, Paulussen T, Kremers SP. Proposing a conceptual framework for integrated local public health policy, applied to childhood obesity-the behavior change ball. Implement Sci. 2013;8:1–17.
90. Onyenwe CA, Onwumere C, Odilibe IP. Socioeconomic determinants of mental health and substance use: a review and conceptual solutions for public health policy. Int J Appl Res Soc Sci. 2024;6:409–20.
91. Hanushek EA, Schwerdt G, Woessmann L, Zhang L. General education, vocational education, and labor-market outcomes over the lifecycle. J Hum Resour. 2017;52:48–87.
92. Duncan GJ, Magnuson K. Investing in preschool programs. J Econ Perspect. 2013;27:109–32.
93. Yoshikawa H, Weiland C, Brooks-Gunn J, Burchinal MR, Espinosa LM, Gormley WT, Ludwig J, Magnuson KA, Phillips D, Zaslow MJ. Investing in our future: the evidence base on preschool education. Society for Research in Child Development; 2013.
94. Chung RY-N, Chung GK-K, Gordon D, Mak JK-L, Zhang L-F, Chan D, Lai FTT, Wong H, Wong SY-S. Housing affordability effects on physical and mental health: household survey in a population with the world's greatest housing affordability stress. J Epidemiol Community Health. 2020;74:164–72.
95. Sharam A, Byford MC, Karabay B, McNelis S, Burke T. Matching markets in housing and housing assistance. 2018.
96. Fenelon A, Mayne P, Simon AE, Rossen LM, Helms V, Lloyd P, Sperling J, Steffen BL. Housing assistance programs and adult health in the United States. Am J Public Health. 2017;107:571–8.

97. Nath S, Shyanti RK, Nath Y. Influence of anthropocene climate change on biodiversity loss in different ecosystems, Global climate change. Elsevier; 2021. p. 63–78.
98. Romero-Ocaño AD, Cosío-León M, Valenzuela-Alcaraz VM, Brizuela CA. The impact of gradually replacing fossil fuel-powered vehicles with electric ones: a bi-objective optimisation approach. Expert Syst Appl. 2022;194:116546.
99. Greer K, Zeller D, Woroniak J, Coulter A, Winchester M, Palomares MD, Pauly D. Global trends in carbon dioxide (CO2) emissions from fuel combustion in marine fisheries from 1950 to 2016. Mar Policy. 2019;107:103382.
100. Göddeke D, Krauss K, Gnann T. What is the role of carsharing toward a more sustainable transport behavior? Analysis of data from 80 major German cities. Int J Sustain Transp. 2022;16:861–73.
101. Ikwuagwu CV, Ajahb SA, Uchennab N, Uzomab N, Anutaa UJ, Sa OC, Emmanuela O. Development of an arduino-controlled convective heat dryer. UNN International Conference: Technological Innovation for Holistic Sustainable Development (TECHISD2020); 2020. p. 180–95.
102. Etukudoh EA, Adefemi A, Ilojianya VI, Umoh AA, Ibekwe KI, Nwokediegwu ZQS. A review of sustainable transportation solutions: innovations, challenges, and future directions. World J Adv Res Rev. 2024;21:1440–52.
103. Roberts C. Easy street for low-carbon mobility? The political economy of mass electric car adoption, electrifying mobility: realising a sustainable future for the car. Emerald Publishing Limited; 2022. p. 13–31.
104. Shi L, Sethi SP, Çakanyıldırım M. Promoting electric vehicles: reducing charging inconvenience and price via station and consumer subsidies. Prod Oper Manag. 2022;31:4333–50.
105. Fournel J-F. Electric vehicle subsidies: cost-effectiveness and emission reductions. 2023.
106. Pareek S, Sujil A, Ratra S, Kumar R. Electric vehicle charging station challenges and opportunities: a future perspective. In: 2020 international conference on emerging trends in communication, control and computing (ICONC3). IEEE; 2020. p. 1–6.
107. Halder P, Babaie M, Salek F, Haque N, Savage R, Stevanovic S, Bodisco TA, Zare A. Advancements in hydrogen production, storage, distribution and refuelling for a sustainable transport sector: hydrogen fuel cell vehicles. Int J Hydrog Energy. 2023;
108. Uddin SU, Chidolue O, Azeez A, Iqbal T. Design and analysis of a solar powered water filtration system for a community in Black Tickle-Domino. In: 2022 IEEE international IOT, electronics and mechatronics conference (IEMTRONICS), vol. 2022. IEEE. p. 1–6.

Part III
Public Health: Environment and Gender Concerns

Chapter 9
Policy and Governance in Public Health: Gender Concerns and Remedies

Anu Mehra

9.1 Introduction

Public health in India grapples with a multitude of challenges and opportunities owing to its expansive and diverse population. The health landscape varies drastically from densely populated urban centres to remote rural regions, shaped by socio-economic disparities, cultural norms, and infrastructure constraints. Major health concerns encompass communicable diseases such as tuberculosis and malaria, alongside a rising burden of non-communicable diseases like diabetes and cardiovascular conditions. Access to healthcare services remains uneven, particularly affecting marginalized communities such as tribal populations and residents of urban slums, who often face significant barriers in accessing essential healthcare. Nevertheless, India has made considerable advancements in healthcare delivery through initiatives like the National Health Mission, which aims to strengthen healthcare infrastructure, expand immunization coverage, and improve maternal and child health outcomes. Addressing these complex health challenges moving forward necessitates concerted efforts towards ensuring equitable access, implementing preventive healthcare strategies, and formulating robust public health policies that prioritize the health and well-being of all Indians.

Gender considerations profoundly shape public health in India, exerting significant influence on healthcare access, health outcomes, and overall well-being. Women encounter formidable barriers such as limited healthcare access due to cultural norms, economic constraints, and lack of decision-making autonomy. These disparities contribute to elevated maternal mortality rates, inadequate reproductive health services, and lower health literacy levels among women compared to men. Effective interventions must prioritize enhancing healthcare accessibility through

A. Mehra (✉)
Law Centre 1, Faculty of Law, University of Delhi, New Delhi, India

S. Malik et al. (eds.), *Public Health Issues: Theory and Practices*,
https://doi.org/10.1007/978-981-96-6650-8_9

community-driven initiatives, boosting health literacy among women, advocating for gender-sensitive policies, advancing research on gender-specific health issues, and fostering community engagement to challenge harmful gender norms. Addressing gender disparities not only enhances health outcomes for women but also fortifies the broader healthcare system, promoting equity and inclusivity in healthcare provision across India.

The 2017 National Health Policy underscores the critical importance of women's health and integrating gender perspectives into public health endeavours. It identifies gender-based violence as a significant public health concern and calls for the establishment of women-friendly healthcare facilities. Addressing gender inequities in health is pivotal for achieving fair health outcomes. Women often confront distinct challenges, including limited access to healthcare facilities, lower health literacy rates that impact their ability to seek timely medical care, and cultural barriers that hinder their healthcare choices. Conversely, societal norms of masculinity may deter men from seeking preventive care. Recognizing and addressing these gender-specific health issues are fundamental to fostering inclusive health policies and interventions that cater to the diverse needs of all genders in India, ultimately leading to improved health outcomes and enhanced overall well-being for the entire population.

The National Family Health Survey (NFHS-4) brought out several key challenges in implementing gender-sensitive health policies in India:

1. Gender Disparities in Health Outcomes: Maternal Mortality Rate.
2. Gender Inequality in Health Insurance Coverage: Publicly Funded Health Insurance Schemes (PFHIS).
3. Gender-Based Violence (GBV): NFHS 4 and 5 Data.
4. Limited Access to Healthcare Services: Rural-Urban Divide.
5. Gender Norms and Social Expectations: Traditional Gender Roles.
6. Data Collection and Analysis: Data Limitations.
7. Implementation and Sustainability: Institutional Support.
8. Community Engagement and Empowerment: Women's Empowerment.

These challenges highlight the need for comprehensive policies that address gender disparities and promote gender equity in healthcare systems. Effective implementation and sustainability of these policies require institutional support, community engagement, and a commitment to disrupting harmful gender norms.

9.2 Gender-Specific Health Concerns in India

Gender-specific health concerns in India highlight significant disparities and challenges that impact the well-being of women and men differently. Women in India face unique health challenges, including higher rates of maternal mortality due to complications during childbirth and limited access to reproductive health services in certain regions. Cultural norms and economic constraints often restrict women's decision-making power regarding their health, leading to disparities in health literacy and preventive care. Moreover, gender-based violence remains a pervasive issue affecting women's physical and mental health. On the other hand, men in India confront health issues such as higher prevalence rates of tobacco and alcohol use, contributing to increased risks of respiratory diseases and liver cirrhosis. Addressing these gender-specific health concerns requires targeted interventions that enhance healthcare access, promote health literacy, challenge harmful gender norms, and advocate for gender-sensitive policies across the healthcare system. By prioritizing gender-specific health needs, India can strive towards a more equitable and inclusive approach to public health that improves outcomes for all genders.

Gender bias in access to healthcare is prevalent in India, with women often facing barriers to quality healthcare services. These barriers include a lack of education, limited decision-making power, and cultural norms that prioritize men's health over women's. Addressing gender bias in healthcare access is crucial to ensuring that all individuals have equal opportunities to receive the care they need. High rates of malnutrition among women and a growing cancer epidemic, particularly breast cancer, highlight these disparities. Maternal mortality, poor nutrition, and lack of access to quality healthcare facilities are significant issues [1, 2].

NFHS data reveals that traditional gender norms, deeply ingrained in Indian society, significantly affect women's health. These roles often dictate that women prioritize family responsibilities over their own health, leading to neglect of their health needs. For instance, women's participation in household decision-making is still limited. NFHS-5 shows that only about 42% of women participate in key household decisions, indicating a lack of autonomy that impacts their ability to seek timely and appropriate healthcare. Women in India experience higher levels of multimorbidity compared to men, attributed to biological, sociocultural, economic, and environmental causes. Understanding gender disparities in NCDs is crucial for effective health policy and intervention [1]. Deep-seated sociocultural norms and stigma surrounding GBV also pose significant challenges. Many survivors face societal pressure to remain silent about their experiences, fearing ostracization and further victimization. This stigma not only discourages women from reporting incidents of violence but also from seeking medical and psychological help, perpetuating a cycle of silence and suffering.

9.3 Structural Determinants

Economic status, education, social status, and age are closely interrelated factors influencing access to maternal and reproductive healthcare. Gender norms and social structures restrict women's access to these services, exacerbating health inequities [1]. Efforts to reduce maternal mortality must consider these determinants to address inequities effectively. Additionally, cultural beliefs and traditional practices can also play a role in limiting women's access to necessary healthcare services. By addressing these structural determinants comprehensively, interventions can be more targeted and impactful in reducing maternal mortality rates. It is crucial for healthcare policies and programs to be culturally sensitive and inclusive in order to effectively reach all women in need of maternal and reproductive healthcare. By understanding and addressing these various factors, we can work towards improving access to essential services for all women, ultimately reducing maternal mortality rates.

9.4 Maternal and Child Health

India has achieved its National Health Policy targets, notably reducing the Maternal Mortality Ratio (MMR) to 97 per lakh live births as per the latest SRS' 2018–2020. Efforts are now focused on achieving Sustainable Development Goal (SDG) target 3.1, aiming to further reduce MMR to less than 70 per 100,000 live births by 2030. To address maternal and child health issues comprehensively, the Government of India has implemented various policies and programs. These initiatives ensure optimal healthcare for pregnant women, starting from early pregnancy through postpartum care. The Surakshit Matritva Aashwasan (SUMAN) scheme guarantees dignified, respectful, and quality healthcare at no cost, aiming to eliminate preventable maternal and newborn deaths [3]. Under SUMAN, 41,010 facilities have been notified to provide essential care. Additionally, the Janani Suraksha Yojana (JSY) promotes institutional deliveries among socio-economically disadvantaged pregnant women, with approximately one crore beneficiaries benefiting from the scheme. The Janani Shishu Suraksha Karyakram (JSSK) ensures free deliveries and other essential services for pregnant women in public health institutions, benefiting over 1.37 crore beneficiaries in 2023–2024 alone. The Pradhan Mantri Surakshit Matritva Abhiyan (PMSMA) offers free, quality antenatal checkups, extended to support high-risk pregnancies and ensure safe deliveries through financial incentives for identified women and their accompanying health workers. These efforts are complemented by quality certification initiatives like LaQshya, which ensures respectful care during childbirth across certified facilities. To further enhance maternal health, the Midwifery Initiative promotes natural birthing through skilled Nurse Practitioner Midwives (NPMs) trained in accordance with international competencies. These initiatives are bolstered by the establishment of First Referral Units (FRUs) and Maternal and Child Health (MCH) wings to provide emergency obstetric and newborn care. Outreach activities, maternity waiting homes, and performance-based incentives for health workers in remote areas further improve access to maternal and child health services. Despite these advancements, challenges persist, necessitating continued efforts to bridge socio-economic gaps and ensure equitable access to healthcare for all pregnant women and newborns in India [1].

9.5 Family Planning and Contraception

Family planning and contraception play crucial roles in shaping India's demographic and health landscape. With a population exceeding 1.3 billion, India faces significant challenges related to population growth, maternal health, and socioeconomic development. Family planning programs in India aim to empower individuals, particularly women, with the knowledge and access to contraceptive methods that suit their reproductive choices. Government initiatives such as the National Family Planning Program and the Mission Parivar Vikas focus on expanding access to a wide range of contraceptives, including oral pills, injectables, condoms, intrauterine devices (IUDs), and sterilization procedures. These efforts are vital in enabling couples to plan their families effectively, reduce unintended pregnancies, and improve maternal and child health outcomes. Despite progress, barriers such as cultural beliefs, inadequate healthcare infrastructure, and disparities in access to information remain. Addressing these challenges requires sustained investments in healthcare services, education, and community engagement to promote informed decision-making and ensure equitable access to family planning resources across diverse socio-economic and geographic contexts in India. Family planning and contraception have seen significant changes, with modern methods becoming more accepted and accessible. However, issues related to sexual and reproductive health rights (SRHR) remain complex and contested. Operationalizing these rights in policies and programs is crucial for improving health outcomes [1].

9.6 Safe and Legal Abortion

Safe and legal abortion in India is governed by the Medical Termination of Pregnancy (MTP) Act, enacted in 1971 and amended in 2021 to expand access and ensure women's reproductive rights. Under this law, abortion is permitted up to 20 weeks of gestation under specific conditions, such as risk to the life or physical or mental health of the woman, foetal abnormalities, rape, or contraceptive failure. Beyond 20 weeks, abortion is allowed only if it is necessary to save the woman's life. The MTP Act also mandates that abortions must be performed by registered medical practitioners in approved facilities to ensure safety and minimize risks. Access to safe abortion services is critical in reducing maternal mortality and morbidity from unsafe procedures, which historically posed significant health risks to women. Efforts continue to educate women about their rights and available services while addressing social stigma and barriers that can deter access to safe and legal abortion care across different regions and communities in India. Despite the legalization of abortion in 1971, unsafe abortions continue to pose a significant public health issue. Improved access to safe abortion services is essential to reduce mortality and morbidity among women [1].

9.7 Menstrual Hygiene Management

Menstrual hygiene management (MHM) in India remains a critical public health issue affecting the well-being and dignity of women and girls. Socio-cultural taboos and limited access to affordable menstrual products often lead to inadequate hygiene practices, posing health risks such as infections and discomfort. In recent years, efforts have intensified to promote awareness about menstrual health, debunk myths, and provide access to menstrual products, including sanitary pads and menstrual cups. Government initiatives like the Menstrual Hygiene Scheme aim to distribute subsidized sanitary napkins to schoolgirls and women in rural areas, enhancing their access to menstrual hygiene products. Community-based programs and educational campaigns also play a pivotal role in fostering positive attitudes towards menstruation and encouraging hygienic practices. However, challenges persist, including sanitation infrastructure limitations, economic constraints, and cultural norms that influence menstrual practices. Addressing these challenges requires sustained efforts to ensure comprehensive MHM education, access to affordable and sustainable menstrual products, and supportive policies that prioritize menstrual health as a fundamental aspect of women's well-being in India. Menstrual hygiene management among adolescent girls is a significant concern, with various studies highlighting the challenges faced by girls regarding menstrual hygiene [1]. Comprehensive sex education is crucial for addressing these issues and promoting overall health and well-being among adolescents.

9.8 Gender-Based Violence

Gender-based violence (GBV) remains a pervasive issue in India, affecting women and girls across diverse socio-economic and cultural backgrounds. This form of violence encompasses physical, sexual, emotional, and economic abuse, often rooted in unequal power dynamics and entrenched gender norms [4]. Instances of GBV include domestic violence, sexual harassment, dowry-related violence, and trafficking. Despite legal frameworks and initiatives aimed at prevention and protection, such as the Protection of Women from Domestic Violence Act and the Sexual Harassment of Women at Workplace (Prevention, Prohibition and Redressal) Act, challenges persist in effectively addressing and reducing GBV. Factors contributing to this issue include societal stigma, lack of awareness, inadequate support services, and barriers to seeking legal recourse. Efforts to combat GBV in India involve multi-sectoral approaches that prioritize education, empowerment, legal reforms, and community mobilization to challenge harmful gender stereotypes and ensure the safety, dignity, and rights of all individuals affected by gender-based violence. Domestic violence negatively impacts the health and nutritional status of women, contributing to poor health outcomes. National- and state-level health policies must address domestic violence to improve women's health [1].

9.9 Sexual Violence and Trauma

Gender-based violence (GBV) is another critical issue highlighted by NFHS-4 and NFHS-5, deeply rooted in traditional gender norms. The surveys report that approximately 30% of women have experienced physical violence since the age of 15. GBV not only directly affects women's physical and mental health but also hinders their ability to access healthcare services. Women subjected to violence often face stigma and lack of support, preventing them from seeking necessary medical and psychological care.

Sexual violence and its associated trauma represent significant challenges in India's societal landscape, affecting individuals across age, gender, and socio-economic divides. Instances of sexual violence range from rape and sexual assault to harassment and exploitation, often perpetuated by cultural norms, patriarchal attitudes, and power differentials. Survivors of sexual violence may endure profound psychological and physical trauma, compounded by societal stigma and barriers to seeking justice and support [5]. While legislative measures like amendments to the Criminal Law Act have strengthened penalties for sexual offences and expanded definitions of consent, implementation gaps and social barriers continue to hinder effective redressal and prevention efforts. Addressing sexual violence requires a holistic approach encompassing legal reforms, survivor-centred support services, education on consent and gender equality, and community mobilization to challenge harmful attitudes and promote a culture of respect and safety for all individuals in India. Sexual violence is a significant issue in India, with underreporting due to cultural and societal factors. Intimate partner violence (IPV) during pregnancy has serious reproductive health consequences and is linked to poor mental health outcomes [1, 2].

9.10 Non-Communicable Diseases (NCDs)

Non-communicable diseases (NCDs) pose a growing health challenge in India, affecting individuals across all age groups and socio-economic backgrounds. These diseases, which include cardiovascular diseases, diabetes, cancer, and chronic respiratory conditions, account for a significant proportion of morbidity and mortality in the country. Factors contributing to the rise of NCDs in India include rapid urbanization, lifestyle changes, unhealthy dietary habits, tobacco use, and increasing life expectancy. The burden of NCDs is compounded by limited healthcare infrastructure, disparities in access to diagnosis and treatment, and socio-economic inequalities. Efforts to address NCDs in India involve comprehensive strategies focusing on prevention through health education, promotion of healthy lifestyles, tobacco control measures, early detection through screening programs, and strengthening healthcare systems for effective management and care. By prioritizing NCD prevention and management, India aims to mitigate the impact of these diseases on public health and enhance the overall well-being of its population. NCDs contribute to around 60% of all deaths in India, with cardiovascular diseases, chronic respiratory disease, cancer, and diabetes being major contributors. The National Programme for Prevention and Control of Cancer, Diabetes, Cardiovascular Diseases, and Stroke (NPCDCS) addresses these issues [1].

9.11 Mental Health Concerns

Mental health concerns in India present a significant yet often overlooked public health challenge, affecting individuals across diverse demographics and communities. Factors such as rapid urbanization, socio-economic disparities, cultural stigma, and life stressors contribute to the prevalence of mental health disorders like depression, anxiety, schizophrenia, and substance use disorders. The stigma surrounding mental illness often deters individuals from seeking timely diagnosis and treatment, exacerbating the burden of these conditions [6]. Limited mental health infrastructure and a shortage of trained professionals further impede access to quality care, particularly in rural and underserved areas. Efforts to address mental health concerns in India include advocacy for mental health awareness, de-stigmatization campaigns, integration of mental health services into primary healthcare, and implementation of national mental health policies. By prioritizing mental health as a fundamental aspect of overall well-being, India aims to improve access to care, support affected individuals, and promote a healthier and more inclusive society [7]. Mental health disorders such as depression, anxiety, bipolar disorder, and schizophrenia are prevalent in India. The National Mental Health Program (NMHP) and the Mental Healthcare Act of 2017 aim to improve mental healthcare services and protect the rights of individuals with mental illness [8].

9.12 Gender and Mental Health

Gender plays a crucial role in shaping mental health outcomes in India, influencing both the prevalence of mental health disorders and access to treatment and support. Women and men experience mental health issues differently due to various social, cultural, and biological factors. Women often face higher rates of depression and anxiety, linked to factors such as gender-based violence, unequal power dynamics, and socio-economic disparities [9]. Cultural expectations and roles can limit women's autonomy and contribute to stress and psychological distress [3, 10]. On the other hand, men may experience mental health challenges related to societal pressures of masculinity, which can deter them from seeking help for conditions like depression or substance abuse. Addressing gender disparities in mental health requires targeted interventions that promote gender equity, challenge harmful stereotypes, and ensure equitable access to mental health services. By recognizing and addressing the intersection of gender and mental health, India can foster a more supportive environment that promotes mental well-being for all individuals. Women report higher levels of mental distress compared to men, influenced by factors like roles, responsibilities, and gender inequity. The COVID-19 pandemic exacerbated mental health issues for women globally, highlighting the need for gender-disaggregated data and resources to address mental health needs [1, 2, 11].

9.13 Stigma and Discrimination

The NFHS data reveal pronounced disparities in healthcare access between rural and urban areas, affecting the implementation of gender-sensitive health policies. Women in rural areas face substantial barriers to healthcare, including fewer health facilities, a shortage of healthcare professionals, and inadequate infrastructure. In contrast, urban areas generally offer better healthcare services, but these are often overcrowded and expensive, limiting access for economically disadvantaged women.

Stigma and discrimination remain pervasive issues in India, affecting various aspects of society including health, education, employment, and social interactions [12]. Individuals from marginalized communities such as Dalits, tribal populations, LGBTQ+ individuals, and persons with disabilities often face discrimination based on caste, gender identity, sexual orientation, and physical or mental abilities. Stigma surrounding health conditions such as HIV/AIDS, mental illness, and leprosy further marginalizes affected individuals, leading to social exclusion, reduced access to healthcare, and limited opportunities for economic and personal growth. Efforts to combat stigma and discrimination in India involve legislative measures, awareness campaigns, and advocacy for human rights and social justice. Promoting inclusive policies, fostering empathy and understanding, and challenging discriminatory attitudes are essential steps towards building a more equitable and accepting society where all individuals can live with dignity and access equal opportunities. Stigma and discrimination against people with mental illness create barriers to service utilization and help-seeking. Cultural beliefs and lack of trained professionals contribute to the treatment gap, necessitating further research and interventions to reduce stigma [2, 11].

9.14 Nutrition Challenges

Nutrition challenges in India pose significant obstacles to public health and overall development, impacting individuals across different age groups and socio-economic backgrounds. Malnutrition remains a persistent issue, with high rates of undernutrition, micronutrient deficiencies, and stunting among children under five years old. Poor dietary diversity, inadequate access to nutritious food, and socio-cultural factors contribute to these challenges, particularly in rural and marginalized communities

[13]. Conversely, there is a rising prevalence of overweight and obesity, driven by changing dietary patterns, urbanization, and sedentary lifestyles. Addressing nutrition challenges in India requires a multifaceted approach, including improving food security, promoting breastfeeding practices, enhancing access to fortified foods and micronutrient supplements [14], and advocating for nutrition-sensitive policies across sectors like health, agriculture, and education. By prioritizing nutrition as a fundamental aspect of public health, India aims to improve the well-being and future prospects of its population while striving towards achieving global nutrition goals. India faces a dual burden of undernutrition and overnutrition. Programs like the National Food Security Act aim to address these issues, but challenges remain, especially in reducing anaemia and addressing wasting in children [1, 2].

9.15 Gender Disparities in Nutrition

Gender disparities in nutrition persist as a critical issue in India, significantly affecting the health and well-being of women and girls. Cultural norms, unequal access to resources, and discriminatory practices often result in poorer nutritional outcomes for females compared to males. Women and girls frequently face limited access to nutritious food due to economic constraints, unequal distribution within households, and traditional practices that prioritize male members. This disparity is particularly evident in regions with deep-rooted gender inequities, where women's dietary needs are often neglected, impacting their overall health and productivity. Addressing gender disparities in nutrition requires targeted interventions that empower women economically, promote gender-sensitive policies, enhance access to education and healthcare, and challenge harmful social norms that perpetuate inequalities. By ensuring equitable access to nutritious food and promoting gender equality, India can improve the nutritional status and health outcomes of women and girls, contributing to their overall well-being and empowerment. Gender disparities in nutrition are influenced by inequities, norms, and practices that impact women's access to education, income, and nutrition. Malnutrition among women affects their health, productivity, and the well-being of future generations [1, 2].

9.16 Health Policy and Implementation (National Health Policy of 2017)

The National Health Policy (NHP) of India serves as a comprehensive framework guiding the country's healthcare initiatives and priorities [15]. Updated periodically, the policy outlines strategies to address public health challenges, promote universal healthcare access, and improve health outcomes across diverse demographics. Key pillars of the NHP include enhancing preventive healthcare, strengthening healthcare infrastructure, promoting quality healthcare services, and ensuring equitable access for all citizens. The policy emphasizes the integration of traditional medicine with modern healthcare systems, fostering partnerships with private sectors, and leveraging technology for healthcare delivery. By prioritizing disease prevention, health promotion, and addressing social determinants of health, the NHP aims to achieve universal health coverage and improve the overall health and well-being of India's population, thereby laying the foundation for a healthier and more resilient nation. The National Health Policy emphasizes health research, innovation, and alignment of policies for medical devices and equipment with public health goals. Improving public sector capacity for manufacturing essential drugs and vaccines is also highlighted [1].

9.17 Strengthening Healthcare Access

Strengthening healthcare access in India is a multifaceted endeavour aimed at overcoming barriers to quality healthcare services across the country. India's healthcare landscape is characterized by disparities in infrastructure, healthcare workforce distribution, and affordability, which pose challenges particularly in rural and underserved areas [16, 17]. Efforts to improve access include expanding healthcare infrastructure through the establishment of new facilities and upgrading existing ones, especially in remote regions. Initiatives like the National Health Mission focus on enhancing primary healthcare services, immunization coverage, and maternal and child health outcomes. Telemedicine and digital health platforms are being increasingly leveraged to bridge geographical gaps and improve access to specialist care. Additionally, schemes like Ayushman Bharat aim to provide financial protection to vulnerable populations through health insurance coverage, reducing out-of-pocket expenditures and enhancing affordability [18]. By adopting a holistic approach that integrates preventive, promotive, and curative healthcare services, India strives to ensure equitable access to quality healthcare for all its citizens, thereby improving health outcomes and fostering inclusive development. Efforts to improve healthcare infrastructure, regulatory mechanisms, and quality improvement culture are crucial for enhancing access to healthcare. Programs like infrastructure development, healthcare workforce expansion, and telemedicine aim to increase healthcare access [11].

9.18 Gender Integration in Health Programs

Gender integration in health programs in India is essential for addressing the unique health needs and challenges faced by women and men across the country. Recognizing the impact of gender norms and roles on health outcomes, initiatives are increasingly designed to promote gender equity and inclusivity in healthcare delivery. These efforts involve integrating gender-sensitive approaches into health policies, programs, and services to ensure that they respond effectively to the specific needs of both genders. For instance, maternal and child health programs now emphasize women's empowerment, access to reproductive healthcare, and maternal nutrition. Similarly, men's health programs focus on addressing issues such as tobacco use, mental health, and workplace safety. Strategies include training healthcare providers in gender-responsive care, conducting gender analysis to inform program design, and engaging communities to challenge harmful stereotypes and promote positive gender norms. By mainstreaming gender considerations into health programming, India aims to enhance health outcomes, reduce disparities, and create a more equitable healthcare system that meets the diverse needs of all individuals. The GP M program focuses on integrating gender into health interventions, emphasizing the importance of addressing gender inequality. Scaling up gender-integrated programs remains a challenge, requiring systematic approaches [1, 2].

9.19 Role of NGOs in Community-Based Interventions and Partnerships

Non-governmental organizations (NGOs) play a crucial role in community-based interventions and partnerships across India, particularly in addressing diverse social, health, and environmental challenges. These organizations often fill gaps in government services by implementing targeted programs that cater to specific community needs, such as healthcare access, education, women's empowerment, environmental sustainability, and disaster relief [19]. NGOs leverage local knowledge, cultural sensitivity, and community trust to implement grassroots initiatives that promote sustainable development and social justice. They facilitate partnerships with local governments, businesses, and international organizations to amplify their impact and ensure holistic community development [20]. Through advocacy, capacity building, and direct service delivery, NGOs contribute significantly to improving the quality of life and promoting inclusive growth in India, fostering resilient communities and empowering marginalized populations. NGOs play a critical role in addressing gaps in healthcare provision, focusing on marginalized and vulnerable populations. They partner with the government to provide universal coverage in health and education [1].

9.20 Public-Private Partnerships (PPPs)

Public-Private Partnerships (PPPs) in India are instrumental in addressing public health gender concerns and implementing effective remedies [21] These partnerships bring together the expertise and resources of both government entities and private organizations to tackle complex health issues related to gender disparities. In the realm of public health, PPPs play a crucial role in enhancing healthcare access, improving service delivery, and advancing gender-sensitive health care policies.

They enable the development and implementation of innovative programs that prioritize women's health, maternal care, and reproductive rights. By leveraging the strengths of both sectors, PPPs can bridge gaps in healthcare infrastructure, promote health education, and empower women through community engagement and advocacy. These collaborative efforts not only improve health outcomes but also contribute to sustainable development goals by fostering inclusive healthcare systems that prioritize equity and dignity for all individuals in India. PPPs leverage the strengths of both public and private sectors to improve healthcare access, quality, and efficiency. However, challenges like poor management, lack of human resources, and corruption hinder their success [1, 2].

9.21 Conclusion

In conclusion, addressing gender concerns within India's public health framework is crucial for achieving equitable health outcomes and fostering inclusive development. By recognizing and addressing the unique challenges faced by women, including barriers to healthcare access, maternal mortality risks, and disparities in health literacy, India can strengthen its healthcare systems and promote the well-being of all its citizens. Remedial actions such as gender-sensitive policies, community-based interventions, and initiatives aimed at empowering women and challenging harmful norms are essential steps towards bridging these gaps. Through concerted efforts to integrate gender considerations into public health programs and policies, India can aspire to create a more just and resilient society where everyone, regardless of gender, has equal opportunities to lead healthy and fulfilling lives.

Addressing gender-specific health concerns in India is crucial for achieving health equity and universal health coverage. Gender norms and roles influence health outcomes, making it essential for policymakers to consider gender-sensitive approaches. Continued investment in health research, innovation, and infrastructure is necessary to improve healthcare access and quality. Integrating gender into health programs and strengthening community-based interventions and partnerships will play a vital role in addressing public health challenges in India.

References

1. PCI, India. Addressing gender barriers impacting health and nutrition of women. 2024. https://www.pciglobal.in/addressing-gender-barriers-impacting-health-and-nutrition-of-women/. Accessed on 13 Oct 2024.
2. Sen G, Iyer A, Chattopadhyay S, Khosla R. When accountability meets power: realizing sexual and reproductive health and rights. Int J Equity Health. 2020;19:111.
3. Ministry of Health and Family Welfare, Government of India. Maternal Health Programme. 2024. https://nhm.gov.in/index1.php?lang=1&level=2&sublinkid=822&lid=218. Accessed on 5 Dec 2024.

4. Kumar S, Jeyaseelan L, Suresh S, Ahuja RC. Domestic violence and its mental health correlates in Indian women. Br J Psychiatry. 2005;187(1):62–7. https://doi.org/10.1192/bjp.187.1.62.
5. Bhaumik U. Rape trauma syndrome: a retrospective study of post-traumatic stress disorder after sexual assault among Indian women. ASEAN J Psychiatry. 2022;23(3):1–9. https://www.aseanjournalofpsychiatry.org/articles/rape-trauma-syndrome-a-retrospective-study-of-post-traumatic-stress-disorder-after-sexual-assault-among-indian-women.pdf.
6. Breaking the stigma: addressing mental health in India. Times of India Blog, 2023. https://timesofindia.indiatimes.com/readersblog/myamusings/breaking-the-stigma-addressing-mentalhealth-in-india-49561/. Accessed on 15 Oct 2024.
7. Patel V, Kieling C, Maulik P, Divan G. Improving access to care for children with mental disorders: a global perspective. Arch Dis Child. 2013;98(5) https://doi.org/10.1136/archdischild-2012-302079.
8. Ministry of Health & Family Welfare, Government of India. National Mental Health Programme. https://nhm.gov.in/index1.php?lang=1&level=2&sublinkid=1043&lid=359#:~:text=The%20Government%20of%20India%20has%20launched%20the%20National,to%20stimulate%20efforts%20towards%20selfhelp%20in%20the%20community. Accessed on 12 Nov 2024.
9. National Institute of Mental Health. Women and Mental Health. https://www.nimh.nih.gov/health/topics/women-and-mental-health. Accessed on 29 Nov 2024.
10. Kundal AB. Fundamental health services for women: analysing gender disparities, 2023. https://www.orfonline.org/expert-speak/fundamental-health-services-for-women-analysinggender-disparities. Accessed on 15 Nov 2024.
11. Health Policy Plan. 2017;32(1). Ministry of Health and Family Welfare, Government of India. National Health Policy, 2017. https://mohfw.gov.in/sites/default/files/9147562941489753121.pdf. Accessed on 17 Oct 2024.
12. Barik D, Thorat A. Issues of unequal access to public health in India. Front Public Health. 2015;3(245):1–3. https://mpra.ub.unimuenchen.de/77224/#:~:text=Barik%2C%20Debasis%20and%20Thorat%2C%20Amit%20%282015%29%3A%20Issues%20of,luxury%20and%20only%20the%20rich%20can%20afford%20it
13. Global Nutrition Report | Country Nutrition Profiles – Global Nutrition Report, 2024. https://globalnutritionreport.org/resources/nutrition-profiles/?country-search=India. Accessed on 20 Nov 2024.
14. Gupta N. Malnourishment in Indian women: the hidden crisis. 2022. https://timesofindia.indiatimes.com/blogs/voices/malnourishment-in-indian-women-the-hidden-crisis/. Accessed on 11 Nov 2024.
15. Grover A, Singh RB. Health Policy, programmes and initiatives. Urban Health Wellbeing. 2019;26:251–66. https://doi.org/10.1007/978-981-13-6671-0_8. https://pmc.ncbi.nlm.nih.gov/articles/PMC7122919/.
16. Chawla NS. Unveiling the ABCs: identifying India's healthcare service gaps. Cureus. 2023;15(7):42398. https://doi.org/10.7759/cureus.42398. https://pubmed.ncbi.nlm.nih.gov/37621782/. Accessed on 11 Nov 2024
17. Healthcare access in rural communities in India. Ballard Brief, 2019. https://ballardbrief.byu.edu/issue-briefs/healthcare-access-in-rural-communities-in-india. Accessed on 19 Nov 2024.
18. Akhtar MN, Haleem A, Javaid M. Scope of health care system in rural areas under Medical 4.0 environment. Intell Pharm. 2023;1(4):217–23. https://doi.org/10.1016/j.ipha.2023.07.003.
19. Jayaraman A, Fernandez A. Role of civil society in health care: Mechanisms for realizing universal health coverage in vulnerable communities of India. Front Public Health. 2023:11. https://doi.org/10.3389/fpubh.2023.1091533. https://www.frontiersin.org/journals/public-health/articles/10.3389/fpubh.2023.1091533/full.
20. Asian Development Bank. Civil society brief: India. 2023. https://www.adb.org/sites/default/files/publication/879896/civil-society-brief-india.pdf. Accessed on 20 Oct 2024.
21. Asian Development Bank. Improving health and education service delivery in India through public-private partnerships. 2010. https://www.adb.org/sites/default/files/publication/27495/health-education-delivery-india-ppp.pdf. Accessed on 10 Nov 2024.

Chapter 10
International Environmental Treaties and Public Health in the Context of Global Climate Change Crisis: Challenges and Mitigation

Ram Alagan, Seela Aladuwaka, Sandhu Aladuwaka, Parul Dubey, Shalie Malik, and Manoj Kumar Mishra

10.1 Background

The health of the planet and the health of its inhabitants are intricately intertwined. Environmental degradation can lead to a variety of public health issues, ranging from air and water pollution to biodiversity loss. In response to these challenges, international institutions and governments have developed various environmental treaties aimed at mitigating environmental harm and protecting public health [1–3]. Although there are well over 2000 treaties signed still, environmental deterioration is increasing in many areas [4].

We live in an age of globalization where health epidemics exceed national borders. According to Cain Burdeau (2020) [5], scientists are cautioning that climate change, deforestation, population growth, industrial farming, and globalization are shaping the world into a new era of viruses where those like the novel Coronavirus emerge from unnoticeable breaks of nature. In this global enterprise, the global pandemic breaks all norms, spreading beyond international boundaries. One of the best examples was COVID-19—it killed well over seven million people so far from

R. Alagan · S. Aladuwaka
Department of Advancement Studies and W.E.B. Du Bois Honors Program, Alabama State University, Montgomery, AL, USA

S. Aladuwaka
Department of Political Science (MPA), University of Alabama, Tuscaloosa, AL, USA

P. Dubey · M. K. Mishra (✉)
Cancer Research Center, Department of Biological Sciences, Alabama State University, Montgomery, AL, USA
e-mail: mmishra@alasu.edu

S. Malik
Department of Zoology, University of Lucknow, Lucknow, Uttar Pradesh, India

S. Malik et al. (eds.), *Public Health Issues: Theory and Practices*,
https://doi.org/10.1007/978-981-96-6650-8_10

the outbreak [6]. Still, the global communities are not out of the woods of COVID-19 or another unknown novel global virus. This underscores the challenges for inter-governmental agencies and international organizations to seek solutions to protect their vulnerable populations.

International collaboration around climate change is an instrument for fighting diseases. International environmental treaties are the most important spots of the statute with the potential to advance public health goals [4, 7, 8]. Human-environment interactions have a long history; how we choose to co-exist with it can have immense consequences. Crowe and Fennelly (2013) [9] stated that perhaps it was more straightforward for ancient human beings to appreciate and respect their reliance on the environment. The environment delivered care, and it provided challenges to survival. Based on the given condition, humans depend on, adapt to, and modify the environment. During these interconnections, humans had a huge influence on the environment. However, this dependency on resources from natural systems has intensified beyond healthy co-existence throughout the years, and we are seeing adverse effects today. Although at present there are many international treaties in place, human activities continue to intensify unhealthy living conditions for people, animals, and ecosystems. The current increasing trend in environmental damage in water, land, and air has developed borderless viral infections at an alarming rate around the globe.

The Health and Environmental Interplay Database (HEIDI) prepared and identified 2280 environmental treaties concluded between the eighteenth century and 2017 [4] and those are both multilateral treaties including biological diversity and climate change; the majority are bilateral and regional treaties such as fisheries conservation, freshwater management, oil spill, and nuclear waste. The Database shows that there are more than 300 environmental treaties that have health-related provisions. Schirnding, Onzivu, and Adede (2002) [10] asserted that international environmental laws provide "a viable strategy" to enhance public health by promoting increased awareness of the connection between health and environment, allocating technical and financial resources, promoting research and monitoring, enforcement of health-related standards, and establishing global cooperation. During the last several decades, numerous publications have come out on global environmental treaties and public health from individual scholars to international agencies [11–16]. Bridging environmental treaties and public health is vital in the era of global warming and climate change. Willetts et al. (2022) [17] published a report in Health in the Global Environmental Agenda-Guide that contends the world faces a triple planetary crisis of environmental degradation in the form of biodiversity loss, climate change, and pollution. These environmental crises led to a burden of people lacking access to healthcare, needing enhanced protection from health emergencies, and falling behind the health and well-being metric. The report emphasizes the need to merge both the global environment and health governance, arguing that "sound environmental policymaking can improve and expedite positive health outcomes." It is a comprehensive topic to investigate; we aim to outline a few major international treaties and how they are associated with public health issues. To better comprehend the opportunities and challenges of making the association between treaties and public health, this research aims to outline a framework for climate change as the primary factor between the two.

10.2 Impact of Global Climate Change on Public Health: Significance of International Treaties on Public Health

Although global ecological and climate change transformations have occurred for millions of years, the Industrial Revolution was the turning point where humans contributed to a significant level of environmental modifications and threatened the existence of the planet Earth. Most of the human applications are focused on economic development and financial achievement while lacking proper environmental protection for decades. Modern political discourse on environmental challenges from many parts of the world has contributed to a lack of interest in commitments to address the dire challenges of climate change. Collectively, global communities encounter greater threats to living environments and public health. Thus, recognizing the seriousness of public health and environmental problems from both national to international boundaries is a must.

International environmental treaties are keystone legislations for preserving the planet's natural environment, biodiversity, and public health. Furthermore, international environmental treaties are focused on reducing the environmental impacts of climate change by lowering harmful emissions and lowering the global temperature. International organizations and governments are involved in adopting environmental treaties and collaborations to protect public health from harmful impacts. However, people face greater challenges due to a lack of common agreements to protect the planet. For example, due to the high demand for fossil fuel resources, several major oil-producing nations are facing challenges from major fossil fuel users, many of whom are well-developed nations. Another instance is the destruction of priceless tropical resources in areas like the Amazon Rainforest, and the loss of many established ecosystems. The high demand for tropical forest products (trees, animals, and minerals) is causing a rapid depletion of the environment. The forest loss has created threats to public health as everything is closely interconnected such as food, water, medicine, and shelters.

According to Ritchie (2021) [18], at the end of the last ice age—10,000 years ago—the world had lost one-third of its forests. Forest loss is not just the loss of resources, but the loss of countless natural relationships that support human lives on Earth. Ritchie (2021) [18] also expressed those two billion hectares of forest (an area twice the size of the United States) have been removed to grow crops, raise livestock, and harvest fuelwood. We have inherited serious challenges such as novel global health pandemics, infectious diseases, water scarcity, famine, desertification, soil erosion, increased CO_2, unusual precipitation and floods, and rising sea levels. Since all these negative consequences are affecting people's health and livelihoods, particularly in the developing parts of the world, these impacts lead to forced migration from poor countries to developed countries. These migrators are "climate migrants," a subcategory of environmental migrants. Climate migration is defined as a singular type of environmental migration, where the change in the environment is due to climate change [19]. The migrant population faces unprecedented suffering and enormous health risks including increased illness and death rates due to "the lack of policies needed to make migration a healthy and socially productive process" [20]. In terms of a public health perspective, "it will have "serious ramifications" for the people that move, the family they leave behind, and the communities that host the newcomers."

To comprehend the adverse consequences of human-induced environmental impacts, we have put together a model of six major environmental impacts of global climate change and its impacts on public health (Fig. 10.1).

Along with these six complex climate change issues, we also want to explore another intricate relationship between climate change and tropical cyclones/hurricanes. Whether it is tropical cyclones or Atlantic hurricanes, warming ocean temperatures act as the common factor. As the Earth's climate warms due to increased CO_2 and greenhouse gas emissions, sea surface temperatures rise, providing more energy to fuel tropical cyclones or hurricanes. Tropical cyclones or hurricanes form over relatively warm sea surfaces, which has led to notions that global warming will increase hurricane activity globally [21]. This heightened energy can intensify storm strength, leading to more frequent and severe tropical storms. Climate change also affects other aspects such as atmospheric circulation patterns and moisture availability. Landfall of tropical cyclones or hurricanes is closely associated with external damage including human lives and economic loss. Both affluent and impoverished communities suffer serious casualties and multi-billion dollars of property damage. To illustrate, we generated the top ten hurricanes and their impacts on economic and life loss (Fig. 10.2).

Regardless of economic status, class, race, and gender, economic damage is universal. It highlights our concentration in this research on international environmental treaties and their significant role in mitigating such damage and protecting public health. The most consequential question: to what extent are we as global communities ready to accept these treaties for their applications to protect public health? On a positive note, regardless of the political climate, dedicated scientists continue to investigate these connections to better understand and predict future tropical storm behaviors in a warming world. The advent of international agreements to advance research can help advance these avenues for protection.

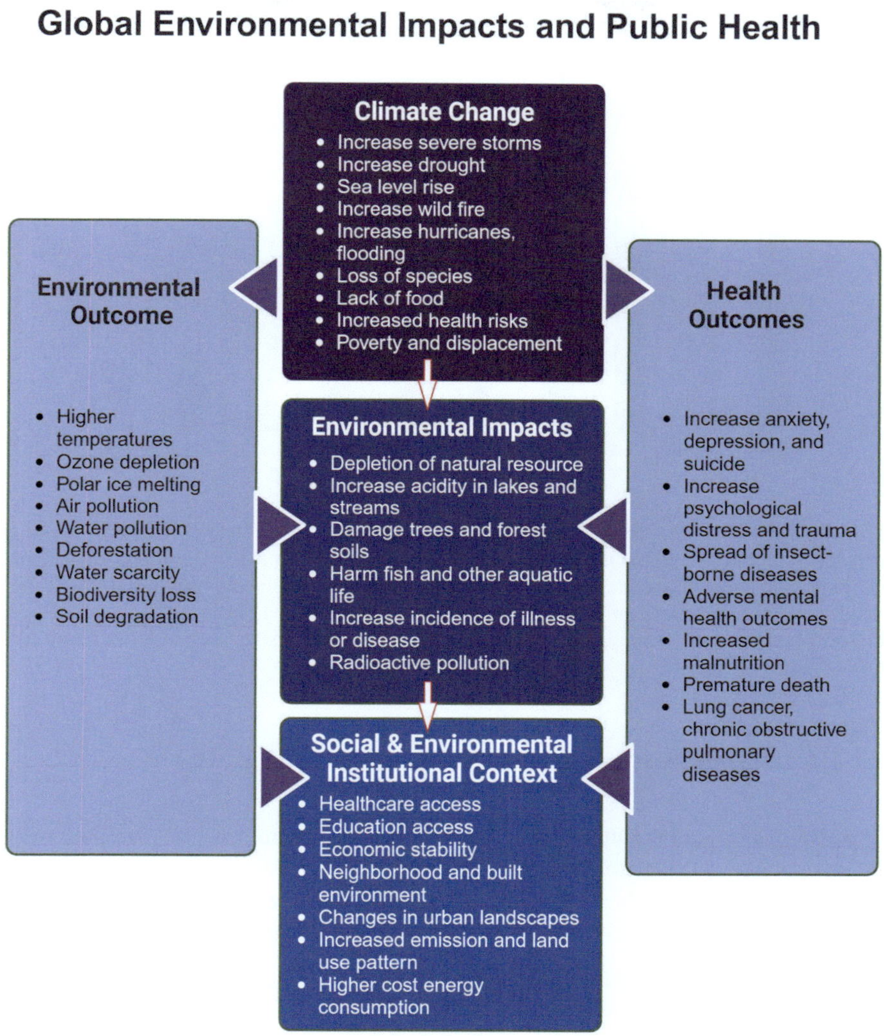

Fig. 10.1 The interconnectivity of global climate change and its impacts on public health. Five major interconnectivities are identified and the extended outcomes of those major connectivities are also outlined. The model strongly recommends that international environmental treaties are a milestone in tackling these complexities of public health. It is also advised that a single government or an agency can't tackle this alone. The more neglect that takes place to mitigate the negative impacts of illegal migration will increase on the national and international scale due to disadvantageous living conditions. (Design of the diagram adapted from U.S. Global Change Research Program, 2016)

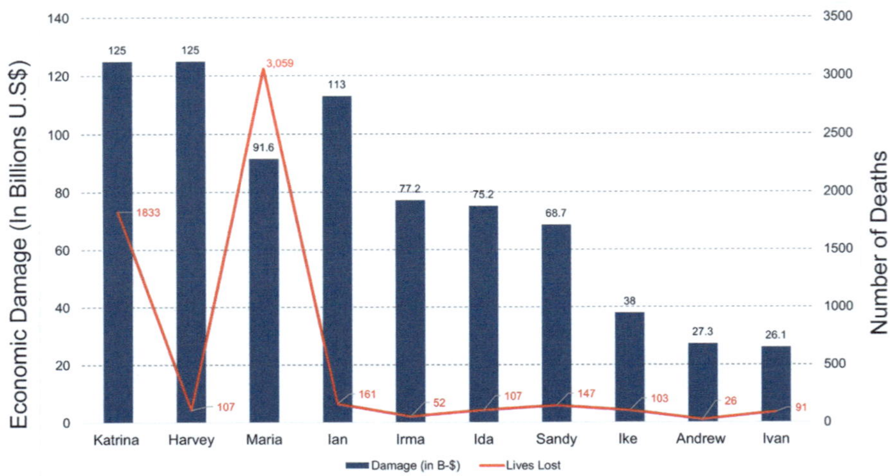

Fig. 10.2 The world's top ten hurricanes and damage. Deaths (on the right excess) and economic damage in billion dollars (on the left excess). The research aims to provide this data to elaborate on the significance of natural disasters due to climate change and the unprecedented losses. The trend of such hurricanes continues each year, with the causes of these storms only worsening. Policy formulation around mitigating climate change is an urgent goal to prevent future trends like this. (Source: [22–30])

10.2.1 Hypothesis

Implementation and commitment to international environmental treaties positively impact public health outcomes by mitigating climate change impacts and promoting sustainable practices, thereby leading to improved overall well-being of public health and decreased rates of environmentally induced diseases.

10.2.2 Methodology

The methodology for this research involved several steps. First, we conducted a thorough literature assessment to identify existing studies and gaps in research. Second, we executed data collection from diverse published sources on global environmental impact issues and public health to understand their relationships to environmental treaties. Third, we used quantitative data analysis of environmental and health data from a timeline of 1990 to 2020. Fourth, we prioritized the top vulnerable nations (top 10 and top 20) due to severe human influence on the climate to comprehend the significance of environmental treaties. Finally, we aimed to synthesize findings that allow for recommendations to strengthen future treaty effectiveness in promoting public health.

10.3 Discussion

10.3.1 The Intersection of Environmental Treaties, Public Health, Climate Change

Environmental degradation poses significant risks to public health on a global scale. The associations between the environment and public health have been vastly studied. Environmental threats have been proven to have a major impact on human health [31]. Due to various reasons, it is hard to estimate the correct mortalities and diseases created by environmental damage. However, the World Health Organization (2009) [32] has estimated that 13 million deaths annually are attributable to preventable environmental causes. The World Health Organization (2009) [32] also estimates that 24% of the global disease burden and 23% of all premature mortalities are attributable to environmental factors. Developing countries are 15 times more vulnerable to these damages than developed countries, due to differences in exposure to environmental threats and access to health care.

The impact of climate change on human health is significant (USGCRP, 2016) [33]. The US Global Change Research Program explains that exposure to health hazards related to climate change affects different people and communities on different scales. When often assessed individually, exposure to multiple climate change threats can occur simultaneously and it creates surging health impacts. The impacts of climate change include increasing temperatures, changing precipitation, extreme weather patterns, and rising sea levels. These impacts threaten human health by stifling food production, air quality, and water resources. The United States Environmental Protection Agency (2016) [34] pointed out that the severity of these health risks will depend on the ability of health departments public and safety systems to address or prepare for these changing threats, as well as factors such as an individual's behavior, age, gender, and economic status. Furthermore, "climate change multiplies risks and existing health problems; potential health effects depend largely on population vulnerability such as elderly and people with particular disease and deprived population" [35].

Environmental pollution from industrial activities, deforestation, and the burning of fossil fuels contributes to respiratory diseases, cardiovascular problems, and various other health issues. Climate change exacerbates these problems by altering ecosystems, increasing the frequency and severity of natural disasters, and facilitating the spread of infectious diseases. Recognizing the urgent need to address these challenges, countries and international organizations around the world have come together to intervene and execute international environmental treaties. These agreements aim to reduce greenhouse gas emissions [36, 37], commit industrialized countries and economies in transition to limit and reduce greenhouse gasses [38], promote sustainable development [39], and the landmark multilateral environmental agreement that regulates the production and consumption of nearly 100 man-made chemicals referred to as ozone-depleting substances [40]. The Montreal Protocol, finalized in 1987, was known as innovative and successful [41]. It was a global agreement to protect the stratospheric ozone layer by phasing out the production and consumption of ozone-depleting substances (ODS) such as refrigerators, air conditioners, fire extinguishers, and aerosols. The unique aspect of the Montreal Protocol was that "it is the first treaty to achieve universal ratification by all countries in the world." The Environmental Protection Agency (EPA) [12], "estimates that Americans born between 1890 and 2100 are expected to avoid 443 million cases of skin cancer, approximately 2.3 million skin cancer deaths, and more than 63 million cases of cataracts, with even greater benefits worldwide" [41]. Although several of these treaties do not speak word-for-word about public health as a central concern, they all hold direct and indirect implications for public health, knowing how connected the environment is to human health and well-being.

10.3.2 The Paris Agreement vs Public Health: Special Focus on CO_2 and Lung Cancer

The Paris Agreement was adopted on December 12, 2015, by 196 parties within the UN Climate Change Conference (COP21), going into effect on November 4, 2016. It is one of the largest and most impactful environmental treaties in the entire world. The treaty's goal is to reduce greenhouse gas emissions across the world to get the global temperature increase below 2 °C above pre-industrial levels and eventually get to 1.5 °C [42].

The Paris Agreement requires countries to develop nationally determined contributions (NDCs) every five years from 2020 to strategize how they'd respectively tackle climate change in the areas of finance, technology, and capacity-building. Recent discussions within the Paris Agreement at COP28 in 2023 led to governments agreeing to speed up the development of wind and solar power towards 2030 to transition away from fossil fuels [42]. The agreement helps fund nations on their path to decarbonization and ideally zero-carbon industries, with many countries hoping to turn carbon neutral by 2050 [42].

Unlike the Kyoto Protocol (1997) [38] which focused mainly on developed nations only, the Paris Agreement (2015) [36] includes commitments from both developed and developing countries, reflecting a more inclusive and equitable approach to addressing climate change. This goal is crucial for safeguarding properties and public health on multiple fronts. By promoting the transition to renewable energy sources and encouraging sustainable land use practices, the Paris Agreement not only helps mitigate climate change but also improves air quality and reduces the prevalence of respiratory diseases associated with pollution from fossil fuels.

Campell-Lendrum (2018) [43], the WHO Lead on Climate Change and Health, argues that the Paris Agreement is a "fundamental public health agreement, potentially the most important public health agreement of the century." Campell-Lendrum warns that without tackling climate change, we "undermine" the world's water supplies, air, and food security—and the Paris Agreement is a unique opportunity to help solve global warming and health, [42]. Specifically, the Paris Agreement's decarbonization efforts pave the road for reducing air pollution. A recent assessment during the COP24 predicted that meeting the Paris Agreement's targets for reducing air pollution would save over 1 million lives a year by 2050 [44]. To illustrate, a *Lancelet Planet Health* study using GCAM predicted that the health net benefits that would follow from a reduction in emissions by 2050 would mitigate the costs of innovation for decarbonization [45].

Air pollution as identified is one of the top culprits for human life mortality from respiratory disease and toxins. According to WHO/UNEP Health and Environment Linkage Initiative (2004) [46] every day, nearly 1800 people in developing cities die of urban air pollution. The data also underlines that every month, nearly 19,000 people in developing countries die from unintended poisonings. To illustrate such disastrous health challenges, we employed a prioritization strategy to select the top ten CO_2 production nations in the globe to highlight their contribution to global climate change regarding air pollution and CO_2 production (Fig. 10.3).

The Paris Agreement's goal is to decrease greenhouse gas emissions across the globe and reduce global temperature. Carbon dioxide (CO_2), one of the most prevalent greenhouse gases, has become a considerable threat to human health. It alters atmospheric composition, affecting air quality and endangering human populations. Elevated CO_2 levels aggravate respiratory and cardiovascular diseases, intensifying smog formation, increasing the temperature of the Earth's surface, and impairing visibility. Moreover, CO_2 interacts with other pollutants, amplifying their adverse effects on the environment and ecosystems. Addressing CO_2 emissions is crucial in mitigating air pollution's wide-ranging impacts, from urban areas to remote regions, safeguarding both current and future generations from the detrimental consequences of degraded air quality.

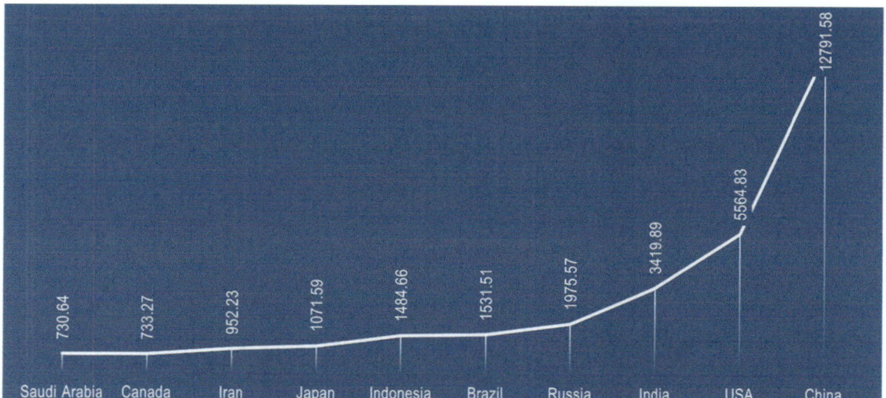

Fig. 10.3 The top ten CO_2 production (in Metric Tons) nations for 2020 to 2022. Carbon dioxide (CO_2) has been identified as one of the top factors for atmospheric pollution and global climate change [47]. It is noted that the top six nations that produce CO_2 from this diagram are also the leading global population nations

Climate change-induced air pollution causes numerous health problems. The EPA indicates that "climate-driven changes in weather conditions, including temperature and precipitation, are expected to increase ground-level ozone and particulate matter (such as windblown dust from droughts or smoke from wildfires). These changes aggravate existing air pollution," [48]. Air pollution profoundly impacts health by exacerbating respiratory and cardiovascular diseases [31, 49–54]. Although many toxins have adverse consequences on public health, pollutants with the strongest evidence for public health concern include particulate matter (PM), carbon monoxide (CO), ozone (O3), nitrogen dioxide (NO2), and sulfur dioxide (SO2) [55]. Fine particulate matter is an especially prevalent source of health risks, as these very small particles can penetrate deep into the lungs, leading to respiratory infections, asthma, bronchitis, and eventually reduced lung function [55].

Pollutants induce inflammation, oxidative stress, and systemic effects, affecting vulnerable populations like children, the elderly, and those with pre-existing conditions [56, 57]. Urban areas, industrial zones, and dump yards with toxic materials could create amplified risks, but even rural regions can experience pollution drift because of landfills. Studies underscore that poor economic regions, politically underrepresented neighborhoods, and disempowered minority-populated locations are more vulnerable to such health disparities [58–61]. According to the US Census Bureau American Community Survey (2009–2020) [62], 24 million US residents live in impoverished, disadvantaged neighborhoods. These are neighborhoods in which one-fifth of all community members live below the federal poverty line [63]. Around the world, millions of people reside in the same circumstances simply because they were born in a poor background without adequate financial support and political will. It is vital to recognize proper mitigatory measures to regulate benchmarks such as the reduction of toxic materials, cleaner energy adoption, and public health strategies to minimize exposure to toxins. The vulnerability of populations to these effects underscores the need for international and national environmental treaties that tackle complex health challenges. Safeguarding populations worldwide from the adverse impacts of air pollution can improve the quality of life and life expectancy for millions.

Figure 10.4 explains the top ten populated countries' lung cancer status in 2022. The data also demonstrates there is a close relationship between nations that produce large amounts of CO_2 emissions (Fig. 10.3) and face greater challenges in lung cancer epidemics such as China, the USA, Russia, and Brazil. Nations such as China, the USA, and Japan are major economies in the world, but there is another confounding variable.

The reason these larger nations are leading in lung cancer is that one of the most consequential factors to lung cancer is tobacco smoke exposure. China has the largest smoking population in the world, with around 316 million adult smokers, and accounts for nearly one-third (30%) of smokers and 40% of tobacco consumption worldwide [65]. Despite this, it is also the fact that these top ten populated nations are industrially major players and large producers of CO_2. Another major point of discussion stemming in recent years about environmental conservation and global climate change dialogues has been politically motivated and disregards the imminent threat of climate change across the world. Still, many people and global

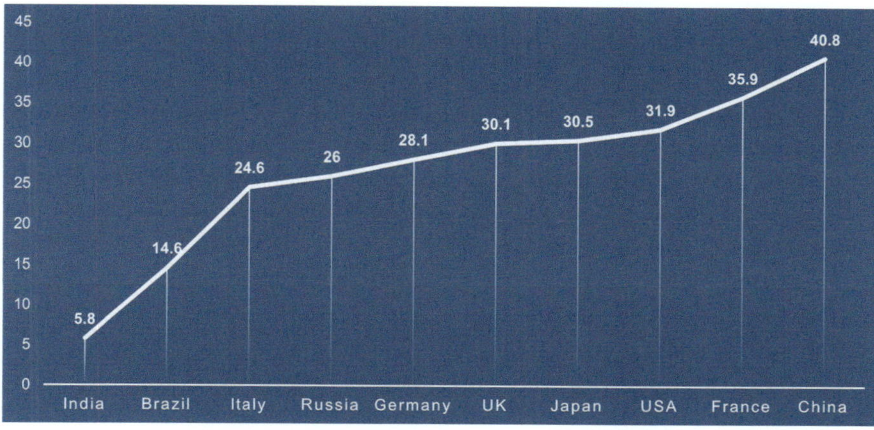

Fig. 10.4 Total global lung cancer incidence rate (%) for the top ten populated nations and rates in 2022. According to World Cancer Research Fund International (2022) [64], Hungary had the highest overall rate of lung cancer in 2022, followed by New Caledonia. We employed the prioritized method to highlight how the most populated and influential nations contribute to global environmental protection and saving public health

political figures believe there is no truth in it. According to Funk and Kennedy (2016) [66], there is a wide political division in views of the potential for devastation to the Earth's ecosystems and what might be done to address any climate impacts.

The toxic political discourse around climate change has created a polarized environment online. Political partisans interpret the current scientific findings on climate change with a lack of trust in the information they get from professional researchers; it ends up creating different views on climate science, turning scientific fact into a political discussion point instead [66], the United States of America, China, Germany, Japan, and India are the most powerful economies in the world. They are also leading in CO_2 emissions and environmental damage. Yet even the United States briefly exited the Paris Climate Agreement in 2020 until reinstated in 2021 [67]. If one of the major players fails to take the leadership to bridge the trust in scientific findings due to short-term political gain and fossil fuel cooperation interests, it will be a major challenge for international scientific communities to convey what is right and wrong in environmental policies.

10.3.3 Climate Change, Public Health, and Lower-Income Nations: Special Focus on Malaria Outbreaks

The environmental factors are mostly responsible for health problems in developing nations, specifically among poor and vulnerable groups due to the risk of exposure to environmental hazards linked to poverty, industrialization, and increasing urbanization [10, 68, 69]. The Paris Agreement conveys this urgency. A

2021 study published in the medical journal *The Lancet* investigated how many nations mentioned health engagement in their Paris Agreement NDCs [70]. The study found affluent nations were less likely to mention health engagement than low- and middle-income nations; the journal also concluded that countries that are more affected by climate change engaged with health in their NDCs more as well [71]. The damages from climate change may be far more dire in these less affluent nations, while larger nations may not have that urgent of a clock due to their resources and resiliency. However, there are international resources already in place that prioritize poorer nations. The Green Climate Fund (GCF) [72] exists as the "world's largest climate fund" to help developing nations strategize and invest in green technology. Policy institutions like the GCF created from international treaties are essential for lower-income nations that may lack the infrastructural defense against climate change's health risks, and there is always room for more protections like the GCF.

Environmental treaties, at their core, seek a safer and better world to live in their objectives and missions—and public health ultimately benefits from that fight. Global climate change reduction treaties are interconnected with public health, especially in vulnerable populations of women, children, the elderly, and minority ethnicities. The Paris Agreement exclusively articulated about reducing greenhouse gas emissions across the world to get the global temperature under control. Regardless of the partisan divide on climate change, it is a real and systemic global threat to public health, the natural environment, and biodiversity. In other words, climate change poses a profound global health emergency, especially for underdeveloped nations. These regions experience exacerbated weather events and health-related issues such as weak health infrastructure, tropical storms, water scarcity and contamination; desertification, food insecurity; undernutrition, malaria, diarrhea, and heat stress outbreaks. The World Health Organization (2023) [73] states that these climate threats influence health both directly and indirectly, increasing the risk of deaths, non-communicable infections, the emergence and spread of infectious diseases, and health emergencies. In many parts of the underdeveloped world, rising temperatures and changing precipitation patterns have already disrupted agriculture production and migration patterns, worsening maternal health and child nutrition. The fallout of these health crises leads to regional economic instability and political instability. In addition, the increasing floods and droughts increase waterborne diseases such as malaria and cholera in many parts of the underdeveloped world, particularly in the African Continent. Fig. 10.5 displays the top 25 nations with malaria disease deaths in the world. Out of the top 25, 24 of the nations are from the African continent conveying how fragile poorer nations' infrastructures are against climate change and waterborne infections. To compare the malaria outbreak with economically poor nations, we compiled data for the top 25 poor nations.

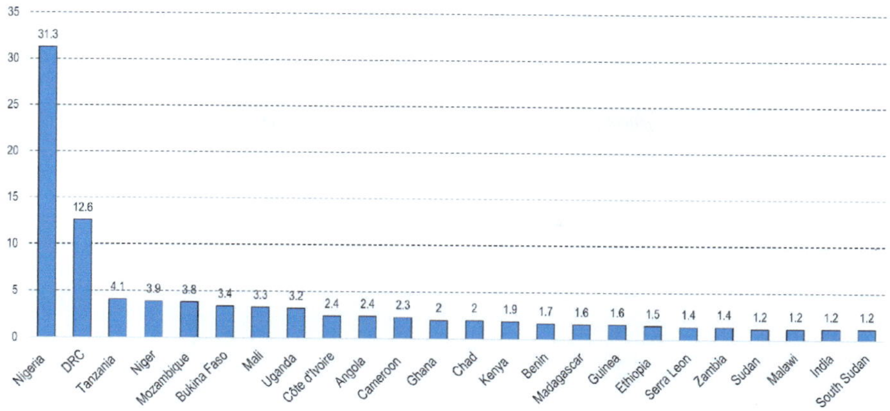

Fig. 10.5 The top 25 nations' deaths by Malaria infection. The WHO Data (2022) [74] displays the total deaths in percentage. Except for India in the 24th lowest range, every other 24 countries are located in the African Continent—which recaps the challenges for these poor nations to overcome public health outbreaks as they are not in a position to encounter these challenges due to the poor economy, infrastructure, and lack of scientific expertise. (Source: WHO (2022))

10.3.4 Climate Change, Public Health, and Lower-Income Nations: Special Focus on Cholera Outbreaks

Vector-borne infections like cholera are another public health issue that impacts less affluent nations globally. Africa in particular faces recurrent cholera outbreaks due to inadequate water, sanitation, and hygiene infrastructure in many regions [75]. Cholera thrives in areas with poor access to clean water and sanitation facilities, leading to contaminated drinking water and food sources. In many parts of Africa, cholera outbreaks have become common due to a lack of infrastructure facilities, weak health systems, urban slums, political instability, and a lack of environmental policies. The World Health Organization (2023) [75] also remarks that political conflicts, unplanned urbanization, and climate change all increase the risk of cholera. The current ongoing global climate and political conflicts could worsen the cholera outbreaks, especially in Africa, contributing to high mortality rates among affected populations. Altogether, the health epidemics and social/political instability issues worsened the illegal migration trend in and out of Africa. The research compiled the top 25 countries that are facing cholera outbreaks globally (Fig. 10.6). World Health Organization (2023) data displays that out of 25, 17 nations are from the continent of Africa.

These cumulative effects disproportionately affect marginalized populations in Africa more than any part of the world and exacerbate social and health disparities. On the one hand, it is very unfortunate that impoverished populations go through such a remarkable health crisis when the damage largely comes from major producers of contaminant substances and CO_2 emissions—mostly developed countries. However, major developed nations also hold the largest positive leverage in global

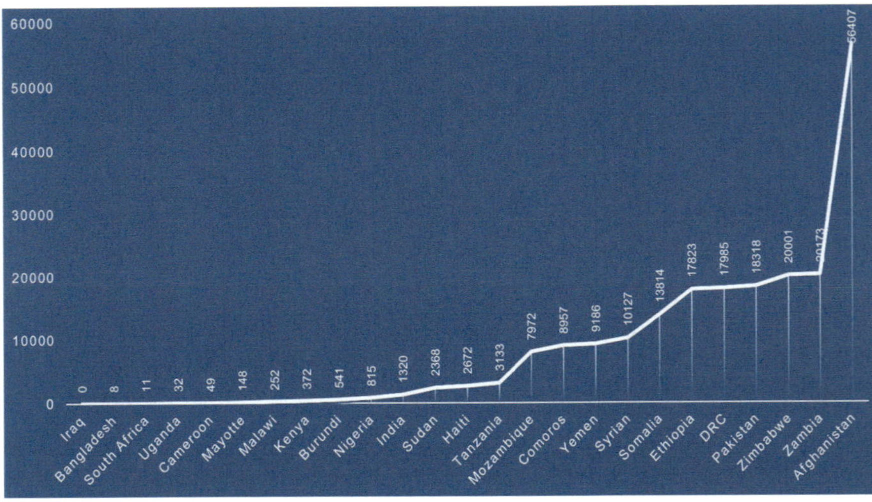

Fig. 10.6 Globally the top 25 nations' cholera outbreaks. Out of the 25 nations, 17 are situated in the African continent [75]. Afghanistan also has higher cases of cholera infections due to various reasons such as long years of conflict and displaced people living in crowded camps that have poor sanitation and hygiene [76]. Unfortunately, these camps may provide a significant outbreak of threat for disease transmission to the general population

economic, environmental, and development determinations. Addressing climate change and public health is not an easy undertaking for the majority of underdeveloped nations. Instead, tackling global health emergencies requires coordinated efforts from global economies to reduce greenhouse gas emissions, adapt infrastructure and health systems, and enhance resilience in vulnerable communities. International cooperation is paramount to provide technological and financial support for mitigation strategies. Prioritizing equity ensures that underdeveloped nations receive the necessary assistance to mitigate and manage the health impacts of climate change, promoting global health security and sustainable development.

10.4 Challenges and Future Directions

International environmental treaties and agreements play a pivotal role in addressing global challenges, both for the health of the planet and its people. We have invaluable opportunities to address decades of damage through treaties like the Paris Agreement, along with contemporaries like the Kyoto Protocol, Montreal Protocol, and many others. Moreover, international environmental treaties aim to promote collaborative efforts among nations to set standards, share knowledge, and implement policies that safeguard ecosystems and improve public well-being.

However, these treaties face significant challenges. Issues like inadequate enforcement mechanisms, insufficient funding, corporate greed, lack of political leadership, and disparities in commitment among nations hinder their effectiveness. Geopolitical tensions and differing priorities also pose further obstacles to achieving consensus and meaningful action on critical environmental and safety of public health issues.

The United Nations Framework Convention on Climate Change Report (2017) [77] underscores that global communities should set strong mandates for a transition to low-carbon, climate-resilient societies. It also implores countries to work towards common goals while focusing on national and international opportunities, and challenges regarding public health. Looking ahead, future directions for international environmental treaties involve enhancing monitoring frameworks, integrating health considerations more explicitly into ecological policies, and fostering innovation in sustainable development practices. Addressing emerging challenges, such as the intersection of environmental degradation and public health, will require continued global cooperation and a breadth of policies to ensure a resilient and healthy future for all. Finally, to achieve sustainable environmental treaties and protect the planet's health, targeted changes need to be adopted in political, social, and economic systems around the world.

10.5 Conclusion

This chapter explored the complex relationship between international environmental treaties, climate change, and public health. International environmental treaties are the keystone to safeguarding the public and the planet's health. Exploring the intersection between these three areas is paramount in the contemporary geopolitical climate. By investigating the diverse literature and empirical research, this research highlighted the direct and indirect impacts on environmental degradation of public health, including the production of CO_2, respiratory disease, exposure to toxic substances, waterborne illnesses, and the exacerbation of climate-related health threats (Fig. 10.7).

Environmental degradation can lead to a myriad of public health issues, which only continue to grow worse over time. However, successful collaboration on treaties has demonstrated that there is still hope for systematic change. International treaties can protect nations with the direction and actionability to transition to a greener future. Despite facing many challenges such as enforcement issues, geopolitical tensions, and public trust, these treaties and agreements remain essential for fostering cooperation, setting standards, and promoting sustainable development practices. Looking forward, enhancing monitoring mechanisms and integrating health considerations more robustly into environmental policies are crucial steps. By addressing these challenges and adapting to emerging issues, international treaties can continue to be effective tools in safeguarding our environment and improving the well-being of populations worldwide. When our well-being is tied to the health of the planet, we must put aside our differences to protect it. We do not have another Earth to depend on.

Fig. 10.7 An overview of international environmental treaties, challenges, threats, comprehensive preventive measures, and programs. The figure summarizes the challenges, missions, and preventive measures that need to be considered to mitigate environmental threats and protect biodiversity and public health [78]

References

1. North Atlantic Treaty Organization. Environment, climate change, and security. 2024.; Available from: https://www.nato.int/cps/en/natohq/topics_91048.htm
2. Bozorgmehr K. Rethinking the 'global' in global health: a dialectic approach. Glob Health. 2010;6:1–19.
3. Dry S. Epidemics for all? Governing health in a global age. STEPS working paper 9. 2008, STEPS Centre.
4. Morin JF, Blouin C. How environmental treaties contribute to global health governance. Glob Health. 2019;15(1):47.
5. Cain B. Scientists expect more pandemics in age of globalization, climate Change & Assault on Nature 2020.; Available from: https://www.courthousenews.com/scientists-expect-more-pandemics-in-age-of-globalization-climate-change-assault-on-nature/
6. Coronavirus Death Toll. 2024.; Available from: https://www.worldometers.info/coronavirus/coronavirus-death-toll/
7. Szlezak NA, et al. The global health system: actors, norms, and expectations in transition. PLoS Med. 2010;7(1):e1000183.
8. Holzscheiter A, Bahr T, Pantzerhielm L. Emerging governance architectures in global health: Do metagovernance norms explain inter-organisational convergence? Politics and Gov. 2016;4(3):5.
9. Crowe TD, Fennelly LJ. Using the environment to affect behavior, crime prevention through environmental design. 3rd ed. Butterworth-Heinemann; 2013. p. 71–88.
10. von Schirnding Y, Onzivu W, Adede AO. International environmental law and global public health. Bull World Health Organ. 2002;80(12):970–4.
11. Environmental agreements environmental effectiveness, European Environment Agency, Copenhagen, Denmark. 1997.; Available from: https://www.eea.europa.eu/publications/92-9167-052-9/page002.html

12. EPA (United States Environmental Protection Agency), EPA's 33/50 Program, Sixth Progress Update: Continuing Progress Toward Ultimate Reduction Goal, EPA 745-K-95-001. 1995.
13. Gostin LO, Mok EA. Grand challenges in global health governance. Br Med Bull. 2009;90:7–18.
14. Fidler D. The Challenges of Global Health Governance. 2010. International Institutions and Global Governance Program, the Council on Foreign Relations Inc. Available from: https://www.cfr.org/report/challenges-global-health-governance
15. Frenk J, Moon S. Governance challenges in global health. N Engl J Med. 2013;368(10):936–42.
16. Hill PS. Understanding global health governance as a complex adaptive system. Glob Public Health. 2011;6(6):593–605.
17. Willetts E, Grant L, Bansard J, Kohler PM, Rosen T, Bettelli P, Schröder M. Health in the global environmental agenda: a policy guide. International Institute for Sustainable Development. 2022. Available from: https://www.iisd.org/publications/health-global-environment-agenda-policy-guide
18. Ritchie H. The world has lost one-third of its forest, but an end of deforestation is possible. 2021.; Available from: https://ourworldindata.org/world-lost-one-third-forests
19. The International Organizationfor Migration (IOM), Migration, Environment and Climate Change (MECC) Division. 2024.; Available from: https://environmentalmigration.iom.int/environmental-migration
20. Carballo M, Nerukar A. Migration, refugees, and health risks. Emerg Infect Dis. 2001;7(3 Suppl):556–60.
21. Knutson T. Global warming and hurricanes: an overview of current research results, NOAA/GFDL. 2024.; Available from: https://www.gfdl.noaa.gov/global-warming-and-hurricanes/
22. Santana R, Deslatte M, and McConaughey J. After Ida, small recovery signs amid daunting destruction. 2021.; Available from: https://apnews.com/article/business-environment-and-nature-louisiana-392d8001a9c69df607d9a7b5b84474fa
23. Blake ES, Landsea CW, Gibney EJ. The Deadliest, Costliest, and Most Intense United States Tropical Cyclones from 1851 to 2010, National Hurricane Center, (NOAA Technical Memorandum NWS NHC-6). 2011; Available from: https://www.nhc.noaa.gov/pdf/nws-nhc-6.pdf Archived.
24. Blake ES, Kimberlain TB, Berg RJ, Cangialosi JP, Beven II JL. Hurricane Sandy: October 22–29, 2012, Tropical Cyclone Report. 2013, United States National Hurricane Center.
25. Blake ES, Zelinsky DA. Tropical cyclone report: hurricane Harvey: august 17—September 1, 2017. National Hurricane Center; 2018.
26. Knabb RD, Rhome JR, and Brown DP. Hurricane Katrina: August 23–30, 2005 Tropical Cyclone Report 2005.
27. Brown DP, Beven JL, Franklin JL, et al. Atlantic hurricane season of 2008. Mon Weather Rev. 2010;138(5):1975–2001.
28. Rappaport Ed. Hurricane Andrew, preliminary report. 1993.; Available from: https://www.nhc.noaa.gov/1992andrew.html
29. Hurricane Committee. Twenty-seventh session, final report. World Meteorological Organization; 2005.
30. Stewart SR. Hurricane Ivan September 2–24, 2004. United States NAtional Oceanic and Atmospheric Administration's NAtional Weather Service 2004.
31. Remoundou K, Koundouri P. Environmental effects on public health: an economic perspective. Int J Environ Res Public Health. 2009;6(8):2160–78.
32. World Health Organization, Public Health and Environment 2009.; Available from: https://www.who.int/data/gho/data/themes/public-health-and-environment
33. Crimmins A, et al. The impacts of climate change on human health in the United States: a scientific assessment. The impacts of climate change on human health in the United States: A Scientific Assessment, 2016.
34. The United States Environmental Protection Agency, climate impacts on human health 2016.; Available from: https://climatechange.chicago.gov/climate-impacts/climate-impacts-human-health

35. The European environment state and outlook 2010-chapter 5: environment, health and quality of life. 2010, Copenhegan: The European Environment Agency.
36. Paris Agreement 2015. United Nations framework convention on climate change (UNFCCC). URL: https://unfccc.int/sites/default/files/resource/parisagreement_publication.pdf
37. Convention on Biological Diversity. Secretariat of the convention on biological diversity. United Nations Environment Program; 1992.
38. Kyoto Protocol to The United Nations Framework Convention On Climate Change, United Nations. 1997.
39. Earth Summit, Rio de Janerio, Brazil. The Rio Conventions, The Interconnected Challenges of Climate Change, Desertification and Biodiversity Loss. 1992.; Available from: https://unfccc.int/process-and-meetings/the-rio-conventions
40. Montreal Protocol. About Montreal Protocol. 1989. UN Environment Programme, Environmental Rights and Governance. Available from: https://www.unep.org/ozonaction/who-we-are/about-montreal-protocol
41. The U.S. Department of State, The Montreal Protocol on substances that deplete the ozone layer. 1988.; Available from: https://www.state.gov/key-topics-office-of-environmental-quality-and-transboundary-issues/the-montreal-protocol-on-substances-that-deplete-the-ozone-layer/
42. UNFCCC, The Paris Agreement is a Health Agreement – WHO. United NAtions Cliamte Change. 2018; Available from: https://unfccc.int/news/the-paris-agreement-is-a-health-agreement-who
43. Campell-Lendrum. Climate Action Studio SB48: WHO, Climate Change and Health. 2018.
44. World Health Organization. COP24 special report: health and climate change, (WHO). 2023; Available from: https://www.who.int/publications/i/item/cop24-special-report-health-climate-change
45. Markandya A, et al. Health co-benefits from air pollution and mitigation costs of the Paris Agreement: a modelling study. Lancet Planetary Health. 2018;2(3):e126–33.
46. World Health Organization Health and environment: tools for effective decision-making: review of initial findings/the WHO-UNEP Health and Environment Linkages Initiative (HELI). World Health Organization. 2004. https://iris.who.int/handle/10665/43177.
47. Climate Watch. Historical GHG emissions, human-caused greenhouse gas (GHG) emissions drive climate change. 2021.; Available from: https://www.climatewatchdata.org/ghg-emissions?end_year=2021&start_year=1990
48. The United States Environmental Protection Agency, Climate change impacts on air quality. 2024.; Available from: https://www.epa.gov/climateimpacts/climate-change-impacts-air-quality.
49. World Health Organization. Preventing disease through healthy environments: a global assessment of the burden of disease from environmental risks. 2018; Available from: http://www.who.int/quantifying_ehimpacts/publications/preventingdisease/en/index.html
50. Pearce D. Economic valuation and health damage from air pollution in the developing world. Energy Policy. 1996;24(7):627–30.
51. Liu Q, et al. The influence of air pollution on happiness and willingness to pay for clean air in the Bohai Rim area of China. Int J Environ Res Public Health. 2022;19(9)
52. Wang H, Mullahy J. Willingness to pay for reducing fatal risk by improving air quality: a contingent valuation study in Chongqing. China Sci Total Environ. 2006;367(1):50–7.
53. Alberini A, et al. Valuing health effects of air pollution in developing countries: the case of Taiwan. J Environ Econ Manag. 1997;34(2):107–26.
54. Pervin T, Gerdtham UG, Lyttkens CH. Societal costs of air pollution-related health hazards: a review of methods and results. Cost Eff Resour Alloc. 2008;6:19.
55. World Health Organization. Air quality, energy, and health 2024; Available from: https://www.who.int/teams/environment-climate-change-and-health/air-quality-and-health/health-impacts/types-of-pollutants

56. Milani C, et al. Systemic exposure to air pollution induces oxidative stress and inflammation in mouse brain, contributing to neurodegeneration onset. Int J Mol Sci. 2020;21(10)
57. Becaria A, et al. Aluminum and copper in drinking water enhance inflammatory or oxidative events specifically in the brain. J Neuroimmunol. 2006;176(1–2):16–23.
58. Christie-Mizell CA. Neighborhood disadvantage and poor health: The consequences of race, gender, and age among young adults. Int J Environ Res Public Health. 2022;19(13)
59. Rodrigues DE, et al. Exploring neighborhood socioeconomic disparity in self-rated health: a multiple mediation analysis. Prev Med. 2021;145:106443.
60. Ross CE, Mirowsky J. Neighborhood disadvantage, disorder, and health. J Health Soc Behav. 2001;42(3):258–76.
61. Cohen DA, et al. Neighborhood physical conditions and health. Am J Public Health. 2003;93(3):467–71.
62. U.S. Census Bureau American Community Survey 5-Year Data 2009–2020. 2022.
63. Firebaugh G, Acciai F. For blacks in America, the gap in neighborhood poverty has declined faster than segregation. Proc Natl Acad Sci USA. 2016;113(47):13372–7.
64. World Cancer Research Fund International, Lung cancer statistics. 2022.; Available from: https://www.wcrf.org/cancer-trends/lung-cancer-statistics/
65. Parascandola M, Xiao L. Tobacco and the lung cancer epidemic in China. Transl Lung Cancer Res. 2019;8(Suppl 1):S21–30.
66. Funk C, Kennedy B. The politics of climate. Pew Research Center; 2016. Available from: https://www.pewresearch.org/science/2016/10/04/the-politics-of-climate/
67. Berwyn B. The US Rejoins the Paris Agreement, but rebuilding credibility on climate action will take time. Inside Climate News 2021.; Available from: https://insideclimatenews.org/news/21012021/biden-paris-climate-agreement/?gad_source=1&gclid=EAIaIQobChMIsZLg3aCEhwMVKDYIBR2UJAArEAAYASAAEgLrVfD_BwE
68. McMichael AJ. The urban environment and health in a world of increasing globalization: issues for developing countries. Bull World Health Organ. 2000;78(9):1117–26.
69. World Health Organization. The World Health Report 1998: life in the 21st century: a vision for all. 1998.
70. Romanello M, et al. The 2021 report of the lancet countdown on health and climate change: code red for a healthy future. Lancet. 2021;398(10311):1619–62.
71. Dasandi N, et al. Engagement with health in national climate change commitments under the Paris Agreement: a global mixed-methods analysis of the nationally determined contributions. Lancet Planetary Health. 2021;5(2):e93–e101.
72. Green Climate Fund, About GCF. 2023.; Available from: https://www.greenclimate.fund/about
73. World Health Organization. Disease Outbreak News, Cholera—Mozambique. 2023; Available from: https://www.who.int/emergencies/disease-outbreak-news/item/2023-DON443
74. World Health Organization. World malaria report 2022, global report 2022; Available from: https://www.who.int/publications/i/item/9789240064898
75. World Health Organization. Global Cholera and Acute Watery Diarrhoea (AWD) Dashboard. 2023; Available from: https://who-global-cholera-and-awd-dashboard-1-who.hub.arcgis.com/
76. Amnesty International. Afghanistan: country's four million internally displaced need urgent support amid pandemics. 2021.; Available from: https://www.amnesty.org/en/latest/press-release/2021/03/afghanistan-countrys-four-million-internally-displaced-need-urgent-support-amid-pandemic/
77. United Nations Framework Convention on Climate Change. Opportunities and options for integrating climate change adaptation with the Sustainable Development Goals and the Sendai Framework for Disaster Risk Reduction 2015–2030. 2017.
78. Aladuwaka S, Alagan R, Singh R, Mishra M. Health Burdens and SES in Alabama: Using Geographic Information System to Examine Prostate Cancer Health Disparity. Cancers (Basel). 2022;14(19):4824. https://doi.org/10.3390/cancers14194824. PMID: 36230747; PMCID: PMC9563407.

Part IV
Public Health: Policy and Law

Chapter 11
Wellness Programs

Chahal Anjali and Sandeep Kumar

Your life does not get better by chance. It gets better by change.

Jim Rohn

11.1 Background

In the 1950s, public health in India was known as the Hygiene Department and was managed by sanitary inspectors. Hygeia was the ancient Greek goddess of health, wisdom, and purity, who propounded the philosophy of hygiene in Athens in 600s BC. She was the daughter of *Asklepios*, the Greek god of medicine. The cult of Hygeia spread during 400 BC after the first appearance of plague in Greece. In Greek, "*Hygeia*" meant "soundness" or "wholeness." In medicine, hygiene was about maintaining the "wholeness" of the body and keeping it fit. At that time, most people died from **infectious diseases**. **Injuries** must have been the second most common cause of death due to tribal battles. People died young. Nowadays, noncommunicable diseases are taking a toll on the majority of people, as infectious and communicable diseases have been contained with sanitation, public health measures, and vaccinations. Road traffic accident injuries have taken over war injuries. Life expectancy has increased, but noncommunicable diseases in India have become a major cause of concern. Health-seeking behavior has grown beyond sanitation and hygiene into more devious lifestyle changes to be adopted. Maternal and child health and nutritional disorders must additionally be tackled with equal fervor.

C. Anjali (✉)
Dr. Giri Lal Gupta Institute of Public Health and Public Affairs, University of Lucknow, Lucknow, India

S. Kumar
Surgery and Epidemiology, King George's Medical University, Lucknow, India

AIIMS Bhopal, Bhopal, India

S. Malik et al. (eds.), *Public Health Issues: Theory and Practices*,
https://doi.org/10.1007/978-981-96-6650-8_11

India is experiencing an epidemiological transition from communicable diseases to silently progressing noncommunicable diseases [1]. As per the WHO-NCD India profile (2018), the **leading noncommunicable diseases**, cardiovascular diseases (27%), chronic respiratory diseases (11%), cancers (9%), and diabetes (3%), account for more than 63% of total deaths in India [2, 3]. These diseases have become a global epidemic and a prominent cause of premature death and disability in both urban as well as rural populations, affecting all socioeconomic strata and contributing to the loss of productive years of life. NCDs impose a large financial burden, as only a minority are able to claim medical insurance benefits for these conditions, causing higher out-of-pocket (OOP) expenditures. Also, 80% of all disability-adjusted life years (DALYs) are lost before the age of 60 due to the impact of NCDs [4]. Additionally, people indulge in substance abuse including tobacco and alcohol, poor nutrition, junk food consumption, and delays in seeking treatment for NCDs further compound the problem. The poor are equally affected by NCDs. As per the WHO, about 80% of the world's population lacks the resources required for palliative care [5] in the advanced stages of NCDs. **Cardiovascular disease** contributes the maximum burden of NCDs both worldwide and in India. The World Bank estimates that India will lose 6–10% of its GDP each year due to premature deaths and preventable diseases caused by NCDs [6]. India lost $237 billion between 2006 and 2015 from premature deaths due to heart disease, stroke, and diabetes [7]. **Diabetes** is becoming a particular concern; between 1990 and 2010, the annual number of DALYs attributable to diabetes in India nearly doubled, from about 4.1 million to nearly 8 million. Meanwhile, the annual number of deaths due to diabetes in the country increased more than twofold, from about 100,000 in 1990 to 223,999 in 2010 [8]. In 2012, India had more than 63 million (6.3 crores) people living with type 2 diabetes, earning the country the title of *diabetes capital of the world*. Furthermore, the International Diabetes Federation (IDF) estimates that 33% of adults with diabetes in India are undiagnosed at any given time [9]. The EPIC model forecasted that India will lose $4.58 trillion between 2012 and 2030 due to disease burden on its population [10].

Another important NCD is mental disorders, accounting for 3.5% of deaths. Thus, a greater emphasis on the social and emotional well-being of the population needs to be placed in the health policy. **Thus, there is no single solution; need-based, well-researched interventions and pro-poor programs to tackle risk factors (behaviors) and NCDs (disease) need to be executed**. These can be tackled largely through lifestyle modification. Half of cancer cases can be downstaged by screening, and some can be prevented by curtailing tobacco use. Environmental pollution is largely responsible for respiratory diseases and tuberculosis. These lifestyle risks and environmental factors require non-health sectors and interdepartmental collaboration between state and central governments, with community participation in wellness programs. Wellness programs should resolve the issues of **equity** and health services **accessibility**. The full utilization of government Vaccination programs; nutrition, iron and calcium supplementation; mass drug administration for filaria, malaria and worm infestations, and Maternal and Child Health services should occur through the Wellness Clinic participation.

11.2 Concept and Components of Wellness

Health was defined by the WHO in 1948 as "*a state of complete physical, mental and social well-being and not merely the absence of diseases or infirmity*" [11]. "**Well-being**" refers to a positive state, framing **health as a positive aspiration** [12]. Wellness is an active process through which people become aware of and make choices for a more successful and healthy life. Conrad defines wellness as a conscious and deliberate approach to achieving an advanced state of physical and psychological/spiritual health [13]. Global Wellness Institute (GWI) defines wellness as the **active pursuit of activities, choices, and lifestyles that lead to a state of holistic health** [14]. Wellness is related to an individual's behavior, lifestyle, choices, and activities. It is an organized set of activities designed to support individuals and their family members to make positive changes in their behavior to reduce health risks and enhance their ability to perform actions.

Key principles of wellness include a conscious, self-directed, and evolving process of achieving one's full potential, positive and affirming attitudes toward living a long, meaningful, and healthy life, and multidimensional fueling the body, engaging the mind, and nurturing the spirit [15].

Ashtachakra (Swasthya-Aayaam) describes mutually independent and interconnected dimensions of wellness [16], which are self-explanatory (Fig. 11.1) and help individuals understand the acronym **WELL** as **W**hole person, **E**nvironment, **L**ifestyle, and **L**earning [17].

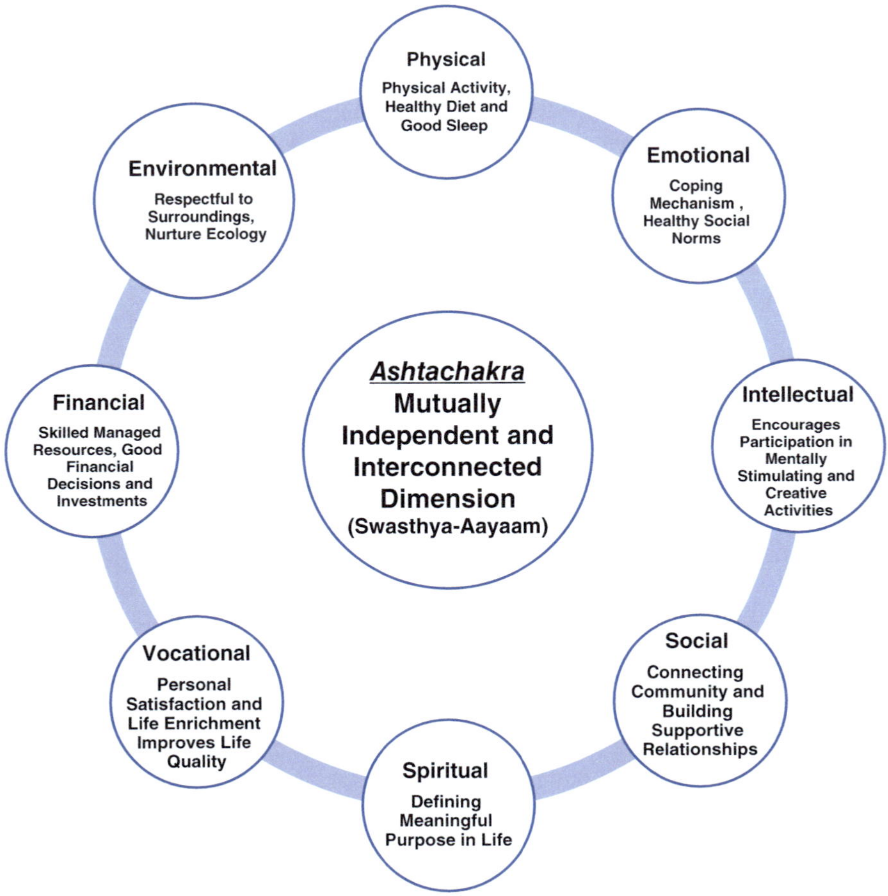

Fig. 11.1 Ashtachakra (Swasthya-Aayaam) mutually independent and interconnected dimensions of wellness [16]

11.3 Wellness as We Inherit from Ancient Indian Culture

Indian culture not only discerned and described wellness in the *Vedas* but also inculcated it in the lifestyle of millions of Indians. The holistic wellness described in Ayurveda and the six principles of "*Yog*" is an ancient version of wellness that was programmed in the lifestyle of inhabitants in the land of *Bharatvarsh*.

Ayurveda Chikitsa (vk;qosZn fpfdRlk)—The term "Ayurveda" originates from the Sanskrit words "*ayus*" (**vk;ql**), meaning "*life*" or "*longevity*," and "*veda*" (**osn**), meaning "**knowledge**." Thus, etymologically, *Ayurveda* means the "**science of life and longevity**." This ancient system of medicine was developed in the Indian subcontinent over 6000 years ago and provides a holistic approach to health, emphasizing prevention, wellness, and longevity.

The source of ancient Indian wisdom is the foundational texts known as the four Vedas: *Rigveda*, *Yajurveda*, *Samaveda*, and *Atharvaveda* (**_Xosn] ;tqosZn] lkeosn o vFkoZosn**). Composed between 4000 and 6000 BC by *Rishi Vyas*, these scriptures encapsulate the principles of what is now known as *Sanatan Dharma*. Among these, the *Rigveda* preserves some knowledge of *Ayurveda*. The *Atharvaveda*, on the other hand, is particularly dedicated to the medical systems of that era.

Yog-Pranayam (iz.kk;ke) Chikitsa—*Pranayam* is one of the eight limbs (**vax**) of Yog. Generally, people misinterpret *Pranayama* as *Yog*. People practicing *Pranayama* in their daily life are heard saying that they are practicing Yog. However, these two terms are not synonymous. Yog is a complete lifestyle science for capacity building in achieving good health. *Pranayama* is the fourth limb of Yog. This is to elucidate further that practicing *Pranayam* without the knowledge of *Aasan*, i.e., physical exercises, cannot provide the benefits anticipated by *Patanjali* and current proponents of the science of Yog. Aasan (**vklu**) is the third limb of Yog. **Aasan** and Pranayama are complementary to each other. **Pranayama** is defined as a set of respiratory, i.e., breathing **exercises** in various breath dimensions. **Yog**, in its different limbs (**vax** ang), has been extremely popular in India since time immemorial. Yog is held in high esteem throughout the world now. This science is being valued as a panacea for several physical and mental illnesses. This is to further reiterate that the life structure of Bhartiya people has evolved around dietary balance, physical exercises, abstinence, fasting, and meditation. But the great sage **Patanjali** is credited with forming the life structure of Bharatvarsha around the science called **Yog**. Eight limbs of ***Yog*** are as follows: *Yam* (**;e**)—emphasizes nonviolence, truth, honesty, celibacy, and non-accumulation, i.e., abstinence; "*niyam*" (**fu;e**)—includes hygiene, satisfaction, perseverance and austerity, self-study, and concentration on God; "*Aasana*" (**vklu**)*—doing physical exercises in different postures; Pranayam-regulating and controlling the breath of life such as slow/deep breathing by alternating inhaling from nostrils, holding and exhaling from mouth and vice versa. Thereby, controlling inner force- mind and body through pranayam. "*Pratyahar*" (**izR;kgkj**)—withdrawal of the sense and motor organs from worldly objects.

Desire or infatuation with worldly objects is an impediment to achieving wellness through Yog; "*Dharana*" (**/kkj.k**)—objects of the world attract our senses and cause modification in our mind. Concentrating on non-worldly sublime objects is a way to maintain equilibrium in the mind, which is a remedy from agony and distress; "*Dhyan*" (**/;ku**)—evolving and developing the flow of consciousness toward creativity; "*Samadhi*" (**lekf/k**)—meditating to immerse and submerge in vacuum or nothingness. Sublimation with *Pratyahar*, *Dharana*, *Dhyan*, and *Samadhi* allay anxiety and mental diseases. By practicing **Yoga** in all its eight components, oxygenated blood circulates in the body, abstinence from sensual infatuation develops, and mental equilibrium and peace are achieved, which leads to stronger immunity, helps to ward off mental stress, and supports the realization of oneness with the absolute reality. Thus, if the Asan and Pranayam are done according to the rules of abstinence, the state of *Dhyan* and *Samadhi* is achieved spontaneously. Describing all the "asanas" is not the subject matter of this book. A few **illustrations** of some Asanas, like *siddhasana*, *padmasana*, *bhadrasana*, *swastikasana*, and *vishram-karak asana*, are as follows:

Yog can be understood with the following *Shlok* (**'yksd**):

योगः चित्तवृत्तिनिरोध, योगः समाधिश्च ।
योग चित्त की वृत्ति का निरोध एवं योग समाधि है,
योग लय है सांसारिक व्यक्ति का पूर्ण चेतना अर्थात परम् सत्ता से।

Yog has been extensively studied for various ailments jointly by practitioners of modern medicine, and many randomized clinical trials have been conducted. Conditions like bronchial asthma, paraplegia, and chronic respiratory disorders have been treated with add-on Yog and Pranayama with the best supportive treatments and have been found beneficial. **Wellness is a holistic, multidimensional aspect of life that helps an individual awaken and make decisions toward optimal health and well-being** [18]. Wellness is succinctly captured in Indian health traditions by the Sanskrit term "*Svasthya*" (Sva—individual, sthya—stability), that is, "the state of being in harmony with oneself." This state would vary with person and context [19].

11.4 Wellness in Contexts of Vulnerable Groups [20]

Special crusades in wellness programs have been identified in the following five groups.

1. *Maternal Health*: Maternal ill-health and disability are not just medical problems but outcomes of a complex interplay of eco-social forces, lifestyles, exposures, and individual-level factors. Focusing on all direct and indirect factors will help in combating maternal malnutrition and morbidity.
2. *Elderly*: Geriatric patients have special needs and requirements that should be understood by the young generation, who must be resilient to addressing the emotional aspects of old age. The vertical (across family) and horizontal (intra-familial) integration of the elderly is augmenting their life.
3. *People with Diabetes and Hypertension*: The uphill menace of diabetes and increasing comorbidities needed much-awaited attention. These people can benefit hugely from lifestyle modifications, and this needs to be communicated to all in society through a mass communication approach.
4. *Malnutrition (Under- and Overnutrition)*: Malnutrition during critical growing periods has long-term complications that cannot be reversed subsequently, even with the help of expert intervention. There are many underlying factors responsible for undernourishment, and these should be addressed with a scientific and collaborative strategy. Simultaneously, overnutrition is being addressed through changes in food policy and the marketing of processed foods by educating the population of the ill effects of ultra-processed but cheap products.
5. *Children with Adverse Childhood Experiences (ACEs)*: Adverse childhood experiences include varied forms of abuses—physical, mental, social, and sexual. Studies have reported a direct link between ACEs and CVDs, nonallergic asthma, depression, fatty liver, and many other ailments. The increased stress disturbs physical, mental, and emotional well-being.

11.5 Objectives in Wellness Programs

Watt et al. [21] defined wellness program as a **structured intervention** focused on achieving wellness in the physical, psychological, or spiritual realm. These programs help people engage in self-care and better control their health and health care. Wellness incorporates sociocultural, work *ipso facto*, psychological, and disease-related factors. Wellness programs are an organizational approach to improving individual health outcomes by means of **medical** and **nonmedical** initiatives. The medical components of wellness programs include health screenings, counseling sessions, episodic care, etc., and the nonmedical initiatives may include team outings, fun activities, retreats, fitness sessions, and sports activities like marathons. The main aim of these programs is to help the population stay healthy, productive, and resilient and to attain well-being in life. The **objectives** are to improve the health of the members by incentivizing healthy lifestyle behaviors and, consequently, reduce downstream healthcare resource utilization. Wellness programs primarily concentrate on **risk factor reduction** (behavioral risks) by adopting interventions across populations to promote healthy living habits. Disease management in high-risk individuals should be an equally important attribute of a wellness program [22]. A **key point to consider while planning a wellness program** is that prevention should be prioritized over cure. Efforts to be channelized toward the **working population,** considering the **sedentary working environments** at many workplaces, and **long working hours** that lead to an obesogenic environment. The special needs of working places are recognized. **WHY** the program is needed? **WHO** the target population is? **WHAT** components does the intervention of the wellness program offer? are the usual why, who and what. Three components are identified in most of the wellness programs, viz, evaluating health status and identifying areas for improvement, encouraging action to improve health, and reactive incentives means incentives for regular screeings and rewards for regular exercising [23].

11.6 Various Wellness Programs in India

In India, wellness programs are offered in diverse formats by governments, insurers, employers, and corporates. **Government wellness programs** may not be popularized as "wellness program," but they are planned to improve population health or as a strategy to strengthen public health care. The overall objective is to improve the health of the target population and reduce the healthcare costs. These programs have varied approach from improving health indicators i.e. Reproductive Maternal Neonatal Child Health (RMNCH+A) and Adolescent, Infant and Young Child feeding, Supplementary feeding, food security, Uzzwala Scheme to recently launched (2018) flagship program of health systems strengthening of primary health care through establishment of "Health and Wellness Centers" with the principal of healhcare at door step and 'time to care' in no more than 30 minutes. A brief overview of each program from the latest to the past is as follows.

1. **National Health Protection Mission (Ayushman Bharat Yojana/Pradhan Mantri Jan Arogya Yojana—PMJAY): With the motto of *Arogyam Paramam Dhanam***, the world's largest health insurance scheme, Ayushman Bharat or Healthy India, with its twin pillars of Health and Wellness Centers (Ayushman Arogya Mandir) for the provision of comprehensive primary health care and the Pradhan Mantri Jan Arogya Yojana (PMJAY), was launched in 2018. It promises health coverage worth Rs. 500,000 per year to poor family for the treatment of serious ailments. Health and Wellness Centers (HWCs) are envisaged to address the basic primary healthcare needs, spanning preventive, promotive, curative, rehabilitative, and palliative care, of the entire population in the area, rather than focusing on population subgroups, through a range of

services up to the last mile. The two components of Ayushman Bharat together will mark a significant milestone in India's path toward Universal Health Coverage (UHC) [20]. A life-course approach and the empanelment of individuals and families ensure wellness for all through programs, viz, **Maternal and Child Health**, by assuring Maternal and Reproductive Health Services. **Care during Pregnancy and childbirth** by identifying high-risk pregnancies and follow-up, counseling on care during pregnancy and ensuring antenatal care checks, identifying complications during childbirth, postpartum complications and timely referral, enabling access to Take Home Ration from Anganwadi center, follow-up to ensure compliance with IFA in normal and anemic cases, facilitating institutional delivery and supporting birth planning, and postpartum care visits. **Neonatal and infant health** with home-based newborn care through specified number of visits for home and institutional deliveries, identification and care of high-risk new born, counseling and support for exclusive breastfeeding, supplementary feeding practices, adoption of WASH practices, growth monitoring, and continued IYCF enables access to food supplementation and provides counseling for early childhood growth and development through ICDS, identification of birth asphyxia, sepsis, and congenital anomalies, appropriate referral, immunization, family/community education for prevention of infections, and many more.

2. **Family Planning, Contraceptive Services, and Other Reproductive Care Services**.
3. **Immunization**: This enables newborn and child health services.
4. **Tele-Consultation**: Use of technology to improve care coordination and facilitate the continuum of care.
5. **Yoga**: Recognized as a system of medicine Yoga promotes health and well-being by making the body, mind, and soul united with one another, in harmony with the universe. This helps in the prevention and treatment of chronic diseases, including cardiovascular diseases, diabetes, and musculoskeletal diseases, as well as in combating anxiety and depression. Ashtanga yoga has eight stages or components to attain the ultimate well-being, and practicing it helps in developing a positive attitude toward oneself and society.
6. **Health Awareness**: Interventions related to a healthy diet, physical activity, stress management, meditation, and tobacco and alcohol cessation are conducted at the individual, family, and community levels to promote healthy behaviors.
7. **Dietary Patterns**: These have been linked to the risk of developing obesity, hypertension, cardiovascular diseases, diabetes, and cancer in various studies. Whole-food, plant-based diets are rich in bioactive compounds, which play an important role in controlling genetic and other biological factors that contribute to the development of chronic diseases. They are rich in antioxidants, which help in neutralizing free radicals that damage cells and tissues [24, 25]. Age-group-specific diet is recommended based on evidence-based findings. People who used to have a nonvegetarian diet may consider incorporating egg, lean meat, lean poultry, and fatty fish in moderation.

8. **Physical Activity**: This has been found to be positively associated with functional independence, mobility, glucose homeostasis, bone health, psychological well-being, and overall quality of life [26]. At least 150 min of moderate-intensity aerobic physical activity per week or at least 75 min of vigorous-intensity aerobic physical activity per week, along with muscle-strengthening activities twice a week, is recommended for adults aged 18–64 years. Age-group specific recommendations for physical activity are available on the WHO website https://www.who.in/publications/i/item/9789240015128
9. **Stress Management**: As per the National Mental Health Survey of India in 2016, 1 in 20 people in India suffers from depression. Human behavior and well-being are markedly influenced by stress and mental health issues. The management of stress is achieved through positive psychology (PERMA), Pranayam, and mindfulness meditation ("*Swachh Mann-Swasth Tan*"), and psychological well-being through practicing Yoga regularly [12, 15, 27].
10. **Behavior Change for Holistic Healthy Life Style**: This involves adopting positive behavior in a day-to-day life and forbidding harmful behaviors like tobacco use in any form, alcohol consumption, and dependence on narcotics. Follow *dinacharya* (daily regimen), *ritucharya* (seasonal regimen), and personal hygiene for good health and well-being [28–30].
11. **Positive Parenting for Adolescent Health and Well-Being**: This ensures a safe and reassuring environment for holistic child development. Since adolescents adopt attitudes and practices similar to their parents, it is very important to demonstrate positive behavior to inculcate safety, self-esteem, self-reliance, and self-confidence in adolescents [31].
12. **Management of Substance Abuse Disorders** by following the ABC approach: **A**sking proactively about substance abuse, giving **B**rief advice to choose positive behavior in life, and providing support for **C**essation help them bring a change in behavior [32].
13. **Health and Wellness Centers to Strengthen Primary Health Care**: To ensure delivery of comprehensive primary healthcare services, existing subhealth centers and primary health centers would be converted to health and wellness centers (HWCs) and care would be provided to all people at no cost and nearer to their homes. The program included wellness through outreach activities, mobile medical units, health camps, home visits and community-based interaction on the principle of seamless continuum of care, ensuring principles of equity, quality, universality, and no financial hardship [33].
14. **Expanded Range of Services Through Health and Wellness Centers (HWCs)**: HWCs provide an expanded range of services, including drug distribution for the elderly and other subpopulation groups to provide care for chronic diseases; family planning, contraceptive services, and other reproductive healthcare services; management of communicable diseases, including those covered under National Health Programs; screening, prevention, control, and management of noncommunicable diseases; care for common ophthalmic and ENT problems; basic oral health care; elderly and palliative healthcare services;

emergency medical services; screening and basic management of mental health ailments.

15. **Infant and Young Child Feeding Program** [34]: This program promotes early initiation of breastfeeding, feeding of colostrum, exclusive breastfeeding for 6 months, and complimentary feeding from 6 months onward with gradual introduction of food from all food groups along with continued breastfeeding.
16. **National Program for Health Care of the Elderly (NPHCE)**: Older adults comprise 7.5% of the population, with two-thirds living in villages and almost half in poor socioeconomic conditions [35]. The NPHCE was initiated in 2010 with a vision to provide the best comprehensive, long-term, and dedicated services for active and healthy aging [36]. The chief strategies include preventive and promotive care by experts and routine domiciliary visits including educating family to maintain the health of bedridden or older adults who are disabled. PHCs conduct routine health checkups, raise health awareness, and offer rehabilitation in villages and at health sanitation camps. At CHCs, twice-weekly geriatric clinics are organized, with physiotherapy and counseling units for older persons, services to bedridden patients, and referrals to DHs. Special focus is placed on intensive care services and acute rehabilitation for patients aged 75 years and above. Dedicated geriatric OPD services are available at the district hospital and the regional geriatric center (RGC). NPHCE has launched 19 RGCs at selected medical colleges in 18 states to provide tertiary care services under the Rashtriya Varishtha Jan Swasthya Yojana. The myths, stereotypes, and social stigma are addressed by educating and sensitizing stakeholders cognizant of geriatric care. Boys and girls from tribal communities having little formal education can be educated as community health workers and encouraged to work in their local neighborhoods for bridging the healthcare gap between tribal and non-tribal residents.
17. **School Health and Wellness Program**: For the holistic development of school-going children, health, well-being, and life skills are globally perceived as an important requisite. The WHO defines life skills as "the psychosocial competencies and abilities for adaptive and positive behavior that enable individuals to deal effectively with the demands and challenges of everyday life [37]." India has around 26 crore schoolchildren in the age group of 6–18 years. Investments in the health and life skills of children empower them to understand own self and others and help them discover their strengths and weaknesses, besides motivating them to improve further. They are not only prepared to face the difficult situations/pressures in life but also equipped with coping strategies of decision making for self and be confident. Children need to handle physical, psychological, social, and emotional changes for healthy transitions from childhood to adolescence and from adolescence to adulthood by rapidly adjusting to the pace of external and internal stimuli in the absence of truly reliable resources, which renders them especially vulnerable. To align with this context, the School Health component of the Ayushman Bharat initiative has been conceptualized, which will equip children with life skills (*Jeevan Kaushal*) and prepare them to

handle unknown challenges by integrating with different developmental learning stages of students. The objective is to increase knowledge, inculcate positive and progressive attitudes, and enhance life skills to promote informed, responsible, and healthy behaviors among school-going children [38].

The **chief/core skills** to be developed in schoolchildren include self-awareness, a problem-solving attitude, critical thinking, creative thinking, a willingness to learn, empathy, the ability to handle emotions in every situation, interpersonal skills, and effective communication.

Various theme-based projects to create Healthy and Happy Students include: growing up healthy (psychosocial changes and being comfortable with them), emotional well-being and mental health, interpersonal relationships, values and responsible citizenship, gender equality, nutrition, health and sanitation, prevention and management of substance abuse, promotion of a healthy life style, reproductive health and HIV prevention, safety and security against violence and injuries, and promotion of safe use of internet and social media, relevant laws and policies will be incorporated to suitably utilize the above themes. **Health screening and services in schools** include screening children for 30 identified health conditions through Rashtriya Bal Swasthya Karyakaram (RBSK), mobile health teams, administration of IFA and Albendazole tablets to combat iron deficiency anemia, provision of sanitary napkins, access to adolescent-friendly health clinics, and maintenance of electronic health records for each child.

18. **Wellness in Higher Education Institutions**: The WHO has revealed that mental health accounts for 13% of the global disease burden and that suicide is the second leading cause of death among 15–29 year olds [39]. When wellness is cultivated at the student level, stressors associated with pursuing education are likely to be reduced. Few events have embodied wellness like the Fit India campaign, ***Khelo India***, and ***Yoga Day***, but more is needed to train students for the challenges of life [40].
19. **Other Government and State-sponsored Schemes**: These schemes are not directly a wellness program but help in the management of health and the prevention of diseases in a population subgroup. **Central Government Health Scheme**—The comprehensive healthcare program for working and retired employees of the Central Government of India and their dependents. Introduced in 1954, this government mediclaim policy offers a range of medical facilities, including dispensary services, specialist consultations, and hospitalization [41]. Similarly, several state governments have comprehensive healthcare infrastructure and policies. **The Employees' State Insurance Scheme (ESI)**—ESI is a social security and health insurance scheme for employees of organized sector, provided by the State Insurance Corporation under the Ministry of Labor and Employment, GOI. The scheme is beneficial to employees and their families in availing medical and cash benefits and offers a pension for the dependents in case of any unfortunate event.

11.7 Insurance Integrated Wellness Programs

A proactive approach to health is designed to promote healthy behavior and lifestyles among employees, thereby reducing the likelihood of illness and simultaneously costly medical interventions. Herein, insurers (for example, ACKO) give rewards to the people consistently involved in health-promoting activities. These programs offer a wide range of activities, from gym memberships, incentives, comprehensive coverage to maintain well-being, and nutrition counselling to stress management and mental health support. The insurers may provide discounts on medical consultations and health check-ups, redeemable vouchers for tours, entertainment, fitness centers, and heavy discounts on the policy premium or upon policy renewal. Components of the insurance-integrated wellness program include reward points, smoking cessation programs, exercise programs and fitness activities, membership in reputed clubs, personalized wellness mentor, weight-loss programs, stress management activities, viz., meditation, Yoga classes, vaccination drives, and second medical opinion in case of disease condition.

11.8 Insurance Regulatory and Development Authority of India or IRDAI

Insurance Regulatory and Development Authority of India or IRDAI has given guidelines for wellness and preventive benefits associated with health insurance products in 2019 [42]—improvement of health is an important intent of wellness program, rewards should be given to consistent customers in the wellness programs, no discrimination in providing benefits to the customer, errors, if any, should be quickly addressed in calculating reward points and confidentiality pertaining to information of the customers should be maintained. If wellness-integrated insurance is offered by the company, insurers may gain by decreasing the probability of health-related claims if a person's vulnerability to illnesses is decreased by regularly practicing health-promoting activities. Examples of such insurers include Kotak Health Insurance, Niva Bupa Heartbeat plan, ACKO, ICICI Lombard, HDFC ERGO, and many more.

11.9 Workplace Wellness Programs

These are important for successful prevention strategies as long hours are spending at work, work is increasingly sedentary and supportive environment has potentially raised the productivity in the long run. Employees get numerous benefits from improved health, reduced out-of-pocket expenditures, enhanced productivity, and a positive workplace culture, thereby increasing job satisfaction and the company benefits through cost savings, reduced absenteeism, improved market ratings, improved retention of employees, and may get legal and ethical benefits.

In India, the 2023 work well-being report (indeed—thriving at work) revealed that only 24% of employees experience high workplace well-being, which is below the global average. Among occupational hazards, the maximum (37%) is suffering from back pain, 16% from hearing loss, and others from chronic conditions. These health issues result in an economic loss of 4–6% of GDP due to absenteeism and presenteeism.

Wellness program	Program description
Aditya Birla Health Insurance's Health Rewards [43] https://www.adityabirlacapital.com/multiply-wellness/home **India**	Health is assessed by administering an online questionnaire, and health rewards are given for "Active Days" through prescribed activities. 0–30% discount on policy premium is rewarded based on the number of active days or a "Final fitness Result Assessment"
Wipro GearUp and Behavior Spotting programs [44] Source: www.wipro.com **India**	**GearUp**, a preventive approach, equips employees with the right attitude, knowledge, and behavior toward mental health and well-being engagements. It includes nutrition consulting, arena (health centers), medical camps, etc. **Behavior spotting program**, a psychological first aid program designed for leaders (front line managers) to be equipped with the skills to identify signs of distress and align strategies to support members in need **We Re (well-being and resilience)**, a team for employee well-being. **Mitr (friend)** initiative to provide counseling for employees
Infosys **HALE** (health assessment and lifestyle enrichment)—"A proactive approach to health and life enrichment aimed at increased awareness and overall well-being, resulting in good health, reduced stress levels, a safe work environment, and improved productivity levels" [45] Source: www.infosys.com **India**	Events under HALE have four pillars—Health, Safety, Leisure, and Emotional Well-being **Health** includes health assessments, focused interventions, work environment, and health education **Safety** focuses on awareness building, skill development, and community development **Leisure** includes club connect and hobby week, primers and workshops, online channels, InfyRadio For **emotional** well-being HALE tool, hale hotline, etc.
TCS care [46] Source: www.tcs.com **India**	**TCS care's building on belief** program offers physical health, yoga, fitness and nutrition, mental and emotional health, personal safety, financial health, purpose, and engagement **Fit4Life** initiative engages in multiple physical activities through interactive group initiatives and personalized yoga **Ergonomics team** focuses on ergonomics engagement program **Purpose4life program** for volunteering efforts to contribute to societal well-being

(continued)

Wellness program	Program description
LivFit by Oman Insurance Company (OIC) [47] Source: www.tameen.ae/PDFs/Livfit **Middle East**	LivFit conducts a health assessment survey, and a customized report is sent to the member to discuss with their wellness coach. Incentives, discounts on health check-ups and fitness products, along with specific health interventions for weight loss, smoking cessation, and stress management are given
Vitality wellness program [48] Source: www.discovery.co.za/portal **South Africa, United Kingdom, United States, China, and Australia**	Evidence-based interventions and behavioral economics are used, and members earn vitality points by getting active, eating well, and health screening. Based on points scored, discounts on healthy food, travel, wearable devices, etc., are given
Volkswagen Poznan Health Strategy [49] **Poland**	Program offers personalized health recommendations, stress management, and information campaigns. Experts from a specialized field prepare motivational content for employees on a regular basis. Engagement in healthy lifestyle behaviors is rewarded by increasing base remuneration as well as free vouchers

Source: Adapted from Milliman report (2019) [23]

The idea is to promote health, increase productivity, reduce absenteeism and presenteeism with a focus on healthy workforce, and provide on-site wellness days and workshops to maximize convenience and positive outcomes. Workplace wellness gives an opportunity to participate in the program and group exercises along with dedicated medical facilities on-site and engagement from within company facilitate positive well-being in the employees.

11.10 Corporate Wellness Program

In today's hustle and bustle world, for success and fame, time for self-care is ignored by most people. To maintain work–life balance, people are looking for solutions in a corporate wellness program. This is what they are designed to tackle—giving rejuvenating solutions and setting forth a journey to understand oneself and inherent priorities to tackle the situation and embrace well-being. A corporate wellness program not only offers solutions to the organization but also offer a tailored approach to individuals. A few names to discuss here are as follows:

(a) *Patanjali* pioneered mass education in wellness teaching with 40–60 minute sessions in Yog and Pranayam, mostly through television channels. Baba Ramdev regularly conducts early morning sessions in Yog and sermons on lifestyle at his center near Haridwar, where there is a huge auditorium, and also in camps in other cities.
(b) *HaBuild Healthcare Private Limited*—A Nagpur-based high-tech company owned by Mr. Saurabh Bothra, an IITian, is promoting wellness using high technology on social media platform, mostly on WhatsApp and YouTube,—currently serving 1.5 million subscribers who regularly practice in 45 min ses-

sions, a very soft version of *Yog* amalgamated with health and wellness talks that are highly scientific. The number of people joining the live stream HaBuild sessions has been accredited by the Guinness Book of World Records two times.

(c) *Avyukt Healthcare Solutions Pvt Ltd*—With a team of over 200 paramedical staff, 100 doctors, and 200 lab and diagnostic center tie-ups, this organization is spreading the concept of employee wellness in private institutions and multinational corporations. They manage over 180 Occupational Health Centers across India.

(d) *HealthifyMe*—It provides corporate wellness programs for multinational companies, helping them manage the health of their employee for better well-being. Also, it helps the companies in increasing productivity by focusing on employees' physical and mental condition and maintaining a safe and healthy work environment.

(e) *NanoHealth*—One of the burgeoning health problems of twenty-first century is noncommunicable diseases, which account for the highest deaths and disabilities across the world; a one-stop solution is provided by NanoHealth for healthy today to ensure a happier tomorrow.

(f) *Stepathalon*—A 12-month employee wellness program designed for organizations of all sizes, across all industries and countries, to help employees lead healthier, happier, and more productive lives. Their aim is to move the nation toward a healthier living through behavioral changes to manage health and well-being.

(g) *Infinite Health Studios*—It offers health and wellness solutions to workplaces. Their aim is to provide good nutrition and wellness to workplaces and help people in managing diabetes at the individual level across India.

(h) *The FullerLife*—It has been providing mood trackers, workout sessions, online seminars, therapy sessions, and nutrition advice for two decades to big businesses.

(i) *VantageFit*—The ultimate package to boost employees' well-being by offering an easy-to-use control center, a reward system, a live scoreboard, and super fancy health tracking and organizing competitions for the workers. The problems and their consequences in today's fast-paced world make wellness difficult to achieve, but these and many more Corporate Wellness Programs are here to support and enhance the potential of the workforce. There are numerous benefits of conducting such wellness programs to boost productivity, reduce absenteeism, and maintain overall well-being in the organization.

11.11 Comparison of Wellness Programs in India and United States

Notwithstanding its large population and compelling challenges, India is providing free basic healthcare facilities to one billion people. Health is affected by varying factors, from social to environmental, and therefore, actions to address these problems do not come within the purview of health systems alone, and thus, intersectoral convergence and participation of the community are needed to achieve "Health for All" from "Health in All" approach. Many striking differences are present between US and Indian Wellness Programs.

Insurance coverage For low-income people, the government recently launched the tax-financed National Health Protection Scheme (*Ayushman Bharat—Pradhan Mantri Jan Arogya Yojana* or PM-JAY) in which they are given the facility of cashless treatment at private hospitals. There are also a handful of health insurance programs aimed at benefitting population subgroups. The overall estimated penetration of insurance coverage in India is about 25%, which is approximately 91.4% in the United States.

Access and affordability The United States has better access to healthcare facilities and infrastructure, but the challenge is affordability. Healthcare facilities and insurance premiums are far more expensive. In India, both accessibility and affordability are important issues. The quality of care in remote areas, lack of awareness, resource constraints, and not enough trained workforce are other issues of equity.

Outcomes-based reward/penalties in wellness programs can disproportionately penalize groups that already face barriers to participating in health activities and improving health. For example, racial and ethnic minorities are more prone to suffer from NCDs. If they do not attend wellness and disease screening programs, their health insurance premiums may go up or certain penalties may be imposed, which can unfairly harm the low-economic individuals. Whereas in India, people are following both modern treatment and alternative therapies, wherein a preventive approach with Ayurveda, naturopathy, and homeopathy is successfully explored as well. Wellness clinics have only recently started. There are no such penalties in India, but the poor infrastructure of public hospitals pushes the people toward private health care, increasing their out-of-pocket expenditure, which is 62.6%, the third highest in the world.

Health culture in the United States runs on a private and public insurance system, with employers investing more than 60% of insurance for Americans [50]. Organizations receive more incentives to provide wellness programs due to the investment each employee represents. The United States takes wellness seriously.

In India, public organizations lay their focus on occupational health, smoke-free policies, and employee health insurance but lack in defined wellness program at the workplace. Transnational corporations have wellness programs mostly focused on insurance and medical benefits, but from last decades they too are now investing in employee well-being and is in a nascent stage. Few corporates organize walkathons, health runs, Yoga, and meditation classes as part of their wellness programs. Also, some have policies focused on diet and nutrition; however, talking about mental health is a big taboo in Indian society.

11.12 Future Directions/Suggestions

Create a healthy built-in environment, a healthy city, in place of smart cities, as our modern designed environment—both urban and rural—is obesogenic, where many interrelated factors are responsible for sedentary behavior. Limited social interactions, online work, and online activities are causing loneliness with reduced engagement. The worsening physical and mental health conditions and stressful working environment need immediate action on a priority basis. Indian organizations must prioritize employee wellness, align leadership practices, and bridge the generational gap for increased productivity, economically and healthy workplace to retain talent. Policy interventions that focus on a healthy environment, prioritize in-house walkability and physical movement in urban/regional planning, and promote healthy infrastructure can have long-lasting effects on the entire population of a community. Targeted policies to benefit the disadvantaged and marginalized can be a game changer.

11.13 Conclusion

India has embarked, after due diligence by *Niti Ayog*, on establishing over 1 lakh **Health and Wellness Centers (HWCs)** throughout the country. In February 2018, the Indian Government announced the **Ayushman Bharat Program (ABP)** with two components: (i) **Health and Wellness Centers (HWCs)**, to deliver comprehensive primary healthcare (PHC) services to the entire population and (ii) **Pradhan Mantri Jan Arogya Yojana (PMJAY)** for improving access to hospitalization services at secondary and tertiary level health facilities for the bottom 40% of total population. The HWC component of ABP aims to upgrade Government Primary healthcare facilities and presently(5th April 2025),there are over 1.76 lakh active Ayushamn Arogya Mandirs (HWC) in India, providing comprehensive primary healthcare. The HWC component was launched on April 14, 2018, and by March 31, 2020, a total of 38,595 AB-HWCs were operational across India.

Wellness centers are the *Sanctum Sanctorum* for improving the health of people, reducing the burden of illness, and ultimately helping society and country prosper. Health services evaluation of HWCs by a third party is still awaited. Impact estimation on the reduction of total disease burden, downstaging of cancer, and reduction in overall usage of health facilities is an extremely difficult task, and we do not think that mere establishment of HWCs in 2018 will show results as quickly. Appropriate facilities in HWCs, their proper utilization, sustained political will, community and civil society participation, with mid-course corrections, are the path ahead. Experience from India is extremely important for other low- and middle-income countries that are waiting to see the effect of such a large-scale launch. As such, society at large and in general discussions in Indian household remain oblivious to the wellness programs launched by the government. However, as *Bharatwasi*, we are proud inheritors of our traditional system, which is the ingredient of almost all the components of wellness programs as determined by modern medical science.

As such, society at large and in general discussions in Indian household from disease to ease, healing to health, and health to wellness- a state of being wel lis a long road ahead of India. As such, society at large and in general discussions in Indian household from disease to ease, healing to health, and health to wellness- a state of being wel lis a long road ahead of India. However, with inclusive public policy—from me and my (myself, my family, extended family) to my country (my country without borders) and from human being to well-being, a strategic wellness program that may act at individual, interpersonal, and community levels can help the population to positively impact their health and well-being by using communication for behavioral modification. To conclude, a comprehensive setting and proper synchronization between programs, environmental supports, policies, and community motivation are needed to fulfill the health needs of each and every one.

References

1. WHO. Non-communicable diseases. 2022. Available from: https://www.who.int/newsroom/factsheets/detail/non-communicable%20diseases. Accessed 20 Apr 2023.
2. The Lancet GBD. Global burden of disease. 2022. Available online: https://www.thelancet.com/gbd. Accessed 12 July 2021.
3. Non-communicable diseases country profiles 2018. Available from: WHO India, https://www.who.int. Accessed 24 Sept 2022.
4. WHO. Impact of out-of-pocket payments for treatment of NCDs in developing countries: a review of literature. 2011. Available from: https://www.who.int/publications/i/item/impactof-out-of-pocket-payments-for-treatment-of-non-communicable%20diseases-in-developing-countries-a%20review%20of-literature. Accessed 24 Sept 2022.
5. Comprehensive National Nutrition Survey. Fact sheets. Available from: https://nhm.gov.in/index1.php?lang=1&level=2&sublinkid=1332&lid=713.
6. Stuckler D. Population causes and consequences of leading chronic diseases: a comparative analysis of prevailing explanations. Milbank Q. 2008;86(2):273–326. Available from: http://www.ncbi.nlm.nih.gov/pubmed/18522614.
7. World Health Organization (WHO). Preventing chronic diseases: a vital investment. Geneva: World Health Organization; 2005.
8. Institute for Health Metrics and Evaluation (IHME). Global burden of disease study 2010: India global burden of disease study 2010 (GBD 2010) results 1990–2010. Seattle: IHME; 2013.
9. International Diabetes Federation (IDF). Diabetes atlas. 5th ed. Brussels: International Diabetes Federation; 2015.
10. Abegunde D, Stanciole A. An estimation of the economic impact of chronic non-communicable diseases in selected countries. Geneva: WHO; 2006.
11. World Health Organization. Summary reports on proceedings minutes and final acts of the International Health Conference held in New York from 19 June to 22 July 1946. World Health Organization; 1948. https://apps.who.int/iris/handle/10665/85573
12. Green L, Ashton K, Bellis MA, Clemens T, Doughlas M. "Health in all policies" – a key driver for health and well-being in a post Covid-19 pandemic world. Int J Environ Res Public Health. 2019;18(18):9468.
13. Conrad P. Wellness as a virtue: morality and the pursuit of health. Cult Med Psychiatry. 1994;18:385–401.

14. Global Wellness Institute. Build well to live well: wellness lifestyle real estate and communities. 2018. https://globalwellnessinstitute.org/industry-research/wellness-real-estate-communities-research/.
15. LiveWell. https://www.nhs.uk/live-well/.
16. Stoewen DL. Dimensions of wellness: change your habits, change your life. Can Vet J. 2017;58(8):861–2.
17. 8 Dimensions of wellness [Internet]. LiveWell@UMD.2015 [cited 2022 Apr 6]. Available from: https://unwellness.wordpress.com/8-dimensions-of-wellnes/.
18. McGrady A, Brennan J, Lynch D, Whearty K. A wellness program for first year medical students. Appl Psychophys Biof. 2012;37(4):253–60. https://doi.org/10.1007/s10484-012-9198-x.
19. Yeung O, Johnston K. Resetting the world with wellness. Miami: Global Wellness Institute; 2020.
20. Ayushman Bharat-Comprehensive Primary Health Care Through Health and Wellness Centres. Guidelines for health and wellness centres in India. Nirman Bhawan, New Delhi: Ministry of Health and Family Welfare, Government of India; 2018.
21. Watt D, Verma S, Flynn L. Wellness programs: a review of the evidence. CMAJ. 1998;158(2):224–30.
22. Caloyeras JP, Liu H, Exum E, et al. Managing manifest diseases, but not health risks, saved PepsiCo money over seven years. Health Aff. 2021;33:124–31. https://www.healthaffairs.org/doi/full/10.1377/hlthaff.2013.0625
23. Baveja L, Counihan A, Hayward T, Lis M, Taneja N. Milliman report. How to implement a wellness programme. International Health Research Series of "How to" papers. 2019.
24. Kim H, Caulfield LE, Garcia-Larsen V, Steffen LM, Coresh J, Rebholz CM. Plant-based diets are associated with a lower risk of incident cardiovascular disease, cardiovascular disease mortality and all cause mortality in a general population of middle-aged adults. J Am Heart Assoc. 2019;8(16):e012865.
25. Tuso PJ, Ismail MH, Ha BP, Bartolotto C. Nutritional update for physicians: plant-based diets. Perm J. 2013;17(2):61–6.
26. Stranahan AM, Lee K, Martin B, Maudsley S, Golden E, Cutler RG, et al. Voluntary exercise and caloric restriction enhance hippocampal dendritic spine density and BDNF levels in diabetic mice. Hippocampus. 2009;19(10):951–61.
27. Seligman MEP, Steen TA, Park N, Peterson C. Positive psychology progress: empirical validation of interventions. Am Psychol. 2005;60(5):410–21.
28. Woodyard C. Exploring the therapeutic effects of yoga and its ability to increase quality of life. Int J Yoga. 2011;4(2):49–54.
29. Science of Behavior Change [Internet]. 2013. [cited 2022 April 7]. Available from: https://communfund.nih.gov/behaviorchange.
30. Thakkar J, Chandhari S, Sarkar PK. Ritucharya: answer to the lifestyle disorders. Ayu. 32(4):466–71. Available from: https://www.ncbi.nlm.nih.gov/pmc/articles/PMC3361919/.
31. Tripathi JS. Deole YS. Indriyopakramaniya Adhyaya. In Reddy PS, Deole YS, Basisht G. (Eds.) Charak Samhita New Edition. 1st Edition, CSRTSDC;2020. https://www.carakasamhitaonline.com/index.php?title=Indriyopakramaniya_Adhyaya&oldid=44474.
32. Eberle C, Kirchner MF, Herden R, Stichling S. Paternal metabolic and cardiovascular programming of their offspring: a systematic scoping review. PLoS One. 2020;15(12):e0244826.
33. NHSRC. Operational guidelines for PM Ayushman Bharat health infrastructure mission. New Delhi: Government of India; 2018.
34. Ministry of Health and Family Welfare. MAA program for infant and young child feeding guidelines. Available from: https://wcd.nic.in.
35. Lena A, Ashok K, Padma M, Kamath V, Kamath A. Health and social problems of the elderly: a cross-sectional study in Udupi taluk, Karnataka. Indian J Community Med. 2009;34:131–4.
36. National Programme for Health Care of the Elderly. Operational guidelines NPHCE. New Delhi: Government of India; 2011. Available from: https://main.mohfw.gov.in/sites/default/files/operationalguidelinesforNPHCE2010.pdf.

37. WHO. Life skill education in schools. Geneva: WHO (Division of Mental Health and Prevention of Substance Abuse); 1997.
38. NCERT. Curriculum on health and wellness of school-going adolescents: under the aegis of School Health Programme of Ayushman Bharat. New Delhi: MHRD, Government of India.
39. WHO. World mental health report: transforming mental health for all. Geneva: WHO; 2022.
40. Goss HB, Cuddihy TF, Tomson-Michaud L. Wellness in higher education: a transformative framework for health-related disciplines. Asia Pac J Health Phys Educ Recreat. 2010;1(2):29–36.
41. National Government Services Portal. Find Government Services Faster. New Delhi: Government of India.
42. IRDAI. Exposure drafts on guidelines on wellness and preventive features/benefits. Insurance Regulatory and Development Authority of India; 2019.
43. Aditya Birla Health Insurance's Health Rewards. https://www.adityabirlacapital.com/multiply-wellness/home.
44. Wipro GearUp and Behavior Spotting programmes. www.wipro.com.
45. Infosys HALE (health assessment and lifestyle enrichment). www.infosys.com.
46. TCS Care. www.tcs.com.
47. LivFit. A corporate wellness program for a healthier workforce. Oman Insurance Company (OIC). 8 Dec 2019. www.tameen.ae/PDFs/Livfit.
48. Vitality wellness programme. www.discovery.co.za/portal.
49. Podhorecka W, Niedbalska D. Health care program at Volkswagen Poznan. Harvard Business Review. 8 Dec 2019. https://www.hbrp.pl/b/program-opieki-zdrowotnej-w-volkswagen-poznan/P10eH4eR8?NO_COOKIES=1.
50. Baicker K, Cutler D, Song Z. Workplace wellness programs can generate savings. Health Aff. 2010;29(2):304–11.

Chapter 12
Infectious Disease and Emergency Response Planning

Vipul Shah, Chahal Anjali, and Shalie Malik

12.1 Introduction

At the onset, we must take the opportunity to both congratulate you and thank you. Congratulations on reading the book so far; we are sure you must have learned some fascinating facts about public health, and thank you for being interested in public health.

In the next few pages, we will try to bring you the core knowledge on pandemic planning at a global level, while the nitty-gritty of outbreak prevention and management will be dealt with in a separate chapter. We will liberally use both anecdotes and parallelisms in this journey to drive home these important lessons. Let us start with simple examples from the animal world—suppose a herd of elephants living in a forest is trying to protect itself from a group of predators—who will it take care of the most? The answer is easy—the infants, the pregnant mothers, the elderly, and those who have some sort of disability. The vulnerable cannot defend themselves; however, in an example of immense solidarity and cohesiveness, the stronger members in the herd keep the weaker ones at the centre and try to repulse all attacks by the predator or group of predators.

Let us take another parallel example from the world of deer; they have similar issues, and to fight off predators, they have developed keen olfactory senses that act

V. Shah (✉)
R.P. Shah Memorial Trust for Global Health and Paediatric Disabilities, Lucknow, Uttar Pradesh, India

C. Anjali
Dr. Giri Lal Gupta Institute of Public Health and Public Affairs, University of Lucknow, Lucknow, Uttar Pradesh, India

S. Malik
Department of Zoology, University of Lucknow, Lucknow, Uttar Pradesh, India

S. Malik et al. (eds.), *Public Health Issues: Theory and Practices*, https://doi.org/10.1007/978-981-96-6650-8_12

as early warning systems, they communicate with each other, gather information from all sources and when they have made a collective decision that there is real danger, they use their best asset—speed and agility—to dash for safety.

The predator is endowed with certain advantages to counter such moves; in the wild, it is a fight for survival is constant and brutal, and though humans have increasingly been able to modify their environment, interactions between humans and animals and/or novel infectious agents are becoming more common as humans increasingly foray into the wild. We will allude to the lessons drawn from these examples in the text later, but let us first understand pandemics from historical references.

12.2 Background of Pandemic Planning

The word "pandemic" comes from the Greek root word "pan," i.e. all, and demos, i.e. "people" or "population." Thus, pandemics affect all of the population. Mankind has been ravaged by infectious diseases throughout antiquity. Infectious diseases such as malaria, which may have aggregately killed 50–60 billion people throughout human history [1], are not considered pandemics anymore because of their high prevalence in the population over centuries. The vagaries of pandemics can be measured by a composite measure of what percentage of people were killed and what was the geographical spread. Historical accounts of the same are often inexact due to the absence of census activities or being only limited to the young male population. In earlier times, states were mostly concerned with the headcount of people they could mobilize in case of external aggression, for census activities, or for purposes of taxation, which underestimated the death count to a large extent. Among large-scale epidemics that killed more than a million people, the Cocoliztli epidemic of 1545–1548 is estimated to have killed 27–80% of the Mexican population of the time, brought about by a probable combination of climate change and an infectious agent [2]. The Black Death pandemic (Bubonic Plague) is estimated to have killed 30–60% of the European population between 1346 and 1353 AD [3]. The plague of Justinian (Bubonic plague) has historically been estimated to have wiped out 25–60% of the European population between 541 and 549 AD with a death toll of 15–100 million people (though that has been challenged recently) [4]. The deadly Spanish flu killed 1–5% of the infected (mostly young) individuals; however, because of its global spread, it killed, according to variable estimates, between 17 and 100 million people [5]. Another important issue when assessing the impact of the pandemics is the need to take the base population numbers into account, the world population has been rising significantly, and coupled with accelerated aging [6] due to demographic shifts, even a small change in the mortality rate can cause an exponential increase in overall deaths in future pandemics. Most estimates of the effects of pandemics have taken only mortality into account; there is only meagre longitudinal follow-up literature on alleged long-term sequelae, for example encephalitis lethargica (Spanish Flu) and Post-Acute COVID-19 Syndrome (PACS) [7, 8], while the literature on societal and economic effects of long-term sequelae is very minuscule and needs to be studied comprehensively to factor in while making decisions during acute phases of the next pandemic. Cognitive literature has repeatedly shown us that biases creep into most of our decisions [9], and therefore, concrete data is needed to prevent such biases and create a better decision-making matrix.

The story of mankind's response to acute pandemic threats and its mitigations thereof is even more interesting. The historical answer to outbreaks, in most cases, was a primal flight reaction, those who had the means to leave would immediately leave the area; outbreaks were carried from one geographical region to another by these migratory groups of people (which included traders), and this led our forefathers to create strict rules of conduct as to how to socially behave with both those who travelled from such areas of outbreaks and those who cared for their sick relatives. The methods of both prevention and treatment were based on either intuitive reactions or accrued knowledge which was transmitted across generations in the form of social and cultural rules, including quarantine and efforts at personal and environmental hygiene. Historically, vaccination was also tried in both India and China [10], but it was not until much later that immunization campaigns became a primary part of the repertoire of techniques for pandemic preparation [11].

A heartwarming story with many lessons for modern public health professionals and students occurred when a smallpox outbreak in 1947 threatened New York City, just before an Easter Sunday parade, which led Israel Weinstein, the city's health commissioner then, to call for everyone to get vaccinated, even if they had received the vaccination as children. The rollout was swift and well orchestrated. Vaccination was provided in school settings, and with overwhelming public support, in less than a month, more than six million New Yorkers were apparently vaccinated while the city ended up recording only 12 infections and two deaths [12]. It is a recurrent lesson during pandemic planning (and experience during the recent COVID-19 pandemic) that societal cohesion and social capital (both bridging and bonding types) are probably among the most important factors in eventual success. During the recent COVID-19 pandemic, oriental societies that leveraged their sense of public decency and morality with the uptake of technology were able to sustain their fight against the onslaught of infection much better [13].

In 1960, at the height of the Cold War and amidst serious concern about the threat of bioterrorism, the US Surgeon General L.E. Burney prepared a framework for responding to the next pandemic, including surveillance, immediate large-scale manufacture and distribution of vaccines, and the identification of key areas of research, but nothing much happened at the ground level, since at the political level it was felt that other priorities were more important and that the risk of the threat was politically "expendable" [14]. Every new influenza variant would bring a flurry of activity, but on the whole, this reactive mode continued. In 1967, the World Health Organization announced the Intensified Smallpox Eradication Programme, which aimed to eradicate smallpox in more than 30 countries through surveillance and vaccination. Despite the ongoing Cold War, during which both sides did not want to look each other in the face, it was heartening to see the United States and the Soviet Union united in support of the programme, leading to the global eradication of smallpox, which along with polio eradication represents the crowning jewels in the achievements of public health in general and WHO in particular, and create a roadmap for sustained international efforts in pandemic preparedness planning.

In January 1976, a novel swine-origin influenza virus was found to infect soldiers at Fort Dix, New Jersey, USA; this new development among the army complex galvanized the highest decision-making echelons to mount a pan-US national immunization programme leading to US Congress-funded vaccine production and liability indemnification of manufacturers (to help quicken response without fear among the manufacturers since the Cutter incident was still fresh in memory), quick vaccine production, and a mass immunization campaign, lead to a massive 45.65 million persons vaccinated in the United States. After approximately 2 months of intense action on the vaccination front, the programme was suspended since the threat was contained and the risk of a link between the "swine flu" vaccine and Guillain–Barré syndrome had emerged (later confirmed). This experience of being able to modulate or naturally control a potential threat, along with a more nuanced understanding of the risk posed by risk-mitigating action taken, led to a more cautious approach to interpreting initial data and consequent nuanced risk communication to the lay public, greater investment in research and preparedness, a better understanding of US interagency operational responsibilities, a push towards better intragovernmental communication between planners, better logistic ground-level preparation for execution, and improved mechanisms for programme evaluation in the face of emergency in the United States and slowly across the globe [14].

By 1986, legislation created the US National Vaccine Program Office (NVPO), and in 1992, a meeting was held in Courchevel, France, which led to the formation of a US Federal Interagency Group on Influenza Pandemic Preparedness Response. In 1993, for the first time, non-federal consultants were included in the effort of pandemic planning in the United States, which ultimately led to the creation of a global core group of public health experts dedicated to pandemic planning with diverse educational and national backgrounds [14].

In 1997, the first outbreak of avian influenza A (H5N1) virus infections in humans was found in Hong Kong, with more than 30% mortality in infected humans, which caused global alarm and led to the culling of more than 1.5 million chickens [14]. This grave risk gave a further fillip to global pandemic planning. At this juncture, it is important to reiterate that this chapter in no way claims to be or meant to be a compendium of complete knowledge of pandemic planning, and the reader interested in delving deeper into the subject is encouraged to read the various references that have been alluded to in the text along with the relevant chapters in the textbook for a comprehensive understanding of the principles and scope of the planning efforts.

12.3 Impact of Prior Pandemic Planning Efforts

The World Health Organization (WHO) published its first formal pandemic plan in 1999 [15] and subsequently promoted pandemic planning globally among member states, but apparently, this had a limited global effect, geographically limited to the global north. The year 2003 saw a reemergence of the H5N1 virus [16], which led to concerns among those involved in pandemic planning that the next pandemic would be caused by the spread of the H5N1 virus, with a nidus in Asia and spillover into Africa and Europe. The International Partnership on Avian and Pandemic Influenza was formed to coordinate support for developing countries' efforts to control the spread of the (H5N1) virus and to prepare for an influenza pandemic; these efforts generated monetary support and pledges, both in money and educational services from the Global North to support global pandemic preparedness, elevated readiness in governmental circles across the globe, and also spurred private entrepreneurial activity in terms of research and expansion of testing and manufacturing capacities on a global level. In addition to direct financial assistance, the US government also provided direct technical assistance to help countries develop capacities for rapid response, laboratory diagnosis, and surveillance. The US government focused on the creation of a Strategic National Stockpile sufficient to treat 25% of the US population, procurement of ventilators and PPE (including respirators), advanced development agenda for vaccines, therapeutics, and diagnostics with the 5-year aim of creating the capacity to produce sufficient vaccine to protect the entire US population within 6 months of the onset of an influenza pandemic, modernizing diagnostic technologies for public health laboratories [14]. The UK Influenza Preparedness Strategy 2011 [17] and the European thrust to pandemic preparedness were modelled on almost similar lines with cross-government exercises to test the response. In 2015, the WHO implemented a comprehensive global research strategy and preparedness plan known as the WHO R&D Blueprint for Epidemics and the formation of a WHO pathogen priority list, which ensured that research efforts were concentrated on diseases with epidemic or pandemic potential where medical countermeasures were limited or non-existent [18]. The aforementioned strategies helped the WHO to halt the spread of Ebola Virus and Monkeypox infections from Africa into the world; however, prior experiences of the influenza waves showed that stockpiling vaccines was useless and there was a shift in the thought process on pandemic planning, which entailed moving beyond vaccine-only strategies [19].

The experiences of the COVID-19 pandemic bared the glaring mistakes and gaps in global pandemic planning efforts, and since November 2022, the WHO has started focusing on entire classes of viruses or bacteria rather than individual pathogens related to 30 viral families, one core group of bacteria, and "Pathogen X"—an unknown pathogen with the potential to trigger a severe global epidemic. This new approach is also expected to help identify representative viruses (or prototypes) within a viral family as a pathfinder in generating evidence and filling knowledge gaps that may then be applied to other viruses of threat in the same family, with the end goal of improved pandemic preparedness by proactively managing emerging viruses and other threats on a global scale [20].

In April 2023, under the aegis of the International Health Regulations (2005), the WHO launched an initiative that provides guidance on integrated planning for responding to any respiratory pathogen such as influenza or coronaviruses. The new Preparedness and Resilience for Emerging Threats Initiative (PRET) incorporates the latest tools, shared learning of best global practices, and advocates for collective action established during the COVID-19 pandemic and other recent public health emergencies, using an entirely new method, focussing on the mode of transmission approach to guide countries in pandemic planning instead of individual diseases more so since many capacities and capabilities are common among groups of pathogens. It is also envisaged that the aforementioned guidance will include technical guidance and support for promoting and strengthening integrated preparedness and response, as outlined in World Health Assembly resolutions [21].

Coming back to the two examples from the animal world that we started off with, it is not out of place to remember that in the fight against all infections, we need to ethically prioritize the needs of the vulnerable; the ring formed by the stronger elephants in the herd parallels the "ring vaccination" technique used to stop an infection, and the deer example offers us valuable lessons in early detection, developing strong communication system, and the value of speed and agility triumphing over perfection.

To a casual reader entering the vast ocean of pandemic planning, it would be of interest to know that of the whole gamut of pathogens known to infect humans, >70% are zoonotic and viral in nature [22]. Animals can not only infect humans directly but can also serve as reservoirs of the infectious agent or as amplifier hosts, easing the initial leap from animals to humans through direct or indirect interactions. In a large number of instances, humans act as dead-end hosts to these agents; however, either by chance or spurred by a bid to survive within the new human host, some pathogens acquire genetic mutations to sustain human-to-human infection [23]. In extremely rare circumstances, new host exclusivity is eventually acquired and subsequently sustained; however, most acute viral zoonoses require constant reintroduction from non-human hosts [24] to begin human-to-human transmission, which in recent days has largely been triggered by human influences such as climate change, deforestation, farming, population, and societal dynamics, leading to a dangerous upward trend [25] (for further understanding the reader is urged to refer to chapter 12 in the textbook by Alagan R et al.). It is needless to repeat that globalized interconnected economies, the need for international travel, along with the increased speed of climate change, have increased the speed at which potential outbreaks can spread multifold.

The global pandemic effort and the framework of the WHO Pandemic Preparation were based on the following learnings, which finally led to advanced discussions on the pandemic accord [26] and finally culminated in a historic Pandemic Agreement in May 2025.

1. Countries will have full sovereignty in addressing public health matters, including pandemic prevention, preparedness, response, and health systems recovery

2. Focus on international cooperation and obligations for states regarding international laws and human rights during emergent situations
3. Equity will be a principle, indicator, and outcome of all pandemic-related activities, including prevention, preparedness, and response
4. Enjoyment of the highest attainable standard of health is a fundamental right without any discrimination and global health inequality is a common danger
5. WHO will have a central role in directing and coordinating authority in pandemic prevention, preparedness, response, and recovery of health systems and will focus on generating scientific evidence through multilateral cooperation
6. Pandemics require member countries to prioritize effective and enhanced cooperation with development partners and other relevant stakeholders
7. The international spread of disease is a global threat with serious effects on public health, human lives, livelihoods, societies, and economies, necessitating global participation of countries and relevant stakeholders in an effective, coordinated, appropriate, and comprehensive manner
8. International Health Regulations of the World Health Organization need to be used in ways that are commensurate with and restricted to public health risks, and avoidance of unnecessary interference with international traffic and trade is required
9. National action plans should be inclusive, with a focus on communities and persons in vulnerable situations, places, and ecosystems
10. Pandemic preparation and response must be systemically integrated into whole-of-government and whole-of-society approaches, ensuring adequate political commitment, resourcing, and cross-sectoral coordination to break the cycle of "panic and neglect"
11. The accord and planning will take into consideration past experiences of global outbreaks, e.g. coronavirus disease (COVID-19) HIV, Ebola virus disease, Zika virus disease, Middle East respiratory syndrome, and monkeypox/mpox, in a bid to improve future response and close identified gaps
12. Recognizing the COVID-19 experience that urban settings are especially vulnerable to infectious diseases and epidemics, and the important role that communities have in preventing, preparing for, and responding to health emergencies
13. Women were disproportionately impacted by the burden of the pandemic; they constituted more than 70% of the global healthcare workforce (both formal and informal), and therefore, diverse, gender-balanced and equitable representation is necessary at all levels of pandemic preparation and response
14. There is concern that those affected by conflict and insecurity are particularly at risk during pandemics and need to be prioritized
15. Multisectoral collaboration is needed through whole-of-government and whole-of-society approaches at all levels; collaboration, coordination, and global solidarity are important achieving sustainable improvements in pandemic prevention, preparedness, and effective response
16. There needs to be an acknowledgment that the effects of pandemics are not limited to death and health alone but spill across a broad array of sectors, including economic growth, employment, trade, transport, gender inequality, food insecurity, education, environment, and culture

17. The determinants of health impact the vulnerability of communities/persons in vulnerable situations to the spread of pathogens and the evolution of an outbreak
18. Multilateral regional cooperation and good governance are essential in pandemics, which are cross-border in nature and require collective action and solidarity
19. Policies and interventions should be supported by the best available scientific evidence and adapted to take into account resources and capacities at subnational and national levels
20. Access to timely information and efficient risk communication to counteract pandemics (and infodemic) is of utmost importance
21. There needs to be a recognition of the fact that most emerging infectious diseases originate in animals, including wildlife and domesticated animals, and then spill over to people; therefore, there is a need for a synergistic "One Health" approach with an urgent need to detect and prevent health threats at the animal and human interface, in particular zoonotic spillover and mutations, and to sustainably balance and optimize the health of people, animals, and ecosystems through the creation of the Quadripartite (WHO, the Food and Agriculture Organization of the United Nations, the World Organisation for Animal Health, and the United Nations Environment Programme) given the growing possible drivers
22. Antimicrobial resistance is a silent pandemic and could be an aggravating factor during a pandemic
23. Building and strengthening resilient health systems to advance universal health coverage as the foundation for effective, equitable pandemic response, and recognizing that health is a precondition for, and an outcome and indicator of social, economic, and environmental dimensions of sustainable development and the 2030 SDG Agenda
24. Pandemics have a disproportionately heavy impact on frontline workers (particularly health workers), the poor, and vulnerable people in vulnerable situations, which hampers the achievement of universal health coverage and the Sustainable Development Goals
25. Global solidarity, effective global coordination, accountability, and transparency are necessary to reduce shocks, especially for countries with limited capacities and resources, since gross inequities hindered timely access to medical and other COVID-19 pandemic-related products, and a better pandemic response will need common but differentiated responsibility from all States Parties and relevant stakeholders
26. Health equity needs to be achieved through resolute action on social, environmental, cultural, political, and economic determinants of health, e.g. eradicating hunger and poverty, ensuring access to health and proper food, safe drinking water and sanitation, employment, decent work, and social protection in a comprehensive intersectoral approach
27. To make quality, people-centred health care for all a reality, equitable access to high-quality health services without financial hardship through a well-trained skilled workforce, adequate investment, and committed policy-makers are needed

28. There has been a growing recognition that publicly funded research and development plays an important role in the development of pandemic-related products and, as such, conditionalities can be imposed. The Doha Declaration on the Trade-Related Aspects of Intellectual Property Rights (TRIPS Agreement) and Public Health of 2001 does not prevent the World Trade Organization and its members from taking appropriate steps to protect public health and, in particular, to promote equitable access to medicines. Balancing the competing interests of protecting intellectual property rights for the development of new medical products, while recognizing concerns about their effects on prices and using innovative options to increase global efforts towards equitable and timely production, access, and distribution of health technologies, vaccines, drugs, and diagnostic know-how, preferably by enhancing local production during pandemic situations, is warranted"
29. Recognizing the structural barriers at the institutional and operational levels during the global response to the COVID-19 pandemic, an urgent need has been felt to establish a clear roadmap for a non-charitable model of pandemic preparation and response while recognizing the need for sustainable mechanisms to support the transfer of technology and know-how to support the same while balancing the competitive interests but not to the detriment of public health (resolution WHA61.21 (2008) in a pandemic situation
30. The importance of promoting early, safe, transparent, and rapid sharing of samples and genetic sequence data of pathogens cannot be underscored as well as ensuring fair and equitable sharing of benefits arising therefrom under international laws (International Health Regulations, the Convention on Biological Diversity and its Nagoya Protocol) and the efforts made by all international bodies and relevant stakeholders towards this goal should be continued.

Central to the pandemic response are issues of speed, cost, and trust. Science and technology can help solve the first two problems, but it is of paramount importance that we have consensus on global coordination, communication, and governance to ensure the use of foolproof mechanisms to produce and deploy quality interventions rapidly on a global scale, which generate trust in the products' safety and efficacy. It has to be reiterated at this point that pandemic preparedness will need to include bio-surveillance and viral discovery (with its associated risks of lab leaks), fundamental research (pathogenesis, immunology, antigen design, delivery, reagents, and assays), and research and development of prototype vaccine platforms, therapeutics, and diagnostics so that they can be deployed at the earliest.

The WHO, on its part, has advocated the need to establish a Global Alliance for Preventing Pandemics and an International Collaborative Public Health Research Centre, which would establish sustainable infrastructure for infectious disease discovery, surveillance, diagnostics, and response, with sample receipt to pathogen identification in less than 8 h, with the added ability to identify several new pathogens using agnostic serological assays and to detect the footprint of past infections in the immune system, elucidate the causes of outbreaks, and provide early evidence of cross-species transmission [27]. It is expected that the pandemic agreement adopted by the World Health Assembly will boost global collaboration in the field and has the potential to lead to a stronger, more equitable response to future pandemic prevention, preparedness, and response.

It has been pointed out that while we currently have a wealth of genomic data, we have limited full-genome data and limited translational information on connections between surveillance and discovery. Often, critical data needed for forecasting is either unavailable or not used for public health measures [28]. Choosing between multiple candidates for clinical trials of vaccines is based on prioritization and availability. There has been a shift in regulatory approach in favour of immunobridging (evidence showed that neutralizing Abs from different platforms were protective) which was used in COVID-19 vaccine approvals. Issues during such emergent conditions will include an urgent need to understand protection, vaccine effect, and population immunity, which would require high-quality assays. While antibody responses are important, T-cell responses are more durable and more cross-reactive than antibodies. For public health professionals, it is important to keep in mind that the best strategy for prioritization will depend on the specific agent at that point. In a bid to reduce the bench-to-bedside time, new technologies to define the atomic-level details of surface proteins likely to be vaccine targets and the use of artificial intelligence/machine learning combined with high-throughput screening to allow accelerated development of vaccine antigens for important human pathogens, along with the rapid development of monoclonal antibody and protein reagents, are urgently needed Such aforementioned technologies are in advanced stages of use, research, and development [29, 30]. At this juncture, it will be interesting for public health professionals to know that monoclonal antibodies during the COVID-19 pandemic were discovered and approved for emergency use authorization within a short duration of 3 months between the discovery and the first human dose underlying the effectiveness of such strategies [31, 32].

The public health planner also needs to remember that there are poor responses to vaccines in the most vulnerable, and therefore, the value of monoclonals and medications cannot be understated; thus, it will be foolhardy to pursue a vaccine-only strategy. Recent experiences over the last two decades have shown that time-tested public health strategies cannot be thrown out of the window and that the breadth of protection needs to be considered in the context of goals—whether we are targeting broad protection against infection vs severe disease, which again will depend on the agent.

12.4 Issues Plaguing Global Pandemic Preparation and the Way Forward

Before we delve further into the issues plaguing global pandemic planning, we need to understand that the major population of the world lives in the Global South, where increased pressure on land and abject poverty make increasing interactions with the animal world a daily necessity. The Global South is also facing a double whammy of a high load of prior infectious diseases and increased lifestyle diseases; this milieu is a perfect condition for infectious outbreaks. Any infectious agent also has more hosts to spread to and therefore higher chances of finding a mutation which may help the agent become sturdier and more capable of further spread. Poor infrastructure and poor spending on public health make early detection difficult. Poor nutrition due to poverty complicates things, and poverty creates further structural, emotional, and cultural barriers to access, which further delay the early detection of outbreaks.

The Global South believes that further emphasis on transparency and promptness in the declaration process at the WHO level is needed, while simultaneously recognizing that the WHO currently enjoys very little flexibility in the use of funds. The Global South also believes that there is an urgent need to ensure that extra-budgetary or voluntary contributions are unearmarked to ensure that the WHO has the necessary flexibility for their usage in areas where they are required the most, without putting an overwhelming financial burden on developing countries. The discussion on which country contributes how much to the WHO and with what strings attached is a thorny issue, which, alongside issues of the TRIPS waiver during a pandemic outbreak and the speed/volume of distribution of materials (vaccines), plagues global pandemic planning efforts and threatens to derail it completely [33–35]. The Global South also pushes for more representation in the technical committees, transparency in fund utilization, and advocates for alignment of expenditure by the WHO in consonance with country priorities. The Member States have a self-reporting obligation under IHR 2005, and the review of IHR implementation is voluntary; however, there have been voices in the Global North advocating not only to make it mandatory but also to levy strict punishment in case of any issues. There is a growing sense of uneasiness in the Global South, with voices focussing on the fact that building and strengthening capacities in member states is needed based on the self-reporting on IHR 2005 done by the Member States and that the WHO should support the creation of IHR technical and core competencies in each country to facilitate broad global uniformity. A paradigm change is desperately needed, as per the Global South, where the Member States of the WHO should be encouraged to notify the WHO of significant information, including pathogen samples, in the early stages of an outbreak without being shamed or treated unfairly by travel bans due to the same. The subject of travel bans and lockdowns has stirred a lot of debate, even in scientific circles (on aspects of necessity, appropriateness, and/or ability to stop further spread). However, their effectiveness depends on multiple factors, including host factors, agent factors including the mechanism of spread of the infection, and the period during which an infected person can transmit the infection without showing clinical symptoms; therefore, the Global South argues that in case travel bans are effected, there should be an effective means of ensuring that the losses suffered by the reporting country are minimized and, if possible, repatriated at the earliest. The TRIPS waiver has been another point of standoff between the two sides [35]. While the World Health Assembly has adopted the pandemic agreement, the next steps include thorny and contentious negotiations on pathogen access and how the commercial benefits will be shared, and it is where rhetoric will have to stand the test of harsh truth.

One of the biggest learnings for the scientific community during the pandemic is the stark realization of the importance of effective public health and economic measures for health emergencies, which need leveraging a multidisciplinary approach, including social sciences alongside health and natural sciences. It is not out of place here to state that none of the sciences can afford to work in silos. The partnership on pandemic management needs to be supplemented by another necessary partnership for digital health under the aegis of the WHO, according to some countries in the Global South [35].

Another important lesson from the COVID-19 pandemic is that the best treatment is one that is acceptable to the population. For effective pandemic planning, cultural competencies need to be developed at all levels [36–38] with the use of appropriate gatekeepers from cohesive societies to get the whole group to accept treatment, and in this quest, leveraging bridging capital to disseminate information (e.g. using social media influencers) becomes imperative, while bonding capital may help enforce public health policies. Needless to mention here that in such situations, the existence and force of the state are themselves eroded [39–42].

A person in modern society is simultaneously exposed to the neighbourhood [43, 44], workplace [45], kinship [46, 47], or group contexts which may confound, have cumulative or even compensatory influences in decision-making, especially during pandemic situations; understanding the nuances at different contextual levels, for example, home, community, state, and national levels and their intersections, is very important for global bodies and public health workers involved in pandemic planning efforts. The value of building informal channels of communication at all levels cannot be understated. Social media can be a proverbial razor-edged sword and can both make or break efforts, future states will have to balance the twin goals of individual rights and public good when making decisions on media autonomy and that there cannot be a single right prescription for all the myriad conditions that can crop up. The need to keep all channels of discussion open at all times, allowing grief ventilation at all levels, and the need for leadership and statesmanship at all levels cannot be underscored in such circumstances.

Empirical analyses tend to show that strong welfare regimes boost social cohesion, informal social participation, membership in civic associations and a higher level of social trust, with effects on health [48, 49]. Investments in strengthening community bonds without making structural changes may not fully solve public health problems during a pandemic setting, and there is no magic bullet or standard recipe book for how to intervene without carefully considering the local context, as well as the history of the involved population. Prior pandemic management experiences, however, have shown the need to incorporate strong welfare measures and to ensure a continuum of access to regular medical care, especially in the Global South [50].

The lay public, political institutions, and judicial officers, by extension, have been slowly cultured on the idea of "individualized" risk of disease in most countries across the world [51], with a narrow focus on the proximal risk factors for injury and disease. Individualization leads us to identify risks or harms and intervene to prevent or reduce them using surveillance, injury prevention, and infectious disease control (e.g., vaccination, partner notification, and quarantine) [52]. However, due to this approach, political institutions and the judiciary in most countries of the world are unable to find the "distal factors" or the real factors. Health behaviours displayed by the public may be "personal," but the genesis of the behaviours often depends on social factors (including social norms) [53–55], which need to be ameliorated and given due importance to prevent the mal-behaviours from developing in the first place and to try and change the mal-behaviour by social and behavioural methods, including the active reduction of the structural and behavioural barriers which propagate and maintain these health mal-behaviours.

12.5 Conclusions

Advocacy is important for achieving pandemic proofing across political cycles of being elected and has to come from multiple quarters. The WHO, judiciary, civil society, and global public health advocates have the role of providing the nudge and trying to keep the long-term goal in focus. There is often insufficient health data, and activism can help "nudge" policymakers into establishing and maintaining representative data systems. In addition to the above-mentioned stakeholders, the executive has a major role to play in this regard and efforts to sensitize the executive, which can often ride out the waves of political change, are a necessity. Sensitizing the fourth estate (the media) and communities, in particular, is imperative, and major cross-sectoral efforts need to be undertaken to sensitize them to the risks of pandemics and climate change. It is also imperative to state at this juncture that modern lifestyles have reached a level of consumption that makes it impossible for them to scale back; the bulwark of pandemic preparation and fighting climate change effects will fall on leveraging technological advancements, a task which will need long-term commitment, both financial and otherwise. At this juncture, we need to remember that "Black swan events" do occur, and in an "increasingly connected" yet "polarized" world, teetering on the edge of an abyss caused by climate change, such an event caused by a global pandemic has the potential to wipe out a sizeable majority of the human population and collapse human civilization as we know today. The burden to prevent such a catastrophe will have to be borne by an increasingly connected synchronized "global activism" across multiple disciplines, and public health professionals will have to be at the forefront of such efforts alongside activists fighting climate change.

References

1. Whitfield J. Portrait of a serial killer. Nature. 2002. https://doi.org/10.1038/news021001-6.
2. Acuna-Soto R, Stahle DW, Cleaveland MK, Therrell MD. Megadrought and megadeath in 16th century Mexico. Emerg Infect Dis. 2002;8(4):360–2. https://doi.org/10.3201/eid0804.010175. PMID: 11971767; PMCID: PMC2730237.
3. Spyrou MA, Musralina L, Gnecchi Ruscone GA, et al. The source of the Black Death in fourteenth-century central Eurasia. Nature. 2022;606:718–24. https://doi.org/10.1038/s41586-022-04800-3.
4. White LA, Mordechai L. Modeling the Justinianic Plague: comparing hypothesized transmission routes. PLoS One. 2020;15(4):e0231256. https://doi.org/10.1371/journal.pone.0231256. PMID: 32352988; PMCID: PMC7192389.

5. Spreeuwenberg P, Kroneman M, Paget J. Reassessing the global mortality burden of the 1918 influenza pandemic. Am J Epidemiol. 2018;187(12):2561–7. https://doi.org/10.1093/aje/kwy191. PMID: 30202996; PMCID: PMC7314216.
6. World Health Organization. Ageing and health. 2022. Available from: https://who.int/news-room/fact-sheets/detail/ageing-and-health. Accessed 25 July 2024.
7. McCall S, Vilensky JA, Gilman S, Taubenberger JK. The relationship between encephalitis lethargica and influenza: a critical analysis. J Neurovirol. 2008;14(3):177–85. https://doi.org/10.1080/13550280801995445. PMID: 18569452; PMCID: PMC2778472.
8. Chiappelli F, Fotovat L. Post acute CoViD-19 syndrome (PACS) – long CoViD. Bioinformation. 2022;18(10):908–11. https://doi.org/10.6026/97320630018908. PMID: 37654836; PMCID: PMC10465760.
9. Featherston R, Downie LE, Vogel AP, Galvin KL. Decision making biases in the allied health professions: a systematic scoping review. PLoS One. 2020;15(10):e0240716. https://doi.org/10.1371/journal.pone.0240716. PMID: 33079949; PMCID: PMC7575084.
10. Boylston A. The origins of inoculation. J R Soc Med. 2012;105(7):309–13. https://doi.org/10.1258/jrsm.2012.12k044. PMID: 22843649; PMCID: PMC3407399.
11. Mark C, Rigau-Pérez JG. The world's first immunization campaign: the Spanish Smallpox Vaccine Expedition, 1803-1813. Bull Hist Med. 2009;83(1):63–94. https://doi.org/10.1353/bhm.0.0173. PMID: 19329842.
12. Sepkowitz KA. The 1947 smallpox vaccination campaign in New York City, revisited. Emerg Infect Dis. 2004;10(5):960–1. https://doi.org/10.3201/eid1005.030973. PMID: 15216846; PMCID: PMC3323221.
13. Ma M, Wang S, Wu F. Covid-19 prevalence and well-being. In: The world happiness report; 2021. Available from: https://worldhappiness.report/ed/2021/covid-19-prevalence-and-well-being-lessons-from-east-asia/.
14. Iskander J, Strikas RA, Gensheimer KF, Cox NJ, Redd SC. Pandemic influenza planning, United States, 1978-2008. Emerg Infect Dis. 2013;19(6):879–85. https://doi.org/10.3201/eid1906.121478. PMID: 23731839; PMCID: PMC3713824.
15. Gust ID, Hampson AW, Lavanchy D. Planning for the next pandemic of influenza. Rev Med Virol. 2001;11(1):59–70. https://doi.org/10.1002/rmv.301. PMID: 11241802.
16. Chan PK. Outbreak of avian influenza A(H5N1) virus infection in Hong Kong in 1997. Clin Infect Dis. 2002;34(Suppl 2):S58–64. https://doi.org/10.1086/338820. PMID: 11938498.
17. UK Influenza Pandemic Preparedness Strategy. 2011. Available from: https://www.gov.uk/government/publications/review-of-the-evidence-base-underpinning-the-uk-influenza-pandemic-preparedness-strategy.
18. WHO Research and Development Blueprint. WHO research and development blueprint: evaluation of ideas for potential platforms to support development and production of health technologies for priority infectious diseases with epidemic potential. 2016. Available from: https://www.who.int/publications/i/item/who-research-and-development-blueprint-evaluation-of-ideas-for-potential-platforms-to-support-development-and-production-of-health-technologies-for-priority-infectious-diseases-with-epidemic-potential.
19. Radonovich LJ, Magalian PD, Hollingsworth MK, Baracco G. Stockpiling supplies for the next influenza pandemic. Emerg Infect Dis. 2009;15(6):e1. https://doi.org/10.3201/eid1506.081196. PMID: 21970033; PMCID: PMC2727308.
20. WHO. Research response to pathogen X during a pandemic. WHO Report scientific approach pandemic preparedness. 2024. Available from: https://www.who.int/news-room/events/detail/2024/01/19/default-calendar/Research-response-to-pathogen-X-during-a-pandemic.
21. WHO. Report on Preparedness and resilience for emerging threats (PRET). 2023. Available from: https://www.who.int/initiatives/preparedness-and-resilience-for-emerging-threats.
22. Leal Filho W, Ternova L, Parasnis SA, Kovaleva M, Nagy GJ. Climate change and zoonoses: a review of concepts, definitions, and bibliometrics. Int J Environ Res Public Health. 2022;19(2):893. https://doi.org/10.3390/ijerph19020893. PMID: 35055715; PMCID: PMC8776135.
23. Furuse Y, Oshitani H. Viruses that can and cannot coexist with humans and the future of SARS-CoV-2. Front Microbiol. 2020;11:583252. https://doi.org/10.3389/fmicb.2020.583252. PMID: 33042101; PMCID: PMC7530166.

24. Warren CJ, Sawyer SL. How host genetics dictates successful viral zoonosis. PLoS Biol. 2019;17(4):e3000217. https://doi.org/10.1371/journal.pbio.3000217. PMID: 31002666; PMCID: PMC6474636.
25. Marie V, Gordon ML. The (re-)emergence and spread of viral zoonotic disease: a perfect storm of human ingenuity and stupidity. Viruses. 2023;15(8):1638. https://doi.org/10.3390/v15081638. PMID: 37631981; PMCID: PMC10458268.
26. WHO. Report on Ninth meeting of the intergovernmental negotiating body to draft and negotiate a who convention, agreement or other international instrument on pandemic prevention, preparedness and response. Revised draft of the negotiating text of the WHO Pandemic Agreement. 2024. Available from: https://apps.who.int/gb/inb/pdf_files/inb9/A_inb9_3-en.pdf.
27. WHO. Report on WHO Hub on pandemic and epidemic intelligence. Pandemic Hub. Available from: https://pandemichub.who.int/.
28. Stockdale JE, Liu P, Colijn C. The potential of genomics for infectious disease forecasting. Nat Microbiol. 2022;7:1736–43. https://doi.org/10.1038/s41564-022-01233-6.
29. Ruffolo JA, Chu LS, Mahajan SP, et al. Fast, accurate antibody structure prediction from deep learning on massive set of natural antibodies. Nat Commun. 2023;14:2389. https://doi.org/10.1038/s41467-023-38063-x.
30. Brisse M, Vrba SM, Kirk N, Liang Y, Ly H. Emerging concepts and technologies in vaccine development. Front Immunol. 2020;11:583077. https://doi.org/10.3389/fimmu.2020.583077. PMID: 33101309; PMCID: PMC7554600.
31. Jones BE, Brown-Augsburger PL, Corbett KS, Westendorf K, Davies J, Cujec TP, Wiethoff CM, Blackbourne JL, Heinz BA, Foster D, Higgs RE, Balasubramaniam D, Wang L, Zhang Y, Yang ES, Bidshahri R, Kraft L, Hwang Y, Žentelis S, Jepson KR, Goya R, Smith MA, Collins DW, Hinshaw SJ, Tycho SA, Pellacani D, Xiang P, Muthuraman K, Sobhanifar S, Piper MH, Triana FJ, Hendle J, Pustilnik A, Adams AC, Berens SJ, Baric RS, Martinez DR, Cross RW, Geisbert TW, Borisevich V, Abiona O, Belli HM, de Vries M, Mohamed A, Dittmann M, Samanovic MI, Mulligan MJ, Goldsmith JA, Hsieh CL, Johnson NV, Wrapp D, McLellan JS, Barnhart BC, Graham BS, Mascola JR, Hansen CL, Falconer E. The neutralizing antibody, LY-CoV555, protects against SARS-CoV-2 infection in nonhuman primates. Sci Transl Med. 2021;13(593):eabf1906. https://doi.org/10.1126/scitranslmed.abf1906. Epub 2021 Apr 5. PMID: 33820835; PMCID: PMC8284311.
32. King DF, Groves H, Weller C, et al. Realising the potential of correlates of protection for vaccine development, licensure and use: short summary. NPJ Vaccines. 2024;9:82. https://doi.org/10.1038/s41541-024-00872-6.
33. Juneja Gandhi T, Dumka N, Kotwal A. Is the proposed global treaty an answer for public health emergencies? BMJ Glob Health. 2023;8(9):e012759. https://doi.org/10.1136/bmjgh-2023-012759. PMID: 37709300; PMCID: PMC10503390.
34. WHO. Report on Pandemic prevention, preparedness and response accord. Available from: https://www.who.int/news-room/questions-and-answers/item/pandemic-prevention%2D%2Dpreparedness-and-response-accord. Accessed 10 June 2024.
35. Government of India. Report on India's approach on WHO reforms from the website of Ministry of Health and Family Welfare. Government of India. Available from: https://main.mohfw.gov.in/?q=newshighlights-29. Accessed 27 July 2024.
36. Brashear CA, Thomas N. Core competencies for combatting crisis: fusing ethics, cultural competence, and cognitive flexibility in counseling. Couns Psychol Q. 2020;35:215. https://doi.org/10.1080/09515070.2020.1768362.
37. Lee E, Kourgiantakis T, Hu R. Teaching note—teaching socially just culturally competent practice online: pedagogical challenges and lessons learned during the pandemic. J Soc Work Educ. 2021;57(sup1):58–65. https://doi.org/10.1080/10437797.2021.1935367.
38. Papadopoulos I. The Covid-19 pandemic and cultural competence: global implications for managers, nurses and healthcare workers during major health disasters and emergencies. J Nurs Manag. 2022;30(7):2451–2.
39. Bilal A, Hoogensen Gjørv G, Lanteigne M, Brancaleoni R, Gjørv J, Gui D, Kielar JK, Aluola C, Magalini S. Comprehensive security, disinformation, and COVID-19: an analysis of the impacts of mis- and disinformation and populist narratives during the pandemic. Open Res

Eur. 2023;3:209. https://doi.org/10.12688/openreseurope.16733.1. PMID: 38515932; PMCID: PMC10956505.
40. Roels NI, Estrella A, Maldonado-Salcedo M, Rapp R, Hansen H, Hardon A. Confident futures: community-based organizations as first responders and agents of change in the face of the Covid-19 pandemic. Soc Sci Med. 2022;294:114639. https://doi.org/10.1016/j.socscimed.2021.114639. Epub 2021 Dec 17. PMID: 34998135; PMCID: PMC8683095.
41. Wong AS, Kohler JC. Social capital and public health: responding to the COVID-19 pandemic. Glob Health. 2020;16:88. https://doi.org/10.1186/s12992-020-00615-x.
42. Alfano V. Does social capital enforce social distancing? The role of bridging and bonding social capital in the evolution of the pandemic. Econ Polit. 2022;39:839–59. https://doi.org/10.1007/s40888-021-00255-3.
43. Noppert GA, Clarke P, Hoover A, et al. State variation in neighborhood COVID-19 burden across the United States. Commun Med. 2024;4:36. https://doi.org/10.1038/s43856-024-00459-1.
44. Rigolon A, Németh J, Anderson-Gregson B, Miller AR, deSouza P, Montague B, Hussain C, Erlandson KM, Rowan SE. The neighborhood built environment and COVID-19 hospitalizations. PLoS One. 2023;18(6):e0286119. https://doi.org/10.1371/journal.pone.0286119. PMID: 37314984; PMCID: PMC10266617.
45. Nafilyan V, Pawelek P, Ayoubkhani D, et al. Occupation and COVID-19 mortality in England: a national linked data study of 14.3 million adults. Occup Environ Med. 2022;79:433–41.
46. Snyder M, Alburez-Gutierrez D, Williams I, Zagheni E. Estimates from 31 countries show the significant impact of COVID-19 excess mortality on the incidence of family bereavement. Proc Natl Acad Sci USA. 2022;119(26):e2202686119. https://doi.org/10.1073/pnas.2202686119. Epub 2022 Jun 23. PMID: 35737829; PMCID: PMC9245632.
47. Reed MN, Li L, Pesando LM, Harris LE, Furstenberg FF, Teitler JO. Communication with kin in the wake of the COVID-19 pandemic. Socius. 2023;9:1–15. https://doi.org/10.1177/23780231231199388.
48. Rostila M. Invited commentary: social cohesion, depression, and the role of welfare states. Am J Epidemiol. 2020;189(4):354–7. https://doi.org/10.1093/aje/kwz207. PMID: 31573029; PMCID: PMC7274177.
49. Andrews R, Jilke S. Welfare states and social cohesion in Europe: does social service quality matter? J Soc Policy. 2016;45(1):119–40. https://doi.org/10.1017/S0047279415000513.
50. Madhav N, Oppenheim B, Gallivan M, et al. Pandemics: risks, impacts, and mitigation. In: Jamison DT, Gelband H, Horton S, et al., editors. Disease control priorities: improving health and reducing poverty. 3rd ed. Washington, DC: The International Bank for Reconstruction and Development/The World Bank; 2017. Available from: https://www.ncbi.nlm.nih.gov/books/NBK525302/, https://doi.org/10.1596/978-1-4648-0527-1_ch17.
51. Krippner GR. Unmasked: a history of the individualization of risk. Sociol Theory. 2023;41(2):83–104. https://doi.org/10.1177/07352751231169012.
52. Cardona B. The pitfalls of personalization rhetoric in time of health crisis: COVID-19 pandemic and cracks on neoliberal ideologies. Health Promot Int. 2021;36(3):714–21. https://doi.org/10.1093/heapro/daaa112. PMID: 33025018; PMCID: PMC7665453.
53. Cislaghi B, Berkowitz AD. The evolution of social norms interventions for health promotion: distinguishing norms correction and norms transformation. J Glob Health. 2021;11:03065. https://doi.org/10.7189/jogh.11.03065. PMID: 34737854; PMCID: PMC8562258.
54. Lang R, Benham JL, Atabati O, et al. Attitudes, behaviours and barriers to public health measures for COVID-19: a survey to inform public health messaging. BMC Public Health. 2021;21:765. https://doi.org/10.1186/s12889-021-10790-0.
55. Hill LM, Davis H, Drewry M, Shelus V, Bartels SM, Gora Combs K, Ribisl KM, Lazard AJ. Barriers to and facilitators of COVID-19 prevention behaviors among North Carolina residents. Health Educ Behav. 2022;49(2):231–41. https://doi.org/10.1177/10901981221076408. Epub 2022 Feb 22. PMID: 35189728; PMCID: PMC9008556.

Chapter 13
Public Health Laws in India: Issues and Challenges in Covid-19

Jyoti Rattan and Anshula Rattan

13.1 Introduction

The COVID-19 pandemic caused public health havoc all over the world, and India was no exception. The WHO played an important role at every stage to tackle this global calamity, declaring the disease deadly and issuing proper guidelines from time to time. Despite various public health laws in India, huge losses related to life and the saving of precious lives were suffered due to various issues and challenges faced during the COVID-19 period. In this chapter, efforts are made by the researchers mainly to answer the following moot questions: What is Public Health? What is the international perspective (related to various international instruments and institutions) regarding Public Health? What are the Public Health laws in India, and what were the issues and challenges to Public Health posed by the COVID-19 pandemic from an international and national perspective?

13.2 Research Methodology

This is a theoretical study in which primary data was collected by analysing various international conventions, international instruments, treaties, the WHO Constitution, the Indian Constitution, Statutes, and Reports available on the Internet. The secondary data was collected by examining various books, journals, articles, etc. available on the Internet.

J. Rattan (✉)
Department of Laws, Panjab University, Chandigarh, India

A. Rattan
University of Auckland, Auckland, New Zealand

S. Malik et al. (eds.), *Public Health Issues: Theory and Practices*,
https://doi.org/10.1007/978-981-96-6650-8_13

13.3 Public Health

Health and public health are two different concepts; health, in general, means treating diseases and injuries of patients, one at a time. On the other hand, public health is the art and science of preventing disease, prolonging life, and promoting physical and mental health, sanitation, personal hygiene, control of infectious diseases, and organization of health services, more in the context of society as a whole. In the case of public health, the researchers try to find the factors responsible for the problems and give solutions. For example, in the case of premature or low birthweight babies (problem), the researchers investigate the factors responsible for this problem and develop programmes to keep babies healthy instead of treating them. Similarly, in the case of high blood pressure, the researchers examine the links among obesity, diabetes, and heart disease and use data to influence policy aimed at reducing all three conditions. Public health covers wide areas such as epigenetics, chronic disease, the science of ageing, mental health, disaster response, refugee health, injury prevention, tobacco control, etc. Significantly, in public health, after identifying a problem or disease, different researchers work in different ways; for example, microbiologists work to find vaccines while behavioural scientists research to find methods to change behaviours. Epidemiologists first see the trend in health and illness and then try to find links, causes, and interventions in areas such as infant mortality and infectious diseases like AIDS and tuberculosis. Environmental scientists work to discover which foods prevent disease, while health policy analysts evaluate health insurance programmes and make recommendations [4]. Social scientists and jurists endeavour to identify the laws that have been breached by competent authorities or in cases of negligence that have an impact on public health.

Another definition states that Preventive and Social Medicine (PSM)/Community Medicine (CM)/Community Health (CH) is the study of health and disease in the population of defined communities or groups to identify their health need and to plan, implement, and evaluate health programmes to effectively meet these needs. Public health primarily focuses on regulating the environment to promote the well-being of the general population. The main focus is to address the management and regulation of housing, water supplies, food, and other related factors such as fertilizers, inadequate sewage disposal and drainage, construction, defective heating and ventilating systems, machinery, and toxic chemicals that have the potential to impact public health [5].

Public health encompasses the practice of preventing disease, extending lifespan, and advancing physical and mental well-being. It includes efforts to improve sanitation, personal cleanliness, control infectious diseases, and organize health services. The notion of public health encompasses the understanding that community activity plays a crucial role in promoting health, preventing disease, and providing treatment. This realization has arisen from the typical human interactions involved in addressing the various challenges of social life.

13.3.1 Procedure for Promoting Public Health

To promote public health on a wider scale, multiple stakeholders must collaborate and adhere to the appropriate protocols. For instance, initially, epidemiologists apply specific techniques to collect information within a certain geographical region. These data help elucidate and clarify the prevalence of disease in a community by establishing connections between various elements such as food, environment, radiation exposure, or cigarette smoking and the frequency and extent of disease. After receiving important discoveries, the government takes action and enters into business agreements and enacts laws and regulations to put these findings into action. The concerned agencies also conduct official inspections and monitoring of water sources, food processing, sewage treatment, drainage, and pollutants in the specified geographical area. In case there is an epidemic and a breakout of pandemic diseases, the government also has the authority to establish guidelines for suitable medical interventions and isolation protocols, as well as issue travel advisories to prevent the transmission of diseases from afflicted regions [6].

13.4 Public Health: International Perspective (International Instruments and Institutions)

13.4.1 International Instruments

There are various International instruments that declare the right to health as a human right. This basic human right of the right to health has been well advocated and recognized by the International body, the World Health Organization (WHO), and various international instruments such as the Universal Declaration of Human Rights (UDHR, 1948) and the International Covenant on Civil and Political Rights (ICCPR), 1966. Article 6 of the International Covenant on Civil and Political Rights (ICCPR), 1966 declares that every human being has the inherent right to life, and this right is to be protected by law. Here the right to health is inherent in the right to life.

Whereas, according to Article 12 of the International Covenant on Economic, Social and Cultural Rights, the countries that have agreed to this Covenant acknowledge that everyone has the right to enjoy the best possible level of physical and mental health [8],

Article 25 of the Universal Declaration of Human Rights (UDHR), 1948 states that every individual is entitled to a satisfactory level of living that ensures health and well-being of the person, as well as that of the entire family. This includes access to food, clothing, housing, medical care, and essential social services. Additionally, individuals have the right to financial security in situations such as unemployment, illness, disability, widowhood, old age, or any other circumstances beyond their control that hinder their ability to earn a living. These are the major international instruments wherein the right to health is covered expressly.

13.4.2 World Health Organization (WHO)

The World Health Organization (WHO), a specialized agency of the United Nations (UN), is an important international institution that has been playing a significant role in the field of Public Health in all its member States. Notably, the WHO has recognized the right to health as a fundamental human right. The preamble of the Constitution defines health as "... a state of complete physical, mental and social well-being and not merely the absence of disease or infirmity" [7], whereas the WHO Constitution (1946) provides that the enjoyment of the highest attainable standard of health is one of the fundamental rights of every human being.

The main focus of the WHO in public health is that one should not get sick or die due to poverty or because of the non-availability of access to the public healthcare system. It is important to note that the right to health is a wider concept that includes several aspects such as the right to good health, the right to control both health and the body, the right to privacy, the right to live with dignity, and medical experimentation, right of access to the health system, and so on. Briefly, the overall approach of the WHO in this perspective is a people-centric healthcare system [7].

13.4.2.1 Functions of the World Health Organization (WHO) Regarding Public Health

The functions of the World Health Organization (WHO) include three main activities. *First*, it gives information about diseases throughout the world, and for this, it has developed a uniform system for reporting diseases and causes of death. It has established internationally accepted standards for drugs and drawn up a list of "essential" (effective, cheap, and reliable) drugs. It has sponsored and financed many research projects throughout the world. *Secondly*, the WHO promotes mass campaigns to control epidemic and endemic diseases. In this regard, in the past, the WHO had launched several successful campaigns in many countries. *Thirdly*, the WHO has been providing technical advice to the member countries to strengthen the public health administration and services, for which the WHO has sent teams of experts to carry out surveys and demonstrate projects. It has also assisted regional and national health development projects. Apart from technical advice, it has been providing advisory services to governments through its regional staff. The WHO has regional offices in several countries, both developed and less developed. The WHO's local representatives in many less-developed countries help in maintaining contact with problems and sources of financial aid [6].

13.4.2.2 Countries Where the WHO Works

While the WHO operates globally, it primarily focuses on addressing health and disease issues in underdeveloped countries. When building health service systems in a member State, the World Health Organization (WHO) typically takes into account several elements such as public health issues, resource constraints, education of healthcare professionals, and other relevant considerations in countries with similar circumstances.

13.4.2.3 Evaluation of Work Done by the WHO Regarding Public Health

The World Health Organization (WHO) collaborated with the Canadian Government and the Public Health Association of Canada and organized the inaugural International Conference on Health Promotion in 1986. This historic Conference, held in Ottawa, included 212 delegates from 38 different nations. It marked the inception of a global public health movement. The Ottawa Charter, as the conference outcome, placed emphasis on three key areas: advocacy (to enhance the elements that promote health), enabling (to ensure that all individuals have the opportunity to achieve health equity), and mediation (through collaboration across many sectors). Consequently, international organizations, national governments, and local communities initiated a sequence of measures to attain the global objective of "Health for All" by 2000 and beyond.

Thereafter, the WHO Global Health Promotion Conferences have created and advanced the worldwide principles and action areas for health promotion, which cover public health. The Ninth Global Conference, which took place in Shanghai in 2016, was held on the important theme of "Promoting Health in the Sustainable Development Goals: Health for all and all for health". It is significant to note that the Conference emphasized the crucial connections between promoting health and the 2030 Agenda for Sustainable Development. The Shanghai Declaration primarily aimed at implementing decisive political measures to expedite national efforts towards achieving the Sustainable Development Goals (SDGs). In addition to that, the Conference also established a framework for governments to effectively harness the transformative power of health promotion [6].

13.5 Public Health Laws in India

The Public Health Law encompasses a broad range of statutes, regulations, and judicial interpretations. Notably, India does not have a comprehensive public health law, although the Government has made occasional attempts in this area from time to time. Nevertheless, the current legislation pertaining to Public Health is aligned with the international instruments established by the World Health Organization (WHO), either directly or indirectly.

It is significant to point out that the Constitution of India does not explicitly include a provision for the individual's right to health. However, the Supreme Court of India, India's Apex Court of Justice, following the Maneka Gandhi case, has acknowledged the right to health as a basic right under Article 21 through several significant judgements.

Subsequently, the Supreme Court determined that the entitlement to reside with human dignity, as stated in Article 21, originates from the fundamental principles of state policy and consequently included the safeguarding of health. Moreover, it has been established that the entitlement to health is inseparable from the entitlement to life, and the government is constitutionally obligated to furnish healthcare services to the people of the country. The government has a fundamental duty to ensure that the public healthcare system is accessible to the general public. Consequently, the Supreme Court has passed a significant ruling that if a government hospital fails to provide a patient with timely medical treatment, it is considered a violation of the patient's right to life as stated in Article 21 of the Indian Constitution.

The Preamble of the Indian Constitution explicitly refers to the principle of socialism, which aims to enhance the general quality of human life, either directly or indirectly, for people living across the nation. This is amply highlighted in various Directive Principles, such as Article 38, which aims to establish a social order that promotes the well-being of the people. Article 39(e) emphasizes the importance of protecting the health and strength of workers, as well as ensuring that children are not subjected to any form of abuse. It also highlights the citizens' need to be prevented from being forced into unsuitable occupations due to economic necessity. Article 41 requires that the State should make effective provisions, within its economic capacity and development, to secure the right to work, education, and public assistance in cases of unemployment, old age, sickness, disablement, and other forms of undeserved poverty. Article 42 requires the State to create provisions for safe and humane working conditions, as well as provide maternity relief. Article 47 establishes the State's duty to improve nutrition, raise the standard of living, and enhance public health [9].

Notably, the case of Paschim Bangal Khet Mazdoor Samity and Others versus State of West Bengal and Others established that under a welfare state, the government's main responsibility is to ensure the well-being of its citizens and provide sufficient medical services for the people. The government has the responsibility to provide medical assistance to those in such need. The Court emphasized that in India, several clauses in the Constitution state that it is the duty of the Government to uphold public health and ensure access to the public healthcare system.

In addition to the Indian Constitution, there are several statutes that have a direct or indirect connection to public health, particularly the following legislations:[1]

(i) The Epidemic Diseases Act, 1897.
(ii) The Disaster Management Act, 2005.

[1] MoHFW | Home accessed on 7.5.2024.

13.5.1 The Epidemic Diseases Act, 1897

The Epidemic Diseases Act, 1897 is the main public health law in India, which mentions appropriate measures to prevent the outbreak of epidemics.

13.5.1.1 Salient Features of the Act (India Code 2000)

(a) The object of the Epidemic Diseases Act, 1897 is to effectively prevent the transmission of hazardous epidemic diseases.
(b) *Power of the State Government to take special measures and prescribe regulations as to dangerous epidemic disease*: The Act empowers the State Government to take adequate measures to prevent the outbreak of such disease or spread and also power is vested with the State Government to frame the policy for compensation.
(c) *Powers of Central Government*: The Central Government has the authority to take action when it determines that India or a specific region is affected by, or at risk of, a severe epidemic disease and that the usual legal measures are insufficient.
(d) *Penalty*: Any individual who fails to comply with any regulation or order established under this Act shall be considered to have committed an offence that is subject to punishment under Section 188 of the Indian Penal Code.
(e) *Protection to persons acting in good faith under the Act*: No legal action or lawsuit can be brought against any individual for any action taken or intended to be taken in good faith under this Act.

13.5.2 The Disaster Management Act (DMA), 2005

The Disaster Management Act (DMA), 2005 is another public health law in India that enables the government to take appropriate measures to prevent the outbreak of dangerous epidemic diseases in society. It needs to be emphasized here that the Management of Biological Disaster 2008 guideline was subsequently implemented [2].

13.5.2.1 Salient Features of the Act (India Code 2000)

The Act consists of 79 sections with the following important features:

(i) *Objective*: The main aim of the Act is the efficient management of disasters and other matters connected to it, i.e. to minimize the impact of disasters and to promote effective response and recovery measures. This legislation establishes a comprehensive administrative structure for catastrophe preparedness.

(ii) *National Executive Committee*: It consists of high-ranking government officials who represent different ministries, including Finance, Home, Health, Power, and Agriculture. Its responsibility entails the preparation of the National Disaster Management Plan for the entire nation, as well as ensuring its annual review and modification.
(iii) *National Disaster Response Force (NDRF)*: It is India's top rescue response organization with the motto "Aapada Seva Sadaiv Sarvatra". Its main role is to provide a consistent disaster response service in all situations. It is led by the Director General who is selected by the central government.
(iv) *National Disaster Management Authority (NDMA)*: NDMA is a crucial regulatory body at the national level that was established under the Act with the purpose of formulating policies, strategies, and guidelines for effective disaster management. The Chairperson of NDMA, which is the National Disaster Management Authority, is the Prime Minister of India. The NDMA consists of a maximum of nine members, one of whom is the vice chairperson. All members serve for a duration of 5 years.
(v) *State Disaster Management Authority (SDMA)*: It is a regulatory body at the state level that is responsible for developing and executing disaster management plans for the respective state. The chief minister serves as the chairperson of the authority, along with eight additional members.
(vi) *District Disaster Management (DDMA)*: It is a regulatory body at the district level that is responsible for managing and responding to catastrophic situations and their consequences within the district. The Chairperson of DDMA will be either the Collector, District Magistrate, or the Deputy Commissioner of the district.
(vii) *Penalty*: Offenders might face a maximum sentence of 1 year of imprisonment, a monetary penalty, or both, as stipulated in Sections 51–60 of the Act. The legislation defines the violation as the act of impeding or hindering any officer or employee in the execution of their duties, or deliberately refusing to follow their instructions (RSTV Bureau, 2020).

13.6 Public Health and Issues and Challenges in COVID-19: An Indian Perspective

COVID-19 was the biggest global pandemic that was witnessed by the people of the twenty-first century all over the globe. This pandemic caused a monumental loss of human lives worldwide and posed unprecedented challenges to public health, food systems, and work. Unfortunately, many people lost their lives and jobs, and small-scale businessmen ended their businesses, which ultimately resulted in unemployment for millions of people. Empirical evidence has demonstrated that the COVID-19 pandemic has caused a severe and destructive impact on both the economy and society in almost every country. A significant number of individuals, amounting to tens of millions, faced the danger of experiencing extreme poverty. Additionally, the current estimate of undernourished individuals, which stands at approximately 690 million, could potentially rise by as much as 132 million by the end of 2024.

13.6.1 Role of WHO During the COVID-19 Pandemic

During COVID-19, the WHO played a commendable role in trying to effectively manage the out-of-control situation in the world. The WHO collected data from various countries, analysed it, and provided guidance to affected nations on how to take appropriate actions to mitigate the challenge. The WHO teams collaborated with global experts to examine reports, research, and presentations from various nations, scrutinized patterns, sought inputs from additional expert groups, ultimately reaching a consensus on the optimal strategy, and then provided appropriate guidelines to be followed.

In March 2020, COVID-19 was officially declared as a global pandemic by the World Health Organization (WHO). Since then, the WHO has published more than 100 documents about this global tragedy. Of these, more than half are on Public Health and Social Measures (PHSM), offering detailed technical guidance, to suppress or stop the communitywide spread of COVID-19 in affected countries all over the globe.

The major efforts and key objectives of Public Health and Social Measures for COVID-19 were to reduce the transmission of various variants; to reduce the morbidity and mortality due to COVID-19; and to reduce the impact on health systems. These measures primarily focused on identifying and examining cases, delivering secure and suitable medical care, based on the seriousness of the illness, tracking and isolating contacts, preventing transmission between individuals, safeguarding healthcare professionals, and assisting communities in responding effectively to the emerging situation. The main aim of those documents was to inform PHSM to national and local health authorities and other decision-makers at all levels and included actions by individuals, institutions, communities, local and national governments and international bodies, and to limit any possible harm.

Significantly, the Public Health and Social Measures included personal protective measures like physical distancing, also called social distancing; avoiding crowded and poorly ventilated settings; cleanliness and hand hygiene; respiratory etiquette (e.g. always covering the mouth and nose with a bent elbow or a tissue when coughing or sneezing and disposing of the used tissue immediately into a closed bin and then washing hands); wearing a mask; social interactions regulation (e.g. regulating the number and flow of people attending gatherings, maintaining social distance in public or workplaces, domestic movement restrictions); modifying services (e.g. modifying school openings and restricting timings of non-essential businesses); clean environment measures (e.g. cleaning, disinfection, ventilation); active surveillance and response measures (e.g. testing, contact tracing, isolation, and quarantine, as well as genetic sequencing); as well as international travel-related restrictions.

13.7 COVID-19 in India

13.7.1 The First Wave of COVID-19 in India

In India, the first patient of COVID-19 infection was a 20-year-old female from Kerala. She was admitted to the emergency department of the general hospital, with a travel history to China, and the case was reported on 27 January 2020. Since then, COVID-19 has become a serious issue in India and worldwide.

The Government of India announced a nationwide lockdown for 21 days on 24 March 2020 and issued various national advisories from time to time, such as practicing social distancing, wearing masks, and avoiding going out unnecessarily. However, people rendering essential services, such as doctors, nurses, police, and home services, were exempted. Experts believed that such measures allowed the Indian Healthcare Delivery System to handle the situation and stop the further spread of COVID-19 infection. Significantly, these efforts of the Indian Government to prevent the spread of the virus were appreciated internationally [3].

13.7.2 The Second Wave of COVID-19 in India

The second wave, which started in March 2021, was more dangerous and created havoc as preventive measures were taken casually by people, especially youth, due to "pandemic fatigue". This resulted in an increasing number of cases between the ages of 25 and 50 years, as well as a shortage of essential medicine and equipment and medical professionals. So the ever-increasing daily demand for oxygen, Intensive Care Unit (ICU) beds, and oxygen beds could not be met. Consequently, many hospitals refused to admit the patients, resulting in higher mortality rates, leading to the disruption of routine immunization procedures and the treatment of non-communicable and communicable diseases [3].

13.7.3 The Third Wave of COVID-19 in India

The third wave of the COVID-19 pandemic in India was caused by the highly infectious Omicron variant in January 2022. Unfortunately, the majority of the cases were asymptomatic or mildly symptomatic, and the patients admitted to the ICU were mostly unvaccinated or with pre-existing comorbidities. Consequently, there was very little demand for hospital beds, oxygen beds, and ventilators [3].

13.8 WHO Guidelines and Public Health Laws Implemented in India During COVID-19

During the COVID-19 pandemic, the Central Government announced a lockdown for the entire nation, and crores of people were stuck in the same place. Many people lost their lives and careers, and small-scale businessmen ended their businesses, which ultimately resulted in unemployment for lakhs of people across India. Public health and social measures have been implemented across the world to reduce transmission of various variants, morbidity, and mortality from COVID-19 and to prevent the overburdening of the health systems and other critical social functions. India also made sincere efforts to implement those measures.

For instance, important Public health laws, especially the Epidemic Disease Act, 1897 and the Disaster Management Act (DMA), 2005, were enforced. Apart from these laws, for the maintenance of law and order situation, the important provisions of the Indian Penal Code, 1860 (*now replaced by Bhartiya Nayaya Sahinta, 2023 w.e.f. 1 July 2024*), the Criminal Procedure Code, 1973 (*now replaced by Bhartiya Nagrik Surkasha Sahinta, 2023 w.e.f. 1 July 2024*), and the Essential Commodities Act were also applied.

The statewide lockdown of 21 days, declared on 25 March 2020 by the Union Government and prolonged till 31 May 2020, was implemented under the Disaster Management Act, 2005. That law was enforced to effectively manage catastrophes and related concerns.

Specific provisions under the DMA empowered the Central Government to enforce the lockdown and impose restrictions on all forms of transportation throughout the country. Section 62 of the DMA grants the Central Government the authority to issue directives to all ministries or departments of the Government of India, as well as state and union territory administrations. On 11 April 2020, the Central Government utilized Section 69 of the DMA, granting the Secretary of the Ministry of Health and Family Welfare the authority to coordinate activities between ministries and states/UTs, in place of the Home Secretary.

13.8.1 Indian Penal Code (IPC), 1860 (now Replaced by Bhartiya Nayaya Sahinta, 202 w.e.f. 1 July 2024)

The following important provisions of the then in force Indian Penal Code, 1860 were implemented throughout India during the COVID-19 pandemic:

(a) *Negligent acts likely to spread infection of serious disease [Section 269 of IPC, 1860]*: It deals with negligent acts likely to spread infection of disease dangerous to life. This section applies to those who negligently act to spread the virus. They could be penalized with imprisonment, a fine, or both.
(b) *Malignant acts likely to spread infection of serious disease [Section 270 IPC, 1860]*: Malignant acts likely to spread infection of disease dangerous to life. This law applies to those who know that the consequence of their actions could lead to the spread of the virus but still choose to do such an act, such people are liable to be penalized.
(c) *Punishment for disobeying an order issued by a public servant [Section 188 of IPC, 1860]*: It deals with punishment for disobeying an order duly promulgated by a public servant. The above-mentioned law was for those defaulters who disobey the orders of the public servants and roamed around aimlessly during the lockdown.
(d) *Disobedience to quarantine Rule [Section 271 of IPC, 1860]*: Section 271 states that whoever disobeys the quarantine rule is to be punished with imprisonment or fine or both.

13.8.2 Criminal Procedure Code, 1973 (now Replaced by Bhartiya Nagrik Suraksha Sahinta, 202 w.e.f. 1 July 2024)

Section 144 of the Criminal Procedure Code empowers the executive magistrate to issue orders in urgent cases of "nuisance or apprehended danger and direct any person to abstain from a certain act or to take certain order concerning certain property in his possession or under his management to prevent, obstruction, annoyance or injury to any person lawfully employed, or danger to human life, health or safety, or a disturbance of the public tranquillity, or a riot, or an affray". In order to effectively implement the national lockdown, several states had also invoked Section 144 of the Criminal Procedure Code (CrPC). This Section provided the most important preventive measure against coronavirus that restricts a gathering of people at a particular place and thus in a way supported social distancing.

13.9 Issues and Challenges to Public Health Faced in India During COVID-19

Unfortunately, COVID-19 posed several issues and challenges to Public Health all around the world, including India. Despite implementing various measures of the WHO and having an extensive healthcare system in India, the COVID-19 pandemic created havoc on the existing Indian healthcare system by disrupting the supply of essential healthcare services to patients. It also highlighted the significant number of quality discrepancies of healthcare facilities between the rural-urban areas and between public and private healthcare providers. The healthcare system of India was exposed to the lack of oxygen and essential drugs required for the treatment of COVID-19 [2]. Strangely, despite the Epidemic Diseases Act of 1897 and other laws, huge loss of life, employment, and livelihood was suffered in India. During this period, formal employment went up from 33.41 to 38.56 million (about 15%).

13.9.1 Reasons for Issues and Challenges During COVID-19 in India and Efforts by the Government

The Government did not provide enough compensation to the affected persons as there was no comprehensive law to cover such unprecedented challenges posed by the pandemic and also there were some grey areas in the Epidemic Diseases Act, 1897, as well as in the Disaster Management Act, 2005. A brief analysis of these areas and subsequent efforts made by the Government in this regard are as follows:

13.9.1.1 Grey Areas of the Epidemic Diseases Act, 1897

As the name indicates, the Epidemic Diseases Act, 1897 is not applicable normally but is brought into force only during epidemics. Recently, the Act was implemented during COVID-19, and it was realized that the Act has the following major issues:

(i) No protection has been provided to healthcare personnel who are highly vulnerable while combating epidemic diseases.
(ii) No provisions for compensation to be paid to the person if affected due to the epidemics.
(iii) No provisions for protecting a person who suffered loss of income or employment, even after the preventive measures adopted by the state or central government.

Regarding compensation to the affected person, jurists believe that Section 2 of the Epidemic Diseases Act, 1897 merely declares the compensation policy to be prepared by the state but does not expressly impose the legal obligation upon the state to provide it, which ultimately caused injustice to the public who suffer in spite of the preventive measures adopted by the state. Without the remedial measures, it would not be legally appropriate to give preferences to the right to health or life of people over other rights such as the right to go for employment, property or compensation, etc. Law has to make a balance between these two conflicting interests, i.e. the right to public health on one side and the right to employment, property or compensation, etc., on the other side.

13.9.1.2 Grey Areas in Disaster Management Act (DMA), 2005

Whether an epidemic or pandemic can be considered a "disaster": The main criticism of the Act is its narrow definition of disasters under Section 2(d) of the Disaster Management Act (DMA), 2005 as solely sudden occurrences, disregarding progressive disasters like epidemics. Epidemics, such as dengue and tuberculosis, claim numerous lives and cause significant devastation, yet the said law lacks an effective mechanism to combat them. Nevertheless, several legal experts argue that it is possible to understand that a health emergency like the COVID-19 pandemic can be categorized as "grave concerns". However, this view would not be beneficial in efficiently controlling the outbreak [2].

13.10 Efforts of the Government for Comprehensive Public Health Law

The Government has made the following two important efforts in the direction of bringing about a comprehensive Public Health Law.

13.10.1 The Public Health (Prevention, Control and Management of Epidemics) Bill, 2020

In 2009, a Public Health Bill was introduced which acknowledged health as a fundamental right and proposed the creation of a National Public Health Board. The law proposed the creation of planning and implementation authorities at the national, state, district, block, and village levels. The statute explicitly outlined the channels for redressal and communication. Regrettably, the Bill failed to be approved due to the objection of numerous states, citing that health falls under the jurisdiction of the State List. In 2012, the Task Force on Public Health Act was established by the Government to make recommendations, which recommended the draft Public Health Act of the Centre with a state model. Also, by drafting the Public Health Act, a fine balance will have to be struck between the Central government's international obligations and its obligations towards the States [1].

In 2017, the Public Health (Prevention, Control, and Management of Epidemics, Bio-fear based Oppression, and Disasters) Bill, 2017 was introduced. This bill provided specific definitions for epidemics, isolation, quarantine, public health emergency, and social distancing. Finally, the Public Health (Prevention, Control and Management of Epidemics) Bill, 2020 (Bill No. XVIII of 2020) was introduced in March 2020. Unfortunately, this Bill too could not be converted into Law [10].

13.10.2 The Epidemic Diseases (Amendment) Act, 2020

To overcome the grey areas in the EDA, 1897 and to take action during the COVID-19 pandemic, the Epidemic Diseases (Amendment) Ordinance was promulgated on 22 April 2020. Finally, the Epidemic Diseases (Amendment) Act, 2020 was introduced in the Rajya Sabha on 14 September, 2020, to repeal the ordinance and thus amended the Epidemic Diseases Act, 1897. The Act amended the 125-year-old Act, i.e. the EDA, 1897, to include protections for healthcare personnel combating epidemic diseases and also had a provision for compensation. The individuals found guilty of crimes were also obligated to provide compensation to the healthcare service staff, specifically the victims of violence. If there was damage or loss of property, the victim was to be compensated with an amount equal to twice the fair market value of the damaged or lost property, as decided by the Court. The Act also expanded the powers of the central government to prevent the spread of such diseases. Although health is a state subject, the Ministry of Health may issue advisories and directions to implement the Act. The Amended Act also allows the government to inspect any ship arriving at or departing the port. It also gave the government the power to detain any person set upon or arriving in the country [11].

13.11 Conclusion

By and large, the right to health is widely recognized as an inalienable fundamental human right of every person. This basic right has been well recognized by the World Health Organization (WHO) and various international instruments such as the Universal Declaration of Human Rights (UDHR, 1948) and the International Covenant on Civil and Political Rights (ICCPR), 1966.

In India, it is indirectly covered under Article 21 of the Indian Constitution and is a wider concept that includes the right to health and other rights. India's Public Health System has come a long way since independence and comprises mainly of government-funded and run facilities as well as the private healthcare players.

The WHO, a specialized agency of the United Nations, plays a key role in protecting the right to public health. During the COVID-19 pandemic, the WHO issued various guidance documents, which were implemented by all countries to prevent the spread of the disease. India too successfully implemented these guidelines. In India, there are several laws regarding public health, but the most significant ones are the Epidemic Diseases Act, 1897 and the Disaster Management Act, 2005. Amidst the COVID-19 pandemic, the Government of India, in tandem with various state governments, implemented these existing laws to mitigate the spread of the disease and to protect and enhance the well-being of individuals. Additionally, other legislations were also put in place to uphold law and order.

Though successful to a large extent, however, at the same time, it was realized that these measures were not entirely foolproof in effectively addressing the health crisis due to the challenges like the ever-changing nature of the disease, the huge land mass, and the size of the country's population which was to be covered. Nevertheless, certain grey areas in these laws encouraged the Government to introduce Bills so that new laws could better handle the emerging problems that were faced during the COVID-19 crisis, in case of such unprecedented pandemic situations in the future. Fortunately, the Epidemic Diseases (Amendment) Act, 2020 made certain essential amendments in the existing law. Apart from this, the three new criminal laws, Bharatiya Nyaya Sanhita (BNS) 2023, Bharatiya Nagarik Suraksha Sanhita (BNSS) 2023, and Bharatiya Sakshya Adhiniyam (BSA) 2023, have replaced the colonial-era Indian Penal Code (IPC), 1872, the Code of Criminal Procedure (CrPC), 1973, and the Indian Evidence Act 1872, respectively, which are expected to streamline the implementation of sustentative laws. Significantly, the three new criminal laws are people-centric; therefore, the problems that were faced during the implementation of substantive laws during COVID-19 are not expected to arise in the future. However, the Public Health (Prevention, Control and Management of Epidemics) Bill, 2020, is still pending. So the need of the hour is to convert this Bill into an Act and spread awareness as well as ensure strict implementation of these new laws so that the country could deal in a better way with the COVID-19 pandemic-like situations in the future.

References

1. Salunke S. et al. Approach paper on Public Health Act: Task Force on Public Health Act. 2012. https://nhsrcindia.org/sites/default/files/2021-06/10.Task%20Force%20on%20Public%20Health%20Act_2012_approach%20paper.pdf. Last accessed 12 Apr 2024.
2. Gowd KK, et al. COVID-19 and the legislative response in India: the need for a comprehensive health care law. J Public Aff. 2021;21:e2669. https://www.ncbi.nlm.nih.gov/pmc/articles/PMC8250373/. Last accessed 16 Apr 2024.
3. Kapoor M, et al. Impact of COVID-19 on healthcare system in India: a systematic review. J Public Health Res. 2023;12:22799036231186349. https://www.ncbi.nlm.nih.gov/pmc/articles/PMC10345816/.
4. Matranga D, et al. Statistical advances in epidemiology and public health. Int J Environ Res Public Health. 2021;18:3549. https://www.ncbi.nlm.nih.gov/pmc/articles/PMC8036932/. Last accessed 10 Apr 2024.
5. WHO. Review of preventive and social medicine/community medicine/community health curriculum for undergraduate medical education. SEA-HSD-327. WHO. 2010. https://iris.who.int/bitstream/handle/10665/206329/B4482.pdf. Last accessed 12 Apr 2024.
6. WHO. Essential public health functions, health systems, and health security: developing conceptual clarity and a WHO roadmap for action. WHO; 2018. https://iris.who.int/bitstream/handle/10665/272597/9789241514088-eng.pdf?sequence=1. Last accessed 4 May 2024.
7. WHO. Health is a fundamental human right. WHO; 2017. https://www.who.int/news-room/commentaries/detail/health-is-a-fundamental-human-right. Last accessed 6 May 2024.
8. Almeida D. The right to means for adequate health. UMHRC; 2003. http://hrlibrary.umn.edu/edumat/studyguides/righttohealth.html. Last accessed 8 May 2024.
9. Pradipkumar T, Shahista I. Public health laws in India: issues and challenges. Int J Leg Dev Allied Issues. 2021;7:80–8. https://thelawbrigade.com/wp-content/uploads/2021/08/Dr-Pradipkumar-Dr-Shahista-IJLDAI.pdf. Last accessed 9 May 2024.

10. Singh S. The Public Health (Prevention, Control and Management of Epidemics) Bill, 2020. 2020. https://sansad.in/getFile/BillsTexts/RSBillTexts/Asintroduced/pub%20health-E-13320.pdf?source=legislation. Last accessed 12 May 2024.
11. Bhattacharya A. Analysis of The Epidemic Disease (Amendment) Act, 2020. Black n' White J. 2021; https://bnwjournal.com/2021/11/22/analysis-of-the-epidemic-disease-amendment-act-2020/. Last accessed 15 May 2024.

Chapter 14
A Comparative Analysis of Public Health Insurance Laws and Policies in Developing Countries

Manoj Kumar

14.1 Introduction

Public health insurance laws and policies play a pivotal role in shaping healthcare systems globally, serving as essential tools for promoting health equity and ensuring access to necessary medical services [1]. As countries grapple with the challenges of rising healthcare costs, demographic shifts, and the increasing prevalence of chronic diseases, the design and implementation of public health insurance frameworks have become critical areas of focus for policymakers. The diversity of approaches adopted worldwide, from single-payer systems to multi-payer models, reflects the varying economic, cultural, and political contexts that influence health policy decisions.

At its core, public health insurance aims to provide financial protection against healthcare expenditures, reducing the burden on individuals and families while fostering a healthier population [2]. In countries such as Canada and the United Kingdom, government-funded programmes offer comprehensive coverage to all citizens, emphasizing preventive care and equitable access [2]. Conversely, the United States presents a more fragmented model, characterized by a combination of public programmes like Medicare and Medicaid, alongside a robust private insurance sector. These differences highlight the complexities involved in creating effective health insurance systems that align with national priorities and values.

This research paper seeks to explore the general concepts of public health insurance laws and policies across certain countries in the Indian subcontinent. Further, the chapter analyses their structures, funding mechanisms, and sociopolitical factors that shape their development. By examining certain parameters from diverse

M. Kumar (✉)
Dr. Ram Manohar Lohiya National Law University, Lucknow, Uttar Pradesh, India
e-mail: manojkumar@rmlnlu.ac.in

S. Malik et al. (eds.), *Public Health Issues: Theory and Practices*,
https://doi.org/10.1007/978-981-96-6650-8_14

healthcare systems, this study aims to identify the best practices, challenges, and innovations in public health insurance. Furthermore, it will address the implications of these policies for health outcomes, equity, and the sustainability of healthcare systems in the face of global health challenges, such as pandemics and ageing populations. Ultimately, this research aspires to contribute to the ongoing discourse on health policy reform, offering insights that could inform future developments in public health insurance around the world.

The author has determined certain criteria under which the comparison will be drawn between the three developing nations in the Indian subcontinent, namely India, Pakistan, and Bangladesh. Conducting a comparative study on public health insurance laws and policies in India, Pakistan, and Bangladesh can offer valuable insights for several reasons:

- ***Shared regional context***: India, Pakistan, and Bangladesh share historical, cultural, and socio-economic ties as neighbouring countries in South Asia. A comparative study allows the examination of how similar socio-economic conditions have led to different public health insurance systems and legal frameworks.
- ***Diverse approaches to health insurance***: While these countries have common challenges such as poverty, overpopulation, and health infrastructure limitations, their approaches to public health insurance differ. For example, India has schemes like Ayushman Bharat, Pakistan has the Sehat Sahulat Programme, and Bangladesh focuses on a mixed insurance model. Comparing these can highlight the effectiveness of different models [3].
- ***Policy learning***: Lessons learnt from the comparative study could be applied to improve each country's health insurance policies. Successes in one country could inspire reforms in another. For instance, India's digital health initiatives may offer practical solutions for Pakistan or Bangladesh.
- ***Addressing common challenges***: All three countries face challenges like healthcare access, funding, quality of services, and rural healthcare deficits. A comparative study can explore how each nation's policies handle these issues, fostering cooperative approaches to improve healthcare.
- ***Impact on vulnerable populations***: A study comparing health insurance systems could assess their impact on marginalized populations, such as the poor, elderly, and women, identifying gaps in legal frameworks and policies that fail to meet the needs of vulnerable groups [3].
- ***Legal and regulatory frameworks***: Analysing the laws governing public health insurance in these countries can shed light on differences in regulatory oversight, implementation, and accountability mechanisms, suggesting areas for legal reform or better enforcement.
- ***Global and regional health goals***: Comparing the health insurance policies in these countries can also be useful in assessing progress towards achieving international commitments such as the Sustainable Development Goals (SDGs), particularly SDG 3 (Good Health and Well-being).

- ***Cross-border collaboration***: A comparative study can help identify opportunities for regional cooperation on public health, such as joint efforts in combating diseases, sharing resources, or standardizing insurance protocols for migrants and refugees across borders.

14.1.1 Parameters to Conduct the Comparative study

The criteria which will be considered for conducting the comparative study are as follows:

- *Historical context*
- *Current legal framework*
- *Challenges*
- *Recent developments and future directions*

These four criteria offer valuable insights and provide a comprehensive understanding of the field. Here is why each criterion is important:

14.2 Historical Context

Studying the historical context of health insurance laws allows us to understand the evolution of healthcare systems and the reasons behind the adoption of certain policies. It sheds light on the political, economic, and social factors that influenced the development of health insurance in different regions.

By comparing different nations or regions, we can identify patterns, shared milestones, or unique developments that shaped their respective systems, for example, why some countries opted for universal healthcare while others adopted private or hybrid models.

14.3 Current Legal Framework

Analysing the current legal frameworks provides a clear picture of how health insurance systems operate today. This includes understanding eligibility, coverage, funding mechanisms, and the roles of private vs. public actors.

A comparative study highlights differences in coverage, accessibility, and equity. It shows how various systems address modern healthcare challenges, such as cost control, patient rights, and the role of government regulation.

14.4 Challenges

Every health insurance system faces challenges, whether related to funding, inequitable access, or managing costs. Understanding these challenges helps policymakers and stakeholders recognize gaps and areas for improvement.

A comparative perspective shows how different countries tackle common challenges in distinct ways. It offers lessons on best practices and innovative sovlutions that can be adapted or applied in other contexts, for example, how one country's response to an ageing population or rising healthcare costs might inform others.

14.5 Recent Developments and Future Directions

Health insurance systems are dynamic, constantly evolving in response to demographic changes, technological advancements, and political shifts. Keeping track of recent reforms and predicting future trends allows for proactive adaptation [4].

A comparative study of recent developments can reveal trends in healthcare innovation, such as digital health technologies or public-private partnerships. By examining future directions, policymakers can anticipate challenges and explore forward-thinking solutions to improve public health outcomes.

14.6 Public Health Insurance Laws and Policies in India

Public health insurance in India is a crucial aspect of the country's healthcare system, aimed at providing financial protection to individuals against high medical costs. With a diverse population exceeding 1.4 billion, the challenge of ensuring equitable healthcare access is profound. This paper examines the evolution, current frameworks, and implications of public health insurance laws and policies in India, highlighting their significance in promoting health equity and improving overall health outcomes.

14.6.1 Historical Context

The roots of health insurance in India can be traced back to the early twentieth century with the establishment of the Employees' State Insurance Act in 1948, which aimed to provide health benefits to workers in organized sectors [5]. However, comprehensive public health insurance policies were largely absent until the late twentieth century. The liberalization of the economy in the 1990s spurred growth in the private health insurance sector, but disparities in healthcare access persisted, especially in rural areas.

The National Health Policy of 2002 marked a significant shift towards a more structured approach to public health insurance. It recognized the need for universal access to healthcare and laid the groundwork for subsequent initiatives. In 2018, the government launched the Ayushman Bharat—Pradhan Mantri Jan Arogya Yojana (PM-JAY), a landmark initiative aimed at providing health coverage to approximately 500 million people [5]. This scheme offers an annual coverage of INR 5 lakh per family for secondary and tertiary care hospitalization [6].

14.6.2 Current Legal Framework

India's public health insurance framework consists of several key schemes:

- Ayushman Bharat—PM-JAY: This scheme provides cashless insurance for vulnerable families, enabling access to quality healthcare services. It is implemented through a network of public and private hospitals, ensuring that beneficiaries can avail of services without upfront payments.
- Rashtriya Swasthya Bima Yojana (RSBY): Launched in 2008, this scheme focuses on providing health insurance to Below Poverty Line (BPL) families [6]. It aims to reduce out-of-pocket expenditure, which has been a significant barrier to accessing healthcare.
- Employee State Insurance (ESI): This scheme caters to workers in the organized sector, offering health insurance and medical benefits. It is funded through contributions from employers and employees, ensuring a sustainable model for coverage [7].
- Central Government Health Scheme (CGHS): Targeting central government employees and pensioners, this scheme provides comprehensive medical care, including outpatient and inpatient services, through a network of healthcare facilities [4].
- State-Level Health Insurance Schemes: Various states have initiated their own health insurance schemes tailored to local needs. For instance, the Mahatma Jyotirao Phule Jan Arogya Yojana in Maharashtra and the Kanti Velugu program in Telangana focus on specific population segments and health challenges [4].

14.6.3 Challenges

Despite the progress made in public health insurance, several challenges persist:

- Awareness and accessibility: Many eligible individuals are unaware of their entitlements under various schemes. This lack of awareness often results in the underutilization of available services.
- Quality of care: While insurance can increase access to healthcare, it does not guarantee the quality of services provided. Issues such as overcrowded facilities and inadequate infrastructure can compromise care quality.

- Fraud and abuse: The implementation of public health insurance schemes has sometimes been marred by fraud, with some individuals exploiting loopholes to gain unauthorized access to services.
- Funding and sustainability: Adequate funding remains a challenge. The government's commitment to funding public health insurance schemes is crucial for their sustainability, especially as healthcare costs continue to rise [5].
- Integration with primary healthcare: Ensuring that public health insurance schemes are integrated with primary healthcare services is essential for promoting holistic health outcomes.

14.6.4 Recent Developments and Future Directions

The COVID-19 pandemic highlighted the importance of robust public health insurance systems. The government responded by expanding coverage and streamlining processes to include COVID-19 treatment under existing schemes. Moving forward, several strategies can enhance public health insurance in India:

- Strengthening public awareness campaigns: Increasing awareness about health insurance schemes and their benefits can empower individuals to seek necessary care.
- Improving quality of healthcare: Investing in healthcare infrastructure and training for healthcare providers can enhance service quality, ensuring that insured individuals receive appropriate care.
- Leveraging technology: The use of digital platforms for registration, claims processing, and service delivery can streamline operations and reduce fraud.
- Policy integration: Integrating health insurance with broader health policies can ensure a cohesive approach to healthcare delivery, addressing the social determinants of health.
- Focus on preventive care: Encouraging preventive care through insurance policies can reduce the burden of chronic diseases and lower overall healthcare costs [6].

Public health insurance laws and policies in India are pivotal in addressing healthcare inequities and improving access to medical services for the population. While significant strides have been made, ongoing challenges necessitate targeted reforms and strategic investments. By fostering awareness, improving service quality, and integrating insurance schemes with broader health initiatives, India can move closer to achieving its goal of universal health coverage. The continued evolution of public health insurance policies will play a crucial role in shaping the future of healthcare in the country, ultimately leading to better health outcomes for all citizens.

14.7 Public Health Insurance Laws and Policies in Pakistan

Public health insurance in Pakistan is a critical component of the country's healthcare system, designed to alleviate the financial burden of medical expenses for its population of over 240 million people. With significant disparities in income and access to healthcare services, the need for effective public health insurance policies has become increasingly urgent.

14.7.1 Historical Context

The foundations of health insurance in Pakistan can be traced back to the early years following independence in 1947. Initially, health services were largely funded by government budgets and out-of-pocket payments. The Employees' Old-Age Benefits Act of 1976 introduced some level of health insurance for workers in the formal sector [8]. However, comprehensive public health insurance systems remained largely undeveloped, with the focus primarily on curative care rather than preventive services.

The advent of the Health Policy of 2001 marked a significant shift towards recognizing the importance of health insurance in the broader context of health system reform. However, it wasn't until the late 2010s that substantial strides were made to establish public health insurance mechanisms. The introduction of various provincial schemes aimed at providing health coverage to low-income populations reflected a growing acknowledgement of the necessity for inclusive healthcare financing.

14.7.2 Current Legal Framework

Pakistan's public health insurance landscape consists of several key initiatives and schemes, which vary significantly across provinces:

- Sehat Insaf Card (Khyber Pakhtunkhwa): Launched in 2016, this programme provides universal health coverage to residents of Khyber Pakhtunkhwa. The Sehat Insaf Card offers cashless health services for secondary and tertiary care in both public and private hospitals [9]. The initiative aims to reduce out-of-pocket expenses and enhance access to quality healthcare for low-income families.
- Punjab Health Insurance Scheme: Initiated in 2016, this scheme aims to provide health coverage to families living below the poverty line in Punjab. It covers a wide range of medical services, including hospitalization, surgeries, and outpatient care. The scheme seeks to empower individuals to seek medical care without financial constraints [10].

- Benazir Income Support Programme (BISP): Although primarily a social safety net initiative, BISP has incorporated health insurance components to provide financial assistance for medical treatment to its beneficiaries. This programme underscores the intersection of social welfare and health insurance in addressing the needs of vulnerable populations [10].
- Sindh Health Insurance Programme: Launched in 2018, this initiative aims to provide health coverage to low-income households in Sindh. It focuses on enhancing access to essential health services and reducing the financial burden of healthcare [11].
- Federal Government Health Schemes: The federal government has also introduced initiatives aimed at providing health coverage, such as the Pakistan Medical and Dental Council's regulations on mandatory health insurance for medical professionals [11].

14.7.3 Challenges

Despite the progress made in establishing public health insurance policies, several challenges hinder their effectiveness:

- Awareness and accessibility: A significant portion of the population remains unaware of their rights and entitlements under existing health insurance schemes. This lack of awareness leads to underutilization of services and missed opportunities for accessing necessary care.
- Quality of care: While insurance can increase access to healthcare, it does not inherently guarantee the quality of services provided. Many public hospitals are overwhelmed, leading to inadequate patient care and long waiting times.
- Fragmentation of schemes: The existence of multiple health insurance schemes across provinces, often with different eligibility criteria and benefits, creates confusion and inconsistency in service delivery [12]. This fragmentation complicates efforts to achieve universal health coverage.
- Sustainability and funding: Many public health insurance programmes rely heavily on government funding, which can be unstable. Economic constraints and budgetary pressures can affect the sustainability of these initiatives, limiting their reach and effectiveness.
- Integration with primary healthcare: A holistic approach to health insurance requires integration with primary healthcare services. However, the current focus on secondary and tertiary care often overlooks the importance of preventive and primary health services, which are crucial for overall health outcomes.

14.7.4 *Recent Developments and Future Directions*

In recent years, the COVID-19 pandemic underscored the importance of robust health insurance systems. Initiatives such as telemedicine and the integration of digital health solutions have gained traction, aiming to enhance access to healthcare services in a rapidly changing landscape.

The introduction of the "Health for All" policy in 2020 reflects a renewed commitment to achieving universal health coverage [12]. This policy aims to strengthen health systems, improve financing mechanisms, and ensure that all citizens can access quality healthcare services without facing financial hardship.

To enhance the effectiveness of public health insurance in Pakistan, several strategies should be considered:

- Increasing awareness: Comprehensive public awareness campaigns are essential to educate citizens about available health insurance schemes and their benefits. This can empower individuals to seek care and utilize available services.
- Improving service quality: Investments in healthcare infrastructure, training for healthcare providers, and quality assurance mechanisms are critical to ensuring that insured individuals receive appropriate and high-quality care [8].
- Streamlining policies: Efforts to harmonize and integrate various health insurance schemes can reduce fragmentation, making it easier for individuals to access services and understand their coverage.
- Enhancing digital solutions: Leveraging technology for registration, claims processing, and service delivery can streamline operations and improve the efficiency of health insurance systems.
- Focus on preventive care: Encouraging preventive care through health insurance policies can reduce the overall burden of disease and healthcare costs, promoting a healthier population.

14.8 Public Health Insurance Laws and Policies in Bangladesh

Public health insurance is a vital component of Bangladesh's healthcare landscape, aimed at providing financial protection to individuals and families against the high costs of medical care. With a population exceeding 170 million and a significant portion living in poverty, the necessity for effective public health insurance mechanisms has become increasingly evident.

14.8.1 Historical Context

The origins of health insurance in Bangladesh can be traced back to the early post-independence period in 1971, when the government focused on establishing a healthcare system that could provide basic services to its citizens. Initially, healthcare was predominantly funded through government budgets and out-of-pocket payments, which placed a significant financial burden on families, particularly those in low-income brackets [13].

In the 1990s, the government began to recognize the need for a structured approach to health financing, leading to the formulation of various health policies aimed at expanding access to healthcare. The 2000 Health Policy and subsequent plans acknowledged the importance of health insurance in improving healthcare access and reducing financial barriers, laying the groundwork for future initiatives.

14.8.2 Current Legal Framework

Bangladesh's public health insurance landscape comprises several key initiatives, although it remains fragmented and underdeveloped compared to global standards. Some of the significant schemes include:

1. **Health Insurance Scheme for the Poor**: Launched in 2010, this scheme aims to provide health coverage for low-income families, particularly in rural areas. The programme offers cashless health services in designated hospitals, covering various medical needs, including hospitalization and outpatient care [13].
2. **Social Health Insurance (SHI)**: Introduced in 2015, SHI targets formal sector employees, providing them with health coverage through employer contributions. This model reflects a growing recognition of the role of social insurance in enhancing healthcare access for workers in the formal economy [14].
3. **Community-Based Health Insurance (CBHI)**: Various non-governmental organizations (NGOs) have initiated community-based health insurance schemes to cater to low-income groups, particularly in rural areas. These schemes operate on a cooperative model, where members contribute to a pool that funds healthcare services [15].
4. **Government Health Programmes**: The government has implemented several health programmes focused on specific health challenges, such as maternal and child health, infectious diseases, and nutrition. While these programmes are not insurance schemes per se, they contribute to improving health outcomes and reducing the need for extensive health insurance coverage.

14.8.3 Challenges

Despite these initiatives, public health insurance in Bangladesh faces several significant challenges:

1. **Awareness and accessibility**: A considerable portion of the population remains unaware of their entitlements under the existing health insurance schemes. This lack of awareness leads to underutilization of services and limits access to necessary healthcare.
2. **Quality of care**: Although insurance can increase access to healthcare, it does not guarantee the quality of services provided. Many public hospitals are overwhelmed, leading to inadequate patient care and long waiting times.
3. **Fragmentation of schemes**: The existence of multiple health insurance schemes, often with varying eligibility criteria and benefits, creates confusion and inconsistency in service delivery. This fragmentation complicates efforts to achieve comprehensive coverage for all citizens [16].
4. **Funding and sustainability**: Many public health insurance programmes rely heavily on government funding, which can be unstable. Economic constraints and budgetary pressures may affect the sustainability of these initiatives, limiting their reach and effectiveness.
5. **Integration with primary healthcare**: A holistic approach to health insurance requires integration with primary healthcare services. However, the current focus on secondary and tertiary care often overlooks the importance of preventive and primary health services, which are crucial for overall health outcomes.

14.8.4 Recent Developments and Future Directions

Post-COVID-19, certain initiatives were introduced which include increasing funding for health programmes, enhancing telehealth services, and focusing on preventive care.

Furthermore, the 2021–2025 Health Sector Strategic Plan aims to strengthen the healthcare system by promoting universal health coverage (UHC) and integrating health insurance schemes into a cohesive framework [17]. This strategic plan underscores the government's commitment to improving health financing and expanding access to quality healthcare.

To enhance the effectiveness of public health insurance in Bangladesh, several strategies should be considered:

1. **Increasing awareness**: Comprehensive public awareness campaigns are essential to educate citizens about available health insurance schemes and their benefits. This can empower individuals to seek care and utilize available services.

2. **Improving service quality**: Investments in healthcare infrastructure, training for healthcare providers, and quality assurance mechanisms are critical to ensuring that insured individuals receive appropriate and high-quality care.
3. **Streamlining policies**: Efforts to harmonize and integrate various health insurance schemes can reduce fragmentation, making it easier for individuals to access services and understand their coverage.
4. **Leveraging technology**: The use of digital platforms for registration, claims processing, and service delivery can streamline operations and improve the efficiency of health insurance systems.
5. **Focus on preventive care**: Encouraging preventive care through health insurance policies can reduce the overall burden of disease and healthcare costs, promoting a healthier population.

Public health insurance laws and policies in Bangladesh are vital for addressing healthcare inequities and improving access to medical services. By enhancing awareness, improving service quality, and integrating health insurance with broader health initiatives, Bangladesh can move closer to achieving universal health coverage.

14.9 Comparative Analysis

Public health insurance is a fundamental aspect of healthcare systems in South Asia, particularly in India, Pakistan, and Bangladesh. Each of these countries has made strides towards developing health insurance frameworks to address the financial burdens of healthcare costs on their populations. Despite sharing similar socio-economic challenges and health profiles, the approaches to public health insurance in these nations vary significantly. This analysis aims to compare the laws, policies, and effectiveness of public health insurance in India, Pakistan, and Bangladesh, highlighting their strengths, weaknesses, and potential areas for improvement.

14.9.1 Historical Context

The roots of public health insurance in India can be traced back to the Employees' State Insurance Act of 1948, but comprehensive health coverage was not prioritized until the late twentieth century. The landmark Ayushman Bharat scheme, launched in 2018, represents a significant leap towards universal health coverage, aiming to provide insurance to approximately 500 million people.

Following its independence in 1947, Pakistan's health insurance landscape remained underdeveloped for decades. Initial steps were taken with the Employees'

Old-Age Benefits Act in 1976, but substantial reforms did not occur until the twenty-first century. The introduction of the Sehat Insaf Card in Khyber Pakhtunkhwa in 2016 marked a significant step towards expanding health coverage for the poor.

Health insurance in Bangladesh has historically been limited, with initial efforts focusing on government-funded healthcare services. The Health Insurance Scheme for the Poor was launched in 2010, and various community-based health insurance schemes have been initiated by NGOs, but comprehensive public health insurance has yet to materialize.

14.9.2 Analysis of Current Frameworks

14.9.2.1 Scope of Coverage

The Ayushman Bharat scheme offers extensive coverage for secondary and tertiary healthcare, with an annual limit of INR 5 lakh per family. It aims to include vulnerable populations, but coverage is still primarily focused on hospitalization rather than outpatient services.

The Sehat Insaf Card provides cashless treatment for hospitalization and some outpatient services, focusing on low-income families. However, coverage can vary significantly by province, leading to disparities in access and quality.

The Health Insurance Scheme for the Poor covers essential health services but is limited in scope. Community-based schemes exist but lack standardization and regulatory oversight, leading to inconsistent benefits.

14.9.2.2 Funding Mechanisms

India: Funding for public health insurance primarily comes from government budgets, with the Ayushman Bharat scheme being largely government-funded. There is also an emphasis on public-private partnerships to expand coverage [6].

Pakistan: Funding for health insurance schemes is sourced from government budgets, with some reliance on international aid. The financial sustainability of schemes remains a concern due to budgetary constraints [10].

Bangladesh: Public health insurance is funded through government allocations, with limited involvement from private insurance providers. The reliance on donor funding for community-based schemes further complicates financial sustainability [15].

14.9.2.3 Implementation and Accessibility

India: Implementation is supported by a network of public and private hospitals, but challenges such as bureaucratic inefficiencies and underutilization persist. Awareness of the scheme among potential beneficiaries is also limited.

Pakistan: Implementation varies by province, with some regions having better access to services than others. Awareness campaigns have been initiated, but many eligible individuals remain uninformed about their rights and entitlements.

Bangladesh: Accessibility is hindered by a lack of awareness and limited outreach efforts. The reliance on NGOs for community-based insurance schemes often leads to disparities in coverage across different regions.

14.9.2.4 Challenges and Limitations

- Awareness and education: All three countries face challenges in raising awareness about available health insurance schemes. Many eligible individuals do not fully understand their rights or the benefits provided, leading to underutilization of services.
- Quality of care: While insurance can increase access to healthcare, it does not guarantee quality. In India and Pakistan, overcrowded public facilities often struggle to provide adequate care. In Bangladesh, the quality of services in community-based schemes can vary significantly.
- Fragmentation: The existence of multiple health insurance schemes in each country creates confusion and inconsistency in service delivery. In India, various state-level schemes exist alongside national initiatives, while Pakistan and Bangladesh have fragmented approaches that complicate access.
- Funding and sustainability: The financial sustainability of public health insurance schemes is a common concern. Economic pressures and budgetary constraints can limit the effectiveness and reach of these programmes in all three countries.

14.10 Observations and Findings

- India has made substantial progress with the Ayushman Bharat scheme, providing coverage to a significant portion of its population. Pakistan's Sehat Insaf Card has also expanded access but is less comprehensive. Bangladesh lags behind, with limited coverage and reliance on community-based initiatives.
- While India has a larger network of hospitals under its health insurance schemes, the quality of care remains uneven. Pakistan shows similar patterns, while Bangladesh struggles with quality and accessibility, particularly in rural areas.

- India has implemented some awareness campaigns, but gaps remain. Pakistan is also working to improve awareness, but challenges persist. Bangladesh faces significant barriers in educating the population about health insurance options.

14.11 Conclusion

Public health insurance laws and policies in India, Pakistan, and Bangladesh reflect varying levels of development and effectiveness in addressing healthcare access and equity. While significant strides have been made in recent years, ongoing challenges necessitate targeted reforms and strategic investments. By learning from each other's experiences and focusing on common goals, these countries can move closer to achieving universal health coverage, ultimately leading to better health outcomes for their populations.

To enhance the effectiveness of public health insurance in India, Pakistan, and Bangladesh, some strategies should be considered. Integrating various health insurance schemes into a unified framework can reduce fragmentation and simplify access for beneficiaries.

Moreover, comprehensive public education campaigns are essential to inform citizens about their rights and the benefits of health insurance schemes. Interestingly, investment in healthcare infrastructure and provider training is crucial to ensure that insured individuals receive high-quality care. Furthermore, developing innovative financing mechanisms, including public-private partnerships, can enhance the sustainability of health insurance programmes. Emphasizing primary care and preventive services within health insurance frameworks can improve overall health outcomes and reduce the burden on secondary and tertiary care.

References

1. Chan M. Strengthening health systems to improve health outcomes. World Health Organization; 2021.
2. Weel C, Kidd M. Why strengthening primary health care is essential to achieving universal health coverage. Lancet Natl Libr Med. 2018;2:463–6.
3. Hone T, Macinko J, Millett C. Revisiting Alma-Ata: what is the role of primary health care in achieving the Sustainable Development Goals? Lancet Natl Libr Med. 2018;18:1461–72.
4. Shende V, Wagh V. Public health insurance status and utilization of healthcare services across India: a narrative review. Lancet Natl Libr Med. 2024;2
5. Ahlin T, Nichter M, Pillai G. Health insurance in India: what do we know and why is ethnographic research needed. Anthropol Med. 2016;23:105–8.
6. Salunke S, et al. Approach paper on public health act. Natl Hum Rights Comm India. 2022;1:31–3.
7. Dutt MM. Health insurance sector in India: an analysis of its performance. Vilakshan XIMB J Manag. 2020;17:97–109.

8. Ghaffar A, Salman M. An overview of health care system in Pakistan. J Public Health Med. 2021;22:38–42.
9. Fazal F, Ibrahim M. Healthcare in Pakistan: navigating challenges and building a brighter future. Cureus. 2023;15
10. Khan S, Asif M, Aslam S. Pakistan's healthcare system: a review of major challenges and the first comprehensive universal health coverage initiative. Cureus. 2023;15
11. Gaffar A, Saima H. Health laws of Pakistan: compilation and commentary. J East Mediterr Health. 2021;27
12. Shaikh B, Ali N. Universal health coverage in Pakistan: is the health system geared up to take on the challenge? Glob Health. 2023;12
13. Hasan K, Aziz K. Health insurance for public servants in Bangladesh: a study on its social security implications and challenges. Cabinet Division, Government of Bangladesh; 2022.
14. Hamed A. Health insurance for government employees in Bangladesh: a concept paper. Munich Personal RePEc Arch. 2014;1
15. Khanam M, Azim R. Health insurance for university students in Bangladesh: a novel experiment. Health Sci Rep. 2021;4
16. Haque S. Role of health insurance policies in access to healthcare services in Bangladesh. J Public Policy Adm. 2024;9
17. Hasan Z, Ahmed S. The effectiveness of a government-sponsored health protection scheme in reducing financial risks for the below-poverty-line population in Bangladesh. Health Policy Plan. 2023;39

Chapter 15
Public Health in Developed Countries: A Lesson to Be Learnt from the COVID-19 Pandemic

Varun Chhachhar and Niharika Kumar

15.1 Introduction

The year of 2019 ended with the beginning of one of the deadliest times in the recent past. It was the introduction of a highly pathogenic coronavirus, which was officially declared a global pandemic by the World Health Organization on 11 March 2020. COVID-19 originated in Wuhan in December 2019 and gradually spread across the globe. It caused fatal respiratory infections and soon became a global pandemic, causing a serious health crisis. It affected not only the health of people but also impacted the environment, economy, and human psychology. With lockdown in place, streets were cleared of vehicles and factories were shut down, which ultimately cleared the environment of toxic gases. The home quarantine at the same time also led to mismanaged biohazard waste and caused other solid waste management issues. The huge number of cases called for increased medical equipment and other supplies along with an increased number of the workforce, thereby causing pressure on the country's economy. The countries invested more in public health and research activities during COVID-19, which further strained the economy. Other than this, relief packages and economic vaccines and treatment facilities also led to pressure on the public exchequer.

COVID-19 challenged the public health systems of the world, among other things [39]. It created a public health emergency of international concern, and countries with fragile healthcare facilities suffered the most. SARS-CoV-2 is a highly contagious and infectious virus that causes bioaerosols which transport pathogenic microorganisms and thereby hamper public health. It was found that people with diabetes were at higher risk of pneumonia due to an advanced proinflammatory and prothrombotic state. Further, patients with cardiovascular disease were also at risk

V. Chhachhar (✉) · Niharika Kumar
Faculty of Law, University of Lucknow, Lucknow, Uttar Pradesh, India

S. Malik et al. (eds.), *Public Health Issues: Theory and Practices*,
https://doi.org/10.1007/978-981-96-6650-8_15

of COVID-19 [26]. The COVID-19 pandemic exposed the weaknesses prevalent in public health systems of the world, such as a lack of infrastructure, government preparedness, limited human resources, etc. [12]. The disease outbreak happened mainly due to ill-equipped health facilities, inability of the hospitals to admit a huge number of patients, insufficient training of the professionals to deal with the pandemic and provide adequate patient care. Further, the virus also affected patients with preventable and treatable diseases due to disruptions in health services, with healthcare workers being diverted to support COVID-19 cases. Shortage of medicines, diagnostics, and other technologies was also a reason for such disruptions [17]. Other than this, there was also a lack of coordination between the government at the union and state levels and between the government and healthcare professionals. The public also lacked faith due to inconsistent and unclear communications made to them. Against this backdrop, this chapter will first understand the basic concept of public health and its relationship to the pandemic. It will then proceed to explore the preparedness and combat strategies of a few developed countries during COVID-19, which will throw light on the state of their public health system. It will further see how India managed to handle the situation better with a huge population and limited resources as compared to developed nations. It will be followed by a conclusion.

15.1.1 Methodology

The present chapter is based on doctrinal research and has been prepared through a literature review of various journal articles, books, research reports, and legislations related to public health and the impact of COVID-19 on public health in developed and developing nations.

15.2 Concept of Public Health

The history of public health is almost as old as civilisation. There is considerable evidence on the presence of drainage systems, sewers in ancient societies. The Book of Leviticus (1500 BC) has texts about personal cleanliness, hygiene of maternity, sanitation of campsites, etc. The Code of Hammurabi contains the rules of medical practice. Mosaic law talks about the overriding duty of saving life as a religious imperative among other things. Other similar texts can be found in relation to Greece, Rome, Europe, and Asia. The concept of public health as such has undergone many changes, and therefore to arrive at one universal definition is not easy. One of the most relevant definitions was given by C.E.A. Winslow, a popular figure in the history of public health:

> the science and art of preventing disease, prolonging life and promoting health and efficiency through organized community efforts for the sanitation of the environment, the control of community infections, the education of the individual in personal health, the organisation of medical and nursing services for the early diagnosis and preventive treatment of disease, and the development of the social machinery which will ensure to every individual in the community a standard of living adequate for the maintenance or improvement of health... [43]

The above definition was given in 1920 and was good for its time. It is noteworthy that many of the contemporary definitions build on this one with a few twists. The American Public Health Association (APHA) defines public health as the practice of preventing disease and promoting good health within groups ranging from small communities to entire nations. Health professionals from diverse fields working together with the common goal of achieving good health for the population are also included in this definition. The objective of any healthcare professional or a community is to enhance the number of healthy years in a population's life. It is with this intention that the government and the medical infrastructure tend to those first who are in need. Public health also involves investigation into disease outbreaks by using the trends and occurrences of disease in the population and population subsets to infer the risk of disease in individuals. The identification of risk or risk factor is somewhat based on the work of Koch. Koch's postulates talk about the disease caused by a living organism and state that the following four relationships must occur regarding the causes of the disease:

(a) The causative organism must be observed in every case of the disease.
(b) It can be grown in a pure culture.
(c) This pure culture, when inoculated into a susceptible host animal, must reproduce the disease.
(d) The microorganism must be observed in, and recovered from, the experimentally diseased animal [13].

This will help in a better understanding of epidemics and pandemics. The term epidemic is used when the number of cases of a particular disease is higher than what is normally expected or is out of proportion in a particular geographical area. When the disease breaches a specific region and spreads to multiple areas or the entire globe, it is known as a pandemic. There have been several epidemics and pandemics in the last hundred years, the most recent one being the Severe Acute Respiratory Syndrome Coronavirus -2 (SARS-CoV-2) that caused Coronavirus disease 2019 (COVID-19). The first case emerged in Wuhan, China in December 2019, and it affected millions of people globally. It was labelled as a pandemic by the WHO on 11 March 2020.

The definition of public health is very critical in the light of other major issues that are impacting public health, such as global warming leading to climate change, which is thereby causing changes in seasonal cycles, an increase in temperature leading to hot waves, and urban heat islands. Factors like melting of glaciers are posing a threat of another pandemic, with the threat of releasing disease-causing organisms. The extreme weather conditions are causing events like floods, droughts, fires, earthquakes, etc., which are also posing a threat to the lives of billions of people in the world. A clear definition of public health may reflect whether such cases can be included in it. Considering such a phenomenon as a public health issue will raise the concern of addressing it at a collective or governmental level, in contrast to individual action. In public health issues, there is prioritisation and treatment with urgency. The concept of public health is multifaceted and in constant flux. The constant change requires continuous reassessment and amendments to its definition.

The UK Faculty of Public Health (FPH) in its strategy for 2020–2025 provides a concise but wide-reaching encapsulation of public health, which may originally be attributed to epidemiologist Donald Acheson:

> public health is the science and art of preventing disease, prolonging life and promoting health and wellbeing, through the organised efforts of society. [6]

This crisp definition reflects that public health is a cluster of things that fall under both science and art. It has multiple aims, i.e., avoidance of disease, achieving greater longevity, and promotion of a positive state of health and well-being. Further, it is not the responsibility of a single actor but requires efforts across society.

15.3 COVID-19 vs. Public Health in Developed Countries

The COVID-19 pandemic posed serious challenges to public health across the globe. Such situations impact the developing nations more, given the lack of adequate funds and sufficient medical essentials for the population. It is generally presumed that developed nations such as the United Kingdom, the United States, Australia, Canada, etc., are better prepared to sail through public health emergencies such as a pandemic. However, the pandemic exposed the fragility of the healthcare system not only in public health and long-term care but also in primary care in such nations. This section will look into the status of public health in the aforementioned four well-resourced countries. It will help in understanding how these countries differed in terms of pre-existing universal health coverage, pandemic readiness, and the level of government and public support for public health measures.

Before proceeding to this, a table can be referred to which was prepared by Huston P and others in their research, which shows how the COVID-19 cases were handled. The data collected from the primary care physicians and people with possible COVID-19 map out the approach that was followed to tackle the pandemic. It shows how often the patients were called up for follow-up visits in the physician's office, and how they were offered remote assessments either by telephone, email, videoconferencing, or assessment in assessment centres (Table 15.1).

Now the situation and measures taken by the governments of the four selected nations will be discussed in detail.

Table 15.1 Site of primary care assessment of potential COVID patients in six countries[a]

Country	Virtual[b] (off-site)	Primary care offices	Assessment centres	After-hours clinics	Emergency departments	Home visits
Australia	Common	Occasional	Common[c]	Sometimes	Common	Occasional
New Zealand	Common	Sometimes	Common	Sometimes	Occasional	Sometimes[e]
Canada	Common	Occasional	Common	Sometimes	Common	Occasional
The Netherlands	Common	Common	Occasional	Common[d]	Common	Sometimes
UK	Common	Occasional	Common	Sometimes[d]	Sometimes	Occasional
USA	Common	Sometimes	Common	Sometimes	Sometimes	Occasional

Source: Ref. [20]

[a]This is based on knowledge of national pandemic plans, professional communications and anecdotal evidence amassed by the authors in order to give a general picture; it does not reflect the heterogeneity that may occur within each country

[b]Virtual assessments were conducted to advise patients as to whether it was necessary to be clinically assessed and, if indicated, to direct them to the appropriate venue

[c]Known as GP respiratory clinics

[d]Seeing patients in off-hours is part of primary care system

[e]Commonly done for the sub-population of vulnerable older persons

15.3.1 Australia

The first case of COVID-19 in Australia was recorded on 25 January 2020. In February 2020, the Australian Health Sector Emergency Response Plan for Novel Coronavirus (COVID-19) was announced by the Prime Minister. The cases peaked in March 2020, and then on 8 April 2020, a select committee was established by the Australian Senate to look into the government's response to the pandemic. The relevant legislation in connection with the Commonwealth's health system response to COVID-19 is the Biodiversity Act 2015 and the National Health Security Act 2007. In comparison to its global counterparts, Australia had a small number of COVID-19 cases and deaths associated with it. The reason behind this may be twofold: (i) it is geographically remote, and (ii) the tremendous efforts on the part of the government and public health advisors [22]. There are many factors responsible for Australia's effective management of the disease, such as early physical distancing measures, stable wealth, and a stable political system. The measures were successful due to the immense public support and the government's assistance in return to those businesses and individuals who were worst affected by the disease. Some specific steps taken by the Australian government towards the management of COVID-19 are mentioned below:

(i) A national partnership on COVID-19 response was announced on 6 March 2020 between the Australian and state and territory governments. Under this, the federal government bears 50% of the costs incurred by the state and territory health systems for the diagnosis and treatment of confirmed and suspected cases of the virus and other activities meant to prevent its spread. This partnership further provides for the state and the territories to enter into agreements with private hospitals to ensure support for the public health system.

(ii) In May 2020, the Australian government entered into an agreement through an addendum to the National Health Reform Agreement (NHRA) (2020–2025) under which a funding guarantee was given to all the states and territories by the Morrison Government to ensure that no jurisdiction is left affected by COVID-19 [12].

(iii) A draft legislation, "The Privacy Amendment (Public Health Contact Information) Bill 2020", which was passed by the Parliament on 14 May 2020, was brought to provide support to the government's COVIDSafe mobile contact tracing app and to extend privacy protections.

(iv) All the courts and tribunals minimised in-person appearance in the light of the safety of the parties and court staff. A COVID-19 List was created in the Family Court of Australia and the Federal Circuit Court of Australia under which only urgent parenting-related disputes that arose due to the pandemic were dealt with.

(v) Reforms were made to the bankruptcy law to provide immediate relief to those who were in financial difficulty due to the economic effects of the coronavirus. Temporary debt relief measures were introduced to support individuals and small businesses.

(vi) The Australian Human Rights Commission found that there was a rise in racial discrimination complaints and encouraged people to report coronavirus-fuelled racist attacks. It also developed online resources to help children and teenagers and to address the gendered impact of COVID-19.

(vii) The Office of the Australian Information Commissioner published COVID-19 privacy guidance for organisations covered by the Privacy Act, 1988. A National COVID-19 Privacy Team was also convened.

(viii) Several measures were taken towards primary healthcare for diagnosing and managing confirmed and potential cases of SARS-CoV-2. One of the key measures under this was temporary Medicare Benefit Schedule (MBS) items for telephonic or video consultations.

(ix) Several changes were made to the existing medicines regulations such as allowing an authorised pharmacist to supply appropriate medicines to those in immediate need and who were unable to get a Pharmaceutical Benefits Scheme Prescription, allowing pharmacists to give substitute medicines (without prior approval of the prescriber) in case the prescribed medicine was in short supply, and enabling image-based prescriptions.

(x) The Australian government entered into supply agreements with several companies for COVID-19 vaccines such as AstraZeneca, Novavax, Pfizer, and Moderna.

In conclusion, a variety of measures were taken across different government departments of Australia. The available literature points towards well-informed decision-making and strategic planning on the part of the government for effective handling of the pandemic.

15.3.2 Canada

The public health system of Canada was rebooted after the outbreak of SARS in 2003 [29]. Following the national and provincial inquiries, the national Public Health Agency of Canada (PHAC) was established to deal with the country's public health threats [34]. Public health agencies were also created at the subnational level to function as regional centres for disease control. This reflects Canada's strong preparedness towards any epidemic/pandemic that may ensue in the future. Despite these changes, Canada didn't perform as expected during COVID-19. Canada's overall COVID-19 death rate as of June 2023 exceeded the global average but was lower than that of the United Kingdom. Its death rate was worse than Australia's but was better than that of the United States [25].

There were many factors behind Canada's poor handling of the COVID-19 situation, such as even though it had universal health coverage, the country was not well prepared. The number of affected cases in Canada was moderate in 2020 [44] due to the initial delay in testing and implementation of travel restrictions. It also struggled in maintaining PPE supplies and in suboptimal infection control in long-term care facilities. Further, it failed to take into account previous reports, due to which it lost many older patients and staff in long-term care homes [11]. It also faced challenges in the procurement and delivery of COVID-19 medications such as remdesivir, ritonavir-nirmatrelvir, and tocilizumab, which led to provinces and hospitals rationing use [16]. There was a shortage of healthcare staff as well which put pressure on the existing ones [10]. Absence of research infrastructure in healthcare prevented Canada from participating in or carrying out clinical trials and other international studies [18]. Moreover, the absence of data sharing agreements across federal and provincial or territorial jurisdictions slowed data sharing [35]. Public health data comes from various sources such as electronic health records, administrative data on healthcare services utilisation, and public health surveillance data. The government at all levels collects, accesses, and uses it for informed decision-making. But data were in short supply, which prevented making public health decisions during COVID-19. Public health decisions varied across jurisdictions and were further impacted by outdated health information systems and a lack of integration [4].

There were some positive developments also. The pandemic plan of Canada was updated to identify primary care as responsible for assessing ambulatory patients [33]. It was among the most vaccinated countries with >83% of the population receiving at least one dose in February 2023 [15]. People living and working in long-term care homes and the indigenous population were given vaccination on priority soon after the country's approval of Pfizer-BioNTech and Moderna COVID-19 vaccines in December 2020. Research collaborations were also undertaken to address urgent issues such as devising mitigation techniques, engagement of patients in research, understanding the correlation between infection and immunity, and creation of the COVID-19 Immunity Task Force [40]. Further, certain federal legislations were also enacted to address the health issues of Canadian citizens during the COVID-19 pandemic, such as:

(i) An Act to amend the Financial Administration Act (special warrant) (S.C. 2020, c.4)
(ii) An Act respecting certain measures in response to COVID-19 (S.C. 2020, c. 5)
(iii) A second Act respecting certain measures in response to COVID-19 (S.C. 2020, c. 6)
(iv) Time Limits and Other Periods Act (COVID-19) (S.C. 2020, c. 11, s. 11)
(v) An Act respecting Canada emergency student benefits (coronavirus disease 2019) (S.C. 2020, c. 7)
(vi) An Act to amend the Canadian Dairy Commission Act (S.C. 2020, c. 8)
(vii) An Act respecting further COVID-19 measures (S.C. 2020, c. 11)
(viii) An Act relating to certain measures in response to COVID-19 (S.C. 2020, c.12)
(ix) An Act to amend the Criminal Code and the Identification of Criminals Act and to make amendments to other Acts (COVID-19 response and other measures) (S.C. 2022, c.17)

There are a few general flaws in the public health system of Canada that need to be fixed for the future, such as:

(i) The PHAC (Government of Canada: Public Health Agency of Canada), which was created in 2004, is responsible for drafting national clinical and public health guidelines, as well as providing technical assistance, border quarantine services, and specialised services for early pathogen detection tests [27]. But it lacks the power to issue directions to provincial and territorial health agencies or any other body of similar nature to implement its recommendations.
(ii) For every province, there is a chief medical officer or public health officer who is empowered to delegate their functions related to public health to regional or municipal health authorities, irrespective of the resources available to them. It leads to a lack of coordination between decision-makers at different jurisdictional levels.
(iii) The healthcare professionals used different media to spread awareness during COVID-19, such as a few joined official advisory committees, while some used social media platforms. It led to a conflicting situation and created confusion and trust issues among the public [5].
(iv) The organisations representing health professionals pointed out the shortage in medical supplies and raised their voice, calling for measures to strengthen the health workforce.
(v) The absence of a coordinated pandemic planning authority caused doubt as to the official nature of the rules in place. The National Advisory Committee on Immunisation (NACI) made evidence-based recommendations on COVID-19 vaccine eligibility but failed to say anything about implementation [28]. Due to this, every province created its own vaccine eligibility plans, allocation, and mandates.

15.3.3 United Kingdom

In 2020, the United Kingdom was among the countries that had a high number of COVID-related deaths. The large number of COVID-19 cases can be attributed to the initial lack of testing and PPE supplies, certain steps that created public uncertainty, and other socio-demographic factors that led to the spread of the infection. The United Kingdom has universal health coverage, but its pandemic strategy took effect from 2011, which was last updated only in 2014 [9]. The pandemic strategy of the nation mainly focused on an influenza-style pandemic and ignored the suggestions from previous planning exercises, which could have been useful. With a decade of underfunding of the public health sector, the United Kingdom entered the pandemic without sufficient resources or a workforce, capacity, or voice that was needed to manage the pandemic. An SAS doctor in England stated: *"The running down of public health funding progressively over last decade left the public health service understaffed and under-resourced and this inevitably reduced their ability to manage the pandemic"*. The overall approach of the nation may be understood in the form of its actions taken during different waves of the pandemic.

In the first wave (February 2020–September 2020), the response of the UK government was slow and there was no clear policy in place. There was laxity in initial contact tracing and the social distancing strategies were also introduced very late. The whole of 2020 was laced with delays in action towards the pandemic, such as face covering advice being implemented 2–3 months after it was first recommended by the global health agencies. There was confusion in public health messaging, and the broader political narrative focused on ending the restrictions rather than caution and preparation for the second wave. The government failed to use the time at hand for testing and contact tracing that led to a backlog and ultimately to outsourcing, which was a costly affair.

Second Wave (September 2020–April 2021): The first lockdown ended without any measures for containing the spread of the infection. When the local lockdown and localised restrictions were put in place in summer 2020, they were of no help. The communication was also poor between the national and local governments, which also affected the implementation of the restrictions. Public communication became worse in the second wave and people faced problems in understanding the local measures. The trust in public messaging was severely impacted. One positive development was the vaccination rollout. The NHS-led vaccination programme was a welcome step during the second wave.

During the third wave (May 2021–December 2021), most of the population was vaccinated, but despite this, there were many cases of COVID-19 and hospitalisations remained on the higher side. The rapid spread of the Delta variant created a lot of pressure on the health services of the United Kingdom. The UK government's approach of removing the restrictions in the name of 'freedom' further worsened the situation.

Fourth wave (December 2021–Present): The spread of Omicron put pressure on UK health services during the winter. To tackle the rising threat and address the rising staff absence rates, it was advisable for the government to reintroduce the earlier measures. All four UK government published strategies for replacing the legal restrictions with guidance. The government's decision to remove public health measures, such as free testing, monetary support for self-isolation, and statutory sick pay provision, created a situation in which only those who could afford to protect themselves were able to do so. These strategies have impacted public messaging as well. The absence of clear government guidance and gaps in vaccine coverage question the state of those who are at high risk or are unvaccinated. The dismantling of the pandemic infrastructure seems premature without future consideration for a possible case spike of COVID-19 [3].

Some of the positive steps taken by the UK government are:

(i) The Coronavirus Act 2020 was enacted with "emergency powers" to enable the public authorities to respond to the COVID-19 pandemic [37]. It was later withdrawn in 2022.
(ii) The government announced 6.6-billion-pound funding from the Coronavirus Emergency Fund on 13 April 2020 to support the health and social care response. It was in addition to the budget of the Department of Health and Social Care that was being allocated for the same purpose.
(iii) The government also announced the write-off of 13.4 billion pounds of NHS debts from 1 April 2020 to ensure that the NHS has appropriate funding and support to respond to the COVID-19 pandemic.
(iv) Further, additional medical equipment, along with ventilators, was also procured. Support was also increased for the adult social care workforce [19].
(v) The NHS COVID-19 App, which automates the process of contact tracing, was also funded.
(vi) The government made provision for mental health support as well. It came up with a life assurance scheme where the family of an eligible health and social care worker would receive a certain sum in case they died from coronavirus in the course of their frontline work.
(vii) An infection control fund was also introduced to manage the spread of the virus.
(viii) The government also provided support in the form of evacuation and return flights to the United Kingdom to its citizens who were stranded in other territories [30].

15.3.4 United States

The United States had the largest number of cases, almost a quarter of the world's count of COVID-19, which was mainly due to delays in testing, variable social distancing guidelines, decreased access to healthcare [8], and varied support for public health guidelines by governments and the public [2]. It does not have universal health coverage. The updated pandemic plan does not prescribe the role of primary care [42]. Further, the National Security Council Directorate for Global Health

Security and Biodefense, established to handle the United States' approach towards disease outbreaks and pandemics, was also disbanded in 2018. Primary care physicians were actually on their own to tackle the pandemic in terms of assisting in the response, dealing with the changing, uncertain, and at times conflicting recommendations from local, State, medical specialty, and federal authorities [23]. They had to find their own PPE supplies and were mostly dependent on service-based funding.

This pandemic response of the United States came as a surprise because before this, the global evaluations of pandemic preparedness had rated the country as one of the well-prepared countries [7]. It started well to manage COVID-19 cases by creating an Incident Management System to track and coordinate the public health response. The Centres for Disease Control (CDC), which is the nation's leading public health agency, was also performing its duties. A 'Coronavirus Task Force' was created, and a public health emergency was declared by the State as soon as the first confirmed case was reported. Measures like screening of passengers at airports and directions for self-isolation to those returning from high-risk areas were also issued in January and February 2020. Despite these efforts, the United States faced a high number of cases and mortality rate. It experienced a 'trimodal wave' in COVID-19, where each peak was higher than the previous one. It is noteworthy that racial and ethnic minorities and the poor were more affected, with higher infection and death rates reported among the Blacks and Hispanics [32]. The hospitalisation rate was higher among people with lower incomes. There are a variety of factors responsible for such mismanagement, such as:

(i) Even after receiving a warning of the unusual spread of a pathogen from the CDC officials based in Thailand, the United States counterpart did not do anything to track the transmission in the United States. In that crucial time, the virus spread undetected, and the insistence of the CDC on adopting its own test kits was another blunder as they were later found to be contaminated.

(ii) The initial target population for testing was limited to those who had travelled from China and showed symptoms, which further allowed the spread of the virus through communities. CDC was incapable of supporting the management of COVID-19 in the United States through delayed testing, scientific errors, and misjudgements.

(iii) There was political interference as well that affected the working of CDC. The White House was irresponsible in implementing CDC guidelines regarding school and business reopenings, religious gatherings, and further allowed questionable treatments. It also pushed the agency to change its guidelines in August 2020 and review the agency's weekly reports of mortality before publication.

(iv) The self-isolation rules in the United States neglected the reality of its low-income population who live in crowded households. The United States failed to adopt supported isolation and institutionalised isolation policies at scale despite having the resources.

(v) The initial statements from the CDC and public health personnel rejected the use of face masks for preventing the spread of the disease [31]. These statements were later clarified, but the damage was done as it led to confusion among people and later on divided them on the efficacy of the use of face masks. Shockingly, people were also alleging a violation of civil liberties when asked to use face masks.

(vi) The guidelines on large public gatherings were also different across different jurisdictions. While many nations put a strict ban on public gatherings, the United States did not issue any such strict guidelines; rather, it emphasised the preparedness of the crowd, and in some places the number of people was limited. Such an approach also contributed to an increase in COVID-19 cases.

(vii) Studies have shown that compliance with social distancing norms was largely dependent on political affiliation. Like people who voted for Trump complied less as compared to those who voted for Hillary Clinton [14].

(viii) The United States also failed to implement a strict border control policy during COVID-19 pandemic. Earlier, the screening was only limited to people travelling from China, which also failed as a large number of infected people still managed to enter the United States. Further, airport screenings were also not very stringent and consistent. The steps were improved, but by then it was too late.

The above factors made United States the country worst hit by COVID-19. Mitigation efforts came into play on 21 January 2021 when the Biden administration proposed 1.9 trillion dollars to support a unified National Strategy for the COVID-19 Response and Pandemic Preparedness. It aimed at ensuring free vaccination for everyone residing in the United States, implementation of masking nationwide through executive order, along with ensuring that everyone had access to reliable and free testing. It emphasises the provision of emergency relief funding to states and focuses on increasing the PPE supply. The strategy also focuses on the safe reopening of schools, local businesses, and communities by laying down specific guidelines. Further, a COVID-19 Health Equity was also proposed to be established. The funding to COVAX was also ensured for the equitable distribution of vaccines. Finally, clear public communications and decision-making driven by evidence were also encouraged [21].

Out of the four countries mentioned before, Australia was best prepared as it had both universal health coverage and up–to-date pandemic plans [36]. It has guidelines for general practitioners (GPs) for both pandemic influenza and public health emergencies. The government swiftly prepared for widespread testing and also assisted in providing personal protective equipment (PPE) to general practice [41].

15.4 COVID-19: Glorious Emergence of India as a Leader in Times of Crisis

The COVID-19 pandemic caused severe suffering to the lives of people, along with economic loss and social disruption. In crises like these, everything is dependent on the public healthcare system of a nation. India, being the second most populous country in the world, faced a tremendous challenge to contain the situation. It was later seen that India managed the situation miraculously by containing the virus within its borders and keeping the infection and mortality rates low relative to the population size. But this success changed when the second wave hit India in March 2021. The cases of infection deaths rose tragically, making India the second highest COVID-19 case count in the world, with over 25% of the global deaths from COVID [38].

Various reports from the COVID-19 times suggest that India still managed to do better than the developed nations, such as the United States and the United Kingdom, whose mitigation techniques were unorganised and haphazard. India, being the largest democracy, was faced with a critical challenge at that time, which was to balance the protection of public health and saving of lives, on the one hand, with safeguarding individual rights and freedom on the other. A variety of steps were taken by India during this time, such as issuing guidelines for hand washing, mandatory mask wearing, social distancing, self-isolation, etc. Further, measures like comprehensive testing, contact tracing, thermal screening of all incoming airline passengers, limiting foreign arrivals by imposing visa restrictions, and a mandatory 2-week quarantine for all incoming travellers. India also made efforts to evacuate all its citizens from high-risk nations such as China, Italy, Japan, etc. The government initially banned the export of medical equipment and pharmaceuticals, which would be needed by citizens. It also conducted targeted testing to find out the asymptomatic and pre-symptomatic individuals and segregated them accordingly. In order to prevent community transmission, the government issued directions for the closure of schools, malls, gyms, restaurants, and other public places. Steps were also taken to raise awareness and discourage the spread of misleading information relating to the treatment of the infection. The nationwide lockdown was extended in different phases, and districts were divided into three zones depending on the extent of the spread of the virus so that appropriate control and mitigation measures could be taken. Further, the Epidemic Diseases Act, 1897 and the National Disaster Management Act, 2005 granted power to the Central Government to take decisions best suited to fight the prevalent situation of the time. It also allowed the States to take immediate preventive emergency measures to control the situation.

Despite taking all these measures, the cases gradually rose, and the lockdown forced several migrant labourers to return to their homes on foot in the light of the situation. The poor and the migrant workers suffered immensely with limited food and water. Many people lost their jobs as businesses and factories shut down. India also faced a shortage of hospital staff, hospital beds, and oxygen support. These shortages caused the most damage to those who are hit by socio-economic inequalities and poverty. Now, till this point, there was no hope or cure. The pressure on the Indian economy was also increasing, and the GDP growth rate also dropped.

The Indian government tried to handle this socio-economic shock of COVID-19 by boosting its economy with economic stimulus packages along with measures to compensate the workers for their income loss and assisted small and medium businesses by extending liquidity and financial support. The government announced a relief package worth 1.7 trillion rupees to help the poor and migrant workers through cash transfers and food security. The public health measures of the government helped in bringing down the infection cases. Steps such as quarantine of symptomatic patients in healthcare facilities, declaration of containment zones for the infected neighbourhood, and stepping up on medical equipment such as ventilators, oxygen cylinders, diagnostic and testing kits, sanitisers, masks, etc. helped a lot. The National Health Protection Scheme or *Ayushman Bharat Yojana,* launched in 2018 as the world's largest government-funded health programme, also contributed to the facilitation of COVID-19 testing. Although the testing and treatment was free at public facilities when the pandemic first broke, this health scheme allowed free testing at private labs and treatment for COVID-19 at 'empanelled' or certain specific hospitals. It boosted widespread testing and mitigation of existing or new cases.

Other than the above-mentioned steps, India did something remarkable in 2021. The Drugs Controller General of India gave an emergency approval to two vaccines (Covishield and Covaxin) for restricted use against COVID-19 on 3 January 2021. Later, on 16 January of the same year, India started the world's largest vaccination drive using domestically produced vaccines. Prime Minister Narendra Modi also announced 'vaccine maitri' or 'vaccine friendship' initiative on the same day, under which India was set to deliver free supplies of COVID-19 vaccines to those countries that are in line with New Delhi's 'neighbourhood first' policy. These 'gifts' were later on to be delivered to the rest of the world. The two vaccines, as authorised by India, were developed by the University of Oxford and a British-Swedish company AstraZeneca, one from each. They granted a licence to the Serum Institute of India, which is the world's largest vaccine maker (by volume), to produce the vaccine locally under the label of Covishield and also to manufacture 60% of the global supply under AstraZeneca's name. The vaccines thus produced were cost effective and didn't require delicate storage, in contrast to the United States, Pfizer-BioNTech, and Moderna. It made it feasible to be delivered to other countries with a low storage infrastructure. The other vaccine was produced by Bharat Biotech, an Indian Firm, in collaboration with the Indian Council for Medical Research and the National Institute of Virology under the label Covaxin, which is India's first homemade vaccine against the virus. These vaccines were bought by nations like Brazil, Morocco, Saudi Arabia, and South Africa. The leaders of these States, including the WHO director general, expressed their gratitude to India for its support in the pandemic.

The Deputy Chairman of the Rajya Sabha, Harivansh Narayan Singh, stated at the 26th Conference of Speakers and Presiding Officers of the Commonwealth in Canberra, Australia that India helped 150 nations through vaccines and medical supplies during the pandemic. India also evacuated stranded foreign nationals in India to their home countries. Under the "Vaccine Maitri" initiative, India supplied more than 282 million vaccines to 101 countries and two UN entities in the first week of the initiative [24].

15.5 Conclusion

COVID-19 has posed a significant challenge to the public health systems of all nations across the globe. The developed and powerful nations that prima facie appeared to be well prepared turned out to be struggling with proper strategies to combat the pandemic. The lack of coordination between the union and state and local governments was prominent, which led to different COVID-19 guidelines at different levels and caused implementation problems. This approach also contributed to creating confusion, distrust, and frustration among the public. It can be deduced that the initial response to the pandemic in almost all the nations mentioned above was very slow, which led to the community spread of infection and ultimately worsened the situation. The developed nations referred to in this chapter displayed a lack of leadership and good governance qualities in terms of a lack of information sharing, delays in testing, failure in contact tracing, poor implementation of closure and lockdown guidelines, inadequate measures at the airports and borders to prevent the spread, etc. Moreover, the political affiliation, particularly in the United States, emerged to be one of the reasons for public defiance of face masking and social distancing rules, abstaining from public gatherings and self-isolation of suspected cases, reluctance towards vaccination, and so on. The understaffing of public health officials also appeared to be a significant issue in most of the nations, which impacted not only the COVID-affected patients but also those who were suffering from other diseases.

When talking about developing nations like India, it can be said that it has comparatively managed a little better given the huge population and lack of adequate and advanced medical infrastructure. People followed the government guidelines and abstained from public gatherings and maintained social distancing. The face masking rules were also followed, and schools and other public places were also shut down on time. The most noticeable step came in the form of vaccine maitri wherein India helped many nations with the supply of COVID-19 vaccine and other medical supplies. Times like the pandemic teach that the public of the entire nation is dependent on a well-funded public health system.

References

1. About the Public Health Agency of Canada. https://www.canada.ca/en/public-health/corporate/mandate/about-agency/history.html. Accessed 25 Mar 2024.
2. Berchick ER, Barnett JC, Upton RD. Health Insurance Coverage in the United States: 2018, 2019. https://www.census.gov/library/publications/2019/demo/p60-267.html. Accessed 21 May 2024.
3. BMA. The public health response by UK governments to COVID-19, 2023. https://www.bma.org.uk/advice-and-support/covid-19/what-the-bma-is-doing/the-public-health-response-by-uk-governments-to-covid-19. Accessed 18 May 2024.

4. Bubela T, Flood CM, McGrail K, et al. How Canada's decentralised covid-19 response affected public health data and decision making? 2023; https://doi.org/10.1136/bmj-2023-075665.
5. Caulfield T, Bubela T, Kimmelman J, et al. Let's do better: public representations of COVID-19 science. FACETS. 2021; https://doi.org/10.1139/facets-2021-0018.
6. Coggon J. What is public health? London: Faculty of Public Health; 2023. https://www.fph.org.uk/media/2afgi1gm/what-is-public-health.pdf. Accessed 22 May 2024
7. Crosby S, Dieleman JL, Kiernan S, et al. All bets are off for measuring pandemic preparedness. Think Global Health; 2020. https://www.thinkglobalhealth.org/article/all-bets-are-measuring-pandemic-preparedness. Accessed 26 May 2024
8. Cutler D. How will COVID-19 affect the health care economy? JAMA. 2020;323(22):2237–8. https://doi.org/10.1001/jama.2020.7308.
9. Department of Health. Scientific summary of pandemic influenza & its mitigation, 2011. https://assets.publishing.service.gov.uk/media/5a75baaeed915d506ee810d4/dh_125333.pdf. Accessed 27 May 2024.
10. Drummond D, Sinclair D, Gratton J (2022) Troubles in Canada's health workforce: the why, the where, and the way out of shortages. Howe Institute. https://www.cdhowe.org/public-policy-research/troubles-canadas-health-workforce-why-where-and-way-out-shortages. Accessed 25 May 2024
11. Estabrooks CA, Straus SE, Flood CM, et al. Restoring trust: COVID-19 and the future of long-term care in Canada. FACETS. 2020;5(1) https://www.facetsjournal.com/doi/10.1139/facets-2020-0056. Accessed 20 May 2024
12. Filip R, Puscaselu R, Norocel L, et al. Global challenges to public health care systems during the COVID-19 pandemic: a review of pandemic measures and problems. J Pers Med. 2022;12(8):1295. https://doi.org/10.3390/jpm12081295.
13. Friis RH, Sellers TA. Epidemiology for public health practice. Jones and Bartlett Publishers; 2020.
14. Gollwitzer A, Martel C, Brady WJ, et al. Partisan differences in physical distancing are linked to health outcomes during the COVID-19 pandemic. Nat Hum Behav. 2020;4(11):1186–97. https://doi.org/10.1038/s41562-020-00977-7.
15. Government of Canada. COVID-19 vaccination: vaccination coverage, 2024. https://health-infobase.canada.ca/covid-19/vaccination-coverage/. Accessed 29 May 2024.
16. Grant K. Hospitals running out of key drug for COVID-19 patients. The Globe and Mail; 2021. https://www.theglobeandmail.com/canada/article-drug-critical-to-covid-19-patients-being-rationed-in-ontario/. Accessed 25 May 2024
17. Haileamlak A. The impact of COVID-19 on health and health systems. Ethiop J Health Sci. 2021;31(6):1073–4. https://doi.org/10.4314/ejhs.v31i6.1.
18. Hanney SR, Straus SE, Holmes BJ. Saving millions of lives but some resources squandered: emerging lessons from health research system pandemic achievements and challenges. Health Res Policy Syst. 2022;20:99. https://doi.org/10.1186/s12961-022-00883-6.
19. HM Government. COVID-19 response: living with COVID-19, 2022. https://assets.publishing.service.gov.uk/media/621400ede90e0710b73fd459/COVID-19_Response_-_Living_with_COVID-19.pdf. Accessed 19 May 2024.
20. Huston P, Campbell J, Russell G, et al. COVID-19 and primary care in six countries. BJGP Open. 2020;4(4) https://doi.org/10.3399/bjgpopen20X101128.
21. Institute for Global Health Sciences. The United States' response to COVID-19: a case study. https://ycsg.yale.edu/sites/default/files/files/The%20United%20States'%20Response%20to%20COVID-19.pdf. Accessed 24 May 2024.
22. Johnston I, PHAA (2020) Australia's public health response to COVID-19: what have we done, and where to from here? Aust N Z J Public Health 44(6):440-445. doi: https://doi.org/10.1111/1753-6405.13051

23. Kamerow D. Covid-19: don't forget the impact on US family physicians. BMJ. 2020; https://doi.org/10.1136/bmj.m1260.
24. Livemint. India helped over 150 nations in form of Covid vaccines: Rajya Sabha Dy chairman, 2023. https://www.livemint.com/news/india/india-helped-over-150-nations-in-form-of-covid-vaccines-rajya-sabha-dy-chairman-11672820542481.html. Accessed 28 May 2024.
25. Mathiue E, Ritchie H, Guirao LR, et al. Coronavirus (COVID-19) deaths. Our World in Data; 2020. https://ourworldindata.org/covid-deaths. Accessed 21 May 2024
26. Miyah Y, Benjelloun M, Lairini S, et al. COVID-19 impact on public health, environment, human psychology, global socioeconomy, and education. ScientificWorldJournal. 2022; https://doi.org/10.1155/2022/5578284.
27. Mowat DL, Butler-Jones D. Public health in Canada: a difficult history. Healthc Pap. 2007; https://doi.org/10.12927/hcpap..18755.
28. National Advisory Committee on Immunization (NACI): Statements and Publications. Archived 1: Recommendations on the use of COVID-19 vaccine(s), 2020. https://www.canada.ca/en/public-health/services/immunization/national-advisory-committee-on-immunization-naci/recommendations-use-covid-19-vaccines/december-12-2020.html. Accessed on 26 May 2024.
29. National Advisory Committee on SARS and Public Health. Learning from SARS: Renewal of Public Health in Canada. Health Canada; 2003. https://www.canada.ca/content/dam/phac-aspc/migration/phac-aspc/publicat/sars-sras/pdf/sars-e.pdf. Accessed 23 May 2024
30. National Audit Office. Overview of the UK government's response to the COVID-19 pandemic, 2020. https://www.nao.org.uk/wp-content/uploads/2020/05/Overview-of-the-UK-governments-response-to-the-COVID-19-pandemic.pdf. Accessed 20 May 2024.
31. Netburn D. A timeline of the CDC's advice on face masks. Los Angeles Times; 2021. https://www.latimes.com/science/story/2021-07-27/timeline-cdc-mask-guidance-during-covid-19-pandemic. Accessed 28 May 2024
32. Oberlander J. Introduction to "COVID-19: politics, inequalities, and pandemic". J Health Polit Policy Law. 2020;45(6):905–6. https://doi.org/10.1215/03616878-8641445. Accessed 21 May 2024
33. Pan-Canadian Public Health Network. Canadian Pandemic Influenza Preparedness: Planning Guidance for the Health Sector, 2018. https://www.canada.ca/content/dam/phac-aspc/migration/phac-aspc/cpip-pclcpi/assets/pdf/report-rapport-02-2018-eng.pdf. Accessed 26 May 2024.
34. Public Health Agency of Canada Act, 2006.
35. Reports of the Auditor General of Canada. COVID-19 pandemic: COVID-19 vaccines, 2022. https://www.oag-bvg.gc.ca/internet/docs/parl_oag_202212_09_e.pdf. Accessed 26 May 2024.
36. Royal Australian College of General Practitioners. Managing emergencies in general practice: a guide for preparation, response and recovery, 2017. https://www.racgp.org.au/getattachment/07c89324-780e-473a-8f13-6e4a4ea5c0ce/Managing-emergencies-in-general-practice.aspx. Accessed 24 May 2024.
37. Secretary of State for Health and Social Care. The Coronavirus Act analysis, 2020. https://assets.publishing.service.gov.uk/media/6245c4b88fa8f52776e12241/withdrawn-coronavirus-act-analysis-print-ready.pdf. Accessed 19 May 2024.
38. Sharma SD. India's fight against the COVID-19 pandemic: lessons and the way forward. SageJournals. 2022;78(1) https://doi.org/10.1177/09749284211068470.
39. Tabari P, Amini M, Moghadami M, et al. International public health responses to COVID-19 outbreak: a rapid review. Iran J Med Sci. 2020;45(3):157–69. https://doi.org/10.30476/ijms.2020.85810.1537.

40. The COVID-19 immunity Task Force. 2020. https://www.covid19immunitytaskforce.ca/. Accessed 28 May 2024.
41. Tsirtsakis A. PHNs to receive 2.3 million masks to help fight coronavirus. newsGP, 2020. https://www1.racgp.org.au/newsgp/professional/primary-health-networks-to-receive-2-3-million-mas. Accessed 27 May 2024.
42. U.S. Department of Health and Human Services. Pandemic influenza plan, 2017. https://www.cdc.gov/flu/pandemic-resources/pdf/pan-flu-report-2017v2.pdf. Accessed 26 May 2024.
43. Winslow CE. The untilled fields of public health. Science. 1920;51(1306):23–33. https://doi.org/10.1126/science.51.1306.23.
44. Worldometer. Coronavirus cases, 2020. https://www.worldometers.info/coronavirus/. Accessed 22 May 2024.

Index

A

Air pollution, 12, 120, 151, 152
Ancient Arabic System of Public Health, 5
Ancient Chinese System of Public Health, 4
Ancient Egyptian System of Public Health, 4
Ancient Greek System of Public Health, 5
Ancient Indian System of Public Health, 4
Ancient Mesopotamian System of Public Health, 4
Ancient Public Health, 3–4
Ancient Roman System of Public Health, 5
Artificial intelligence, 120, 196
Ashtachakra, 167, 168
Australian Health Sector Emergency Response Plan for Novel Coronavirus, 241
Avian influenza, 190, 191
Ayushman Bharat, 15, 103, 107, 139, 172, 173, 175, 222, 225, 232–234
Ayushman Bharat-National Health Protection Mission (AB-NHPM), 103, 107
Ayushman Bharat - PM-JAY, 172, 173, 181, 225
Ayushman Bharat Yojana, 172, 173, 250

B

Benazir Income Support Programme (BISP), 228
Bhore Committee, 7–9
Biological Diversity (Amendment) Act, 2015, 241
Black Death, 5, 18, 19, 188

C

Cancer, 30–34, 53, 82, 86, 112, 113, 131, 135, 136, 166, 167, 173, 182
Central Government Health Scheme (CGHS), 10, 99, 102, 176, 225
Centres for Disease Control, 85, 243, 247
Cholera outbreaks, 20, 155, 156
Chronotherapy, 51–53
Circadian, 39–53
Climate migration, 146
Clock, 15, 40, 43, 45, 46, 48, 50–52
Code of Criminal Procedure (CrPC), 1973, 214, 218
Communication, 27, 28, 32, 41, 81, 116, 171, 176, 183, 190, 192, 194, 195, 198, 216, 238, 241, 245, 248
Community-Based Health Insurance (CBHI), 106, 230, 233
Comparative analysis, 221–235
Coronavirus Act 2020, 246
COVID-19, 6, 15, 70, 71, 74, 85, 102, 106, 114, 137, 143, 189, 191–196, 198, 203–218, 226, 229, 231, 237–251
COVID-19 Immunity Task Force Public Health Agency of Canada, 243

D

Declaration of Alma-Ata, 99
Developed nations, 145, 150, 155, 238, 240, 249, 251
Disorder(s), 39, 45–52, 80, 82, 85, 87, 112, 117, 136, 165, 166, 170, 174

S. Malik et al. (eds.), *Public Health Issues: Theory and Practices*,
https://doi.org/10.1007/978-981-96-6650-8

Disruption, 39, 40, 44–48, 51, 212, 238, 248

E
Early childhood education, 86, 115–116
Economic impact, 65, 114–116
Economic inequality, 98–99, 135, 249
Economic stability, 79–80, 114, 117, 120
Education quality, 80
Employee State Insurance (ESI), 11, 225
Employee State Insurance Scheme, 99
Empower individuals, 27, 84, 133, 226, 227, 229, 231
Environment, 3, 4, 17, 39, 40, 44, 49, 65–68, 70, 72–75, 81–83, 111, 114–118, 120, 144–146, 149–151, 153, 154, 157, 172, 174, 177, 178, 180, 182, 188, 193, 204, 205, 211, 239
Environmental sustainability, 66, 74, 140, 194
Environmental Sustainable development goals, 67
Environmental treaties, 143–158
Epidemic Disease Act, 1897, 7, 208, 209, 213, 215, 217, 249
Epidemiological transition, 24, 166, 204
Epidemiology, 19–20, 24
Evolution of Public Health in India, 8–16
Expenditure on health as a percentage of GDP, 92

F
Federal Government Health Schemes, 228
Financial burden, 84, 92, 111, 112, 166, 197, 227, 228, 230, 232
Food security, 82, 138, 150, 172, 249
Funding mechanisms, 221, 223, 233

G
Gender disparities, 130, 131, 136, 138, 140
Gender-specific health issues, 130
Germ and Miasma theory, 18
Global alliance, 150, 156, 195
Global climate change, 143–152, 154–157, 188, 192, 199
Global health, 23, 102, 145, 154, 156, 193, 207, 222, 245
Global policies, 85–87, 99, 118
Global Public Health Initiatives, 99, 101–102
Global South, 96, 100, 101, 196–198
Global warming, 144, 146, 151, 239
Government-Funded Health Insurance schemes (GFHIS), 103
Government Health Programs, 230
Gross domestic product (GDP), 91–95, 101, 103–105, 114, 166, 178, 249

H
Health, 3, 165, 189
  concerns, 80, 129–131, 136, 141, 152
  determinants, 79, 87, 101, 194, 226
  disparity, 28, 82, 84, 85, 97–99, 102, 107, 111, 112, 118, 131, 141, 152, 155, 224
  economics, 91, 97, 99, 107, 194, 197
  emergency, 15, 154, 156, 192, 193, 197, 216, 237, 240, 247, 248
  equity, 84–87, 98, 107, 111, 112, 118, 141, 167, 194, 207, 221–224, 235, 248
  expenditure, 24, 91, 92, 94–97, 101, 104, 221
  financing, 91, 92, 97, 99, 101, 107
  inequalities, 84, 102, 114, 118, 193
  insurance, 23, 97, 98, 102–107, 111, 114, 115, 130, 139, 172, 176, 177, 181, 204, 221–235
  literacy, 27–34, 81, 118, 129–131, 141
  outcomes, 31, 33, 81, 84, 106, 111–113, 115, 116, 118, 119, 129, 130, 133–136, 138–141, 144, 148, 171, 222, 224, 226, 228, 230, 231, 235
Health for All, 6, 11, 12, 24, 100, 103, 107, 181, 194, 207, 229
Health Silk Road, 102
Healthcare, 80, 81, 91, 111, 144, 172, 175, 180, 181, 193, 221
  access, 29, 79, 81–82, 99, 112, 129, 131, 135, 137–141, 181, 222, 224, 225, 227–231, 234, 235
  affordability, 81, 97, 139, 181
  financial uncertainty, 97
  quality, 81–82, 84, 101, 111, 131, 132, 139, 181, 225–229, 231, 234
Health care system, 206, 208
Healthy habits, 5
History of Public Health, 4–5, 165
Holistic health, 167, 168, 174, 175, 226
Housing quality, 83
Human well-being, 79, 174, 183

I
Implementation and accessibility, 234
Income inequalities, 98, 107
Indian Penal Code, 1860, 213
Industrial revolution, 145
Infectious diseases, 18, 21–22, 70, 149, 154, 165, 187–199, 204, 230

International Covenant on Civil and Political Rights (ICCPR), 1966, 205, 217
International Covenant on Economic, 205
International health regulations, 192, 193, 195, 205
International Public Health Events, 5–6

J
Janani Shishu Suraksha Karyakram (JSSK), 132
John Snow, 6, 20

K
Kyoto Protocol, 150, 156

L
Lifestyle modifications, 44, 165, 167, 171
Light, 39–41, 44, 47–52, 66, 222, 223
Light therapy, 51–52
Longevity, 4, 24, 168
Low-cost healthcare, 99
Low-income, 28, 80, 99, 102, 107, 115, 119, 153–155, 182, 227, 228, 230, 233
Lung cancer, 150–153

M
Malaria Outbreaks, 153–155
Maternal and child health (MCH), 22, 129, 132, 133, 139, 140, 154, 165, 173, 230
Maternal Mortality Ratio (MMR), 132
Medical Termination of Pregnancy (MTP), 11, 133
Melatonin, 43, 44, 47–52
Menstrual hygiene management (MHM), 134
Mental health, 12, 15, 49, 85–87, 114, 131, 133, 135–137, 140, 174–178, 181, 182, 204, 205
Metabolic, 44, 50, 51, 53, 82
Milk station, 22
Misalignment, 44–46, 49, 51
Mission Parivar Vikas, 133
Montreal Protocol, 149, 156

N
National Disaster Management Act, 2005, 216, 249
National Disaster Management Authority (NDMA), 210
National Disaster Response Force (NDRF), 210
National Health Policy (NHP), 12, 13, 15, 92, 103, 104, 130, 132, 138–139, 225
National Health Protection Scheme (NHPS), 15, 103, 172, 173, 181, 250
National Health Security Act, 2007, 241
National Public Health Board, 216

O
Out-of-pocket (OOP) payments, 92, 97, 104, 107, 114, 115, 166, 177, 181, 227, 230
Out-of-pocket Expenditure (OOPE) on health, 92, 101, 105, 139, 225

P
Pandemic, 5, 6, 9, 14, 15, 20, 65, 69–71, 74, 76, 80, 85, 102, 114, 137, 143, 145, 187–199, 203, 205, 210–218, 222, 226, 229, 237–251
  accord, 20, 143, 192, 193
  treaties, 191, 193, 195, 242
Paris Agreement, 150, 151, 153, 156
Period, 4, 10, 17, 39–41, 44, 48–50, 53, 69, 70, 104, 112, 114, 171, 197, 215, 230, 244
Phase, 13, 41, 47–49, 51–53, 86, 103, 119, 189, 249
Phase-shifts, 46, 52
PM-ABHIM, 15
Policy learning, 222
Poor health outcomes, 79, 98
Pradhan Mantri Surakshit Matritva Abhiyan (PMSMA), 132
Preparedness response, 190–193, 195, 238, 243, 247, 248
Press Information Bureau, 91, 93, 103
Primary care assessment, 241
Public health, 27, 70, 86, 91, 117, 129–141, 143, 165, 187, 203, 221, 237–240
  in Ancient Period, 17–18
  in British India, 7
  in developing countries, 99, 221–235, 237–251
  insurance, 221–235
  law, 20, 203–218
  in Medieval Period, 17–18
  in Modern Period, 19–20
Public health initiatives (PHI), 91, 99, 102–104, 106
Pulse Polio Immunization, 13
Punjab Health Insurance Scheme, 227

Q

Quality of life, 34, 79, 140, 152, 174

R

Racial and ethnic minorities, 28, 181, 247
Rapid Estimate of Adult Literacy in Medicine (REALM), 29
Rashtriya Swasthya Bima Yojana (RSBY), 103, 104, 106, 225
Resilience, 83, 86, 114, 156, 178, 192
Rhythms, 39–41, 43–53
Right to health, 100, 101, 205, 206, 208, 215, 217
Risk factors, 6, 31, 118, 166, 172, 198, 239

S

Sanitation, 3, 4, 12, 16, 20–21, 24, 134, 155, 156, 165, 175, 176, 194, 204, 238, 239
School health, 9, 175, 176
Sehat Insaf Card (Khyber Pakhtunkhwa), 227, 233, 234
Semashko system, 99
Shared regional context, 222
Sindh Health Insurance Programme, 228
Sleep, 41, 45–50, 52
Sleep disorders, 51, 81
Sleep-wake cycle, 43, 44, 46–49, 51–52
Smallpox, 189, 190
Social and Cultural Rights, 189, 205
Social capital, 83
Social determinants of health (SDH), 28, 79, 87, 101, 111, 115–117, 120, 139, 226
Social discrimination, 81, 87, 112–114
Social Health Insurance (SHI), 100, 230
Social isolation, 83, 112, 113, 118, 119
Social networks, 114, 118
Socioeconomic status (SES), 27, 84, 86, 111, 114
State-Level Health Insurance Schemes, 225
Suprachiasmatic nucleus (SCN), 41–43, 46, 51, 52
Surakshit Matritva Aashwasan (SUMAN), 132
Sustainable Development Goal (SDG), 14, 66, 107, 132, 141, 194, 207, 222
Swasthya Aayaam, 29, 167, 168
Symptoms, 21, 28, 46–49, 51, 52, 82, 86, 197, 247

T

Tele MANAS program, 15
Test of Functional Health Literacy in Adults (TOFHLA), 29, 30
The Disaster Management Act (DMA), 2005, 208, 209, 213, 215–217
The Epidemic Diseases (Amendment) Act, 2020, 217, 218
The Health Insurance Scheme for the Poor, 230, 233
The National Family Health Survey, 13, 14, 130, 131, 135, 137
The Public Health (Prevention, Control and Management of Epidemics) Bill, 2020, 216, 218
Transportation, 82, 97, 102, 116–118, 120, 213

U

UNICEF, 10, 23, 100
Universal Declaration of Human Rights (UDHR), 85, 205
Universal health coverage (UHC), 92, 99–102, 104, 107, 139, 141, 173, 194, 226–229, 231, 232, 235, 240, 243, 245, 246, 248
U.S. Department of Health and Human Services (HHS), 28, 34, 79

V

Vaccination, 7, 8, 10, 19, 21, 22, 24, 28, 81, 119, 165, 177, 189, 190, 192, 198, 243, 245, 248, 250, 251
Vector borne diseases, 14, 21, 155
Vulnerability, 115, 149, 152, 177, 194

W

Well-being, 3, 23, 24, 32, 65, 76, 79, 80, 83, 86, 97, 98, 101, 107, 111, 112, 114, 115, 119, 129, 130, 134, 136–139, 141, 144, 148, 150, 156, 157, 166, 167, 170, 171, 173–181, 183, 204–206, 208, 217, 222, 240
Wellness, 15, 103, 107, 167–171, 173, 176, 177, 179–182
Wellness program, 23, 32, 97, 111, 130, 136, 138, 165–178, 180–183

Women health, 22, 130, 131, 133–136, 138, 139, 141
Workplace wellness, 177–180
World Bank, 6, 80, 100, 102, 112, 114, 166
World Health Organization (WHO), 3, 6, 8, 10, 11, 13, 14, 23, 70, 79, 82, 85, 86, 95, 96, 100, 102, 107, 115, 119, 149, 150, 154, 155, 166, 167, 172, 174–176, 189, 191–195, 197–199, 203, 205–207, 211, 213–214, 217, 239, 250

Y

Yog+, 168–170, 179, 180

MIX
Papier aus verantwortungsvollen Quellen
Paper from responsible sources
FSC® C105338

If you have any concerns about our products,
you can contact us on
ProductSafety@springernature.com

In case Publisher is established outside the EU,
the EU authorized representative is:
Springer Nature Customer Service Center GmbH
Europaplatz 3, 69115 Heidelberg, Germany

Printed by Libri Plureos GmbH
in Hamburg, Germany